Roasting

ALSO BY BARBARA KAFKA

Party Food

The Opinionated Palate

Microwave Gourmet Healthstyle Cookbook

Microwave Gourmet

Food for Friends

American Food and California Wine

AS EDITOR

The James Beard Celebration Cookbook

The Four Seasons

The Cook's Catalogue

The Cuisine of Toulouse-Lautrec

Roasting

A SIMPLE ART

Barbara Kafka

PHOTOGRAPHS BY

Maria Robledo

William Morrow and Company, Inc.
NEW YORK

LIBRARY OF CONGRESS CATALOGING-IN-PUBLICATION DATA

Kafka, Barbara.
Roasting / Barbara Kafka.
p. cm.
Includes index.
ISBN 0-688-13135-2
1. Roasting (Cookery)   I. Title.
TX690.K34 1995
641.7'1—dc20   95-18259
CIP

PRINTED IN THE UNITED STATES OF AMERICA

First Edition

1 2 3 4 5 6 7 8 9 10

BOOK DESIGN BY ALISON LEW/VERTIGO DESIGN

For Ernie

a n d

A L L   M Y   C H I L D R E N

Nicole   Michael

and   *and*

Richard   Jill

ACKNOWLEDGMENTS

I salute with pleasure the men and women who through millennia have roasted and those who left records and recipes for what they did, thereby enriching the unspoken background behind this book that I hope enriches it.

In the present, I thank my longtime editor and friend, Ann Bramson. My books would not have existed without her. There really are not enough words.

At William Morrow, I also thank the chairman/CEO, Al Marchioni. Most writers seem to feel hurt by their publishers. I, on the other hand, have received only support and affection. Lisa Queen redefines the role of sub-rights director. Kim Yorio got the word out in splendid fashion. Deborah Weiss Geline, leader of copyeditors, has made order from madness. Karen Lumley, production manager, did the impossible and ushered this book into the world. Alison Lew designed the book beautifully, and Maria Robledo, the photographer, understood the rich glories of brown.

In my lair, I have talented assistants. There is Esti Marpet, who has been a friend for several years and seen me through two books, making everything possible by keeping my life in order. Stephana Bottom has been my excellent assistant on this book, testing and keeping the manuscript in order. Johanna Semple has tested recipes and dealt with my many vicissitudes with the increasingly complex world of computers. All too briefly, Suzanne Yearley was a general assistant.

Beyond my door, I have been fortunate to have warm friends and supporters in the world of food. I thank the people at TVFN, the Television Food Network, who have brought a new and highly enjoyable dimension to my working life: Tony Hendra (my sparring partner), Reese Schoenfeld, Pat O'Gorman, Ricki Stofsky, Joe Langan, John McGarvey, and Sue Huffman, who introduced me to it all. Additionally in my working life, there are the friends and very professional editors at *Gourmet:* Gail Zweigenthal, Zan Zackroff, Alice Gochman, and others too numerous to mention. *The New York Times*, recently in the person of Trish Hall and many others over the years, has been supportive.

My friends have tasted and passed judgment, sometimes of as many as four versions of the same dish. Irene Sax ate, but she also pointed me to the notes of Karen Hess. Paul and Penny Levy sheltered me in Oxford. Brigitte cooked with me, young and today, in New York, Geneva, and Paris with her matchless style. Corby Kummer has been a constant and faithful custodian of my words. Chefs and fine food writers in the Americas, Europe, and Australia have been companions and inspirations. There is sadly no way to thank all of them.

Contents

BEFORE LIGHTING THE OVEN

W HY ROAST?

OVER THE YEARS I HAVE GOTTEN SCADS OF FRANTIC PHONE CALLS AND BEEN ON THE RECEIVING END OF WISTFUL LUNCHTIME PLAINTS. The theme is usually the same and made up of unhappy elements you can sew together as you wish: "I can't cook; I have to entertain—friends, business. What can I do? There's just no time. The kids, husband, or wife deserve a meal; but I'm exhausted when I get home. I must return a few invitations. There's just no time to shop." My answer, I hope helpful, has almost always started with: "Anybody can roast a chicken. Almost any family or guest will be happy to eat one."

When the next call comes—"What do I give them this time? I gave them chicken last time"—my answer comes back, "Leg of lamb." By now I can give the instructions in a few pithy sentences and set them fairly happily off to the kitchen. Except in the case of the rude, I usually get a relieved call in a few days describing success. Within a year or two, there will be follow-up calls telling me how the new roasters have changed, improved, or transformed my recipe into their own. That's ideal. For me, recipes are ways of getting people to cook, eat together, have pleasure, learn, and adopt. Recipes are not eternal, nor do I think that I own them.

One dividend is that friends, associates, and editors have all contributed to this book over the years of its preparation. Once they got the hang, as the reader will, of the basic technique, they have tried different ingredients and adapted recipes often to splendid effect. I hope that I have thanked them all.

Lack of ownership is particularly true when it comes to roasting. What I am writing is a distillation of my own experiences, what I observed in professional kitchens and have read about and tried. This continuity gives me great pleasure. Recently, I read these notes by Karen Hess in *What Mrs. Fisher Knows About Old Southern Cooking*, a reprint of an 1881 book by what Hess has shown, with excellent research, to be the first African-American cookery-book author in America:

> One of the most admirable aspects of Abby Fisher's work is her roasting technique. She learned to cook when roasting was still carried on before ... the hearth, either on a spit or using a contraption called a Dutch oven (not what we know as a Dutch oven today). [It was a heat-reflecting box placed in front of the fire.] Proper roasting produces a wonderful, lightly caramelized crust on the out-

side, but leaves the meat inside succulent. What is remarkable is that Mrs. Fisher managed to manipulate the iron box of the kitchen range so that it approximated proper roasting methods. Her recipe for "Roast Beef"... is exemplary in this regard: "*A five-pound roast should cook in half an hour and a ten-pound one in one hour.*" [Emphasis added by Hess.] Follow her instructions to the letter if you would have properly roasted beef, rather than the grey, sodden stuff fobbed off as roast beef in our modern cookbooks. Americans have largely forgotten how to roast meat, but Abby Fisher knew.

Well, I believe that some of us still know how today and soon so will you. I have moved roasting into the contemporary home oven; but I have an old cast-iron one in Vermont and it does roast beautifully. I believe, along with Mrs. Fisher, in hot ovens, short roasting times, and rare meat.

When I come home needing to prepare a meal for several people at the end of a busy day, the first thing I do is check that the rack is in the center of the oven and turn the oven on to 500°F. I take the main course out of my shopping bag or out of the refrigerator and set it in a pan and season it. I know that the meal is under way. The last thing I do before I go to bed is to set the oven to clean itself so that the cycle can begin again another day. When the oven doesn't self-clean, I slather it with chemical cleaner.

Going in and out of the kitchen these past few years as I have been almost continuously roasting for this book has been a heady pleasure. The rich aromas in the air make me hungry and remind me of family meals, feasts, and holidays, almost all of which center on a roast.

There is an almost endless list of reasons why I roast: ease, rapidity, lack of fuss, and the enjoyment of guests among them.

*W*HAT IS ROASTING?

PERHAPS THE HARDEST PART OF WRITING THIS BOOK HAS BEEN TO DEFINE WHAT ROASTING ACTUALLY IS, ESPECIALLY IF IT NOW TAKES PLACE IN THE OVEN RATHER THAN ON A SPIT OVER OR IN FRONT OF A FIRE. When is it baking or pot roasting rather than true roasting?

After much thought and consultation with fine cooks and writers, I have come to the decision that "If it looks like a duck..." is my rule. A perfect example of a readily apparent difference is the one between baked potatoes all steamy and fluffy in their dry, brown, crinkled skins and roast potatoes shiny and crusted with the golden fat from roasting birds or meat or butter or oil. The flesh is tender and succulent but not fluffy and steamy. Both are a delight, but not the same.

Paula Wolfert and I came to the conclusion that roasting implies—needs—fat. I would add that the fat need not be added or external. The fat can be that naturally just under the skin or in the flesh of animals.

This is the fat that seduced the eaters—even with burned fingers—in Charles Lamb's (Elia) "Dissertation on Roast Pig." In many cases, less fat is used than would have been in deep-fat frying or sautéing the same food; but the flavor is extraordinary.

The other thing differentiating most baking (not potatoes) and roasting is high temperature. I know that many people are wary of high temperatures and afraid that their meat will shrink away to nothing. However, the high heat is needed. Otherwise the meat, vegetable, fish, or fruit steams in its juices. Also to avoid steaming, the food must be left to cook uncovered. In my third kitchen, the first with an oven, I roasted in an old-fashioned four-inch-deep roaster with a domed lid. Today, it goes unused, as its high sides retain steam.

For the same reasons, to avoid steaming, I rarely baste, except for fruits and vegetables that are getting some of the color and caramelization from a marinade or glaze. However, I frequently turn vegetables, which lack any fat of their own, in the cooking fat in the pan during the roasting.

Roasting began as an open-air activity with a hand-turned spit revolving over a fire. With time, a more satisfactory method evolved of placing the spit in front of the fire so that the drippings would not fall into the fire and be wasted and possibly flare up, scorching the food. Instead, a pan was placed under the spit to collect them. Just as today, the fat was saved for future cooking and the drippings pan was deglazed to make a sauce. Roasting moved into kitchens and in front of fireplaces (see pages 122–123 for more). With the arrival of the patent stove in the nineteenth century, roasting moved into the oven and into Mrs. Fisher's domain. Almost all my roasting is done in an oven, and that is where the recipes in this book are set. As the location changes, so do the techniques. Spit roasting requires careful trussing to keep odd bits from jutting out and burning or falling off. This habit was carried over into the oven; but it is by and large unnecessary and illogical, particularly when it comes to birds. Why would one cram the slowest roasting meat of a chicken—the thigh— against the rest of the bird? Only overdone breast meat or bloody thighs can result. I don't do it.

I roast because I am a naturally hurried person and because I like my meats juicy and rare. The high heat quickly caramelizes the surface of the meat, the skin of the bird or fish, or the outsides of vegetables, evoking rich juices and flavors. If the heat is turned down after the surfaces caramelize, the steam softens the crust. To limit smoking in long-cooking recipes, or those for fatty foods like baby lamb, the heat may be turned down slightly or fat can be removed from the cooking pan. Continuous low-heat cooking is more like steaming or pot roasting than real roasting, which also creates a rich pan glaze that can be degreased and then deglazed with wine or stock to make the best of natural gravies.

Tenting the food with aluminum foil after the food comes out of the oven is useful to keep heat in while the meat rests so that the juices distribute evenly and a little more cooking goes on. It is unnecessary with large pieces of meat, which will retain heat, and I do not recommend it with birds such as roast duck, where a crisp skin is desirable. The retained steam will soften the skin. It is mainly useful with small pieces of food that may get cold while the deglazing sauce is being prepared.

*t*HE CONTINUOUS KITCHEN

IT SEEMS TO ME THAT LESS COOKING IS DONE TODAY THAN USED TO BE AND THAT WHEN IT IS DONE, IT IS SO MUCH MORE WORK BECAUSE WE HAVE LOST THE HABIT OF THE CONTINUOUS KITCHEN. We start each meal from scratch with fresh shopping and a brand-new independent recipe. Our predecessors didn't, and we can save ourselves a great deal of work and have better, more economical food with greater depth of flavor by seeing cooking as an ongoing process. There is no better way to get in the habit than with roast birds, meats, and fish.

"Start with a roast" might be the motto of the continuous kitchen. When the roast is done and eaten, there are usually leftovers that are the home cook's version of a chef's mise en place for future meals.

Bones and scraps should be routinely set to cook for stock at the end of the meal or the morning after (see page 222). This will eliminate the need for cans and cubes except for under the worst of circumstances. Stocks are the bases for soups, stews, and sauces that can contain just a small amount of leftover meat. They keep virtually indefinitely in the freezer and are quickly defrosted in a microwave oven or overnight in the refrigerator and about half an hour in a pot on top of the stove.

Leftovers have gotten a bad name—bad cooking and the British habit of making the Sunday joint and then serving the rest of the meat indifferently prepared throughout the week. Even so, some of the best ideas for using leftovers come from them and from the French. Consider potpies and hashes.

Today's leftover can be turned into tomorrow's elegant first-course salad, a simple sauté, or a curry. Having roasted leftovers is like having a good sous chef in the kitchen, someone who has done half the work before I turn up for the finishing touches. The sauces for these transformations are often based on the stocks. Others can be found—along with a complete listing—on pages 292-309 or in the Index.

*i*NSTANT LEFTOVERS

OFTEN I ROAST WITHOUT ANY SPECIFIC MEAL IN VIEW. I roast to have instant leftovers, food on hand for family and guests to pick at and from which to make sandwiches and salads. Large crowds on a summer weekend eat these all day while I make something else for dinner. A turkey or a loin of pork are favorites.

*t*HE SIMPLE ART

THAT SAID, WHY DO I CALL IT A "SIMPLE ART"? Simplicity when it is good has to be artful, like the little black dress. There is no concealing flaws. What is seen and smelled is what is eaten. There is a method and there are rules; but they are easily mastered. The quality of ingredients is, if anything, more essential to good results in roasting. See page 12 and individual introductions throughout the book for more help than I can give here. But, let us start with the oven, where most of our cooking takes place.

The oven

I USE SIMPLE domestic ovens meant for most homes. I have given up on trying to understand the British Aga. I don't have one. Electric and gas ovens work interchangeably. A cast-iron stove gets even hotter than today's home ovens, and most people don't have one. If that is what is being used, remember that the iron radiates heat through the entire cavity of the oven. Reduce the cooking time.

I prefer separate ovens rather than ovens in stoves. I don't like working on the rest of the meal over the heat of the oven. A stove oven works in exactly the same way as a wall oven. I don't place my independent oven in the traditional position—halfway up the wall. I am short and I have discovered painfully that it requires extra strength to support a pan full of food and potentially burning hot grease when my arms are lifted. I place my ovens under the counter. I do not use a convection oven. If one is in use, the timing should be left as in the recipe, but the heat should be reduced by about 50°F.

Getting to know an oven is much like adjusting to the quirks in a cranky automobile or a friend and just as vital for happiness. Ovens vary markedly in size, depending on the maker and the country of origin. Before deciding to roast a behemoth, check that it will fit in the oven and that the door will close—not always essential—with the pan in place. Knowing the external measurements of the oven is not enough. There are lots of works and insulations in the oven walls and the important measurements are of the interior of the oven. All the recipes in this book fit in a cavity about 16½ inches wide by 18½ inches deep and 15½ inches high. Larger ovens will create no problems.

The temperature in the oven is critical and therefore so is the efficiency of the thermostat that controls it. It is considered normal for ovens to vary in temperature from the set reading by 25°F in either direction, a possible swing of fifty degrees. I consider that less than perfect. It is a good idea to check oven temperatures from time to time with an independent oven thermometer. The service department of the manufacturer or I, using good instructions, can reset the thermostat.

The temperature readings on most ovens start at 100°F when they are turned on. Standard ovens take fifteen to twenty minutes to heat to 500°F. Once hot, ovens will vary in how long they hold the heat, which will make a difference when the oven is opened to relieve the pan of excess fat or so that the food can be turned. If roasting is to continue at the same temperature, it is a good idea to get in the habit of shutting the oven door whenever something is removed from the oven. Conversely, leave the oven door open if it is important to reduce its temperature rapidly. My oven takes a full twenty-five minutes to cool back down to the 100°F setting. I have taken these lag times into consideration in the recipes. Don't wait for oven temperatures to come down. Just follow the resetting and timing instructions.

I prefer self-cleaning ovens for the obvious reason—less mess, less work. Jacques Pépin, who prefers high-heat roasting of chickens as I do, wrote that they "...splatter and make the oven a mess. To cut down on cleaning time after cooking this dish, line the roasting pan with aluminum foil, and if you don't have a self-cleaning oven, lay some aluminum foil on the bottom of the oven as well." I don't line the pan because I want to be able to deglaze it. I do line oven bottoms that are not self-cleaning. Spills will make matters worse.

Dirty ovens are not only unattractive, they also smoke when heated for ensuing roasting. Whether cleaned automatically or by chemicals and scouring, all ovens will need some additional cleaning from time to time. Newer self-cleaning ovens should not be cleaned with chemical oven cleaners particularly around the fabric seal, as the chemicals can rot the seal. Ammonia, scouring pads, and soap and water are the solvents and solutions.

While they will never be as shiny as when new, racks can be left in the oven for cleaning as can an uncoated all-metal pan that is really grotty. If the racks stick rather than slide, it is probably a question of their being too clean. Simply rubbing the edges with a little oil will solve the problem.

Air

WHERE THERE'S SMOKE, there's fire. The opposite is not as ironclad: when there's fire, there may be smoke. I have tried to minimize the amount of smoke resulting from these recipes by proper placement of the pan in the oven so that the food is not overly cooked from the top by radiation, by removing excess fat from the roasting pan, and by reducing the temperature slightly if need be. Nevertheless, it is a good idea to have an exhaust fan and use it and to open a window even with today's better vented ovens.

To keep smoke and smells that are distasteful to some, like those from long-cooked stocks, from escaping the kitchen, close the door. The smell should not be one of burning, which occurs mainly with sugar-laden glazes. The dark brown that forms in the pan is not a proof of burning but rather a valuable roasting by-product. Be sensitive to any smell of burning; it is acrid. The nose is a valuable kitchen ally. Even more sensitive is a kitchen smoke alarm and it can be a nuisance. Turn it off before roasting, being sure to turn it on again after cooking has ceased.

Remember that the oven is like a large cooking pot. When it is opened, there will be a rush of hot, steamy air. Avert the head and wait a minute before removing the pan. Steam fogs glasses and can burn.

Rack placement

WHERE THE RACK and consequently the roasting pan and the food sit in the oven is important. All recipes give rack position. Be sure to put the rack in the proper position before turning on the oven. Having the roasting pan on the top rack browns the food by reflected heat. It is less risky than broiling, with much less chance of scorching the food. Be careful not to place long-cooking foods too high or the same effect will cause burning and smoking. Having the pan on the bottom rack will give a result similar to sautéing, with the strong heat coming from below. Again there is less risk of burning and the pan is larger than a skillet. Foods roasted in the center of the oven, especially for prolonged periods, will cook more evenly.

Different ovens will have different rack positions. They are usually about two inches apart. Generally an inch or so in either direction will not be critical. It is a good idea to get out a ruler and know where the racks of the oven can go. For purposes of comparison, in my oven, measuring from the floor of oven—the heat element is an inch above the floor—the lowest rack is three inches from the floor, the second is six inches (I call this second from the bottom), and the third, or what I call the center rack, is eight inches from the bottom. The top rack will generally be three inches from the top of the oven—two inches below the heating element.

Even the best ovens have hot spots. Often it is best to return a pan that has been taken out of the oven during cooking to remove fat or to turn food pieces with the end that was in back toward the front of the oven.

Roasting pans

USING THE PROPER pan of the proper size is as important to roasting as it is to any other kind of cooking. Pan sizes are indicated in every recipe. If the pan is too large for the amount of food being cooked, burning may take place around the food. If the pan is too small, the food will not fit or it will touch the sides of the pan, risking having it stick to the pan. A too-small pan may also crowd multiple pieces of food so that the sides of the pieces do not brown properly.

Pans should not be as shallow as are jelly roll pans, for example, so that hot fat or juices spill out of them when they are moved. Pans should be no more than an inch and a half to two inches deep or they will steam the food and make it hard to remove from the pan after roasting.

Much of pan choice is based on my desire to have juices for deglazing. I do not use the flat racks that come with the pans shipped with most ovens either. These are meant primarily for broiling. It is impossible to deglaze them and hence much of the good flavor is lost from the roasting process. I also do not use free-standing racks in the pans. I find them hard to clean and of no real aid. Who really cares if where the chicken hits the pan—a small area—has crisp skin?

The pans that come with most ovens have a well and tree or other raised pattern in the bottom. These are not good. Foods do not cook evenly and the pans are very hard to deglaze and to clean. Pans should have flat bottoms and should be thick enough so that they stay flat when hot.

I prefer uncoated pans. They will clean up well when deglazed and then left to soak in hot soapy water. Coated pans tend to lose their coating when deglazed over high heat. My largest pan is aluminum, but I tend to avoid aluminum if possible because of its interactivity with acid foods such as tomatoes, wine, and vinegar. Most aluminum pans, including the coated ones, are porous and they eat up much of the good glaze that is wanted for the sauce. The porosity also makes them hard to clean. Disposable pans are not good: They bend under the weight of large roasts. It becomes expensive to keep buying them. It is impossible to deglaze them. They don't do well over a flame and they can't be scraped hard enough.

In some recipes, particularly for small amounts of food, I use porcelain or oven-proof glass pie and quiche dishes. For other uses I avoid such materials along with earthenware and pottery because they are risky to deglaze on top of a burner. I do have some gorgeous, heavy copper roasting pans. They are very expensive, need special cleaning, and are not in most kitchens. When I use such a pan, I must remember that it takes longer to get hot but that it will then be hotter than other metal pans. Reduce the cooking time slightly.

I use stainless steel with a heat-spreading metal sandwich or mild steel pans that are flat on the bottom. The basic roasting pan available in most stores measures 18 x 13 x 2 inches, which I call large. It is better to buy these large pans with handles that fold down if at all possible to make sure that they will fit into smaller ovens. The other pan sizes that I find useful are 14 x 12 x 2 inches (medium) and 12 x 8 x 1½ inches (small). The small pan has become a treasure of my kitchen. It is perfect for a small bird and for enough vegetables to feed four.

Timing and temperature

AS WITH ALL cooking, timing and temperature are crucial elements in roasting. In addition to the oven temperatures discussed previously, there are the temperatures of the finished foods. Generally the internal temperature is given in the recipe or in the general introductory notes to a chapter or to a given ingredient. The major exceptions are fruits and vegetables. They are done when the tip of a sharp knife slides in easily. Poultry, other than game, geese, and ducks, is done when the juices run clear when the point of a knife is inserted into the joint between the thigh and the body.

Professional cooks can tell by pushing on the outside of a roast with a finger the doneness of the meat inside. The roast becomes firmer to the touch—hardens—as it cooks; but this technique takes practice and sometimes burned fingers.

A thermometer is safer. Don't get a thermometer that tells what well-done or rare is as the markings are invariably wrong. My temperatures are often lower than those recommended by trade associations. They are all totally safe. If I cooked beef and lamb to the recommended temperatures, I would never produce rare meat again. Use an instant-read thermometer. Insert it halfway into the meat, avoiding bone and fat as much as possible. It may be advisable to take the temperature of a large piece of meat in two or more places. Leave the thermometer in place for about ten seconds. It takes time to register. Remove the thermometer if roasting the meat longer. Every once in a while, check the accuracy of the thermometer by sticking the point into boiling water. It should read 210°F. Thermometers can go screwy over time. They are not expensive. If incorrect, buy a new one.

It is not just the size, shape, and amount of bone in a roast that determines the cooking time. If the roast at hand doesn't conform to the recipe, look for a general note either in the introduction to the chapter as in Fish and Some Shellfish or in the introduction to a specific kind of animal as in Birds. Most ovens have a built-in timer. Learn to use it or use an external timer. Relying on memory and the clock can be a risky business. With time and experience, the hints given by smells and sounds coming from the oven will tell the experienced roaster when the food is done. Don't open the oven frequently to check as the oven temperature will go down each time.

My method of roasting may go much more quickly than others. It's better.

Deglazing

PAN JUICES ARE one of the best dividends of roasting, often providing a gravy, the only sauce needed. See page 292 for liquids to use and ways of thickening. Deglazing is a constant technique in this book, and further discussions can be found in the introductions to later chapters. A wooden spoon is the best tool to use to deglaze the roasting pan. Pour or spoon off any fat in the pan. The easiest way, if spooning, is to tilt the pan so that the fat and juices collect in one corner and to use a large, flat metal kitchen spoon to remove the grease. Place the pan over medium-high heat. Pour in the chosen liquid and, holding the pan firmly with a pot holder, scrape vigorously at the bottom of the pan as the liquid boils to remove and dissolve all the marvelous roasting juices. Pour the pan gravy into a sauceboat or bowl or into a two-cup measure, where it can easily be skimmed again.

Other equipment

VERY LITTLE SPECIAL equipment is needed for roasting other than the roasting pans and instant-read thermometer discussed previously. I like to have plenty of thick pot holders around and prefer the mitt kind to avoid burns from inadvertently touching the oven walls.

After roasts are cooked, they need to be removed from the pan. In many instances, the best tools are heavy-duty, large metal spatulas with offset handles, the kind used by grill cooks in restaurants. Two of them will make it easy to pick up even a large fish. Have large platters on hand for large roasts.

While a sharp chef's knife can be used to slice or carve the roast, a good carving set is attractive when I carve at the table (as are small sauce ladles and attractive bowls or sauceboats for the deglazing and other sauces), particularly when bones must be removed from the roast which makes putting the sauce over them rather messy for service.

Some boning may need to be done before roasting. The pin bones of fish and the pin feathers of birds will require a needle-nosed pliers or good tweezers for extraction. Large sharp kitchen scissors or shears are good tools for jointing birds whether in the kitchen—removing wing tips and necks—or at the table. Some sort of cleaver, preferably very heavy so that it does most of the work, is useful for larger animals and bones, especially in stock making.

A flame diffuser is a one of the best small investments possible when making small amounts of stock or simmering mixtures that are liable to scorch. Several sizes of nonstick sauté pans are desirable for hashes and other mixtures that may burn onto the pan. Stockpots, which are tall rather than broad, make more intense stocks, constantly rotating the liquid through the bones. As with other pots, they are best made from stainless steel with a good heat-diffusing bottom, lined copper, or enameled cast iron. A chinois or fine sieve or large colander lined with a dampened and wrung-out cheesecloth or kitchen towel are the ways to get clear stocks.

In recent years, I have become addicted to Japanese wooden lids, otoshi-buta, when making stock. They come in sets with wooden handles. They are meant to fit inside a pot, leaving about a half inch all around them. This keeps the stock or other liquid from reducing too much as it simmers. It also helps to keep the solids under the liquid, where they belong.

A food mill, blender (or mortar and pestle for small quantities), food processor, and spice mill are all helpful.

Ingredients

ROASTING IS SIMPLE, generally using few ingredients, but those should be of the best quality available. This is as true for the fats—olive oil, canola (rapeseed) oil, butter, bacon, and other drippings—as for the principal ingredients. Changing one for another will change not only the flavor but also the cooking. Butter, bacon, and other animal fats, for instance, will brown food more quickly than oil and may burn and smoke.

Fresh fish, meats, and birds are generally preferable to frozen. If frozen foods must be used (game, for instance), place them in a pan in the refrigerator to defrost. They may drip.

Try to buy vegetables, fruits, fish, lamb shanks, and other pieces that are the same size so that they will roast in the same amount of time.

Eggs in these recipes are all "large."

Herbs should generally be fresh. Don't substitute domestic bay leaves, from trees, for the far superior imported bay leaves, from bushes; a different thing entirely.

Both for the sake of the planet and flavor, it is better to buy fruits and vegetables that are local, seasonal, and organic.

Aside from my use of kosher salt for its purity and coarseness, there is little peculiar about the other ingredients I use. I do expect a juicer to be used for lemons and a mill for pepper. If substituting table salt for kosher salt, reduce the quantity by a third.

I hope that I have revealed everything else I know about roasting in the recipes or in the many longish introductions throughout the book. I hope they will be read. It is in them that my artfulness, if any, and information are given. They may be of use.

*b*IRDS

I've never eaten a roast swan, once the prerogative of England's kings, and I've certainly never cooked one; but I have cooked or eaten most of the common table birds, and even a few uncommon ones. High in the Pyrénées at the Super Bagnière de Luchon, I had tiny ortolans, songbirds that were once a delight of the Victorian table, while confused cows, invisible in the mountain fog, stumbled into the dining room, their bells ringing.

I had only read about these birds, which aging gentlemen with substantial stomachs munched, bones and all, a large white napkin draped over head and plate so as to inhale the perfume—a lesson in *Gigi*. Netting the birds is now outlawed, particularly in Italy, where trapping of the seasonal migration had virtually destroyed the songbird population. I'm glad I had the rare opportunity; they were good. I am glad that I have had Scotch grouse from August twelfth (opening of the Queen's Shoot) fresh-ness until the end of the season, when they are hung to what can politely only be called ripeness. I have eaten sage grouse in the West, ruffed grouse in Vermont, and snow grouse, or ptarmigan, from Scandinavia.

Mostly—and with great pleasure—I have cooked chicken, Cornish game hens, turkey, capon, duck, goose, squabs (pigeon), and quail. They are what this chapter is mostly about.

There are choices: wild birds (often frozen), fresh birds, frozen birds, free-range birds, and organic birds. These terms are so loosely applied that it is hard to know what one is really buying. The U.S. government allows chickens that are chilled well below the freezing point to be called "fresh." I have often had the experience of sticking my hand inside a bird only to find ice crystals lodged there along with the bag of gizzards and livers.

Sensational articles in a variety of newspapers have shown supposed "free-range" birds, which we all fondly imagine happily pecking and foraging, living in such tight quarters that an old-fashioned ghetto landlord would be ashamed. Organic birds may be free-range or not. They are supposedly raised on clean water, without antibiotics, and on organic feed. The labeling requirements in these areas are so lax as to mean little except in a few progressive states.

Even "wild" and "game" are comparative terms. As I was testing different birds for this book, I bought "wild" birds such as turkey from a number of suppliers around the country. Stephana Bottom, who is originally from Texas and who worked with me on this book, grew up hunting and has hunted in England and Scotland; she noted with astonishment that none of these birds tasted like the birds at home or abroad. The flavor was much milder. Since the birds available to suppliers are basically farm-raised, it's not surprising. Hunters and demanding buyers of imported birds will get wild birds with buckshot and lots of flavor.

Both fortunately and unfortunately, we have become accustomed to the flavor and tenderness of birds that are totally domesticated—chickens and farmed quail and pheasant. We are pleased by their lower cost and year-round availability. Even in France, home of the famed Bresse chicken, the intensity of chicken flavor has decreased. The birds are no longer raised in Bresse, but are instead sent there to "finishing school" and get the little tag on their legs, much like a diploma. I suspect that if they could fly, they would get the tag for just passing overhead.

Forewarned is forearmed. Gamy birds with extra flavor and less fat on the body mean a decrease in tenderness. Marination (see Marinated Wild Pheasant, page

100), barding (see Simple Wild Turkey, page 93), or stuffing under the skin (see Plump-Skin Chicken, page 29) will tenderize, flavor, and moisten these birds; but they will always be different from domesticated birds. They should be.

Buying and preparing basic roast birds

ROASTING MANY BIRDS has given me the basic techniques for this book. Most important of all is to roast good food. Avoid frozen birds when possible and always reject birds that have been in some way "enhanced" or injected with alien matter.

If the only birds available come in isolation wards of plastic wrap, smell the package to make sure there is no off odor and look at the nasty diaper under the bird to see that there is as little hint of red as possible. All birds should have skins that look made-to-measure for their bodies, not sagging and overlarge or dried out. The skin color of the bird tells you almost nothing about its quality. Feed can be and is manipulated in such a way as to control color.

It is very hard to know exactly how many people any given bird will serve. It depends a great deal on how much else is in the meal and the appetites of the served. I always err on the side of buying more, as leftovers are so delicious. A largish-seeming bird like a wild turkey will serve only four, and a goose three to four; the carcasses as well as the interior cavities are very large. When in doubt about chickens, I prefer to roast two smaller birds rather than a larger one. That way I can accommodate requests for light and dark meat. Approximate servings are indicated in the general introductions to each kind of bird and in individual recipes. Birds needing defrosting, or special in some way, I order well ahead.

If at all possible, allow the bird(s) to come to room temperature before cooking. Otherwise, cooking will take longer and will be less even. All the cooking times are for room-temperature birds. It may take up to two hours for a large turkey to come to room temperature. There is no health danger in leaving a bird out of the refrigerator for that length of time as all cooking times will yield fully cooked birds unless carefully noted. There are no "rare" chickens here, nor will there be any red blood in the cavity of the bird after roasting when it is tilted over the pan to allow the juices to run out.

Frozen birds should be thawed in the refrigerator, and that will take more time than is generally indicated on the package. Any additional information I provide will be given under each bird.

Most birds I roast are cooked without *trussing*, tying up with string or skewers. This may make for birds that look a little less neat on the platter; actually, they look rather bawdy, with legs agape and wings akimbo, their tips whacked off and saved for stock. Poultry shears can be used by those uncomfortable with a cleaver.

Many birds—particularly chicken, duck, turkey, and goose—have pockets of fat inside their tail ends. These pull out easily and should be removed. The other end of the bird—the breast or neck end—is called the crop end. Most birds arrive with a paper packet of giblets (gizzard and heart), liver, and neck thrust into the cavity. Always remove it. Save the liver (page 20). Either start a small stock with the neck, stripped of its skin (which just pulls off), and the other innards (see Basic Chicken Stock, page 42) or freeze these parts for use in future stock. See pages 65–66 for information on cleaning fat from birds and removing wing tips and excess pieces of neck.

Birds with thin skins, such as turkey and me, should be lightly covered with a kitchen towel while coming to room temperature or the skin will dry out. This automatic drying can be an asset when very fatty birds such as duck and goose are to be cooked, whether directly in the oven or after poaching. This is the basic secret of Peking duck, where the drying step is taken a degree further by slightly separating the skin from the bird, often by blowing it up like a soccer ball. Then it is left to dry, swinging gently in a breeze, which can be provided by a fan. There is no recipe here for Peking duck since I don't have a Chinese oven. I'd like one though.

Generally, I season birds just before putting them in the oven, and I mostly omit salt, except for some in the bird's interior. Salt can cause the skin to cook unevenly by drawing out juices in a random pattern. Here is a virtue of another Chinese method in which the whole bird is marinated and the glaze allowed to dry before roasting, adding salt and flavor without softening the skin. Each way of preparing the bird for roasting gives a different crispness. Fat rubbed on skin will soften it except during prolonged roasting, when the skin may burn if an animal fat is used. Lemon juice or another acid on the skin will tend to dry it slightly and make it crisper.

I leave any stuffing for the last minute. If the stuffing is the conventional Thanksgiving kind, it can collect bacteria during a prolonged residence in the bird before it is cooked. I generally cook those stuffings (pages 108–119) as dressings in a separate dish. It is safer, and the bird cooks more quickly and evenly. What I use as stuffings are really flavorings for the cooking bird.

After prolonged and hopeful testing, I sadly decided that there really isn't any advantage in putting stuffing under the skin of a bird except for very small birds or a very simple stuffing of an herb or seasoning. With larger birds, the stuffing causes the skin to burn due to the increase in fat. Conversely, I sometimes *bard* birds, which is to lay or tie fat over or around them. Usually the barding fat—bacon or fatback—is removed at least ten minutes before the bird is taken from the oven in order to even out the browning. By this point any excess fat will have run off the bird, and the skin will not burn.

Roasting birds

I DON'T USE a rack; I'm too lazy to wash something extra. Besides, I save those rich nuggets of flesh without crisp skin, under the bird, for myself. It's too hard to get them out at the table. A rack makes it harder to spoon or pour extra fat out of a pan, as with goose and duck; a bulb baster does the job. If roasting without a rack, it is essential to shake the pan vigorously or push the bird around with a large wooden spatula after the first ten minutes of roasting to be sure that it doesn't stick. Move it around as well each time the oven door is opened for any purpose or when the bird is removed from the oven.

Use high temperatures. At 500°F, the food roasts rather than steams and cooks more quickly. Use a clean oven. Dirty ovens will smoke. Put the fan on or open a window, except during arctic winters. Don't place the bird too high up in the oven. There should be space between the bird and the top of the oven; otherwise the bird will scorch or cook unevenly due to reflected heat. Use a pan just slightly larger than the bird or the juices that seep out may burn.

I often roast two birds at one time in one pan. It is better not to cram two pans into the same oven, as less air circulates and cooking will be uneven. Even three small chickens can be placed in one large pan. To fit the maximum number of birds in a pan, arrange them so that the skinny neck end of one is alongside of the fatter leg side of the next. It is important that the birds fit in the pan without touching each other or the sides of the pan. If the birds touch each other, where they touch will be undercooked and the skin will not be crisp. If they touch the sides of the pan, they are liable to stick. In any case, the skin may be less crisp due to the increased humidity. A little more time—not much—may have to be allowed.

In addition to a tail end and a neck end, each bird has a breast side and a bottom side. The breast side is plumper and rounded. I cook all birds breast side up without turning them over or from side to side. With high heat, I get good all-over browning; I have seen too many disasters when hot and slippery birds are turned.

Except for wild turkeys, which are very oddly shaped, all birds should go into the oven legs first. The rear of the oven tends to be hotter, and the dark meat takes longer to cook. Not trussing—which smashes the thigh, the thickest part of the longer cooking dark meat, against the leg and is irrational—will let the bird cook more evenly.

I almost never baste the birds—spoon fat or liquids over them—as they roast. Basting softens the skin and is unnecessary, because the high heat bastes the birds with their own fat. When that fat is sparse, as it is on quail, or the cooking time is prolonged, as it is for a large turkey, it may be desirable to put some bacon or fat-back—not salt pork—over the breastbone as it cooks or to tent the top of the bird with aluminum foil if the skin seems to be getting overcooked. For crispness remove the foil or the fat for the last ten minutes of cooking.

Birds are done when they have completed the cooking times in the recipes or when a thin knife inserted into the joint between the thigh and the carcass reveals no blood or pinkness.

Serving

AS SOON AS the bird is cooked, remove the pan from the oven; move the bird to a platter somewhat larger than is needed to hold it, which leaves room for carving. A platter is better than a board, since none of the succulent juices are lost when the bird is carved. Removing it immediately from the pan prevents overcooking and sticking. Move the bird by placing a large wooden spoon into the tail end and balancing the bird with a kitchen spoon at the other end. Before moving it, tilt the bird over the roasting pan so that all the juices run out and into the pan.

Larger birds are generally left to sit out of the oven for fifteen minutes to half an hour after roasting. This permits the juices to circulate a bit and the flesh to firm, making it easier to slice. Small birds should be eaten right away, while they are hot.

Deglazing the pan: Today, "no fat" is the name of the game. I must say that I am sometimes tempted to leave a little fat in the sauce for added unctuousness. To remove, tilt the pan so that all the liquid collects in one corner; pour off or spoon out excess fat. Put the roasting pan on top of the stove. Add the water or other liquid and boil, while scraping the bottom vigorously with a wooden spoon. If not using a nonstick pan and the residue is particularly stubborn, use a metal spatula for scraping. Deglazing makes the base of a gravy. It also cleans the pan. Pour the gravy into a sauceboat or bowl or pour it over the finished bird. For more about gravy, see page 292.

How to carve: I don't know why even the most accomplished cooks can get discombobulated at the very thought of carving. Traditionally, it was deemed an accomplishment and a man's job. The bird is always so handsome as it comes whole to the table that the safety net of carving in the kitchen should be abandoned. Today, I find that the cook had better know how to carve the bird.

When the birds are not trussed, there is no string to cut off. Fully cooked birds are much easier to carve than somewhat rare ones. If the platter is large enough, the work will be easier. I always start with the legs, since this frees the battlefield for confronting the breast. I either serve the "dark meat people" first, or near the bird I have a second platter on which to lay the carved pieces.

Anchoring the breast of the bird with a carving fork, I cut the skin between the thigh and the breast and pry the leg and second joint outward. This reveals the joint at the bottom of the thigh, which is easily cut through. If necessary, the end of the leg can be held with a cloth for a surer grip while cutting through the joint. A little jiggling by the hand holding the fork can help to free up the joint—inelegant but efficient.

Depending on the size of the bird, the thigh can be cut away from the leg. If the bird is a large turkey, I slice the meat away from the thigh bone parallel to the bone and, if I'm ambitious, from the leg bone as well. Turning the bird around, I go on to the second leg and thigh.

It is now easy to remove the breast meat from the carcass. If the bird is small, make an incision all along the top of the breastbone and work the knife along the rib cage until the breast half separates almost entirely from the carcass. If the wishbone at the neck end of the breast is large, a small knife may be needed to free the meat from it and from the wing attached to the breast. If serving the wing separately, cut through the joint between the breast and the wing. The sharp edge of the carving knife will be needed to cut through the skin at the platter side of the breast. Some people prefer poultry shears for cutting through joints. A clean kitchen towel can be a savior. When all else fails, holding the towel, grab a piece of the bird such as the leg bone and tug outward so that the knife can get to work.

If the breast is large, cut it in slices on a diagonal to the breastbone, trying to include a little skin on each slice of white meat.

Dividends and extras

NORMAL PEOPLE ROAST birds to eat and serve them. I guess I do too; but in my heart of hearts, it is the soups, hashes, and salads made from leftovers that give me the greatest pleasure. This chapter is stuffed with such recipes.

Speaking of stuffing, there are a few at the end of the chapter. There are also a few extra sauces there and on pages 292–309.

Some sauces and stuffings are made with giblets, the dividends that usually arrive in a paper packet inside the cavity of the bird. The very first chicken I roasted had that packet still inside—not disastrous, but not wonderful. Remove the packet; but do not discard it.

To clean the liver or livers: Livers have two lobes and look like a pair connected by tissue with lots of small blood vessels. Spread the livers flat on a work surface. Hold a lobe in one hand. With the other hand, slide a small sharp knife along the connective tissue, holding it at a forty-five-degree angle away from the lobe being held and toward the other lobe, pushing it off the tissues and vessels that extend into it. Hold the connective tissue and repeat for the second lobe. Discard the tissue.

Soak livers in milk for at least a half hour to remove any bitterness. To amass livers or keep them for the future, put them, cleaned, into a freezer container, cover them with milk, and freeze. Add more livers and milk as more livers become available. To use them, defrost in the refrigerator.

Use the reserved chicken livers in any of the quick pâtés and mousses, to bind sauces, and in Liver-Rich Dressing (page 117).

The other inhabitants of the "extras" bag are usually a piece of neck, whose skin can easily be removed by tugging; the gizzard, which is a firm, two-lobed and hardish dark red kind of bird stomach; and the heart. All of these can be used for stock and Basic Fowl Giblet Gravy (page 45). A good sign that a small stock made from neck, wing tips, gizzard, and heart is done is when the pieces of the neck separate on their own or are easily separated. Gizzards and hearts are cooked as soon as they can be fairly easily pierced with the tip of a sharp knife.

Stock is my favorite roast bird dividend. I ruthlessly take the bones off people's plates, waiting until people are not looking or have gone home, and salvage the carcass from the platter. Into the pot the bones go, cut or torn into pieces if I have the time. The hearts, gizzard, and necks are added—no livers—and liquid to cover. Usually, I start with water, but sometimes canned broth or stock I have made before that wasn't quite strong enough. I cover the stockpot with an otoshi-buta (see page 11) or a lid left ajar. Once the nascent stock has been brought to a boil and then reduced to a simmer, it can keep cooking almost indefinitely. Skim and top up the liquid from time to time.

Not quite a stock and nowhere near as plentiful are the juices that collect around roasted birds as they sit on the platter. The Chinese and Italians love them as I do. I have been known to go into the kitchen and sneak the congealed (lots of bone gelatin) treasures up with a teaspoon. If I can resist, these make fabulous enrichments for sauces and soups.

Co-dependent vegetables: Roasting potatoes along with a chicken may be the most common example (see Roast Chicken with Crispy Potatoes, page 25). Any of the birds can be roasted with potato wedges (a large floury baking potato makes about twelve wedges) added to the pan. Don't cram the pan. If more vegetables are desired, use a larger pan to accommodate them along with the bird. The vegetables should be in a rough single layer. Cook them along with the bird for the last forty to fifty minutes of the roasting time. If the potatoes are added to the pan when the bird begins its roasting or slightly before, they will need to be filmed with a tablespoon of fat. If the bird has roasted for a while before the potatoes are added and has rendered some fat, the potatoes are simply rolled in the fat that has been rendered from the bird. The more fat, the more the potatoes will brown. Scoop up the potatoes once or twice to turn them and keep them from sticking to the pan.

Many other vegetables or combinations of vegetables—see the list on page 315—can roast along with the birds, like the potatoes. Add the vegetables all at once or gradually, depending on their basic roasting times. Whole garlic cloves or shallots can be added with the vegetables.

Salt and pepper vegetables for only the last fifteen minutes of the roasting time. Salt can draw off too much liquid, and pepper becomes bitter if added earlier. Add dried herbs such as rosemary, thyme, winter savory, and oregano at the start of roasting and fresh herbs for only the final five minutes, unless they are in the bird's cavity.

CHICKEN

WHEN IN DOUBT, ROAST A CHICKEN. When hurried, roast a chicken. Seeking simple pleasure? Roast a chicken.

Until fairly recently, a plump chicken tender enough to roast was a sign of luxury. Males, or cocks, were killed when fairly young because only one or two were needed to maintain a flock, and they were generally less tender. Females were seldom killed young since the eggs that they produced well into their hen days were more profitable than the meat.

The French king Henri IV (1553–1610) had a vision of a prosperous rule: "I want there to be no peasant in my kingdom so poor that he is unable to have a chicken in his pot every Sunday." This symbol of utopian opulence was a stewing chicken of no tender prime. (Herbert Hoover echoed the theme about four hundred years later.) Today, we may have great difficulty locating an old hen for stewing; but younger chickens are plentiful, if less flavorful. They are best roasted to concentrate their flavors.

If there is one thing I can say for myself, it's that I can roast a chicken. What's more, mine is a fail-safe recipe that I use repeatedly and that I have gradually understood to be one of the two most popular recipes of the thousands I have written. (The other is for microwave risotto.) A roast chicken suits both children in the family and guests happy to have simple, taste-filled food. It can be elevated to fancy party fare with Champagne Sauce and delight more serious gastronomes in its simplest form.

Varying the deglazing liquid (red or white wine, Champagne, vermouth, Sherry, brandy, water, stock, or cream) stirred into the roasting pan to dissolve all the meat juices easily varies the gravies that can be made, as will a couple of tablespoons of chopped fresh herbs.

Roasting a chicken is quick and requires almost no attention. Once mastered, a roast chicken becomes a frequent visitor to the table. The carcass from a six-pound roast chicken makes over a quart of Basic Chicken Stock (page 42). The shreds of leftover meat make salads and hash.

ROAST
WHOLE
CHICKEN

REALLY, NOTHING IS simpler. Put the rack in the second position from the bottom of the oven, crank the temperature up to 500°F, and go.

The basic roasting time for chickens in the high-heat method is about ten minutes to the pound for a chicken at room temperature, untrussed, which invariably gives a crisp skin and a thoroughly cooked but moist bird. However, it may be necessary to cook free-range chickens with their heavier thighs and legs and greater amount of blood for a longer time. Chickens need to be thoroughly cooked, but not until powdery dry. Interior juices should be clear, and the tip of a knife inserted into the joint between the thigh and carcass should reveal no blood.

All the timings are for unstuffed chickens. In the recipes that follow, many flavorings, such as herbs and garlic, are used inside the chicken cavity. Adapt these recipes to follow the ten-minutes-per-pound rule if the bird at hand is bigger or smaller than that listed in the recipe. Any chicken over seven pounds is a fowl and doesn't roast well. The exception to this is capon (page 51), which is larger but still tender and follows the basic timing for chicken.

To roast more than one chicken at a time, see page 17. To roast vegetables along with chicken, see page 21.

Chickens can be rubbed with a little lemon juice or glazed; but no fat need be applied to the outside as the skin contains a sufficiency.

Simplest roast chicken

SERVES 2 TO 4

TOTAL
ROASTING
TIME
50 *to* 60
minutes

Here it is, the recipe that started the book. If there is no lemon, garlic, or butter on hand, roast the chicken without them. Or play. Use peeled shallots or a small onion, quartered. Add some leaves from the top of a bunch of celery, a couple of sage leaves, or a bay leaf. Try a few juice orange or blood orange wedges.

Vary the deglazing liquid to change the flavor of the gravy or to match what's in the bird. Basic Chicken Stock—or canned—is the starting point; but use part wine—whatever is left over, red or white—or a little vermouth. Make one third of the liquid orange juice if oranges are in the bird. This is not astrophysics. Have fun.

5- to 6-pound chicken, wing tips removed
1 lemon, halved
4 whole garlic cloves
4 tablespoons unsalted butter, optional
Kosher salt, to taste

Freshly ground black pepper, to taste
1 cup Basic Chicken Stock (page 42) or canned, water, fruit juice, or wine, for deglazing

Place rack on second level from bottom of oven. Heat oven to 500°F.

Remove the fat from the tail and crop end of the chicken. Freeze the neck and giblets for Basic Chicken Stock. Reserve chicken livers for another use.

Stuff the cavity of the chicken with the lemon, garlic, and butter, if using. Season the cavity and skin with salt and pepper.

Place the chicken in a 12 x 8 x 1½-inch roasting pan breast side up. Put in the oven legs first and roast 50 to 60 minutes, or until the juices run clear. After the first 10 minutes, move the chicken with a wooden spatula to keep it from sticking.

Remove the chicken to a platter by placing a large wooden spoon into the tail end and balancing the chicken with a kitchen spoon pressed against the crop end. As you lift the chicken, tilt it over the roasting pan so that all the juices run out and into the pan.

Pour off or spoon out excess fat from the roasting pan and put the roasting pan on top of the stove. Add the stock or other liquid and bring the contents of the pan to a boil, while scraping the bottom vigorously with a wooden spoon. Let reduce by half. Serve the sauce over the chicken or, for crisp skin, in a sauceboat.

Simple chicken breasts, legs, and thighs

SERVES 6 TO 8

TOTAL
ROASTING
TIME:
see below

IF CHICKEN IS roasted in pieces instead of as one whole bird, there is no carving to bother with. Chicken pieces roast more evenly than they broil. When broiled, the skin gets dark before the fat renders out and the meat is fully done.

To be pedantic, I remind the cook that a whole breast has two halves. When one buys chicken pieces, the breast is usually already halved into the familiar half-moon shape. Try to choose pieces that have a full covering of skin. The parts are cooked on the bone for more flavor.

This recipe works for any four pounds of chicken parts. A larger pan permits the cooking of more pieces. The largest roasting pan that fits in a standard oven holds sixteen half breast pieces (eight whole breasts) or three whole cut-up chickens.

8 half breasts of chicken with bones, skin on (about 8 to 10 ounces each, 4 pounds) or 4 pounds mixed parts with bones, skin on (half breasts, thighs, and legs)	Kosher salt, to taste Freshly ground black pepper, to taste 1½ cups Basic Chicken Stock (page 42) or canned, wine, fruit juice, or water, for deglazing

Place rack in center of oven. Heat oven to 500°F.

Arrange dark meat, if using, around outer edges and white meat, bone up, toward center of a 14 x 12 x 2-inch roasting pan. Sprinkle with salt and pepper. Roast for 10 minutes. Turn pieces over. Roast 10 minutes more. White meat should be done after 20 minutes. Dark meat will take another 5 to 10 minutes. Remove pieces to platter.

Pour off fat. Deglaze the pan with liquid (page 10) or put pan on top of stove. Add the liquid and bring contents to a boil, scraping the bottom vigorously with a wooden spoon. Let reduce by half. Serve from a sauceboat.

TOTAL ROASTING TIME: white meat, 20 to 25 minutes; dark meat, 30 to 35 minutes

Roast chicken with crispy potatoes

SERVES 4

TOTAL
ROASTING
TIME:
50 to 60
minutes

Throw potatoes into the roasting pan with your chicken, toss a big green salad while it's roasting, and there's dinner for the families of the current crop of harried home cooks. Cut baking potatoes into wedges, use whole small new potatoes, or halve or quarter larger new potatoes. Don't go into anxious spasms trying to turn the potatoes so evenly that each side gets perfectly browned. They will brown enough and be delicious. Taste the potatoes at the end to see if they need more salt and pepper, but be careful because there's a terrible tendency to eat them all up before serving.

There will be very little fat left in the pan. The potatoes will have absorbed it. . . . This is not for the diet conscious.

5- to 6-pound chicken, wing tips removed

1½ pounds Idaho baking potatoes, peeled and cut in half lengthwise, cut in half across, each quarter cut into 3 to 4 wedges (about 28 wedges), or 1½ pounds small red new potatoes, peeled or not and quartered

1 medium onion (8 ounces), peeled, left whole, optional, or 6 cloves garlic, unpeeled, optional

Kosher salt, to taste

Freshly ground black pepper, to taste

1 teaspoon chopped fresh rosemary, optional

Proceed as directed in Simplest Roast Chicken (page 23), using a larger roasting pan so that when you add the potatoes, they will fit. After 10 minutes roasting, move the chicken with a wooden spatula to keep it from sticking. Arrange the potatoes and the onion, if using, around chicken so that they touch as little as possible. Roll the potatoes in whatever fat has oozed out of the chicken. Sprinkle with salt and pepper. Roast for the chicken's remaining time of 35 to 45 minutes, scooping up the potatoes to turn them over every 15 minutes. Add garlic and/or sprinkle potatoes with rosemary, if using, for last 15 minutes. Some potatoes may stick to the pan a bit, depending on the amount of fat from the chicken. This helps form the surface crust. Just be sure to scrape along the pan with the edge of the spatula to unstick the potatoes.

Remove chicken, potatoes, and garlic to a serving platter. The onion may be cut in pieces and served or else thrown into the soup pot with the carcass. Sprinkle potatoes generously with salt and pepper. Deglaze the pan (page 10).

Herb-roasted chicken

TOTAL
ROASTING
TIME:
50 *to* 60
minutes

THE ABSOLUTELY SIMPLEST method is to go to your window box or garden and pick a very large bunch of one or more herbs and cram as much as you can into the cavity of the chicken. Should you be too city bound or lack a green thumb for even a window box, follow the same procedure but harvest the herbs at the local market.

5- to 6-pound chicken, wing tips removed
1½ cups fresh herbs (suggestion: ½ cup thyme leaves, ½ cup winter savory, ¼ cup rosemary, and 6 chives)
Kosher salt, to taste

Freshly ground black pepper, to taste
1 cup Basic Chicken Stock (page 42) or canned, water, fruit juice, or wine, for deglazing

Place rack on second level from bottom of oven. Heat oven to 500°F.

Remove the fat from the tail end and crop of the chicken; freeze the neck and giblets for Basic Chicken Stock. Reserve chicken livers for another use. Stuff the cavity of the chicken with the herbs, salt, and pepper. Season the skin with salt and pepper.

Place the chicken in a 12 x 8 x 1½-inch roasting pan breast side up. Put in oven legs first and roast 50 to 60 minutes, or until the juices run clear. After the first 10 minutes, move the chicken with a wooden spatula to keep it from sticking.

Remove the chicken to a platter. Tilt the chicken over the roasting pan as you move it so that all the juices run out and into the pan. Pour or spoon off any excess fat. Put the roasting pan on top of the stove. Add the stock or other liquid and bring to a boil while scraping the bottom vigorously with a wooden spoon. Let reduce by half. Serve the sauce over the chicken or, for crisp skin, in a sauceboat.

Roast chicken with pomegranate glaze and fresh mint

SERVES 3 TO 4

TOTAL
ROASTING
TIME:
50
minutes

THE RICHNESS OF the deeply brown, glazed chicken, the sparkle of the ruby red pomegranate seeds, and the sweet acidity of the juice combine to make a dish elegant enough for any party. For overkill, serve with Not-on-Your-Diet Potatoes (page 395) or Crispy Creamy Roasted Jerusalems (page 415). More healthfully, go for a simple green vegetable, barely buttered.

Pomegranates vary in size and juiciness. It will take one large or two small pomegranates to make a half cup of juice and the same number again to make a cup and a half of seeds. Watch out for stains.

To juice pomegranates: Cut pomegranates in half like oranges and use a citrus juicer—an electric one is easier—holding the cut sides down firmly and moving the pomegranate half around to extract maximum juice from the seeds.

To seed pomegranates: Cut pomegranates into quarters. Using a small spoon, or your fingers, gently pull seeds away from hard skin. Seeds are bouncy but fragile. As seeds are pulled away, they will separate. Let them drop into a measuring cup. Continue until all seeds are removed. Pick off any white membrane clinging to seeds.

1 bunch (1 ounce) fresh mint
5- to 6-pound chicken, wing tips removed
2 to 3 teaspoons kosher salt
Freshly ground black pepper, to taste
About 4 whole cloves garlic, unpeeled
1½ cups seeds from 1 (or 2 small) large pomegranate

½ cup pomegranate juice from 1 large (or 2 small) pomegranate
1 recipe Rich Chicken Sauce (page 43) or ½ cup Extra-Rich Roasted Triple Stock (page 230) or ½ cup Basic Chicken Stock (page 42) or canned

Place rack on second level from bottom of oven. Heat oven to 500°F.

Remove leaves from half of mint bunch, reserving stems. Stack the leaves, roll, and cut them across into thin strips.

Remove the fat from the tail and crop end of the chicken. Use neck and giblets in sauce. Reserve chicken livers for another use.

continued

Place chicken breast side up in a 12 x 8 x 1½-inch roasting pan. Sprinkle cavity with some of the salt and pepper and stuff with garlic, ½ cup pomegranate seeds, ½ bunch mint with leaves on, and reserved mint stems. Pour ¼ cup of the pomegranate juice over chicken. Sprinkle with 1 teaspoon salt. Put chicken in oven, legs first. Roast 50 minutes, moving the chicken after the first 10 minutes with a wooden spatula to keep it from sticking. The chicken should not burn, but if it smells like it is burning, reduce heat to 400°F and open oven door for a minute to lower the temperature quickly. Continue roasting at lower temperature.

Chicken will be a beautiful mahogany brown color, and any liquid will seem to have disappeared. Tilt the chicken over pan, then remove the chicken to a platter.

Tilt roasting pan and spoon out fat, leaving any juices. Place pan over medium-high heat. Pour in the chicken sauce or stock and the last ¼ cup pomegranate juice. Scrape hard along the bottom of the pan. Use a metal spoon to get all the good brown gunk up from the pan. That brown gunk will dissolve in the liquid to make a sensational gravy.

Add remaining mint leaves. Lower heat. Cook 1 minute. Taste carefully, liquid will be hot. Salt and pepper to taste. Add any juices that have collected on the platter. Cook liquid 30 seconds. Pour about half of the juices over bird on platter, being careful not to overflow platter. Top with half of the remaining pomegranate seeds. Put the rest of the juices in a sauceboat with the rest of the seeds. Mix well. Serve with chicken.

Plump-skin chicken

I DID SAY I don't see much point in doing this. However, we all like to try new things, so here is a model for stuffing a bird under the skin. It is particularly useful for birds that have skins with little fat, such as wild turkey.

Be forewarned that adding butter to the skin of the chicken, on it or under it, will darken it and may cause smoking as the fat drips into the pan.

You will need to liberate the skin from the chicken so that the skin forms a big pocket like an envelope for stuffing. On small birds you can just push your hand in between the skin and the flesh, starting at one end of the bird and moving, with nails curled under, along the breastbone and then snaking your hand down around the breast. Repeat the procedure from the other end and then move your hand as far as possible around the thigh and second joint.

On larger birds where the connective tissue linking the breast to the skin is heavier, take a little knife or scissors and snip at the connective tissue so as to free the skin. At that point, ease in up to one cup of any stuffing. By a large bird I mean a five-pound roasting chicken. The whole amount of the stuffing in this recipe could probably go into a wild turkey or a six-pound whole turkey breast or a nine-pound turkey.

FOR THE MUSHROOM PURÉE (duxelles)

1 pound mushrooms and/or mushroom stems, wiped clean

¼ pound shallots, peeled and sliced (about ⅓ cup)

6 tablespoons unsalted butter

1½ teaspoons kosher salt

½ teaspoon freshly ground black pepper

¼ cup finely chopped fresh flat-leaf parsley

FOR THE CHICKEN

5- to 6-pound chicken, wing tips removed

1 cup Basic Chicken Stock (page 42) or canned, water, fruit juices, or wine, for deglazing

To make mushroom purée: Finely chop the mushrooms and shallots separately. A food processor can be used.

Melt the butter in a large heavy skillet over medium heat. When it foams, stir in the shallots and sauté until softened, about 5 minutes. Stir in the mushrooms and sprinkle with salt and pepper. Sauté, stirring occasionally, until the mushrooms have rendered their liquid, about 6 minutes. Boil off the liquid; this will take from 5 to 10 minutes, depending on the mushrooms and the size of the pan. There should be only butter—no liquid—remaining in the skillet. Reduce the heat to low, stir in the parsley, and cook until the mushrooms are just beginning to brown and no trace of liquid remains in the pan, about 5 minutes. Turn the mushroom purée out of the pan and cool. May be made ahead up to this point. Set aside 1 cup for this recipe. Freeze ¼ cup left over to use another day.

To roast the chicken: Twenty minutes before roasting the chicken, place rack on second level from bottom of oven. Heat oven to 500°F.

Remove the fat from the tail end and crop of the chicken and freeze the neck and giblets for Basic Chicken Stock. Reserve chicken livers for another use.

Liberate skin and form pocket as described on page 29. Slip in stuffing. Place the chicken in a 12 x 8 x 1½-inch roasting pan breast side up. Put in oven legs first and roast 50 to 60 minutes, or until the juices run clear. After the first 10 minutes, move the chicken with a wooden spatula to keep it from sticking.

Remove the chicken to a platter by placing a large wooden spoon into the tail end and balancing the chicken with a kitchen spoon at the other end. Before moving, tilt the chicken over the roasting pan so that all the juices run out and into the pan. Pour or spoon off excess fat. Put the roasting pan on top of the stove. Add the stock or other liquid and bring the contents of the pan to a boil while scraping the bottom vigorously with a wooden spoon. Let reduce by half. Serve the sauce over the chicken or, for crisp skin, in a sauceboat.

Tarragon roast chicken

SERVES 6 TO 8

TOTAL
ROASTING
TIME:
*see facing
page*

THIS SIMPLE, RAPIDLY made dish was one of my triumphs when testing for this book. Although the chicken is roasted in serving pieces, it is as brown and succulent as any whole roast chicken and cooks in about half the time, with no last-minute carving to be done. Sprigs of tarragon are slipped underneath the skin to flavor the chicken and to show faintly through the crisp skin. It is very important to choose chicken pieces that have a nice covering of skin. The recipe will not work with lean and mean skinless breasts. The tarragon needs to be in place a half hour before the chicken is roasted for the meat to end up beautifully perfumed and moist.

Turn the deglazing sauce up a notch or two by making Tarragon-Wine Sauce. Serve with rice or noodles tossed with a little bit of the skimmed-off chicken fat, to soak up all the juices from the ample amount of gravy.

8 half breasts of chicken with ribs, skin on (8 to 10 ounces each, 4 pounds), or 4 pounds breasts and thighs with legs attached

1½ bunches (1½ ounces) fresh tarragon, leaves removed, ½ cup leaves reserved for sauce

½ cup fresh lemon juice

Kosher salt, to taste

Freshly ground black pepper, to taste

1½ cups Basic Chicken Stock (page 42) or canned, water, fruit juice, wine, for deglazing, or, for Tarragon-Wine Sauce, 1 cup Champagne or white wine, ½ cup chicken stock, and ½ cup reserved tarragon leaves

Prepare the chicken ahead so it can marinate. Peel back the skin covering one piece of chicken until most of the meat is exposed. Don't remove the skin completely. If roasting only breasts, start loosening skin from the backbone side and the skin will come right up. Once the skin is pulled away, cover the exposed meat with tarragon leaves. Fan them out and pat them down so they lie flat. Pulling gently, place the skin back over the meat, covering all the tarragon so it won't burn. The more the skin covers the meat, the better it will cook, turning a beautiful golden brown. Continue peeling back skin and stuffing until all pieces are done.

Arrange pieces bone side down so they touch as little as possible in an 18 x 13 x 2-inch roasting pan. Put dark pieces around the outer edges of the pan, white pieces toward the center. Pour lemon juice over and around pieces in pan. Let sit at room temperature for 30 minutes. May prepare up to this point 6 to 8 hours ahead. Make sure time is allowed for refrigerated chicken to return to room temperature (about 1 hour) before roasting, or cooking time will not be correct. Chicken may be salted before roasting or after.

About 20 minutes before roasting the chicken, place rack in center of oven. Heat oven to 500°F.

Roast for 10 minutes. Turn pieces over. Roast 10 minutes more. White meat is done after 20 minutes. Turn over and roast 5 more minutes for browner skin. Dark meat needs another 5 to 10 minutes. Roast chicken just until skin is crisp and juices run clear.

Remove pieces to a serving platter. Pour or spoon off fat from pan. Place over medium-high heat. Add liquid and bring to a boil. Let cook briefly. With a wooden spoon scrape up glaze and any cooked bits. Add reserved tarragon. Let reduce by half. Serve sauce over chicken or in a separate sauceboat.

TOTAL ROASTING TIME: white meat, 20 to 25 minutes; dark meat, 25 to 30 minutes

Simple chicken wings

SERVES 9

TOTAL ROASTING TIME: 20 *minutes*

CHICKEN WINGS ARE inexpensive and can be bought for stock. They are made up of three sections divided by two joints. The tiny wing tips don't have much meat and are best removed and saved for stock. The other two sections can be separated, roasted, and eaten as snack food. Cut through the joints with poultry shears or a heavy knife.

Unless the wings are actually being glazed (see Chicken Wings with Asian Glaze, below), it is best to season them after cooking. Salt and pepper and perhaps a sprinkling of a hot red pepper sauce is all that is needed. They can be served with a side of salsa.

It's hard to know how many to allow per person. I usually figure on five to six pieces per person; that means three whole wings each. A large pan holds three pounds of wings (twenty-seven wings, fifty-four pieces, or enough for nine people). A small pan holds a pound and half (twelve wings, twenty-four pieces, enough for four).

3 pounds chicken wings, jointed into 3 pieces, and tips removed (about 54 pieces)

1 teaspoon canola or other neutral oil

Use the smallest pan that will hold wing pieces comfortably in a single layer. Using your hands, rub oil all around pan. Put wing pieces in pan. Roast on second level from bottom of oven at 500°F for 10 minutes. Turn pieces over. Roast 10 minutes more.

Chicken wings with Asian glaze

SERVES 9; MAKES ½ CUP SAUCE

TOTAL ROASTING TIME: 20 *minutes*

THESE MILDLY SPICY wings make a good dish for an informal party. After the chicken has marinated in the glaze, any extra glaze should be boiled—no nasty raw chicken juices—to serve on the side as a dipping sauce. Hand out plenty of paper napkins. This is almost as messy as it is delicious. The wings can be marinated for up to a day ahead.

Although in this recipe the pan doesn't get deglazed to make a sauce, after removing the wings immediately to a serving dish, place a good two cups of water in the pan and deglaze it to clean it. Extra glaze gets hard at the bottom of the pan, and if it isn't removed immediately it clings stubbornly.

This recipe can be made in larger quantities. Put a second shelf nearer to the top of the oven. After turning the wings, reverse the position of the pans. To make only half the recipe, use a 12 x 8 x 1½-inch pan and half the glaze recipe.

FOR ASIAN GLAZE

4 to 5 cloves garlic, peeled, smashed, and chopped into medium pieces

2½ ounces fresh gingerroot, peeled and cut across the grain into thin slices, then chopped into medium pieces

2 tablespoons soy sauce, preferably tamari

2 tablespoons mirin

2½ tablespoons dark corn syrup or Chinese rock sugar in yellow crystals, crushed

¼ cup rice wine vinegar

1 teaspoon canola or other neutral oil

3 pounds chicken wings, jointed, and tips removed

Put the chopped garlic and ginger in a blender. Add soy sauce and mirin. Blend until a smooth purée. Add the corn syrup and vinegar. Blend until smooth. Using a rubber spatula, scrape into a small bowl and reserve.

Rub the oil inside an 18 x 13 x 2-inch roasting pan. Put wing pieces in pan. Pour on reserved glaze. Toss until all pieces are well coated. Marinate at room temperature about ½ hour. May be made ahead and held at this stage, covered, in the refrigerator, for 1 day. Make sure refrigerated chicken returns to room temperature before cooking or increase cooking time by 5 to 10 minutes.

Place rack on second level from bottom of oven. About 20 minutes before roasting, place the rack in center of oven. Heat oven to 500°F.

Pour or spoon off extra glaze into a saucepan.

Roast wings for 10 minutes. Turn pieces over. Roast 10 minutes more. To prevent sticking, use a spatula to scoop out wings and thickened glaze onto a serving platter as soon as removed from oven.

Boil the extra glaze in the saucepan for 5 to 7 minutes. Place in a small bowl as a dipping sauce.

Chicken leftovers

CHICKEN LEFTOVERS ARE very welcome and useful. They are one of the reasons I prefer to make two smaller chickens, say four pounds each, rather than one large one. I'm more likely to have leftovers. Sometimes, I will make two chickens even if I need only one, to be sure to have enough bones for Basic Chicken Stock (page 42) and to have meat for one of the following dishes. Leftover capon or turkey meat can be used instead.

Even so, there may be times when there simply isn't enough leftover bird meat to make these dishes. When in a jam, poach. The resulting dish will have less intensity of flavor, but still be good. Eight ounces cooked chicken makes one cup meat, cubed in ¾- to 1-inch pieces.

POACHED CHICKEN FOR EXTRAS
1 chicken breast (8 ounces), skinned, boned, and split into half breasts

6 cups Basic Chicken Stock (page 42) or canned, if poaching

To cook in the microwave: Place in pie plate without stock; cover tightly with plastic wrap. Cook 2 minutes 30 seconds at full power (in high-voltage oven). Prick plastic wrap. Remove from oven. Allow to cool and use.

To poach on the stove top: Pour enough chicken stock to cover the breasts in a skillet or shallow pan large enough to hold breasts in a single layer. Bring liquid to a boil, reduce heat to a simmer, and add chicken breasts. Cook about 12 minutes, or until slightly pink inside. Remove from the heat and allow to cool in liquid. Use immediately, or refrigerate overnight in liquid.

Chicken hash with parsnips

THIS IS A delightful midwinter meal. The sweetness of the parsnips is set off by the slight mustiness of the sage. It takes a while for the parsnips to brown. The liquid boils off almost immediately, leaving concentrated flavor.

Using a heavy nonstick pan helps with even cooking and prevents sticking of the finished, browned hash cake.

5 small parsnips (14 ounces), peeled and cut into ¾-inch cubes (2½ cups)

2 tablespoons unsalted butter

1 medium onion (8 ounces), peeled and cut into ¼-inch dice (1¼ cups)

¼ teaspoon allspice

2 teaspoons kosher salt

5 to 6 grinds fresh black pepper

8 medium leaves fresh sage, stacked, rolled, cut across into thin slices (2 tablespoons)

8 to 12 ounces leftover roast chicken meat, cut into ¾-inch pieces (1 to 1½ cups)

½ cup Basic Chicken Stock (page 42) or canned

In a small pan of boiling water, cook the parsnip cubes 10 minutes, or until tender. Drain and reserve.

Meanwhile, in a 10-inch nonstick skillet, melt 1 tablespoon of the butter over low heat. Add the onions, stirring occasionally. When onions begin to brown, add allspice, salt, pepper, sage, and the last tablespoon of butter, and cook until sage is wilted, and onions are brown. Altogether, this should take 10 minutes.

Add the chicken and parsnips. Increase heat to high. Cook until parsnips begin to brown, 5 to 10 minutes, occasionally scooping up sections as they brown and turning over with a spatula.

Add ¼ cup of the chicken stock. Boil 2 minutes, until liquid has evaporated. Do not stir anymore. Reduce heat to low.

Use the spatula to spread out the mixture evenly in the skillet. Press down to compact. Increase heat slightly to medium. Cook 20 minutes. Scoop up large pieces with spatula and turn over. Pour the last ¼ cup of chicken stock into the skillet, and press down mixture once more until solid. Cook over medium heat for 15 minutes.

Turn out onto a serving platter so that crusty browned side is on top.

Chicken curry—hot or cold

MAKES 4 CUPS; SERVES 4 AS A HOT MAIN
COURSE; SERVES 6 AS A COLD FIRST COURSE
WITH GREENS AND PAPADUMS

THESE ARE SUMMER and winter versions of chicken curry. The basic preparation is the same. If there is extra chicken, the recipe doubles easily. If poached chicken is substituted for roast chicken, omit the yogurt.

Any or all of the optional ingredients can be added for the hot or cold version. When papaya is added to the hot version, it should be done at the last minute. Papaya's enzyme breaks down protein and will make the chicken mushy if left in for any length of time. If using coconut for the cold salad, sprinkle on top of the finished dish.

The more items that are added, the larger the amount made.

Many Indian breads are available in packages and can be reheated to serve alongside the curries. The hot version is served with chutney and other condiments. I prefer the fragrant basmati rice.

FOR THE BASIC PREPARATION

2 tablespoons unsalted butter

3 tablespoons curry powder

1 teaspoon whole anise seeds

1 medium onion (8 ounces), peeled and cut into ¼-inch pieces (1¼ cups)

3 cloves garlic, smashed, peeled, and minced

2 ounces fresh gingerroot, peeled and cut into small pieces

¾ cup Basic Chicken Stock (page 42) or canned

2 teaspoons kosher salt

FOR HOT CURRY

1¼ pounds leftover roast chicken meat, cut into 1-inch pieces (2¼ cups)

One 8-ounce container plain yogurt (¾ cup)

2 tablespoons fresh lemon juice

Freshly ground black pepper, to taste

1 fresh pineapple, trimmed, peeled, and cut into 1-inch cubes (1½ cups)

⅓ cup almond slivers

⅓ cup pomegranate seeds, optional

½ papaya, peeled and cut into 1-inch cubes (1½ cups), optional

1 mango, peeled and cut into 1-inch cubes, optional

1 hard green apple (like Granny Smith), cored, peeled, cut into 1-inch cubes, optional, and tossed with 1 teaspoon fresh lemon juice, optional

FOR COLD CURRY

1¼ pounds leftover roast chicken meat, cut into 1-inch pieces (2¼ cups)

One 8-ounce container plain yogurt (¾ cup)

2 tablespoons fresh lemon juice

Freshly ground black pepper, to taste

1 pear, peeled, cored, and cut into ½-inch cubes

½ cup chopped fresh mint (about ½ bunch)

½ cup grated unsweetend coconut, optional

1 banana, peeled and cut into ½-inch slices, optional

¾ cup seedless grapes, cut in half, optional

¼ cup golden raisins, soaked in warm water until softened, optional

¼ cup chopped fresh cilantro, optional

6 cups washed salad greens

In a 10-inch skillet, melt the butter over low heat. Add the curry powder and anise. Cook until aromatic, about 3 to 4 minutes.

Add the onion. Stirring occasionally, cook until transparent.

Meanwhile, put the garlic, ginger, and 2 tablespoons of the chicken stock in a blender. Blend until a smooth paste. Add the remainder of the chicken stock and blend again. Pour into onion mixture. Add salt and mix well. Cook over medium heat 5 minutes until flavors come together. May be reserved at this stage.

For hot chicken curry: Add the chicken to the warm liquid. Add the yogurt and heat until just warmed throughout, 6 to 8 minutes. Do not bring to high heat, or yogurt will curdle. Add lemon juice, pepper, pineapple, almonds, and any optional ingredients, if using. Mix well and heat. Serve with basmati rice on the side and store-bought papadums.

For cold chicken curry: Place warm liquid in a medium bowl. Add chicken and mix well. Let cool. Add yogurt, lemon juice, and pepper. Mix well. Add pear, mint, and any optional ingredients, and mix. Serve on a bed of salad greens with store-bought papadums.

Chicken salads

I HAVE BECOME convinced that even for making chicken salads, roasting is a better way to proceed than boiling. Roasting the chicken gives firm, moist meat with more flavor. It's easy to overcook boiled chicken, with the end product soggy and stringy. The yield of roasted chicken meat will be the same as boiled; nothing is lost by proper roasting. Do not boil unless you are going to prepare a very small amount of meat. Overcooked chicken will taste powdery no matter the method. Roast turkey or capon can be substituted for chicken in a salad.

If enough roasted chicken meat is not available, see page 34. You may want to add more chicken in any case because these salads are designed to use up leftovers and will not feed many hungry people. All are easily multiplied, however.

The texture of most chicken salads is set off by the crispness of a bed of raw greens. About a cup of washed and torn-up greens is needed per person. The choice of greens obviously depends on what is fresh and good and not insanely expensive. It is a good idea to mix firmer greens with softer ones. Many of the firm greens are slightly bitter or peppery, while the soft greens are fairly bland and pleasant. I keep colors as well as flavors in mind when picking greens, balancing the darker—red and green—against the pale.

Firm, dark greens include escarole, dandelion, mizuna, and arugula (slightly bitter); watercress, radish sprouts, shiso, Japanese giant red mustard (peppery); spinach, romaine (including Bibb), and ordinary chicory. Among the light-colored greens are flat chicory, which the French call *frisée*, Belgian endive, and iceberg lettuce. The last two are firm. Firm and also red are the red chicories—radicchios—Treviso and Verona (see page 400), which I seldom use in salad. There are several soft red lettuces for salad in nonheading form, such as oak leaf and Lollo Rossa, and even a butterhead or two. Oak leaf also occurs as a palish green, along with the butterheads, Boston lettuce, and salad bowl. That leaves corn salad (mâche) to represent soft-leaved dark greens.

I don't use cabbage with chicken salad, not even the Chinese varieties, or the red. Aside from the peppery radish sprouts, I use no other sprouts; to me they always look and taste like a lot of tangled hay. I would use mustard and cress, but I never have enough.

Chutney chicken salad

MAKES 1¼ CUPS; SERVES 2 AS
A FIRST COURSE

THE DRESSING FOR this salad has lots of flavor and is about as quick as any I make. Lemon juice can be substituted for lime. The salad is colorful, given the red lettuce and the scallions. The only negative is that it needs to be assembled at the last minute. It doesn't keep well.

The recipe can easily be doubled to serve two as a main course or four as a starter.

6 ounces white or dark leftover roast chicken, cut into ¼-inch-wide strips (1 cup)

2 to 3 tablespoons juice from bottom of chicken pan, leftover gravy, or Basic Chicken Stock (page 42) or canned

2 tablespoons spicy Bengal hot chutney, or milder mango chutney

¾ tablespoon fresh lime juice

10 leaves red leaf or Lollo Rossa lettuce, heavy stems removed from centers

3 inches of greens cut off tops of ½ bunch scallions, cut in very fine lengthwise strips (3 tablespoons)

Put chicken strips in a medium bowl. Combine chicken juices, chutney, and lime juice in a blender. Blend until smooth. With a rubber spatula, scrape the mixture over the chicken. Mix gently with a spoon. The salad will look more attractive if the chicken strips stay intact.

To serve, flatten lettuce leaves slightly. Arrange 5 leaves for each serving so that the red tips of the lettuce fan around the edges of the plate. Put half the chicken into center of each plate. Sprinkle with scallion greens. Tastes best served right away, at room temperature.

Cold-weather chicken salad

MAKES 4 CUPS; SERVES 2 AS
A MAIN COURSE

THIS RECIPE CAN easily be doubled. The warm colors and smoky flavors of the ingredients make it particularly appealing when there is a chill in the air.

1 large or 2 small sweet potatoes (1 pound)

12 ounces leftover roast chicken meat, cut into 1-inch cubes (2 cups)

6 stalks celery, stripped with vegetable peeler and thinly sliced across on the diagonal (⅔ cup)

2 tablespoons chopped walnut pieces

⅓ cup leftover gravy or Basic Chicken Stock (page 42) or canned

3 tablespoons balsamic vinegar

¾ teaspoon kosher salt, or to taste

Freshly ground black pepper, to taste

Large pinch of whole celery seeds

8 to 10 lettuce leaves, heavy stems removed from center

Rinse sweet potato. Prick in several places with a fork.

Cook the sweet potato on 2 layers of paper towel in the microwave, if you have one, for 7 minutes. Let cool and peel. Alternatively, peel the sweet potato and steam over boiling water for 20 minutes. Cool and cut into 1-inch cubes.

In a small bowl, combine chicken, sweet potatoes, almost all the celery (reserve about 2 tablespoons), and half the nuts. In a smaller bowl, combine gravy or stock, vinegar, salt, pepper, and celery seeds. Pour liquid over chicken mixture. Toss gently so the chicken and potato pieces do not crumble.

Arrange lettuce on two plates. Divide chicken evenly and top with a sprinkling of remaining celery and nuts.

Chicken salad with crunch

MAKES 5 ½ CUPS; SERVES 5 TO 6 AS
A FIRST COURSE, 3 AS A MAIN COURSE

A ZIP OF mint, cucumber coolness, and red pepper sweetness and brightness combine in a summer-fresh first course, good before pasta or fish or as an independent main course.

8 ounces leftover roast chicken meat, cut lengthwise into thin strips (2 cups)

1 large red bell pepper (8 ounces), both ends removed, seeded, deribbed, cut in half lengthwise, then cut into thin strips (2 cups)

1 cucumber (10 ounces), peeled, cut into thirds, each third halved, seeded, then cut into thin strips (1½ cups)

1 bunch (1 ounce) fresh mint, washed, leaves removed, and chopped fine (4 tablespoons)

4 tablespoons fresh lime juice (about 2 limes)

2 teaspoons ground cumin

½ cup Basic Mayonnaise (page 303) or store-bought

1 teaspoon kosher salt

Freshly ground black pepper, to taste

1 head lettuce, leaves washed and separated

Put the chicken, red pepper, cucumber strips, and 3 tablespoons chopped mint in a medium bowl. Using your hands or chopsticks, toss gently until combined. In a smaller bowl, whisk together the lime juice, cumin, mayonnaise, salt, and pepper. Pour over the chicken mixture. Mix until all strips are well coated. Sprinkle with remaining tablespoon chopped mint and serve on a bed of lettuce leaves.

Basic chicken stock

MAKES ABOUT 3 QUARTS

CHICKEN STOCK IS the universal solvent of the kitchen and, in the form of chicken soup (page 46), the universal cure. Commercial stocks, frozen or canned, can be used in place of homemade stock, but the taste is thinner. Also they lack gelatin, which can be provided by dissolving a packet of powdered gelatin in a quart of stock. Canned or frozen broths tend to be salty; cubes are almost useless. I have old, moldering, unused packages around for rainy days that never seem to come.

It is worthwhile to make real stock. I make it without vegetables, which can always be added later. Vegetables cloud the stock and can cause it to turn and sour. Besides, I don't know until I use the stock what I want the flavorings to be.

Stock made from the bones saved from plates and the carcass of a roasted bird, with its giblets added, will be richer than stock made from unroasted parts. Tie up the gizzards and hearts in a piece of cheesecloth to fish them out easily after an hour's cooking time. Slice them up to put in gravy (see Basic Fowl Giblet Gravy, page 45) or add to chicken salad. The richest stock of all is Extra-Rich Roasted Triple Stock or Soup (page 230); it's worth saving the carcass for. I also give indications for making stock with chicken backs, necks, or wings—whatever is cheap and available.

Before using the bones of a roast chicken for stock, remove all the good meat and save it for another use. Note that the pieces of tendon and all parts that look and feel unattractive are good for the flavor of the stock. Once a chicken is roasted, it is easy to pull the carcass apart—cut it if you are fastidious. Having the bones in smaller pieces means that less liquid is needed to cover them. Using a stockpot that is tall in proportion to its diameter minimizes the amount of liquid required and constantly rotates the liquid over the bones. Broader pots are useful when a weak stock must be reduced in a hurry to give it strength.

The bones should be covered with liquid by several inches. When I don't have enough time to let the stock simmer for many hours, I cheat by adding canned stock to water for a base. Long simmering is the real trick. It dissolves all the gelatinous bits, and the bones fall apart, having given their all. It takes about eight hours minimum. I like to keep it going up to sixteen hours if I can.

After the initial boiling, don't let the stock boil again. Just let it burp gently from time to time. Boiling risks binding the fat and dissolving solids into the gelatinous liquid. I highly recommend an otoshi-buta, a wooden lid used by Japanese cooks that lets the stock simmer without evaporating too much liquid. Alternatively, cover the pot with a lid, but put it askew—off to one side—so that too much heat doesn't build up, or add half again as much liquid as is needed to cover the bones and let it reduce gradually.

Skim off fat and scum after the first half hour and again whenever you pass by the pot. You can finish skimming the stock at the end of the cooking time. Put the stock through a large colander set over a large metal bowl. (Metal bowls cool more quickly.) Line the colander with a damp cloth before straining the stock for a very clear stock. The stock can be put immediately into the refrigerator or else in front of an open window to cool first. Pour into one-cup and two-cup containers and freeze until needed.

The carcass of a bird that was five pounds before roasting will make about a quart of stock.

Carcass and bones from a 5- to 6-pound roasted chicken, plus uncooked neck and giblets, or 6 pounds chicken bones, necks, and wings	3 quarts water or stock, or to cover by 2 inches

If using a whole chicken carcass, cut it up. Place the chicken parts or bones and parts in a stockpot with water to cover by 3 inches. Cover the pot and bring to a boil. Skim off the fat and scum that rise to the top. Lower the heat so liquid is just barely boiling. Cover if desired. Cook 8 to 16 hours, skimming occasionally, adding more cold water as needed. The more skimming, the clearer the stock.

Pour the stock through a sieve and let cool at room temperature as time permits; then refrigerate. Remove the fat from the surface and any sediment from the bottom.

Use as is, refrigerate for 1 week, or freeze for 6 to 9 months.

Rich chicken sauce

MAKES ½ CUP

Sometimes I want a small amount of very rich chicken reduction, much like a classic glace de viande, to add to or be the base of a sauce. This method of cooking a small amount of liquid, letting it reduce by half, and then adding more liquid and repeating the process gives a much more intense flavor and color than adding all the liquid at once and letting it reduce. Sometimes I let the pot get almost dry before adding more liquid. Unfortunately, unlike normal stocks and sauces, it requires a fair amount of attention. I need to be in the kitchen the whole time or I get a burned mess. It's worth it for a very special dish like Roast Chicken with Pomegranate Glaze and Fresh Mint (page 27).

Wing tips, giblets (heart and gizzards), and neck from 1 chicken	1¾ cups Basic Chicken Stock (page 42) or canned
3 cloves garlic, smashed and peeled	Water, as needed

Put the wing tips, giblets, neck, garlic cloves, and stock in a 3-cup saucepan 4¾ inches in diameter. Cover and bring to a boil. Reduce heat to a simmer. Let cook, uncovered, about 3 hours, adding 1 cup water each time liquid has reduced by half. Skim occasionally when needed. Do not start with more stock, or the sauce will not be a rich, dark color. For the last 20 minutes, cook without adding any more water. Remove and strain. There should be about ½ cup rich chicken sauce.

Champagne sauce

MAKES 1¼ CUPS (ENOUGH FOR A
5- TO 6-POUND ROASTED BIRD)

CHAMPAGNE SAUCE IS a simple deglazing sauce that sounds fancy because it includes Champagne. For me, that is usually something flattish left over from a party. Any good white wine can be substituted. The fancy notes are straining the deglazing liquid and using white pepper to avoid dark splotches.

¾ cup Basic Chicken Stock (page 42) or canned	½ cup heavy cream
1 tablespoon cornstarch mixed with 2 tablespoons cold water, optional	Kosher salt, to taste
½ cup Champagne	Freshly ground white pepper, to taste
1½ tablespoons chopped fresh tarragon leaves, optional	Tiny pinch of cayenne, optional

Remove roasted bird to a platter. Pour or spoon off fat from roasting pan. Put pan on top of stove. Add the stock and bring contents to a boil, scraping the bottom vigorously with a wooden spoon. Let reduce by half. Pour deglazing liquid through a fine sieve into a medium saucepan. If a thicker sauce is desired, pour a little of the hot deglazing liquid into the cornstarch mixture, blend, and stir mixture into saucepan. Add Champagne and tarragon, if using; bring to a boil. Reduce heat to very low. Add cream, salt, pepper, and cayenne, if using. Cook at lowest heat 2 minutes until heated through.

Basic fowl giblet gravy

MAKES 1 TO 2½ CUPS, DEPENDING
ON THE SIZE OF THE BIRD

Giblet gravy is easy if time-consuming, and the basic principle is the same no matter what the size of the bird. The range indicated here would be from a five-pound chicken to a large fifteen-pound turkey. It's not pan gravy; make it up to two days ahead.

Wing tips, giblets (heart and gizzards), and neck from chicken, turkey, or other bird

3 to 6 cloves garlic (depending on size of bird), smashed and peeled

1¾ to 3½ cups Basic Chicken Stock (page 42) or canned, depending on size of bird; or, if available, use stock appropriate to bird

Water, as needed

1 tablespoon chopped fresh herbs or ½ teaspoon celery seeds per cup gravy, optional

Kosher salt, to taste

Freshly ground black pepper, to taste

1 to 2½ tablespoons unsalted butter, optional

1 to 2½ tablespoons all-purpose flour, optional

Put the wing tips, giblets, neck (halved if from a large bird), garlic cloves, and stock in the smallest pan that will hold ingredients comfortably. Cover and bring to a boil. Reduce heat to a simmer and skim. Cook, uncovered, for 1 hour for chicken or up to 2 hours for turkey, until giblets are easily pierced with the point of a knife. Add 1 cup water each time the liquid has reduced by half. Do not start with more liquid or stock, or the gravy will not be a rich, dark color. Skim occasionally. Remove the giblets, allowing them to cool.

Meanwhile, continue to cook stock 1 hour longer for chicken and up to 2 hours longer for turkey, until the neck bones fall apart. Add water as needed. For the last 20 minutes, let cook without adding any more water. Meanwhile, cut the heart and gizzards into thin slices or small cubes and reserve. Strain the stock. Skim off any remaining fat. Just before serving, add giblets and, if you wish, some fresh herbs or celery seeds. Pick meat from neck and add. Heat until warm throughout. Add deglazing liquid from the roasted bird, if available. Season to taste with salt and pepper.

This is now a very rich gravy, but here is an option for thicker gravy. Melt butter and stir in flour. Use a tablespoon of each for every cup of strained stock. Cook, stirring, for 4 minutes. Add giblets and seasonings. Heat until warm throughout.

Chicken soups

CHICKEN SOUP IS one of the world's ubiquitous remedies—I think for the soul as well as the body. It starts with stock. I've tried to tell all in the recipe for Basic Chicken Stock (page 42). It doesn't take much to turn chicken stock into soup. For each cup of soup desired, start with a tablespoon each of chopped onions, carrots, and celery. Cook the vegetables in a tiny bit of fat—some from the chicken is fine—over low heat until the vegetables are soft. Add a cup and a quarter of stock. Bring to a boil; reduce to a simmer, and cook for fifteen minutes. Add a teaspoon of minced parsley or chopped dill. Continue to cook five minutes. Season with salt and pepper. Strain or not, as desired. Serve alone or with cooked rice or noodles.

A few simple recipes for chicken soups follow.

Chicken soup with zing

MAKES 4 CUPS; SERVES 4

THIS IS MY personal home-remedy chicken soup. I eat the whole thing when I feel a cold coming on; but it is good enough to be a light start for a festive dinner. Add a cup and a half of leftover roasted chicken in shreds or cubes to make a hearty soup.

This can easily be doubled or increased further for a large group.

4 cups Basic Chicken Stock (page 42) or canned

½ cup water

2 thin slices of gingerroot, unpeeled (¾ ounce)

2 medium cloves garlic, peeled and thinly sliced lengthwise

1 jalapeño pepper, seeded, deribbed, and chopped fine, or 1 teaspoon seeded and chopped Basic Jalapeños (page 383)

6 fresh mint leaves

3 scallions, trimmed to 5 inches, white and green parts cut separately lengthwise into thin slices

¼ cup fresh lemon juice

¼ cup tightly packed fresh cilantro leaves, finely chopped, plus several whole leaves for topping

Kosher salt, to taste

Freshly ground black pepper, to taste

Put the stock, water, ginger, garlic, and jalapeño in a medium saucepan. Cook, covered, over medium-low heat about 20 minutes. When the garlic is almost cooked through, after about 15 minutes, add mint and scallion whites. After 3 minutes more, add scallion greens, and cook until just wilted, about 1 minute. Add lemon juice, cilantro, salt, and pepper. Warm throughout. Serve broth with a cilantro leaf or two in each bowl.

Home-style chicken soup

MAKES 5 CUPS; SERVES 4

Tʜɪs ɪs ᴛʜᴇ Central European home-cure soup, a world of fully cooked noodles, not Italian al dente pasta. The noodles slither soothingly down grateful sore throats. Don't cook the noodles in the soup or it will get very cloudy and much more soup will be needed.

This recipe presumes a wonderful homemade stock. When making the soup, keep the pot covered. The soup will be rich enough; no evaporation is desired.

1 cup medium egg noodles

4 cups Basic Chicken Stock (page 42)
  or canned

1 small parsnip (1 ounce), trimmed,
  peeled, cut across into thin slices
  (2 heaping tablespoons)

1 medium carrot (2½ ounces), trimmed,
  peeled, cut across into thin slices
  (¼ cup)

2 tablespoons finely chopped white onion

½ cup fresh green peas or ½ cup
  defrosted frozen green peas, optional

2 tablespoons coarsely chopped fresh dill

2 to 3 ounces leftover roast chicken meat,
  cut into ½-inch cubes (¾ cup)

1½ teaspoons kosher salt

Freshly ground black pepper, to taste

Bring a pot of salted water to a boil and cook noodles fully—not al dente. Drain and reserve.

Meanwhile, put the chicken stock in a pot. Heat, covered, over medium heat until simmering. Add parsnip, carrot, and onion. If using fresh peas, add them now. Cook, covered, about 5 minutes, just until carrots may be easily pierced with a knife, but are still firm. Add dill and chicken. If using frozen peas, add them now. Heat until warm throughout. Add drained noodles, salt, and pepper. Serve hot.

Chicken vegetable soup

MAKES 8½ CUPS; SERVES 6 TO 8

THIS IS A quick sort-of-minestrone that is best in summer. It can be served hot or at room temperature. If serving hot, adding grated Parmesan may be a plus. When serving cold, a generous cup of cooked rice can be used instead of the pasta. Want more soup? Add some canned cannellini beans that have been well rinsed, along with the basil, but up the amount of basil.

½ cup ditalini or small elbow macaroni

6 cups Basic Chicken Stock (page 42) or canned

2 tomatoes (12 ounces), deeply cored and cut in chunks

4 carrots (8 ounces), trimmed, peeled, halved lengthwise and cut into roughly 1-inch-long by ½-inch-wide pieces (1 cup)

8 ounces small onions (average diameter ½ inch), peeled and trimmed (1 cup)

4 ounces haricot verts (thin, short, round green beans), ends trimmed

2 small zucchini (8 ounces), halved lengthwise and cut across into ½-inch pieces

3 cloves garlic, smashed, peeled, and chopped

1 cup shredded leftover roast chicken meat, optional

¼ cup packed fresh basil leaves, cut across into thin strips

1½ teaspoons kosher salt

Freshly ground black pepper, to taste

Olive oil, to taste

Cook pasta in a pot of boiling salted water until firm. Drain and run under cold water; reserve.

Pour stock into a medium saucepan. Add tomatoes, carrots, onions, haricots verts, zucchini, and garlic. Cover and bring to a boil. Reduce heat to a simmer and cook, uncovered, for 15 minutes. Add chicken, if using, basil, salt, and pepper. Cook 2 minutes. Stir in olive oil or put olive oil on table so that all eaters add their own. Can be served at room temperature or hot.

Chicken livers

CHICKEN LIVERS ARE a fine extra and dividend. See page 20 for cleaning and storing. Three and a half ounces can be substituted for the goose liver in Goose Liver Mousse (page 82), or twelve ounces for the duck liver in Duck Liver Pâté (page 77). The principle of cooking the livers with boiling fat remains the same.

Cleaned livers, liquefied in a blender with a tiny bit of vinegar, can substitute in Chinese and French recipes that call for thickening sauces with blood.

Chicken livers and three mushrooms

MAKES 2½ GENEROUS CUPS

THIS IS REALLY a simple sauté; don't be put off by the long list of ingredients. It makes a sumptuous filling for several omelets or a festive first course for six, served on top of Roasted Bread (page 367). If the recipe makes more than you need, freeze the extra for another day. Omit the enoki from the part you are going to freeze; add them after defrosting.

6 small dried Chinese mushrooms

6 tablespoons unsalted butter

2½ teaspoons peeled and minced fresh gingerroot

8 ounces fresh mushrooms, sliced ⅛ inch thick

8 ounces chicken livers, rinsed and connective tissue removed (1 cup)

4 thin or 2 fat scallions, green and white parts diagonally sliced into ¼-inch rounds

¼ cup dry white wine

1 teaspoon kosher salt

Freshly ground black pepper, to taste

¼ teaspoon cayenne pepper

1 tablespoon fresh lemon juice

2 tablespoons chopped fresh flat-leaf parsley

4 to 8 ounces enoki mushrooms, trimmed of roots

Put dried mushrooms in a small dish and cover with hot water. Allow to soak for 30 minutes. Squeeze dry. Discard stems and slice caps into strips.

Melt 4 tablespoons of the butter in a large skillet. Add ginger, fresh mushrooms (not the enoki), and soaked mushrooms. Cook over high heat about 30 seconds, until mushrooms are almost tender, stirring constantly. Remove from skillet and set aside.

In the same skillet, heat remaining 2 tablespoons butter. Pat chicken livers dry and add to hot butter with the scallions. Cook 15 to 30 seconds, stirring constantly. Reduce heat to medium, add cooked mushrooms, wine, salt, pepper, cayenne, lemon juice, and parsley. Cook another 10 to 15 seconds. If using as filling for an omelet, stir in enoki mushrooms just before serving. If serving on Roasted Bread as a first course, top pieces of bread with a fair share of the liver-mushroom mixture and top with some enoki.

Chopped chicken liver

MAKES 2 CUPS; SERVES 6 TO 8

THIS IS NO dish for cholesterol watchers or dieters. Those who don't worry will want to know how to render fat (page 83). Sprinkle the drained, rendered cracklings on the liver spread or serve separately, warmed and dusted with kosher salt.

Serve with thin rounds of black radish, crisped in icy water, or good rye bread.

¼ cup rendered chicken fat or store-bought

1 medium onion (8 ounces), peeled and coarsely chopped (about 1¼ cups)

1 pound chicken livers, rinsed and connective tissue removed (2 cups)

2 teaspoons kosher salt, or to taste

¼ teaspoon freshly ground black pepper, or to taste

2 hard-boiled eggs, shelled and quartered

Heat the fat in a large skillet over medium heat. Fry onions until soft and golden, about 15 minutes. Raise heat and add livers. Cook, turning from time to time, until no blood shows and livers are firm when pressed with the back of a spoon.

Remove liver mixture either to a food processor or to a wooden bowl. Add salt, pepper, and eggs. Chop coarsely either by pulsing in the food processor or by chopping in a bowl with a half-moon chopper. Transfer to a serving bowl. Refrigerate, covered, until chilled, preferably overnight.

Simple roast capon

SERVES 4 TO 5

TOTAL
ROASTING
TIME:
60
minutes

Capon is a rooster reconverted into a chicken. It is tender at a larger size than a chicken and has an ample breast that can be thinly sliced. It is usually associated with holidays and parties. Make capon stock like Basic Chicken Stock (page 42). Capon leftovers can be used in any of the recipes for chicken and turkey leftovers.

6½-pound capon, wing tips removed
Kosher salt, to taste
Freshly ground black pepper, to taste

1 cup Basic Chicken Stock (page 42) or canned, wine, fruit juice, or water, for deglazing

Place rack in center of oven. Heat oven to 500°F.

Remove fat pockets from tail and crop ends of the capon. Place capon breast side up in a 12 x 8 x 1½-inch roasting pan. Season cavity with salt and pepper. Put in oven legs first and roast for 60 minutes, or until the juices run clear. After the first 10 minutes, move the capon with a wooden spatula to keep it from sticking.

Remove the capon to a platter by inserting a large wooden spoon into the cavity. Tilt the capon over the roasting pan so that all the juices run out and into the pan. Pour or spoon off excess fat from roasting pan and put roasting pan on top of stove. Add the stock or other liquid and bring the contents of the pan to a boil, scraping the bottom vigorously with a wooden spoon. Let reduce by half. Serve the sauce over the capon or, for crisp skin, in a sauceboat.

Roast capon paprikás with dill

TOTAL
ROASTING
TIME:
60
minutes

CAPON, WHILE A succulent bird, is not one of deep taste. It goes happily with the milder herbs and likes cream. Usually, I make it with tarragon and crème fraîche; but since there are several tarragon and chicken recipes in this book, I tried dill and sour cream with a little paprika instead, and it was just fine. If you want to use tarragon or chervil, substitute them for the dill, substitute heavy cream or crème fraîche for the sour cream, and omit the cornstarch. The sauce is good with noodles or small steamed potatoes.

1 bunch (2 ounces) fresh dill

6½-pound capon, wing tips removed

Kosher salt, to taste

Freshly ground black pepper, to taste

2 teaspoons good paprika, all sweet or half sweet and half hot

1 cup Extra-Rich Roasted Triple Stock (page 230) or Basic Chicken Stock (page 42) or canned

½ cup sour cream, whisked together with 1 tablespoon cornstarch

Place rack in center of oven. Heat oven to 500°F.

Separate dill fronds from the branches and stems and reserve; set aside ½ cup loosely packed fronds.

Remove fat pockets from the tail and crop ends of the capon. Stuff the cavity with the dill stems and branches. Sprinkle with salt and pepper.

Place the capon in a 12 x 8 x 1½-inch roasting pan breast side up. Put in oven legs first. Cook 1 hour, or until the juices run clear, moving the capon with a wooden spatula to keep it from sticking after the first 10 minutes.

Remove the capon from the pan by inserting a large wooden spoon into the cavity. Tilt capon over pan so that all juices run out into the pan and are not lost or running down your arm. Reserve capon on a platter.

Pour or spoon off all but a little fat out of pan. Place pan on top of stove. Add paprika. Smush around and let cook over low heat for 2 minutes. Add stock. Bring contents to a boil, while scraping bottom vigorously with a wooden spoon. Add reserved dill fronds. Reduce heat to low and whisk in sour cream. Add salt and pepper to taste. Heat just until warm but not boiling.

To serve, spoon some of the sauce over the bird. Serve the rest on the side in a sauce-boat. Use extra dill, if available, to sprinkle around serving dish.

Simple roast Cornish game hen

SERVES 2

TOTAL
ROASTING
TIME:
15 *to* 20
minutes

CORNISH GAME HENS are neither game nor Cornish; but they do allow the serving of a single bird for one or two in a world where poussins (very young, small chickens) seem totally unavailable. Cornish hens vary quite a bit in size. I find that birds about a pound in size are most usual and satisfactory. Smaller ones may leave big eaters mildly famished; larger ones are a bit much for one person, but it is possible to cut them in half from stem to stern with large shears.

When preparing several birds, arrange them in the roasting pan with their broader wing ends toward the edges of the pan. Remove the wing tips before cooking; they can be used in Basic Chicken Stock (page 42) along with the leftover carcasses. Two to three birds can fit in a small pan, four to five in a medium pan, and eight to nine in a large pan. Each Cornish game hen serves one person as a main course.

2 Cornish game hens (about 1 pound each), wing tips removed

1 tablespoon unsalted butter or neutral oil, optional

Kosher salt, to taste

Freshly ground black pepper, to taste

½ cup Basic Chicken Stock (page 42) or canned, wine, fruit juice, or water, for deglazing

Place rack in center of oven. Heat oven to 500°F.

Place hens, breast sides up, in a 12 x 8 x 1½-inch roasting pan with legs of 1 next to breast of other. Rub each hen with butter or oil, if using. Season the cavities with salt and pepper. Put in oven and roast for 10 minutes. Move hens around with a wooden spatula so they won't stick. Roast 5 to 10 minutes more. Pour or spoon off excess fat. Put pan on top of stove. Add the liquid and bring contents to a boil while scraping the bottom vigorously with a wooden spoon. Let reduce by half.

Cornish game hen with liver-rich stuffing

SERVES 8

TOTAL
ROASTING
TIME:
25
minutes

THINK OF THESE as neat little packages of well-cooked pâté, surrounded by bird. Stuff the birds just before roasting. The cooking time is longer than that for plain Cornish hens due to the density of the stuffing.

8 Cornish game hens (about 1 pound each), wing tips removed

1 recipe Liver-Rich Stuffing (page 119)

1 tablespoon unsalted butter or neutral oil, optional

1 cup Basic Chicken Stock (page 42) or canned or Mixed Game Bird Stock (page 91)

½ cup red or white wine

Kosher salt, to taste

Freshly ground black pepper, to taste

Place rack in center of oven. Heat oven to 500°F.

Refer to Skewering and Wrapping (page 109) to close neck ends of birds. With birds standing on neck ends, place ½ cup of stuffing in the breast cavity of each hen. Skewer and wrap tail ends of birds.

Rub hens with butter or oil, if using. Place hens, breast sides up, in two 12 x 14 x 2-inch roasting pans. Roast for 10 minutes. Move hens around with a wooden spatula so they won't stick. Roast 15 minutes more.

Remove hens to plates or a platter. Pour off fat from pan. Deglaze with stock and wine, scraping the bottom vigorously. Allow to boil until reduced slightly. Season to taste with salt and pepper. Pass sauce separately.

Roast Cornish game hen and Jerusalem artichokes in tomato-olive sauce

SERVES 4

TOTAL
ROASTING
TIME:
15 *to* 20
minutes

An EARTHY AND refined dinner that can be made with any number of hens by multiplying or dividing the recipe. Allow one bird per person. Two to three will fit in the smallest pan, four to five in a medium pan, and eight to nine in a large pan. I like to use the firm, briny, green olives with their pits firmly in place. If pits in cheeks is not the guests' or family's idea of fun, use small, pitted green Spanish olives. Serve lots of good bread or spoons for mopping up the sauce.

To prepare the Jerusalem artichokes ahead of time, put them in a bowl of water with lemon juice in it to keep them from discoloring. If cooking more than two hens, use 1 tablespoon of red wine (or red wine vinegar or stock) in the sauce for each 2 hens.

4 Cornish game hens (about 1 pound each), wing tips removed

20 large shallots, peeled and trimmed

1 pound Jerusalem artichokes, peeled

¼ cup olive oil

Kosher salt, to taste

Freshly ground black pepper, to taste

2 tablespoons red wine, red wine vinegar, or stock

2 to 3 tomatoes (1½ pounds), cored and chopped in large pieces (4 cups)

½ cup drained medium green olives

Place rack in center of oven. Heat oven to 500°F.

Place the hens, breast sides up, in a 14 x 12 x 2-inch roasting pan. Put 2 shallots in the cavity of each hen. Arrange the remaining shallots and the Jerusalem artichokes in the pan so that they touch as little as possible. Use your hands to rub the oil all over the hens, shallots, Jerusalem artichokes, and the pan. Sprinkle salt and pepper over everything. Roast for 8 minutes. Move hens around and turn vegetables with a wooden spatula so they won't stick. Roast 7 to 12 minutes more, or until hen's juices run clear.

Remove hens and vegetables to a serving platter or individual plates. Tilt pan and remove any grease. Put pan over low heat, add the wine and tomatoes, and cook 1 minute. Add olives and cook 2 minutes over high heat, scraping up any crisp bits with a wooden spoon. Taste for salt and pepper. Pour warm sauce over hens and serve.

*t*URKEY

THIS IS THE BIRD THAT BENJAMIN FRANKLIN WANTED AS THE NATIONAL SYMBOL INSTEAD OF THE PREDATORY EAGLE. When I look at the farm-raised birds wagging their wattles atop scrawny necks and bumbling around, I wonder what kind of image that would have made. Wild turkeys, with their soft brown feathers and rounded forms, are much more attractive as they scuttle softly with their broods down country roads.

Mostly, we eat turkey tame, and at Thanksgiving, which is a bit of a shame as they give a lot of value for the money and, if properly cooked, are moist and firm, unlike most of the birds I have had to eat over the years. Moist meat does not depend on the birds being injected with all sorts of stuff. Fresh turkeys are far better than frozen. When buying, check that the turkey wasn't frozen before it got to you. A frozen turkey will take three days to thaw in the refrigerator. For wild turkeys, see page 93.

Leftover turkey, in addition to all the soup and salad recipes that follow, works well in the chicken salads and in the Chicken Hash with Parsnips (page 35). Thinly sliced, it makes a wonderful dish with Tonnato Sauce (page 285) or Green Goddess Dressing (page 305). The last two could be made into extraordinary sandwiches, or use some Three-Citrus Mayonnaise (page 304) and leftover Cranberry-Orange Relish (page 107); messy but good.

*S*imple roast turkey

SERVES 10 TO 15

TOTAL
ROASTING
TIME:
see page 58

MANY THANKSGIVINGS AT my house have proved the high-heat method to be ideal. A fifteen-pound turkey at room temperature takes two hours to roast. However, it may take several hours for the turkey to reach room temperature. While the turkey is sitting out, cover it loosely with a towel, otherwise the skin will dry out. I prefer a fifteen-pound turkey as it isn't too heavy for me to handle. It usually gives lots of good leftovers and is generally available.

There are certain things to think of to ensure success before beginning: Remove the giblet bag from the interior of the bird. Remove the wing tips. Put everything except the livers into a pot and start Basic Fowl Giblet Gravy (page 45). (Be sure to remove the wing tips before adding the cooked gizzards, heart, and neck meat back into the sauce.) By the time the bird is roasted, the gravy will be done. Use the liver in the dressing/stuffing or store in the freezer, covered with milk (page 20). Make sure there is a pan big enough for the turkey without its touching the sides of the pan. Do not truss.

Consider whether the bird should be stuffed or the stuffing served as a dressing baked separately. If stuffing, think in terms of twelve cups of stuffing for a fifteen-pound bird, which will allow the big cavity to be stuffed and some more stuffing to be crammed under the skin flap at the neck. I seldom stuff because there are real food safety questions about the bird and its stuffing sitting out at room temperature.

The oven must be very clean before roasting, or cooking at this high temperature will cause unpleasant smoke. In any case, there will be some smoke, so turn on the fan or open a window. Don't put the oven rack too high or the skin on the breast will get overcooked. For a twenty-pound turkey, the rack should be in the lowest position. Always put the turkey in legs first—dark meat takes longer to cook and the rear of the oven is the hottest area.

If the top skin seems to be getting too dark, slip a doubled piece of aluminum foil on top of it. Don't move the turkey. Use an oven mitt to protect hands and forearms. Remove the foil with the same oven mitt ten minutes before the turkey comes out.

Large turkeys are most easily removed from the pan by holding them with two pot holders, which will need to be washed. After the meal, get out a large stockpot to boil up the carcass and leftover bones for turkey soup and stock variations.

15-pound turkey, thawed, if necessary, and at room temperature, wing tips removed, reserving giblets and neck for gravy, liver for stuffing	1 cup water, Basic Turkey Stock (page 60), or Basic Chicken Stock (page 42) or canned
Freshly ground black pepper, to taste	Basic Fowl Giblet Gravy (page 45), optional

Place oven rack on second level from bottom of oven. Heat oven to 500°F.

Rinse the turkey inside and out. Pat dry. Sprinkle the outside with pepper. If stuffing, stuff cavity and crop, securing openings with long metal skewers (page 109). Lace them. Do not truss.

Put turkey in an 18 x 13 x 2-inch roasting pan, breast side up. Put in oven legs first. Roast until the leg joint near the backbone wiggles easily, about 2 hours. After 20 minutes, move the turkey around with a wooden spatula to keep from sticking. Remove the turkey to a large platter. Let sit 20 minutes before carving (pages 18–19).

Pour off grease from roasting pan and put pan on top of the stove. Add water or stock. Bring to a boil while scraping bottom of pan vigorously with a wooden spoon, loosening all the crisp bits in the bottom of the pan. These add intensity to the gravy. Let reduce by half. Serve on the side in a sauceboat or add to giblet gravy.

continued

BASIC ROAST TURKEY TIMES AT 500°F

weight	stuffed	unstuffed
9 POUNDS	1 hour 45 minutes	1 hour 15 minutes
12 POUNDS	1 hour 50 minutes	1 hour 20 minutes
15 POUNDS	2 hours 30 minutes	2 hours
20 POUNDS	3 hours 30 minutes	3 hours

Simple whole roast turkey breast

MAKES 3 ¼ POUNDS MEAT; SERVES 6 TO 8
AS A MAIN COURSE, OR ABOUT 24 SLICES—
ENOUGH FOR 10 HANDSOME SANDWICHES
OR MAIN-COURSE SALADS, OR 16 TO 20
FIRST-COURSE SALADS

TOTAL
ROASTING
TIME:
50
minutes

SOMETIMES IT IS just easier to roast a whole turkey breast (available in supermarkets, even unfrozen) instead of a whole bird. It's a great thing to do if guests are coming for the weekend and plenty of sandwich makings are needed. Even "fresh," the breasts will need to sit a good four hours at room temperature to warm enough to roast, due to the heavy bone. This is about the only time I find it best to use a rack in the pan for roasting. If there is no rack, during the longish roasting, the bone touching the pan will char and give an unpleasant taste to the meat. The oven will need to be cleaned afterward, but it's worth it for crisp skin and tender meat.

6-pound whole turkey breast, thawed
  if necessary, and at room temperature

Place rack on second level from bottom of oven. Heat oven to 500°F.

Place turkey, breast side up, on a rack in a 14 x 12 x 2-inch roasting pan. Roast for 50 minutes, or until juices run clear.

Soothing summer turkey salad

MAKES 4 CUPS; SERVES 4 AS
A MAIN COURSE

Even in an air-conditioned room, I can get frazzled on a hot summer day. Give me a day when I've been running around city streets steaming with the heat, bouncing back and forth between tall buildings, picking up the humidity from air conditioners, and I can go wild. Even in the short hills of Vermont, where it is usually a bit cooler and a breeze blows, a day of gardening leaves me spent. These are not the days on which I want a hot meal. I do want this light-as-air salad, whose only dressing comes from the juices of cucumbers and tomatoes. It is good diet food, also.

1 Kirby cucumber (6 ounces), peeled, cut in half lengthwise, seeded, and cut across in ¼-inch-wide pieces

2 small tomatoes (4 ounces each), cored and cut in ½-inch cubes

2½ teaspoons kosher salt

12 ounces 1-inch cubed pieces leftover roast turkey meat (2 cups)

2 scallions, trimmed and white and green parts cut across in ½-inch pieces

3 to 4 radishes, trimmed and sliced into very thin rounds

2 tablespoons chopped fresh dill

Freshly ground black pepper, to taste

Place cucumber and tomatoes in a medium bowl. Add salt and toss. Add other ingredients. Toss gently. Let sit 10 to 15 minutes at room temperature to allow flavors to develop. Serve on a bed of lettuce greens.

Southwest turkey salad

MAKES 4 CUPS; SERVES 6 TO 8 AS A
FIRST COURSE, 4 AS A MAIN COURSE

The Southwest lends its vivid colors as well as its vivid flavors to this salad. Once the salad is made, let it sit for about twenty minutes to let the tastes blend; but don't let it sit for a long time or it will get watery. I like iceberg lettuce, but most people think such a taste should be beneath me. I feel comfortable calling for it here as it's a standard ingredient of Tex-Mex food.

This salad also makes a good filling to wrap up in warm tortillas for very healthful fajitas.

What's that you say? No turkey leftovers midsummer? Well, use chicken, capon, or squab instead.

2 ripe avocados

2 tablespoons fresh lime juice

1½ teaspoons kosher salt

8 ounces leftover roast turkey meat, cut into 1-inch cubes (1 cup)

½ cup cooked corn kernels (1 cooked fresh ear)

2 tablespoons chopped fresh cilantro

1 small tomato (4 ounces), chopped into ¼-inch dice

1 small purple onion (1 ounce), chopped in ¼-inch dice (2 tablespoons)

1 cup cooked dried black beans (or canned, well rinsed)

2 fresh green jalapeño peppers (½ ounce each), seeded, deribbed, and chopped fine (4 teaspoons), or 1½ teaspoons seeded and chopped Basic Jalapeños (page 383)

Head of iceberg lettuce, shredded

Peel and cut avocados into ½-inch cubes. Place in small bowl. Add lime juice and 1 teaspoon of the salt and toss. Combine other ingredients except lettuce in larger bowl. Toss gently until well combined. Let sit 10 to 15 minutes at room temperature for flavors to combine. Taste and season with remaining ½ teaspoon salt if desired. Add avocado and lime juice just before ready to serve. Combine gently to spare the avocado. Serve on a bed of shredded iceberg lettuce with corn chips.

Basic turkey stock

MAKES 6 QUARTS

TURKEY STOCK IS the best part of the turkey, a luscious home for good egg noodles (page 92), just-cooked rice, or, if you are alone, sadly or happily, a poached egg. To have it at its best, it needs to cook a long time to extract all the flavor and gelatin from the bones. It will gel when cold, not firmly but enough to indicate its virtue.

I usually start this the afternoon of Thanksgiving and let it keep going all night until the next afternoon. However, if people are nervous about letting something cook all night, wait until the following day, start the stock first thing in the morning, and strain it just before bedtime.

Carcass and bones from a 15-pound roasted turkey, plus uncooked neck, wing tips and giblets, if available	6 quarts water

Break carcass into pieces. Place in large stockpot with water. Bring to a boil. Reduce heat to a simmer and skim off froth. Use an otoshi-buta (page 11), a wooden lid used by Japanese cooks, or cover with a conventional lid left slightly ajar. Cook 18 to 24 hours. Skim from time to time and add extra cold water to keep the water level constant. Using a small saucepan as a ladle, strain the stock through a colander.

For a clearer stock, dampen a kitchen towel with cold water and ring it out. Line the colander with the towel and strain the stock again. Allow to cool; skim off any fat and ladle stock into well-marked freezer containers, leaving any sediment behind. That's a lot of stock; it can easily be forgotten several months later, which would be a shame.

Turkey soup with carrots and orzo

MAKES 4 CUPS; SERVES 3 TO 4

A SIMPLE LIST of ingredients makes a simply delicious soup. Why complicate things?

4 cups Basic Turkey Stock (page 60)

2 carrots, peeled and grated lengthwise on the large holes of a four-sided grater (about ⅓ cup)

1 cup cooked orzo

4 ounces leftover roast turkey meat, cut into ½-inch cubes (1 cup)

Kosher salt, to taste

Freshly ground black pepper, to taste

Bring stock to a simmer in a medium saucepan. Add carrots. Cook until soft, about 10 minutes. Add orzo and turkey. Cook until warm throughout. Add salt and pepper. Serve warm.

Double-rich turkey soup

MAKES 2½ QUARTS

ALTHOUGH A GOOD turkey soup or stock can be made using just water, it will be richer and fuller if started with turkey or chicken stock. Try this when there is a smaller turkey carcass available.

Carcass and bones from an 8-pound roasted turkey, cut in pieces, plus uncooked neck and giblets, if available

3 quarts Basic Turkey Stock (page 60), canned chicken broth, or water

Kosher salt, to taste, optional

2 cups coarsely chopped celery, with leaves

2 medium onions (1 pound), quartered

4 medium carrots, peeled and cut into chunks

4 fresh sage leaves or 4 sprigs flat-leaf parsley

Few sprigs thyme

¾ pound medium egg noodles (page 92), optional

Place the carcass, neck, giblets, and stock in a stockpot, cover, and bring to a boil. Skim off froth thoroughly. Lower the heat and simmer 12 hours or longer, skimming from time to time and adding water as needed to keep bones covered. If desired, cover with an otoshi-buta (page 11) or a lid ajar. Skim often for a clearer stock.

Strain the stock, discarding the bones. If using for a stock, reserve as is. For soup, salt to taste. Cool to room temperature and skim off all the fat from the top. Refrigerate or freeze if not using right away.

To continue for the soup, add remaining ingredients and cook 45 minutes over low heat. If using noodles, boil separately in boiling salted water until barely cooked. Serve soup as is, heated with noodles, or strain the mixture through a sieve lined with a dampened kitchen towel, pressing on the solids to release all the liquid before adding noodles.

Turkey soup with fennel and mushrooms

MAKES 4½ CUPS; SERVES 4

IF PORTOBELLO MUSHROOMS are not available, substitute white button ones. Reserve the mushroom stems and use instead of part of the mushrooms in Chicken Livers and Three Mushrooms (page 49), using the turkey liver for part of the livers.

1 cup medium-wide or broad egg noodles

1 small fennel bulb (7 to 8 ounces)

1 medium portobello mushroom (2 to 3 ounces), wiped clean, stem removed and reserved for other use

4 cups Basic Turkey Stock (page 60)

2 to 3 teaspoons chopped fresh cilantro leaves

1 teaspoon kosher salt

Freshly ground black pepper, to taste

Bring water to a boil in a medium saucepan. Add noodles and cook for 6 minutes.

Meanwhile, trim fennel. Remove tops and tough outer leaves. Coarsely chop fronds and reserve. Cut bulb into fine strips (about 1 cup).

Cut mushroom cap across into 2 pieces; cut each piece across into fine strips (about 1 cup).

Put the stock in another medium saucepan. Add the fennel strips and mushroom slices. Cover, bring to a boil, then reduce to a simmer. After 3 minutes, add cilantro.

When noodles are cooked, drain and add directly to stock; do not rinse. Increase heat and bring to a boil. Add salt and pepper. Cook 2 minutes. Remove from heat and add reserved chopped fennel fronds. Serve hot.

dUCK

MOST PEOPLE ARE AFRAID TO COOK DUCK, AND IF THEY DO, THEY WANT MOIST MEAT AND CRISP SKIN. BEST ROAST DUCK, WHICH FOLLOWS, IS EASY, AND MAKES A DUCK THAT IS A NICE CHANGE AND IS NOT EXPENSIVE. Just think ahead. For most of us, duck means some variant of Cochin or Peking duck (the breed, not the dish cooked in Chinese restaurants), the white-feathered bird that used to be called Long Island duck. I used to spend time on Long Island, when the duck farms were still there. A three-story-high white cement duck sat beside the highway. It was almost impossible to get a fresh duck. There are versions of the basic roasting for moulard and muscovy ducks; but there are no recipes for true wild ducks such as teal. I don't like them and always find them tough and stringy. The seashore ducks also have a distinctly fishy taste that I find unpleasant.

Even when I get a duck that purports to be fresh, it is chilled almost to the freezing point and requires a day in the refrigerator before I can roast it. If the duck is actually frozen, it will take three to four days in the refrigerator to thaw. Don't worry about bringing it to room temperature. In my method, the duck is precooked in stock. Take it out of the refrigerator when putting the stock on the stove to come to a boil.

Over the years, I have tried an infinity of ways to roast a duck and am convinced that the recipe that follows is the best. (It's the final evolution of the one I wrote in *Food for Friends.*) The precooking method is the same; but when I wrote the earlier version, I chickened out and roasted the duck at a lower temperature than I do today. Now I think I've gotten it right. It works with many varieties.

I tried letting the duck drip in the refrigerator for days, which took up most of the refrigerator and didn't improve the result. I tried slow-roasting, I tried double-roasting, and I tried presteaming. None worked as well.

I tried stuffing the bird with a cast of thousands of aromatic ingredients, among them, lemon grass and other herbs, celery, onion, soy sauce, lemon juice, and garlic. There was no change in the flavor of the meat, so why bother?

A variety of sauces can be served on the side: Ginger and Fermented Black Bean Sauce (page 308), Horseradish Hollandaise (page 306) and Cumberoutlandish Sauce (page 106). Basic Fowl Giblet Gravy (page 45), while not traditional with duck, can be a surprise winner. A few variations will make a host of attractive sauces. For Green Peppercorn Sauce for Duck, add three tablespoons of drained and rinsed canned green peppercorns for the last five minutes of cooking. For a southwestern duck sauce, add a half cup of Cherry Tomato Purée (page 418) or drained and crushed canned plum tomatoes, a teaspoon of chopped Basic Jalapeños (page 383), and three tablespoons of chopped cilantro for the last five minutes. For Something like Bigarade Duck Sauce (a bitter orange sauce), add a half cup of bitter orange marmalade, a half cup of orange juice—blood orange juice would be lovely—and two tablespoons of lemon juice. Green Herb Spread (page 295), Jalapeño-Mango Salsa (page 299), and Jalapeño-Lime Sauce (page 302) all go well with cold duck.

Readying the duck

DUCKS, PARTICULARLY LARGE ones, need some special attention before simmering or roasting. First, cut off any strings that may have been used to truss the bird. Reach inside the bird and remove any loose parts; they may be in a neat paper package. Some of the larger ducks may come without any innards. The neck and giblets (gizzard and heart) should be saved or used for stock or sauce (pages 72-74).

To remove the wing tips: With one hand, hold the wing tip from the side that normally folds in. With the other hand, hold the second joint in the same way. Bring hands down sharply toward each other, which will partially crack the joint. With a large kitchen shears or a cleaver, remove the wing tips. Moulard ducks sometimes arrive without wing tips.

There was a time when birds, particularly game, routinely came with their feet on. It is a rare bird today that comes so festooned. It's a pity, since the feet add much gelatin to the stock. I never roast birds with the feet on; people are squeamish. Instead, I whack the feet off at the ankle joint and save the feet for stock.

Ducks, being fatty birds, secrete pockets of fat that need removal. Melt the fat as for Rendered Goose Fat (page 83). Chunks of fat are located at the tail end, on either side of the pope's nose. On very large birds, such as moulard ducks, and on stronger-tasting birds, I sometimes slice off the triangular pope's nose and discard it, as it is very fatty. At the other end of the bird, the neck end, there may be pockets of fat as well or simply long streaks of fat at the skin edges. Most of this will pull out when firmly grasped. Sometimes, the membrane surrounding the fat and attaching it to the skin may be obdurate. A few snips through the membrane with a good kitchen scissors or the tip of a small sharp knife will release the fat.

Even though there may be a large full piece of neck tucked into the cavity, some of the neck will still be attached. This is true of some game birds and Cornish hens as well. While the birds can be cooked perfectly satisfactorily with the neck piece attached to the bird, it can become unsightly as the flesh shrinks back during roasting. Additionally, I am a greedy stock and sauce maker.

To remove the remaining neck: Ease the skin back from the neck. With sharp kitchen scissors or the point of a knife, cut through the membrane surrounding the neck and, holding it, free it on all sides. When as much neck has been freed as can be done without cutting into the breastbone or into meat, it is time to sever the neck from the bird. With small birds, it is possible to fold the neck over abruptly or to twist it until a crack is heard; then cut through the neck with kitchen shears. Larger necks will require more strenuous effort. I usually saw—somewhat ineffectually—a cut all around the neck to get at the bone. I either pick up a cleaver and sever the neck with a mighty whack or use the kitchen shears to cut through it. My hands get greasy from the duck skin while I'm freeing the neck. I carefully wash scissors or cleaver and hands before picking up the scissors or cleaver so they don't slip. The bird needs to be held with one hand while the other wields the instrument of doom, lest it be my own.

Pricking the skin: In order to let as much fat ooze out of the duck as possible while it simmers and then roasts, the skin needs to be pricked to make little holes in it. Usually a fork with sharp tines is a sufficient instrument. As the bird gets larger, its skin gets heavier and the sharp tip of a paring knife is needed. Prick the skin by holding the implement at an angle, and don't be too vigorous. The skin is supposed to be pierced, not the meat, or it will lose blood and be less juicy after cooking.

Make sure to give extra pricking to the particularly fatty parts of the skin, which are lighter in color and puffy, as if marshmallows were stuffed under the skin. They tend to lurk behind the wings and leg joints. These must be pricked very thoroughly. Do not prick along the backbone or breastbone. There is almost no meat, let alone fat.

This takes care of preparing most ducks. However, some of them arrive in the kitchen with the unsightly stubble of wings sticking out of their skin, like a two-day beard. Heftier bits can be pulled out with a pliers. As soon as the roasted duck comes from the oven, little bits that have eluded plucking can be easily shaved (scrape with a knife). They dry out and come right off.

The cooking times for Long Island duck are for juicy meat. When the duck is cooked, the juices will run clear when the flesh is pricked and a meat thermometer inserted into the center of the breast, but not touching the bone, will register 135 to

140°F. Larger ducks have darker meat and may show a trace of pink, but no blood. If meat without any trace of pink is preferred, increase the roasting times by five to ten minutes, depending on the size of the bird. If bloodier birds are preferred, reduce roasting times by the same amount.

All recipes here will call for simmering the duck as in Best Roast Duck (below) and will proceed with roasting with differences only in simmering and roasting times and seasoning.

Best roast duck

SERVES 2 TO 4

TOTAL
ROASTING
TIME:
30
minutes

THIS IS THE prototype for the two roasted duck recipes that follow.

Despite all the fancy duck recipes around, most of us crave an old-fashioned, simple, crisp roast duck. This recipe deals with the dilemma that by the time the duck skin is crisp enough to please and the fat under the skin has melted away, the meat has become dry, microscopic, and stringy. Poaching the duck before roasting it eliminates most of the fat under the skin. High-heat roasting completes the job. It also keeps the meat juicy and plump. The broth that results from the initial simmering is a delicious duck stock. If made completely of duck and not started with chicken stock—the pleasant outcome of a succession of roastings—it is very rich.

To poach two ducks, find a large stew or braising pan. Put the ducks in and cover with water by an inch to see how much stock will be needed. Remove the ducks and proceed with the recipe. Two ducks can fit in one very large roasting pan; do not let them touch. The only occasion on which I ever successfully made more than two ducks at a time was when visiting a friend with two oversize ovens. Mine are dinky by current standards.

Once the duck has been poached and drained, let it sit in the roasting pan(s) at room temperature for at least thirty minutes. This allows the skin to dry. Next, turn on an exhaust fan or open a window. Put the duck(s) in the clean oven. Surprise! The duck will be perfectly cooked after a brief roasting, and the oven will be clean. Remove the duck from the oven very carefully; the pan contains hot fat.

As I can never predict exactly how much duck each person will eat, I inevitably have leftovers. One half of a cooked duck breast (three ounces) makes a cup and a quarter of shredded meat for soup or salad, as does the meat from one leg and thigh. Don't throw out the bones on people's plates. Remember, recooking will sanitize them. Throw into the remaining broth and boil away.

5- to 5½-pound Long Island duck, thawed, innards removed, wing tips removed, neck trimmed, and extra fat removed

4½ quarts duck stock saved from a prior roasting, or Basic Chicken Stock (page 42), or three 46-ounce cans chicken broth, skimmed, or water

1 teaspoon kosher salt

¾ teaspoon freshly ground black pepper

OPTIONAL INGREDIENTS (instead of salt and pepper)

½ recipe Tandoori Wet Rub (page 294) or ½ recipe ingredients for Muscovy Duck with Blood Oranges (page 69) or ½ recipe Star Anise Rub (page 71)

½ cup skimmed stock from duck or water, for deglazing

Remove the duck from the refrigerator. Let sit at room temperature for the 20 minutes that are needed for the next step.

Pour stock into a tall narrow stockpot. Be sure there is enough room left in the pot for the duck. By using a narrow pot, less stock is needed to cover the duck than in a wider pot. Add the wing tips, neck, giblets, and any blood from the duck. Cover the pot and bring to a boil over high heat.

Meanwhile, using the tines of a fork, thoroughly prick the duck all over, paying special attention to the fattiest areas. Insert the tines at an angle so there is a minimum risk of pricking the meat beneath. Carefully lower the duck into the boiling stock, neck end first, allowing the cavity to fill with stock so the duck sinks to the bottom of the pot. To keep the duck submerged, place a plate or pot cover over the duck to weight it down. The Japanese otoshi-buta—wooden lids that are 1½ to 2 inches smaller than the diameter of the pot—are perfect (page 11).

When the stock returns to a boil, reduce the heat and simmer 45 minutes. Even with the plate as weight, the duck will tend to float to the surface, so check about every 10 to 15 minutes to see that the duck remains submerged. Keep the stock at a gentle simmer; if it boils, the duck will rise to the surface.

When the duck has finished simmering, spoon 1 tablespoon of the duck fat off the top of the stock and spread it in the bottom of a shallow 12 x 8 x 1½-inch roasting pan. Remove the plate and carefully lift out the duck, holding it over the pot to drain any liquid from the cavity. Place duck in roasting pan. Do not tuck the neck flap under the duck. Spread it out in the pan.

Pat the duck thoroughly dry and lightly coat the skin with the salt and pepper or one of the optional ingredients, gently pressing them against the skin. The duck is hot and the skin is tender, so work carefully. The duck may be prepared ahead up to this point and refrigerated for a day. If made ahead, return duck to room temperature. If proceeding with roasting right away, for optimum results, leave the duck sitting out at room temperature for 30 minutes to permit the skin to dry and heat the oven to 500°F with oven rack on the second level from the bottom.

Place duck in oven legs first. Roast 30 minutes. After 10 minutes, spoon out the fat that accumulates in the roasting pan. Move the duck around in the pan with a wooden spatula to prevent the skin from sticking to the bottom of the pan. If it is easier, remove the pan from the oven—careful, hot fat—to spoon off fat. This will avoid getting fat on the inside of the oven, which would smoke. Make sure the oven door is closed, so that the temperature doesn't go down.

After the full 30 minutes, remove the duck from the pan. Pour or spoon off the fat, and deglaze pan (page 10) with stock or water.

When time is available, skim duck stock and place in freezer containers for the next time, or add carcasses and bones back into pan and cook as Duck Stock, Double Rich (page 72).

Muscovy duck with blood oranges

DRAKE SERVES 6 TO 8 AS A MAIN COURSE,
HEN SERVES 4

TOTAL
ROASTING
TIME:
see page 70

I'M PARTICULARLY FOND of this simple counterpointing of rich duck flavor and the sour-sweet taste of richly red blood oranges. If no blood oranges are available, use fresh juice oranges and substitute the juice of a lemon for part of the orange juice. Seville oranges do very well also. The hot sections of orange are served along with the duck. The same procedure can be followed with two Peking ducks.

Muscovy ducks are not birds of great repute since they sometimes have a strong musky scent. They have darker meat than our common Long Island ducks, and are more flavorful as well. The tendency of their meat to become mushy is eliminated with the combination simmering and high-heat roasting method. I generally remove the bit of tail, or pope's nose, at the end of the bird since the musk glands live there.

As with all ducks, the male is the drake and the female the hen. The muscovy drake is significantly larger than the hen, almost twice her size. If a drake is available, I prefer it to a hen because it serves more people and provides more leftovers. A half of a boneless breast weighs eight ounces. The meat from one leg and thigh weighs four to five ounces. If there are leftovers, use them in any of the recipes for leftover duck.

continued

If cooking the smaller hen, consider cooking two at the same time. One hen will probably accommodate only one orange in its cavity. Put the other orange sections in the pan while cooking the cumin and making the sauce.

These ducks often have heavy necks to be removed along with the wing tips (page 66). A paring knife will be needed to prick this skin; and the compensation is no smoke in the kitchen. The meat will be barely pink, the sauce addictive.

1 muscovy duck (drake, 7½ to 8 pounds; hen, about 4 pounds), thawed, innards and wing tips removed, neck trimmed, and extra fat removed; if feet still on, remove

Kosher salt, to taste

Freshly ground black pepper, to taste

2 blood oranges, cut in quarters, white heavy membrane along each sliced edge cut off

4½ quarts duck stock, saved from a prior roasting, or Basic Chicken Stock (page 42), or three 46-ounce cans chicken broth, skimmed, or water

¾ cup skimmed stock from duck or water, for deglazing

1 tablespoon ground cumin

1 teaspoon kosher salt

⅔ cup fresh blood orange juice, from 2 to 3 (6 ounces each) blood oranges

Please see Readying the Duck (page 65) and instructions for Best Roast Duck (page 67).

Simmer as in Best Roast Duck: drake, 45 minutes; hen, 30 minutes. Transfer the bird to an 18 x 13 x 2-inch roasting pan, breast side up. Do not tuck the neck flap under the duck. Pat the duck thoroughly dry and sprinkle the skin with the salt and pepper, gently pressing them against the skin. The duck is hot and the skin is tender, so work carefully. Stuff the orange pieces into the cavity.

Heat the oven to 500° F with oven rack on the second level from the bottom.

Roast 30 minutes for a drake and 20 to 25 minutes for a hen. After 10 minutes, spoon out the fat that accumulates in the roasting pan. Move the duck around with a wooden spatula to prevent the skin from sticking to the bottom of the pan. If it is easier, remove the pan from the oven—careful, hot fat—to spoon off fat. This will avoid getting fat on the inside of the oven, which would smoke. Make sure the oven door is closed so that the temperature doesn't go down.

Remove the duck from pan to serving platter. Pour or spoon off the fat. Deglaze pan with stock or water mixed with cumin and salt. Let reduce by one third. Strain through a fine sieve into a small saucepan, pushing down with the back of a spoon to pass through all of the sauce and as much of the deglazed solids as possible. Add blood orange juice. Boil over high heat. A small amount of fat will puddle in the middle; skim this off. Reduce sauce until there is 1 cup. Just before serving, remove oranges from duck cavity; they will still be warm. Arrange on serving platter around duck. Pass sauce separately.

TOTAL ROASTING TIME: drake, 30 minutes; hen, 20 to 25 minutes

Moulard duck with star anise rub

SERVES 6 TO 8

TOTAL
ROASTING
TIME:
30
minutes

IF A MOULARD duck is unavailable, the rub can be used on two Peking ducks or two muscovy ducks.

Moulards are large ducks, the results of a cross between Peking (Long Island) and muscovy ducks. They easily develop large livers, which is why this breed is used to produce foie gras. Big ducks serve more people, take more simmering time, and need bigger pots. The basic techniques remain the same. Once roasted, half a boned breast will weigh twelve ounces and the boned meat from one leg and thigh will be six ounces.

The duck will be very dark in color when removed from the oven. Do not be dismayed; it is not burned! The color comes from the rub, which tastes and smells delicious. Roast Shiitakes with Soy (page 363) or Mahogany Roasted Endives (page 351) would be good accompaniments.

8-pound moulard duck, thawed, innards and wing tips removed, neck trimmed, and extra fat removed
5 to 6 quarts duck stock, saved from a prior roasting, or Basic Chicken Stock (page 42), or four 46-ounce cans chicken broth, skimmed, or water

STAR ANISE RUB
Scant tablespoon star anise pieces
1 tablespoon sugar
1 teaspoon mustard seeds
8 black peppercorns
1 teaspoon kosher salt

Please see Readying the Duck (page 65) and instructions for Best Roast Duck (page 67). Using a large stockpot, simmer as in Best Roast Duck, 1 hour 10 minutes.

Meanwhile, place all ingredients for the rub in a spice mill. Process until a fine powder, stopping to shake several times for evenness. Makes ¼ cup, enough for a whole duck.

Remove duck to large roasting pan. Pat dry and pat all over with the reserved rub, pressing gently.

Heat the oven to 500° F with the oven rack on the second level from the bottom.

Roast the duck 30 minutes. After 10 minutes, spoon out the fat that accumulates in the roasting pan. Move the duck around with a wooden spatula to prevent the skin from sticking to the bottom of the pan. If it is easier, remove the pan from the oven—careful, hot fat—to spoon off fat. This will avoid getting fat on the inside of the oven, which would smoke. Make sure the oven door is closed so that the temperature doesn't go down.

Remove duck to a platter. Pour or spoon off the fat, and place pan over medium heat. Add 1½ cups skimmed cooking liquid and boil, scraping pan with a wooden spoon. Pass sauce separately.

Duck stock, double rich

A FEW COLD-WEATHER meals with the duck habit, and I have all the duck stock I want, which is a vast amount. The stock gets richer each time a new duck is poached in it. What follows is the model for postmeal enrichment of the stock. The meat from the neck stays very moist, so be sure to save it.

After your guests have enjoyed all the delicious meat, the remaining bare bones provide a glistening amber broth. Don't be timid about snatching back the bones from their plates. Remember, the bones will boil. The more carcasses and bones, the richer the stock. Leave the neck(s) and giblets already in the pot where they are.

Carcasses and bones from 1 to 3 roasted ducks, plus uncooked necks and wing tips, broken into small pieces

3 to 5 quarts stock left over from precooking ducks for roasting, well skimmed

Place the duck carcasses and bones in stockpot that held ducks. Add enough of the poaching liquid to cover bones by 1 inch. Cover, place over high heat; bring to a boil and skim off the scum that rises to the surface.

Reduce the heat so the liquid simmers. Cook, uncovered, skimming the fat and impurities from the surface from time to time. The more skimming, the clearer the stock. Cook about 12 hours, adding water as needed to maintain its level. Discard the solids. Cool the stock, skim again, then refrigerate or freeze.

If using this rich broth as a soup, add salt and pepper freely. Broad egg noodles or blanched, julienned leeks, carrots, celery, and string beans make good additions.

Duck soup with vegetables julienne

THIS IS FOR times when you want a simple, elegant soup. The julienned vegetables dress it up. Add hot red pepper sauce according to your taste. If there is a little leftover duck meat, skin it and cut it into thin strips, and add it along with the leeks.

6 cups defatted Duck Stock, Double Rich (page 72) or Basic Chicken Stock (page 42) or canned

2 to 3 whole carrots (7 ounces), trimmed, peeled, cut into 2¼-inch lengths, and julienned lengthwise (1½ cups)

2 large ribs celery (6 ounces), trimmed, peeled with a vegetable peeler, cut into 2¼-inch lengths, and julienned lengthwise (1 cup)

1 to 3 leeks (12 ounces), green trimmed off, cut into 2¼-inch lengths, and julienned lengthwise (2½ cups)

1 tablespoon plus 1 teaspoon kosher salt

⅛ to ¼ teaspoon hot red pepper sauce

4 to 5 grinds black pepper

Pour stock into a small soup pot. Add carrots and celery. Bring to a boil over high heat. Reduce heat to low and simmer until carrots are just tender, 4 to 5 minutes. Add leeks. Simmer until leeks are limp, 4 to 5 minutes more. Remove from heat. Stir in salt, red pepper sauce, and black pepper.

Elegant duck soup potage

MAKES 5 CUPS; SERVES 4

THIS IS ABOUT as easy and quick as soup gets and very good, too. The white potato cubes and green tarragon leaves swim around in the clear broth. Alternatively, the cooked soup can be put through a food mill for a warming potage. I love lovage, and in season, I substitute it for the tarragon, particularly in the potage version. The recipe can be multiplied endlessly.

2 boiling potatoes (1 pound), peeled, cut in half, and into ¼-inch cubes (3 cups)

4 cups Duck Stock, Double Rich (page 72)

2½ tablespoons fresh tarragon leaves

½ teaspoon kosher salt

6 to 8 grinds black pepper

Bring a medium saucepan filled with salted water to a boil. Add the potatoes. Cook for 5 minutes. Drain and rinse with cool water.

In the same saucepan, pour the stock. Add potatoes. Cover and bring to a boil. Reduce heat to medium-low, cover, and cook for 10 minutes. Add tarragon, salt, and pepper. Cook another 2 minutes. Serve warm.

Roast duck pasta sauce

THIS IS A deeply flavored sauce, a reward to the cook for having made a duck dinner. I prefer small portions as a first course so that the richness is a treat, not cloying. Heartier appetites may prefer to divide this between only two and add a salad of thinly sliced bulb fennel with Simple Light Vinaigrette (page 297). The sauce makes two cups as is; by thinning a little with extra stock, it could be stretched for more portions.

The vegetables can be sautéed on top of the stove instead of in the oven, as they are here.

1 small yellow onion (about 3 ounces), peeled and chopped fine (½ cup)

3 mushrooms with stems (about 3 ounces), cut in small dice (1 cup)

2 stalks celery, trimmed, peeled, and cut into small dice (½ cup)

1 tablespoon duck fat

2 tablespoons chopped fresh flat-leaf parsley, plus extra for topping

4 ounces skinless, boneless roast duck meat, roughly chopped in small pieces (about ¾ cup)

½ cup Duck Stock, Double Rich (page 72), gravy, or Basic Chicken Stock (page 42) or canned

Small piece bay leaf

1 teaspoon kosher salt

½ small clove garlic, peeled, smashed, and chopped fine

Freshly ground black pepper, to taste

8 ounces spaghetti

Freshly grated Parmesan cheese, for topping

Place rack in center of oven. Heat oven to 500°F.

In a small roasting pan, combine onion, mushrooms, and celery with the fat. Cook for 5 minutes. Stir. Cook 5 minutes more until the onions are brown and the mushrooms have given off their liquid. Scrape all vegetables and fat into a medium saucepan. Add parsley. Cook over low heat about 1 minute, or until parsely wilts. Add duck. Continue cooking over low heat 3 to 4 minutes. Add duck stock, bay leaf, salt, garlic, and pepper. Cook for 5 minutes. Remove bay leaf before serving.

Meanwhile, cook the spaghetti in boiling water until done. Strain and toss with warm sauce. Serve in individual bowls, topping each with fresh Parmesan and parsley.

Roast duck salad with black bean sauce

MAKES 1¾ CUPS; SERVES 2 AS
A FIRST COURSE

SEE PAGE 38 for salad greens suggestions for bedding this salad, which is very quick and delicious.

1½ cups skinned leftover roast duck
    meat strips
¾ cup Ginger and Fermented Black Bean
    Sauce (page 308)

¼ cup thin strips of scallion, both green
    and white parts

Place meat and bean sauce in a small saucepan. Heat over medium-low flame until warm throughout, stirring with a wooden spoon or chopstick. Do not leave on heat too long and cook the meat further, as it will dry out. Divide between 2 plates lined with greens and top with scallion.

Asian duck salad

MAKES A SCANT 4 CUPS; SERVES 4

THIS SALAD IS ample enough for a main course and is as good in spring as in winter. The pale green of Napa cabbage, thinly sliced across the head, is a good frame for this rich brown salad if there is a yen for green. Instead of serving as a salad, it can be heated and served over rice.

2 ounces dried black mushrooms
    (shiitake)
3 cups lukewarm water for soaking
    mushrooms
8 to 10 ounces leftover roast duck meat,
    about 2 legs and thighs, or 1 half
    duck, skinned and shredded
    (about 2 cups)

2 to 3 stalks celery, peeled with a vege-
    table peeler, cut across into thirds,
    and then into thin julienne (1 cup)
¼ cup plus 1 tablespoon plum sauce
4 juice oranges
2 tablespoons chopped fresh cilantro
    leaves
1 tablespoon tamari soy
Freshly ground black pepper, to taste

In a medium bowl, put the mushrooms to soak in the warm water. Leave for half an hour. Remove and drain. Cut off stems. Slice caps across into ¼-inch strips. Soaking water may be strained and saved for soup, stews, etc.

continued

In a larger bowl, put the duck meat, celery, mushrooms, and plum sauce. Use hands to mix gently until well coated. Peel the oranges. Using a sharp knife, section each orange, holding it over the large bowl so the juices run into the salad. Add orange sections. Add cilantro, soy, and pepper. Toss gently until mixed. Serve on a bed of lettuce greens.

Bean thread noodle salad

MAKES 3 CUPS; SERVES 4 AS
A FIRST COURSE

I OFTEN HAVE leftover duck, because I never can tell what part of the duck people will eat. Some like only breasts. Consequently, I make more than I need and have plenty for leftovers.

This salad can be made ahead and keeps wonderfully in the refrigerator. It tastes good cold, eaten right out of the fridge, or warm, as soon as it is made.

A whole package of bean thread noodles weighs about eight ounces. The recipe uses just over a quarter of a package. Another night, soak the remainder and serve in duck broth to eight to ten people as a dinner-party first course, with some whole cilantro or thinly sliced lovage leaves floating on top.

2½ ounces bean thread noodles (2 cups when soaked)

2 teaspoons sesame oil

4 ounces (2 medium) carrots peeled, cut in julienne, blanched (½ cup)

¼ cup chopped fresh mint, plus extra for topping (1 small bunch or 1 ounce)

4 to 5 scallions, green part only, cut in 2-inch lengths, then cut lengthwise in thirds (⅓ cup)

1 tablespoon rice wine vinegar

2 tablespoons tamari soy

½ teaspoon freshly grated gingerroot

¼ teaspoon ground Szechuan peppercorns

⅔ cup julienne-cut, skinned leftover roast duck meat

Put dry noodles in a medium bowl. Pour boiling water over noodles, enough to cover well. Leave for ½ hour. Strain noodles and put in medium bowl. Toss with sesame oil. Add carrots, mint, scallions, vinegar, soy, ginger, and peppercorns. Toss until thoroughly combined. Chopsticks are good for this. Serve about ½ cup noodles per plate. Top with a portion of duck meat and sprinkle with chopped mint.

Duck liver pâté

MAKES 2½ CUPS

IF YOU MAKE many ducks, you will collect lots of large livers. It takes only the livers from four ducks to make this creamy, palely beautiful dish. If more livers are saved in milk (page 20), use them to make Liver-Rich Dumplings (page 119), to put into some of your Duck Stock, Double Rich (page 72) or for the pâté variation.

Pretend this is foie gras and serve it with toasted brioche bread or Roasted Bread (page 367), made with reserved duck fat (from poaching and roasting a duck), and a green salad with chopped fresh sage leaves tossed in.

12 ounces duck livers, rinsed and connective tissue removed	1 whole star anise
1 cup milk	2 teaspoons kosher salt
2 cups heavy cream	¾ teaspoon freshly ground black pepper

Place livers in a bowl and pour the milk over them. Allow to stand at room temperature for at least 2 hours unless using frozen, milk-soaked livers, in which case just allow to come to room temperature. Drain and rinse.

Pour the cream into a small saucepan. Add the anise and salt. Bring to a boil, then reduce to a simmer and cook 3 minutes. Remove anise.

Place livers in a blender. Pour a small amount of the hot cream over the livers. Blend to mix well. With blender running, remove cover and pour in remaining hot cream. Blend until very smooth, stopping to scrape down sides once or twice. Add pepper, blend again. Using a rubber spatula, scrape all of mixture into a medium bowl, or several small crocks. Let cool. Cover tightly with plastic wrap and refrigerate at least 1 day. Will keep 2 weeks.

goose

CHRISTMAS GEESE ARE TRADITIONAL. I had remembered goose in Dickens's *Christmas Carol* and couldn't imagine how a bird with so little flesh could be a lavish feed for a hopeful family. When I went back to the text to check, my goose turned into a turkey, which made more sense. Goose makes a solid dinner for four. It just looks large; most of the volume and space is carcass and air. It can be stretched by a good carver to serve six at a fancy dinner with a first course or two and a couple of vegetables. Sauerkraut Noodles (page 172) would be a natural accompaniment.

All the fat—about four cups—let off by the goose is a cook's bonanza for roasting vegetables, particularly potatoes. Let the fat cool slightly and then pour it through a paper coffee filter. The fat will keep virtually indefinitely in the freezer. For a real treat—the kind of self-indulgence that keeps me happy with nothing more than a green salad—I make Melting Potatoes (Not-on-Your Diet)(page 395) with goose fat and Basic Goose Stock (page 80). Potatoes deep-fried in goose fat is a standard of southwestern France.

There aren't a lot of recipes for goose leftovers since there seldom seem to be any. The goose stock from the carcass makes a hearty soup, and any slivers of goose meat can be added. The livers can be saved for Goose Liver Mousse (page 82), or sauté them in a little goose fat; deglaze the pan with red wine vinegar and put the warm livers on top of frisée (pale chicory), with any bits of meat and cracklings that are around. Sprinkle with salt and freshly ground black pepper.

Simple roast goose

SERVES 4 TO 6

TOTAL
ROASTING
TIME:
2
hours
10
minutes

ONE GOOSE MAKES dinner; two geese make a party. Two can be cooked side by side in a large pan. Remember that two will create twice the fat, so proceed with caution. Use oven mitts when removing the pan from the oven to remove the fat. Keep the oven door closed. Turn down the heat after putting the bird(s) back in the oven. Be careful not to spill fat in the oven, or you will get lots of smoke; the goose will not be burning, the fat will.

Poultry farmers have been getting their geese in order. The size, twelve pounds, is fairly standard, and so is freezing. The birds take a full four days to thaw in the refrigerator. The overall cooking time is two hours and ten minutes after the geese have come to room temperature. Deglaze the pan with the richest stock on hand, even meat if there is no goose stock. Even so, the result is more a juice than a gravy.

12-pound goose, thawed and at room temperature, wing tips removed

Kosher salt, to taste

Freshly ground black pepper, to taste

1 cup wine (Port, Sherry, vermouth, or red wine), stock, or half of each, for deglazing

Place rack in lower third of oven. Heat oven to 475°F.

Using kitchen scissors, cut away the fat pockets in the cavity. Keep for Rendered Goose Fat (page 83). Save the neck, wing tips, and giblets for Basic Goose Stock (page 80).

Put the goose in an 18 x 12 x 2-inch roasting pan, breast side up. Salt and pepper. Put in the oven legs first. Roast 30 minutes. After the first 10 minutes, move the goose around in the pan with a wooden spatula so that skin won't stick to the bottom. After the 30 minutes, carefully spoon the melted fat out of the pan; take it out of the oven and close the oven door if nervous about the fat. Then jiggle the goose. Do not let fat splash onto oven floor or it may burn and create lots of smoke. Roast for 40 minutes more. Spoon out fat. Return goose to oven. Turn oven off and, keeping the oven door closed, let the goose continue to roast in the retained heat for 1 hour. Using a sharp knife, prick thigh near body. Juices will run clear. Goose is done.

Transfer goose to a platter and let rest about 20 minutes. Pour or spoon off remaining fat. Put the roasting pan on top of the stove. Add 1 cup of whatever liquid you have on hand, wine, stock, or water. Bring liquid to a boil, while scraping the pan bottom vigorously with a wooden spoon. Unstick all the crispy bits. Whisk liquid to incorporate any drops of blood that remain in the pan. This will thicken the sauce slightly, but it will remain quite thin and light. Let cook 5 minutes, adding salt and pepper to taste. Liquid may be served on the side in a sauceboat or put into the stockpot.

Roast goose with turnips

SERVES 4 TO 6

TOTAL ROASTING TIME: *see page 80*

THERE USED TO be a classic spring bistro dish at Allard, a famous Paris bistro, when Madame was cooking, of roast duck with tiny spring turnips deep-fat-fried to brown, tangy sweetness. I loved the combination of flavors, but didn't like the deep-fat-frying. It's also hard to find tiny turnips. In my climate, the tiny turnips aren't ready in the cold ground until well into summer, when it is too hot for me to be thinking goose or duck. This recipe is my very good attempt to reclaim the past. It does require reheating the turnips at the end of the goose's roasting time; but the goose has to sit there for a while anyhow.

12-pound goose, thawed and at room temperature, wing tips removed

1½ pounds turnips (6, about 4 ounces each), trimmed, peeled, small ones cut into quarters, larger ones cut into 6 to 8 pieces

Kosher salt, to taste

Freshly ground black pepper, to taste

Prepare and start the goose as in Simple Roast Goose (page 78). Roast for 30 minutes. Carefully spoon out fat in pan and arrange turnips in pan around goose. Roast another 20 minutes. Spoon out fat and turn turnips over. Roast 20 minutes more.

With a slotted spoon, transfer turnips from pan to a smaller roasting pan. Keep goose in its pan and return to oven. Turn oven off and let goose continue to cook in the retained heat for 1 hour. Turnips will wait at room temperature. When goose is removed from oven and is resting, heat oven to 375°F. Roast the small pan of turnips 15 minutes. Sprinkle with salt and pepper. Proceed with deglazing as in Simple Roast Goose. Serve hot.

TOTAL ROASTING TIME: goose, 2 hours and 10 minutes; turnips, 55 minutes

Basic goose stock

MAKES ABOUT 2½ QUARTS

Yes, GOOSE STOCK, to use in cooking dry beans or to make a garbure with pieces of leftover goose in it. If several geese are roasted, make more stock. Three carcasses and pieces will make about eight quarts.

Carcass and bones from a 12-pound roasted goose, plus uncooked neck, wing tips, and giblets, carcass and bones broken up into pieces

4 quarts water, or to cover

Place pieces of carcass into large pot; fill with water to cover by 1 inch. Cover and bring to a boil. Lower heat to a simmer. Cover with otoshi-buta (page 11) or lid ajar. From time to time, skim the foam off the top. Cook 9 hours or more, until the bones fall apart. Add more water if needed. This long cooking will impart the best flavor.

Garburesque of goose

MAKES 6 CUPS; SERVES 6

GARBURE IS A THICK, rich soup from France that is often made with confit of duck or goose. This soup, made without goose but with fat and stock from roasted goose, is heavenly, but not authentic—hence, "garburesque." While I have given serving quantities for use as a conventional soup, this is thick with vegetables, beans, and potatoes, and I can share it—reluctantly—with three others and make a meal of it, especially if there is a little leftover goose to toss in and a good green salad and peasanty bread to go alongside.

I prefer to use small, white navy beans in this soup and feel confirmed in my choice by André Daguin of Auch, in southwest France, who prefers them as well. Like the French, I pour some of the red wine in my glass into the last of the thick soup in my bowl, which is to *faire chabrot* and drink it right from the bowl.

½ cup dry small white navy beans

1 to 1½ tablespoons Rendered Goose Fat (page 83)

1 small onion (about 3 ounces), peeled and chopped medium (½ cup)

3 cloves garlic, peeled, smashed, and chopped fine (1 heaping tablespoon)

¼ head green cabbage, cored and sliced across into 1-inch pieces (2 to 3 cups)

3 carrots (3 ounces each), trimmed, peeled, and cut in half lengthwise, then across into 1-inch lengths (1 cup)

2 boiling potatoes (1 pound total), peeled and roughly cut in ¾-inch cubes (scant 2 cups)

1 teaspoon chopped fresh thyme leaves

1 teaspoon thinly sliced fresh sage

3 cups Basic Goose Stock (page 80), or Basic Chicken Stock (page 42) or canned

1½ teaspoons kosher salt

1 small turnip (5 ounces), peeled, quartered, and sliced across into ⅛-inch pieces (1 cup)

First prepare the beans. Place beans in a small saucepan with enough water to cover them by 2 inches. Cover and bring to a boil. Cook for 2 minutes. Remove from heat, cover, and leave for 1 hour. Strain. Cook beans in fresh water for 45 minutes. Strain and reserve.

Melt the goose fat in a medium saucepan. Add onions, cook over medium heat until translucent, about 5 minutes, but don't let them brown. Add garlic. Stir well. Reduce heat to low. Cook 2 minutes. Add cabbage. Cook until it wilts, about 3 minutes. Add carrots and potatoes. Stir for 2 to 3 minutes, until all pieces are slicked with the fat. Add thyme and sage. Add stock, cover, and bring to a boil over high heat. Reduce to medium and cook 10 minutes. Add salt and turnip. Cook 3 minutes. Add beans and any leftover goose meat, if using. Cook 5 more minutes.

Goose liver mousse

THIS IS NOT foie gras; but it will do until my ship comes in. It uses three of the large livers of geese (see page 20 for how to save them up). If that many geese have been cooked, there will be plenty of fat and stock for this recipe.

¾ cup Rendered Goose Fat (page 83), plus extra for sealing, optional

½ medium onion (about 4 ounces), peeled and finely diced

3 goose livers, rinsed and connective tissue removed (3½ ounces total)

2 tablespoons Basic Goose Stock (page 80), or Basic Chicken Stock (page 42) or canned

4 black peppercorns, finely ground

6 juniper berries, finely ground

⅛ teaspoon kosher salt

Place rack in center of oven. Preheat oven to 300°F.

In a small skillet, over very low heat, melt ½ cup of the goose fat. Add onions and cook until very soft and melting, about 45 minutes. Do not let onions brown.

Meanwhile, pack livers into smallest possible ovenproof container. Cover with remaining ¼ cup goose fat. Cook 30 minutes.

Remove livers from oven and cool slightly. Cut livers into small pieces and transfer all livers, with fat, to blender. Blend until smooth, stopping once or twice to scrape down sides of blender with a rubber spatula. Add onions with their fat and continue to blend. Add remaining ingredients. Blend until smooth. Adjust seasoning if necessary.

Transfer mixture to small ramekins. Refrigerate until set. Cover mousse with thin layer of extra goose fat to seal or with plastic wrap. Return to refrigerator. Will keep for a week.

Rendered goose fat

To render fat is to liquefy it by heating. This simple and classic process purifies the goose fat collected from Simple Roast Goose (page 78) by cooking it over low heat until all the water has evaporated and then straining it through a very fine sieve or two layers of dampened cheesecloth. This recipe makes use of the fat only. In the unlikely case that there is skin left, cut it in small pieces and add to fat. After the liquefied fat is strained, there will be a little skin left and a handful of cracklings. Drain the cracklings well on paper towels and pack into a refrigerator container to be briefly heated, sprinkled with salt, and eaten another time or used as a garnish for salads.

Goose fat collected from 12-pound goose, both solid fat cut off before cooking and liquid fat collected during cooking	3 tablespoons water Any extra goose skin, cut in small pieces

Cut solid pieces of goose fat into ¼-inch pieces. Put into a heavy saucepan. Add water and liquid fat. Cook 1 hour over low heat. Strain through a coffee filter. Reserve remaining solid pieces for cracklings. Store in tightly sealed and labeled containers. Will keep in freezer indefinitely.

QUAIL

There are many different kinds of quail. I never know which I'm cooking. I buy them frozen at the market, four to a package. To be safe, allow them to thaw overnight in the refrigerator, although eight to ten hours is usually enough.

Quail are small birds of only about four ounces each with a very, very mild game taste and beige to medium-brown flesh when cooked. While deft eaters can use a knife and fork, I find this food for fingers. I love quail and can eat three as a main course; but if I'm serving a lot of food, two are probably enough, with one making a first course—excellent before a roasted fish.

Nine to ten of these small beasts fit in a small pan, twenty-six to thirty in a large pan—enough for a buffet. Multiply the recipes as need be.

Simple quail

SERVES 3 TO 5 (2 TO 3 QUAIL PER PERSON)
AS A MAIN COURSE, 5 TO 10 (1 TO 2 QUAIL
PER PERSON) AS A FIRST COURSE

TOTAL
ROASTING
TIME:
15
minutes

Quail like spicy flavors and strong herbs. A teaspoon and a half of chili powder can be added to the fat along with a little salt and pepper before smearing the birds. In which case, serve each bird on a round of Roasted Buttercup Squash with Chile Oil (page 412), surround with sprigs of cilantro, and accompany with a wedge of lime or lemon. Guacamole (page 300) on the side would be a plus. A sprig of rosemary thrust into each bird makes for a fine perfume to accompany Roast Red New Potatoes with Garlic and Rosemary (page 393).

The birds can have their tiny legs tied together or not; the timing will not change. It's just an aesthetic question: on a piece of Roasted Bread (page 367) or a bed of vegetables, they will look neater for the trussing. If trussing, snip the string with kitchen shears before serving. If you prefer your quail rare, roast only 8 minutes.

10 quail (about 4 ounces each) thawed, wing tips removed, and legs tied together, if preferred

1 tablespoon unsalted butter or neutral oil

Kosher salt, to taste

Freshly ground black pepper, to taste

1 cup stock, wine, fruit juice, or water, for deglazing

Place rack in center of oven. Heat oven to 500°F.

Arrange quail, breast sides up, in a 12 x 8 x 1½-inch roasting pan. Smear some butter or oil over each quail. Sprinkle with salt and pepper. Roast for 5 minutes. Turn quail over. Roast another 5 minutes. Turn. Roast 5 minutes more.

Remove the quail to a serving platter. Pour off excess fat from roasting pan. Deglaze pan with the stock or other liquid (page 10). Serve the sauce in a sauceboat.

Roast quail with fresh sage and bacon

TOTAL
ROASTING
TIME:
15
minutes

QUAIL COOK A bit more evenly if a piece of string is used to tie the tips of the legs together. If you like your birds rare, cook only 8 minutes.

1 bunch (1 ounce) fresh sage

10 quail (about 4 ounces each), thawed, wing tips removed

7 slices thick-cut bacon, each cut into thirds

Kosher salt, to taste

Freshly ground black pepper, to taste

1 cup water, wine, fruit juice, or stock for deglazing

Place rack in center of oven. Heat oven to 500°F.

Tuck a few small leaves of fresh sage into each quail. Tie legs if desired. Place a large sage leaf on top of each breast. Cover with a piece of bacon. Place each completed quail on a piece of bacon in a 12 x 8 x 1½-inch roasting pan. Sprinkle with salt and pepper.

Roast 5 minutes. Turn over with tongs. Roast 10 minutes more. Remove birds to serving platter. Surround birds with any pieces of bacon that have gotten loose. Pour off grease from pan. Place pan on top of stove over medium heat. Add liquid. Bring to a boil and scrape up crisp bits. Let reduce by half. Serve in a sauceboat on the side. Cut strings, if any, on quail and remove.

Simple roast squab

TOTAL
ROASTING
TIME:
16 *to* 17
minutes

THERE ARE TWO kinds of squabs. One is a small chicken, called a *poussin* in France. If you are lucky enough to find any, cook as for Simple Roast Cornish Game Hen (page 53). I prefer the kind of squab cooked here. It's just a polite name for a domestic pigeon. Unlike the pigeons in the Game Bird section (page 88), these are really not gamy. Like wild pigeon, they have almost no fat of their own and darkish flesh. They need no fat added as they cook so quickly.

Two to three birds can fit in a small roasting pan, the neck ends toward the outside of the pan, four in a medium pan, and six in a large pan. I'm not sure any of us is going to have more pigeon-friendly eaters than that at a time.

Whole anise seeds in the carcass of the bird as it cooks perfumes the entire bird exceptionally. If using anise, deglaze the pan with stock or water; wine will taste too acidic.

2 whole squabs (about 12 ounces each), wing tips removed

Kosher salt, to taste

Freshly ground black pepper, to taste

2 tablespoons anise seeds, optional

1 cup stock, wine, fruit juice, or water, for deglazing

Place rack on second level from bottom of oven. Heat oven to 500°F.

Place squabs, breast sides up, in a 12 x 8 x 1½-inch roasting pan. Sprinkle with salt and pepper. Put 1 tablespoon of the anise seeds into each cavity, if using. Put in oven, legs first. Roast for 16 to 17 minutes, or until juices run clear. Remove to plates. Allow to rest 5 minutes.

Deglaze pan (page 10) with stock or liquid. Reduce slightly and add salt and pepper to taste. Serve the sauce in a sauceboat.

Roast squab with turnips and fresh spinach

SERVES 2

TOTAL
ROASTING
TIME:
16 to 17
minutes

THE REASON THIS recipe is written for two people is that it was the perfect amount of food for me and a friend. To make four birds, use a medium-size pan with bird necks facing toward corners. Use four turnips. Place wedges slicked with one tablespoon fat in the spaces between the birds. Use two pounds of spinach. For six people, use a large pan, six birds, six turnips, one and a half tablespoons fat, and three pounds of spinach.

2 whole squabs (12 ounces each), wing
  tips removed

½ tablespoon unsalted butter or
  neutral oil

3 medium turnips (4 ounces each), peeled
  and cut into 6 to 8 wedges each

Kosher salt, to taste

Freshly ground black pepper, to taste

1 pound fresh flat-leaf spinach, any thick
  stems removed, well washed

Place oven rack on second level from the top. Heat oven to 500°F.

Place squabs, breast sides up, in a 12 x 8 x 1½-inch roasting pan. Slick squabs and pan with butter or oil. Arrange turnip wedges in pan so that they are not touching. Sprinkle salt and pepper over everything. Roast 10 minutes. Move each squab around in pan with a wooden spatula and turn over the turnips. Roast 6 to 7 minutes more.

Remove squab and turnips to a serving platter or plates. Tilt pan to spoon off fat. Place pan over high heat and add spinach. Cook until wilted, 4 to 6 minutes. Transfer spinach and any remaining juices to platter or plates of squab and turnips.

GAME BIRDS

"THE GAME'S AFOOT''; I CANNOT RESIST.

Well, I have really been circling the game for the last few recipes, since quail (page 83–85) and squab (page 86–87) are thought of by many as game, as are the large, dark-fleshed muscovy and moulard ducks. In some ways, they are as much game as many of the "wild" birds that we can buy, since those "wild" birds are farm-raised.

True game is something you have met in the forest that swooshed enticingly from cover (grouse)—but never in small bird season; they seem to know better—or that you have seen flying, or walking down a Southampton road (pheasant) or a Vermont path, or eating the roses (deer). In the United States, it is a sometime thing, especially when fresh, as the license to shoot is strictly limited in order to protect the flocks, and the game must be eaten by the shooter and guests or be given away; it may not be sold. Aside from knowing a hunter or being one, one must find an importer who brings game in from outside the country.

All of the game for this book was strictly legal and hence farm-raised or imported though I have cooked, thanks to hunter friends, local wild venison, particularly the liver, which I love (cook it like Whole Roasted Calf's Liver, page 215), ruffed grouse, and a variety of other animals. I'm not above eating what I will not kill, particularly as I am not to be trusted with a gun, having almost no binocular vision.

If the game is farm-raised, I probably have a pertinent recipe. If it's real wild game, I may or may not have a recipe; look and see what I have and then invent. I was usually confronted by these creatures when I was far from the books in which I could look them up. When in doubt, marinate using the recipe Basic Game Marinade (page 91) for at least twelve hours at room temperature or for a day and a half in the refrigerator. Wipe the bird off and roast at high temperature. Do warn people about buckshot if the game is really wild.

When I get true game from a supplier, it may be frozen or it may be sealed in a Cryovac package. Depending on the size, it will take from one to three days to defrost in the refrigerator. Even if it is tightly sealed, it still needs to be refrigerated, whether defrosting or simply storing. When the package is opened to remove the bird for cooking, be sure to carefully save the blood. It is good in sauces. If not using the blood within the next hour, add a little vinegar—from three drops for the blood of a single pigeon to a quarter cup for the blood from one large or several smaller birds. This will keep the blood from coagulating.

See page 65–66 for more about cleaning birds.

How long will the game keep after defrosting or in Cryovac? This brings up the loaded question of aging or hanging game. I am of many minds about this. I have a vivid memory of the devoted manservant of a large Hungarian gastronome friend named Robi, standing in the kitchen, a surgical mask over his face. He was loyally and carefully cleaning some bird or other that had been hanging outside the window of Robi's apartment for several days and had turned green. I opined that the bird should be jettisoned. It was, despite a spate of dramatic tears.

At one of London's most famous restaurants, I had a grouse so thoroughly hung that it smelled very high, and I became ill after eating it. Yet hanging game can accentuate flavor and tenderize. Since I never seem to get plumed fowl with their innards in—the proper state for hanging—I compromise by allowing the birds to sit in the refrigerator in their plastic packets for two days after they are defrosted. They seem to be fine. I also don't have access to the plumes that French and Russian chefs of the haute époque seemed to delight in sending to the table so the diner wasn't sure the game was dead.

If a bird you expected to see in this section isn't here, look in the Index; it may be someplace else. In a way, it's arbitrary. A wild turkey is only "wild" in so far as it isn't the domestic turkey we have all gotten used to; but I had to put things someplace.

I did learn something important in cooking what seemed like an endless succession of birds (there can be too much of a good thing). Birds that many cooks and writers (among them my favorites, such as Jane Grigson), consider to be dry and requiring barding (covering with fat), larding (inserting strips of fat into the flesh), and/or marinating really don't when cooked by the high-heat method. After many smoke-filled kitchen sessions caused by the melting barding fat, in exasperation I decided to just stick the birds in the oven and see what happened. They were not dry, but rich and perfectly cooked. There was still a tendency to smoke; but pouring off the fat after fifteen minutes of cooking really eliminates almost all of that. With a small bird such as a partridge, remove the fat halfway through the cooking time.

When I add fat to a bird, it is mainly for flavor. I recommend removing solid fat such as strips of bacon ten minutes before the end of the cooking time so that the bird cooks evenly. Since I don't tie the fat into place, this is easy to do with tongs. I try very hard not to munch the bacon, but to keep it to add to the plates of food.

Streaky bacon is a very important asset for cooking game birds and game in general. The flavors marry well, and the bacon adds some fat to slightly dry birds. Besides, it is traditional. The problem is that the bacon usually sold in packages is very thinly sliced and fatty. This adds little flavor and a huge amount of fat, which will smoke. If it is the only bacon available, omit it. I find a butcher who keeps good slab bacon on hand with a very high percentage of lean to fat and have him slice it at least an eighth of an inch thick. In the fall, I usually buy a whole flitch of bacon and keep it wrapped in the freezer until needed. It will soften enough in a very short while at room temperature so that I can slice off what I need and return the rest to the freezer.

The other barding fat I use is thin sheets, about four by six inches, of unsalted fatback. I order this ahead from the butcher, who slices it almost frozen. Individual slices can be separated by thin pieces of paper and returned to the freezer.

As problematical as hanging game is the question of how bloody it should be when served. The game birds in this book are cooked until there is no raw red blood, the juices run fairly clear, and the bird reaches a temperature of about 140°F on an instant-read thermometer inserted into the thickest part of the meat. The meat will still be juicy and faintly pink. If there is any uncertainty about the doneness of the bird, turn it upside down and stick the point of a sharp knife into the area at the base of the thigh joint. There should be no red blood. Any exceptions will be noted in the recipes.

If rare birds are desired, decrease the cooking time by five minutes for small birds and ten for large birds. If the birds are being poached before roasting, increase the poaching time by the time subtracted from the roasting time. That should still provide crisp skin. If no one cares about the skin or residual fat, just reduce the roasting time.

Basic game marinade

MAKES 2 CUPS

I RARELY MARINATE birds, but feel impelled by convention to provide a good, all-purpose marinade for game. As the marinade cooks, it even smells gamy. The marinade needs to cool before use so as not to cook the birds. Birds need to marinate for a fairly long time if they are to pick up any flavor from the marinade. Start at least a day ahead of time. Two might be better.

The amount of marinade given here is enough for up to six quail or two small imported pheasants. The marinade can be multiplied for larger birds. It is also a good liquid in which to defrost frozen cubes of venison when making a stew. Never reuse the marinade unless it is brought to a boil.

This is enough marinade for two pheasants, six quail, four partridge, and the pear tree too. Turn the birds very carefully from time to time.

½ cup red wine

½ cup red wine vinegar

½ cup stock of the kind of game being cooked or Basic Chicken Stock (page 41) or canned, or, for venison, Extra-Rich Beef Stock (page 227) or Extra-Rich Roasted Triple Stock (page 230)

½ cup olive oil

1 piece orange zest (2 x ½ inches)

3 cloves garlic, smashed and peeled

1 pinch ground nutmeg

1 pinch herbes de Provence

1 clove

1 small piece bay leaf

Combine all ingredients in a small saucepan. Bring to a boil. Reduce heat and simmer 5 minutes. Remove from heat. Let cool to body temperature before pouring over bird(s).

Mixed game bird stock

MAKES ABOUT 3 QUARTS

THIS IS THE ideal way to use all the wing tips, necks, and gizzards that have been reserved when preparing game birds (pages 88–90) for roasting as well as the carcasses of most game birds except pheasant, which makes such a good stock on its own (page 104). Most of the other birds are small, and it is best to collect a goodly number in the freezer before making a stock, unless a big dinner party has provided a plethora. Any mixture of birds is fine; but do not use wood pigeon; I found it to make a bitter stock.

Liver-Rich Dumplings (page 119) made with the milk-soaked reserved livers on hand, or boiled fine egg noodles, some salt, pepper, and a sprinkling of a favorite chopped herb turn this into a festive soup. On its own, this stock improves all game bird deglazing sauces.

At least 4 game bird carcasses and all
  bones, reserved wing tips, necks, and
  gizzards

3 quarts water

Brush any seasonings off the carcasses. Break up the carcasses with your hands or a large cleaver. Place bones and parts in a stockpot with water just to cover. Cover and bring to a boil. Skim off the fat and scum that rise to the top. Lower the heat so liquid is just barely boiling. Cover if desired. Cook 12 to 18 hours, skimming occassionally, adding more cold water as needed. The more skimming, the clearer the stock.

Pour the stock through a sieve and let cool at room temperature; then refrigerate. Remove the fat from the surface and any sediment from the bottom. Use as is, refrigerate, or freeze.

About egg noodles for soup

THIS CHAPTER IS full of wonderful stocks, as are the meat and fish chapters. It is helpful to know a little about egg noodles. There are eight uncooked cups in a dry pound of fine noodles and eleven uncooked cups in a pound of dry medium egg noodles. They should both be boiled in three times their volume of boiling salted water—five minutes for fine and seven minutes for medium—and then drained and chilled under cold water unless being used immediately. Each dry cup of fine noodles makes a generous cup when boiled; medium makes three fourths of a cup—less of them dry will fit in a cup.

Simple wild turkey

SERVES 4

TOTAL
ROASTING
TIME:
35
minutes

THESE ARE ALMOST the birds that Ben Franklin admired. If shot by hunters, they really are. However, if they are ordered from a specialty supplier, they taste only slightly wilder than ordinary domestic birds. Most farm-raised birds come frozen and take two full days to thaw in the refrigerator.

Wild turkeys are farm-raised and have very large, heavy carcasses so that, like geese, what seems to be a large bird will serve only a small number of people. They also have skinny little legs set far back on their bodies. It is best therefore to reverse the usual pattern: Put the bird in the oven neck first.

If good bacon cannot be found or is disliked, the turkey can simply be rubbed with a little canola or other neutral oil. As always, keep the wing tips, neck, and innards—except for the liver, which tends to have a strong taste—for stock. Make as Basic Turkey Stock (page 60). Use a game bird stock or at least a chicken stock to deglaze the pan, or there will not be much flavor.

Turkeys hold their legs very tight to their bodies, and the easiest way to carve the bird is to remove the legs first. Hold the end of the leg in a clean towel and rotate away from the body, cutting through the skin with a sharp carving knife. Once the skin is cut, pull fairly sharply on the leg, exposing the joint, which can be cut through fairly easily.

The flesh of the breast will be only slightly darker in color than that of domestic turkey. I would serve Cranberry Mint Dressing (page 114) and Honey-Glazed Turnip Wedges (page 424) along with a good red wine.

Six ¼-inch-thick strips streaky bacon,
   1 strip cut in half across, or
   1 tablespoon canola or other neutral oil
5-pound wild turkey, at room temperature, wing tips removed and neck
   trimmed (see page 65–66)

Kosher salt, to taste
Freshly ground black pepper, to taste
¾ cup stock, for deglazing

Place oven rack on second level from bottom. Heat oven to 500°F.

Place 3 strips of bacon in center of a 14 x 12 x 2-inch roasting pan. Place turkey, breast side up, on top of bacon. Sprinkle with salt and pepper. Place 2 whole strips of bacon over turkey breast and the two half-slices over the legs. Put bird in oven neck first. Cook 10 minutes. Move bird around in pan with wooden spatula to keep from sticking. Cook

10 minutes more. Remove bacon from top of bird. If well-browned, take bacon out of oven. If not, place in pan to cook further. Cook 15 minutes more. Remove.

Transfer turkey to a serving platter. Pour or spoon off excess fat. Put pan on top of stove. Add the stock and bring contents to a boil while scraping the bottom vigorously with a wooden spoon. Let reduce by half. Serve sauce in a sauceboat.

Wild turkey with roasted vegetables

SERVES 4

TOTAL ROASTING TIME: 35 *minutes*

THIS TECHNIQUE PRESUMES an oven that's high enough to hold the turkey on one shelf without touching the top of the oven, with a pan of vegetables on a lower shelf; or a wide enough oven so that both the turkey pan and the vegetable pan can be put next to each other. If that doesn't work, the vegetables can go in a second oven or be popped in the turkey oven as soon as the turkey comes out. Put the turkey on a platter and cover loosely with aluminum foil while deglazing the pan.

1 recipe Simple Wild Turkey (page 93)

2 tablespoons herbes de Provence

Kosher salt, to taste

Freshly ground black pepper, to taste

1 cup bird stock of choice, for deglazing

FOR THE VEGETABLES

1 medium zucchini (9 ounces), halved lengthwise, cut across into 1½-inch pieces (2 cups)

4 to 5 medium carrots (9 ounces), peeled, halved lengthwise, and cut across into 1-inch pieces (1½ cups)

3 medium leeks (9 ounces), trimmed, washed well, white part cut across in 1-inch pieces (2 cups)

4 shallots, peeled and trimmed

2 large floury potatoes, such as Idaho (1 pound total), peeled and quartered, each quarter cut into 3 to 4 wedges (3 cups)

1 tablespoon canola or other neutral oil

1 tablespoon herbes de Provence

Kosher salt, to taste

Freshly ground black pepper, to taste

If the 2 roasting pans will not fit side by side on 1 rack, place 1 rack on second level from bottom and another rack on the lowest level. Heat oven to 500°F.

Prepare turkey as in Simple Wild Turkey. Sprinkle 2 tablespoons of the herbes, the salt, and pepper in the cavity of the turkey. Arrange all vegetables in a second 14 x 12 x 2-inch roasting pan. Sprinkle with the oil, herbes, salt, and pepper. Toss to coat the vegetables.

Place the turkey in oven on second level from bottom. Roast for 5 minutes. Add pan with vegetables on lowest level. Roast 15 minutes. Toss and turn vegetables. Move turkey in pan with a wooden spatula so it won't stick. Roast all 15 minutes more. Move vegetables to a serving platter.

Move turkey to serving platter. Remove bacon from pan. Pour or spoon off excess fat. Place pan on top of stove. Add stock and bring to a boil, scraping bottom of pan with a wooden spoon. Pour in any juices that have collected on turkey serving platter. Let liquid reduce to about ¾ cup. Salt and pepper to taste. Serve on the side in a sauceboat.

Serve 1 piece of bacon per person and a large helping of vegetables.

W OOD PIGEONS (DOVES)

THE BEST GAME BIRDS THAT I HAVE BEEN ABLE TO BUY—THE MOST LIKE GAME AND NOT SOMETHING FROM A CHICKEN COOP—HAVE BEEN WOOD PIGEONS. *Game* is usually a slightly iffy term. These are wild birds, not domesticated pigeon (squab). In Europe, they may weigh up to twelve ounces. The largest of the wild pigeons is the European dove (*Columba palumbus*), which the English call "ringdove," the Scottish, "cushiedoo," and the French, *pigeon ramier*. They can weigh about twelve ounces. The similar-tasting woodcock weighs only slightly less.

The pigeons I got must have been a slightly different species—there are many—and weighed less, just enough to be a portion each. As true game, these deserve to be served rare. Invite only those who will enjoy the feast. Mine were devoured right out of the pan, in my kitchen. If the hunter's bag has only two (watch out for the shot), divide the recipe; but make the birds. They are extraordinarily good.

If cleaning the birds, retain the blood. The urban dwellers like myself who buy wild birds in Cryovac bags should open the packages carefully to retain all the blood, even if it's only a teaspoonful, to bind and enrich the sauce.

Larger wild pigeons cook the same way but require as much as twenty-five minutes. Serve small whole birds on large slices of Roasted Bread (page 367) and pass Bread Sauce (page 105). If the birds are large, put only half a bird on each slice of toast. If the livers came in the birds (not inevitable), clean them; sauté them in a little butter with a little chopped shallot until brown outside and pink inside; mash them with a fork, adding salt and pepper, and spread on one corner of the toast.

Roasted wood pigeon stuffed with grapes

SERVES 6

TOTAL
ROASTING
TIME:
15
minutes

FOR WANT OF a wood pigeon, use a squab, but cook it in this way, or use a Cornish game hen and cook it in the same fashion, but for a longer time.

Don't put vegetables on the plate. The pigeon is too messy, and the flavors are perfect as is. Serve salad and cheese later.

6 whole wood pigeons (about 8 ounces each), innards removed, wing tips removed, neck trimmed, and any remaining feathers plucked with pliers or tweezers

3 cups seedless green grapes

6 cloves garlic, smashed and peeled

18 slices lean bacon (12 ounces), halved across

1½ cups apple juice

3 tablespoons cider vinegar

3 tablespoons heavy cream

3 teaspoons kosher salt

8 grinds black pepper

Place oven rack on second level from the bottom. Heat oven to 500°F.

Reserve blood from the package in which the pigeons arrived; each pigeon should have about one teaspoon of blood. Stuff each pigeon with ½ cup grapes and 1 clove garlic. Place birds, breast sides up, in a 14 x 12 x 2-inch roasting pan. Cover each bird thoroughly with bacon. Put in oven legs first. Roast 5 minutes. Move each pigeon around with a wooden spatula to keep from sticking. Roast 10 minutes more.

Remove pigeons to a serving platter or plates. Tilt pan to spoon off fat. Place pan over medium-high heat. Add the apple juice and vinegar. Use a wooden spoon to scrape up any brown bits that stick to the bottom of the pan. Bring to a boil. Remove from heat. Pour in the reserved blood as well as any juices that have collected around the pigeons. Pour sauce into a blender. Blend for 15 seconds. Return liquid to a small saucepan. Over medium heat, gently cook for 2 minutes, stirring constantly. Add the cream and cook 1 more minute. Season with salt and pepper. Serve sauce with pigeons.

PHEASANT

AS A BUYER RATHER THAN A SHOOTER, I AM ABLE TO ACQUIRE ONLY FARM-RAISED PHEASANT AND THE WILD, IMPORTED SCOTCH PHEASANT. The farm-raised birds have been heavier; the cock, as usual, outweighs the hen. Farm-raised cocks have been just under three pounds, and the hens, around two and a half pounds. The much richer and bloodier—think *Macbeth*—Scotch pheasant cocks have been only about a pound and a half, with the hens a quarter pound less. If you go out stalking, you may find the birds to be much larger. The larger the bird, the greater the need for marination and the longer the time it should take.

The imported, truly wild birds have much more flavor and are to be preferred whenever possible. Pheasants were traditionally presented in a brace, a male and female pair, as an ideal house present. While purchasers have their option of requesting all male or all female birds, there is something pleasantly old-fashioned, in the sense of a life I have never lived, about presenting a brace at table. Of the wild birds I have bought, many have arrived with their feet attached. Be sure to save them along with the wing tips for Basic Pheasant Stock (page 104) or Mixed Game Bird Stock (page 91).

It is always particularly important to remove the wing tips from all pheasants to be roasted. The wing tips curl back over the breast of the bird, making it almost impossible to carve if left on.

The larger farm-raised pheasants, if you have any leftovers, will give three ounces of boneless meat per half breast. A whole cock has twelve ounces of cooked meat and the hen, ten. Leftover pheasant meat can be substituted in the Basic Meat Pie (page 155), used in Velouté of Pheasant (page 103) or Winter-Light Pheasant Soup (page 102), or served cold with leftover cold Roasted Japanese Eggplant with Asian Glaze (page 346), Roasted Cippolines Riviera (page 377), or Roasted Red Pepper Spread (page 384).

Simple roast pheasant

MUCH ROASTING OF pheasant has provided me with a surprise. It is not necessary to bard, lard, or marinate the birds. I give such recipes as pleasant variations. This basic recipe technique can be amplified to cook as many birds as can fit in the pan without touching each other or the sides of the pan. See Wood Pigeons (page 95) for serving suggestions. Consider using Star Anise Rub (page 71) for a brace of farm pheasants or four wild ones.

Pheasant always seems happy with sauerkraut that has been drained, rinsed, and heated with some juniper, a piece of a bay leaf, and a little white wine; or try Sauerkraut Noodles (page 172). Cabbage, untransformed by pickling, is just as good, as in Mildly Cardamom Cabbage (page 326), Hungarian Roasted Cabbage (page 327), or Normandy Cabbage (page 330).

1¼- to 1½-pound wild pheasant or 2½- to 3- pound farm pheasant, innards removed, wing tips removed, and neck trimmed

Kosher salt, to taste
Freshly ground black pepper, to taste
½ cup stock, water, or wine, for deglazing

Place rack on second level from bottom of oven. Heat oven to 500°F.

Season skin and cavity of bird with salt and pepper. Place pheasant, breast side up, in a 12 x 8 x 1½-inch roasting pan. Roast farm pheasant 50 minutes for a hen and 1 hour for a cock. Roast wild pheasant 30 minutes. After the first 10 minutes, move the pheasant around with a wooden spatula to keep it from sticking.

Remove pheasant to a platter. Pour off excess fat. Put pan on top of stove. Add the liquid and bring contents to a boil, scraping the bottom vigorously with a wooden spoon. Let reduce by half. Serve sauce in a sauceboat.

TOTAL ROASTING TIME: wild pheasant, 30 minutes; farm pheasant, 50 to 60 minutes

Brace of roast pheasant

A GENEROUS FRIEND who belongs to a hunting club gave me a brace of pheasants he had shot. Fortunately, he had plucked them and drawn them, removed the innards, and bled them. All of that is called "dressing." The pheasants can also be bought, and one of each sex specified. See pages 65–66 for cleaning tips.

Be sure to save the carcasses, wing tips, and neck for Basic Pheasant Stock (page 104) or Mixed Game Bird Stock (page 91).

Brace of pheasants (2¾-pound cock and 2½-pound hen), innards removed, wing tips removed, and necks trimmed

Kosher salt, to taste

Freshly ground black pepper, to taste

2 slices (4 x 6 inches each) barding fat, (page 90)

1 cup Basic Pheasant Stock (page 104), Basic Chicken Stock (page 42) or canned, water, or wine, for deglazing

Place rack on second level from bottom of oven. Heat oven to 500°F.

Season the cavities and the skin of each bird with salt and pepper. Lay the barding fat across the breasts, covering as much of the legs as possible.

Place the pheasants in a 14 x 12 x 2-inch roasting pan, breast sides up, hen pheasant in front of pan, cock in rear. Roast 10 minutes; remove pheasants from oven, closing the door. Remove barding fat from each bird—tongs are helpful—and carefully spoon liquid fat from pan. Return birds to oven and roast hen for 30 minutes and cock for 40 minutes.

When each is done, remove it to a platter by placing a large wooden spoon into the crop end and balancing with a kitchen spoon at the other end. Before moving, tilt the pheasant over the roasting pan so that all the juices run out and into the pan.

Pour off or spoon out excess fat from roasting pan. Place pan on top of the stove. Add the stock or other liquid and bring the contents of the pan to a boil, scraping the bottom vigorously with a wooden spoon. Let reduce by half. Serve the sauce over the pheasants or, for crisp skin, in a sauceboat.

TOTAL ROASTING TIME: hen, 40 minutes; cock, 50 minutes

Marinated wild pheasant

SERVES 2

TOTAL
ROASTING
TIME:
25 to 30
minutes

WHILE THIS RECIPE is written for a single small bird, just enough to feed two when cut in half lengthwise, after roasting, with a pair of large kitchen shears, it can be multiplied. Two small pheasants will fit in a small, 12 x 8 x 1½-inch pan; four in a medium, 14 x 12 x 2-inch pan; and 6 in a large, 18 x 13 x 2-inch pan.

It is important to wipe off the marinade thoroughly before roasting the bird(s) or it will smoke badly. There will be some smoking in any case, which is not the case with Simple Roast Pheasant (page 98). A smaller bird of a pound and a quarter can come out after twenty-five minutes, rather than a half hour; but it seems fine either way. Generally, the imported pheasants are sold with their legs and feet still on. Using a sharp knife, cut off and reserve for stock.

1 Scotch pheasant (cock about 1½
    pounds or hen about 1¼ pounds),
    wing tips removed, innards removed,
    and neck trimmed

1 recipe Basic Game Marinade (page 91)
1 cup Basic Pheasant Stock (page 104),
    Basic Chicken Stock (page 42) or
    canned, water, or wine, for deglazing

Place pheasant in a china or glass bowl just large enough to hold it. Pour marinade over pheasant and rub in. Cover with plastic wrap. Refrigerate 12 to 24 hours, or for at least 6 hours at room temperature. Turn bird in marinade from time to time. Remove from refrigerator and let pheasant reach room temperature, which will take about 2 hours.

Place rack on second level from bottom of oven. Heat oven to 500°F.

Remove pheasant from marinade. Pat dry with paper towel so as to avoid smoke in the oven. The flavor from the marinade will be in the bird by now. Place pheasant in a 12 x 8 x 1½-inch roasting pan, breast side up. Roast 10 minutes; move the bird around with a wooden spatula to keep it from sticking. If there is any fat in the pan, carefully spoon it out. Roast 20 more minutes.

Remove the pheasant to a platter by placing a large wooden spoon into the tail end and balancing with a kitchen spoon at the other end. Before moving, tilt the pheasant over the roasting pan so that all the juices run out and into the pan. Pour or spoon off excess fat. Put the roasting pan on top of the stove. Add the stock or other liquid and bring the contents of the pan to a boil, scraping the bottom vigorously with a wooden spoon. Let reduce by half. Serve the sauce over the pheasant or, for crisp skin, in a sauceboat.

Pheasant with liver-rich dressing

SERVES 8

TOTAL
ROASTING
TIME:
see below

To those few rare readers, blessed by authors, who go straight through a chapter, this recipe will seem very familiar. It is a virtual clone of Cornish Game Hen with Liver-Rich Dressing; but different-size birds require different amounts of stuffing and cooking times.

Since each small bird is being served to two people, it is a good idea to cut them in half in the kitchen; try to cut straight down on either side of the breastbone until the meat is reached. Then cut through the ribs at the top of the meat. The top of the bone is discarded or saved for stock. Continue cutting down on either side of the backbone, which is saved for stock in turn. This accomplishes two neat servings, stuffing inside.

Farm-raised birds will need to be carved, and the stuffing spooned out.

4 wild pheasants (1¼ to 1½ pounds each) or 2 farm pheasants (2½ to 3 pounds each), innards removed, wing tips removed, and necks trimmed

1 recipe Liver-Rich Dressing (page 117), for stuffing

1 cup Basic Pheasant Stock (page 104), Basic Chicken Stock (page 42) or canned, or Mixed Game Bird Stock (page 91)

½ cup red wine

Kosher salt, to taste

Freshly ground black pepper, to taste

Place oven rack on second level from bottom. Heat oven to 500°F.

Refer to Skewering and Wrapping (page 109) to close neck ends of birds. With birds standing on neck ends, place 1 cup of dressing in the breast cavity of each wild pheasant, or 2 cups of dressing in the cavity of each farm-raised pheasant. Skewer and wrap tail ends of birds.

Place pheasants, breast sides up, in a 14 x 18 x 2-inch roasting pan. Roast farm pheasants 50 minutes for a hen and 1 hour for a cock. Roast wild pheasants 30 minutes. After the first 10 minutes, move the birds around with a wooden spoon to keep them from sticking and pour off or spoon out fat in pan.

Remove pheasants to plates or a platter. Pour or spoon off excess fat. Put pan on top of stove. Add the stock and wine and bring contents to a boil while scraping the bottom vigorously with a wooden spoon. Let reduce by half. Season to taste with salt and pepper. Pass sauce separately.

TOTAL ROASTING TIME: farm pheasant hen, 50 minutes; farm pheasant cock, 1 hour; wild pheasant, 30 minutes

Winter-light pheasant soup

MAKES 4 TO 5 CUPS; SERVES 4 TO 5

THIS IS A mild, light soup that lets the flavor of the pheasant stock come through. It's even lighter without the pheasant meat and extra stock. It can easily be multiplied; add a cup of cooked fine egg noodles (page 92) if the version with the meat is wanted as a lunch main course. After reheating the noodles in the soup, check for seasonings.

Half a 4-ounce turnip, peeled and cut into matchsticks (¾ cup)

2-ounce piece of celery root, peeled and cut into matchsticks (1 scant cup)

4-ounce piece of cored white cabbage, preferably young, cut across into thin strips (scant 2 cups)

3 cups Basic Pheasant Stock (page 104) or Basic Chicken Stock (page 42) or canned

½ ounce of the white part of a leek, cut lengthwise into thin strips and soaked in water to remove all dirt (scant ½ cup)

2 tablespoons finely chopped flat-leaf parsley

½ teaspoon chopped fresh thyme leaves

1½ teaspoons kosher salt

2 grinds black pepper

OPTIONAL INGREDIENTS

1 additional cup Basic Pheasant Stock

½ cup thin strips skinned and boned roast pheasant meat

In a 2-quart saucepan, place turnip, celery root, cabbage, 3 cups stock, and, if using optional pheasant, additional cup stock. Cover and bring to a boil. Reduce heat and simmer, uncovered, for 5 minutes. Add leek and herbs and simmer for 2 more minutes. Remove from heat and stir in salt, pepper, and pheasant, if using.

Velouté of pheasant

MAKES 1¼ CUPS; SERVES 2 AS
A FIRST COURSE

SOMETIMES, I WILL have an extra half of a wild pheasant or farm pheasant to use, as there were an odd number of guests. This is not a soup but a very rich and sexy little stew that makes the best of a small quantity of meat and the stock made with all those carcasses and bones as I seldom have much leftover pheasant meat. It goes well with a roasted fish or vegetable main course.

Serve as is over rice or crustless white toast, or double if perchance there is more pheasant. Add two and a half cups of extra stock to this recipe for an elegant soup to serve in cups to four favored guests, or five cups to the doubled recipe, for eight.

1 tablespoon unsalted butter

1 tablespoon all-purpose flour

½ cup Basic Pheasant Stock (page 104) or Basic Chicken Stock (page 42) or canned

½ cup heavy cream

2 teaspoons finely chopped flat-leaf parsley

¼ teaspoon kosher salt

Pinch of ground nutmeg

3 grinds of black pepper

5 ounces leftover roast pheasant meat (light and dark), cut into ¼-inch slices

Melt the butter in a medium saucepan over low heat. Sprinkle the flour over the butter and whisk until well incorporated. Cook 3 to 4 minutes, stirring constantly. While whisking, slowly pour in the stock, then the cream. Stir well, until combined and smooth. Cook over medium-low heat, stirring constantly, until mixture begins to thicken, about 10 minutes. Add parsley, salt, nutmeg, and pepper. Cook another 1 to 2 minutes. Add meat. Stir and cook until warm throughout.

Basic pheasant stock

THIS IS A stock with a beautiful balance of flavors that are assertive, but not aggressive. The scent is almost smoky. The more carcasses you have, the better it will be. At least two are needed. This stock makes the best deglazing liquid, or use it in Winter-Light Pheasant Soup (page 102).

Carcasses and bones from at least two 2½- to 3-pound farm pheasants or four 1¼- to 1½-pound wild pheasants, plus uncooked necks and wing tips, carcasses and bones broken into pieces

3 quarts water, or to cover by 2 inches

Place bones and pieces into a large pot; fill with water to cover by 1 inch. Cover and bring to a boil. Lower heat to a simmer. From time to time, skim the foam off the top. Cook 9 to 16 hours.

Pour stock through a sieve and let cool at room temperature; then refrigerate. Remove the fat from the surface and any sediment from the bottom.

Use as is, refrigerate, or freeze.

SAUCES AND RELISHES

THERE ARE MANY HOT AND COLD SAUCES SPRINKLED THROUGHOUT THE BOOK THAT ARE GOOD WITH HOT OR COLD ROASTED BIRDS. There is a helpful listing on pages 292–309, or look in the Index. Here, I have included a tiny handful of those particularly good with game or expected with turkey.

Bread sauce

MAKES 2¼ CUPS; SERVES 8

A BRITISH CLASSIC for roasted game birds, this mild sauce looks rather like mashed potatoes. I have adapted it from a recipe of the late Jane Grigson's, but she is not responsible. I loved and respected her so much that it gives me pleasure to feel in some way affiliated.

See the note about making a liver mash (page 95) to go on Roasted Bread (page 367) as another accompaniment. Cumberoutlandish Sauce (page 106) will complete the classic triumvirate.

Try to find white bread that is minimally sweetened or not at all.

1 small onion (about 3 ounces), peeled, halved, and stuck with 3 cloves

1¾ cups whole milk

4 ounces white bread, crusts trimmed, pulsed in a food processor to make fresh bread crumbs (3 cups)

Pinch of ground nutmeg

Pinch of cayenne pepper

1 teaspoon kosher salt

Freshly ground black pepper, to taste

2 tablespoons unsalted butter, in pieces

In a small saucepan over lowest heat with a heat diffuser or in a double boiler, heat the onion and milk. Bring to a boil and immediately remove the onion with a slotted spoon. Stir in the bread crumbs and cook until the milk is absorbed and the sauce is thick and hot, but not boiling. Stir in the nutmeg, cayenne, salt, pepper, and butter. Simmer just until butter disappears.

If the sauce needs reheating, bring back to the simmer over lowest heat. Serve warm.

Cumberoutlandish sauce

MAKES 2 CUPS; SERVES 6 TO 7

THERE IS so much debate—see Elizabeth David—about the proper composition and history of England's classic game sauce, Cumberland sauce, that I thought as an outsider, it behooved me to moderate the name of my own version. It is a sweet and spicy, acid red beauty, not unlike American red pepper jelly, which would make a good substitute, melted, with some Port added. (Good Port is better; go up another tablespoon.) The sourer the oranges, the better.

Those who like thicker sauces can add two tablespoons of cornstarch dissolved into a slurry with a quarter cup of water. Temper the slurry by stirring some of the hot sauce into it. Stir it into the sauce along with the zests.

2 blood or Seville oranges, washed zest of 1 removed with a vegetable peeler with as little white pith as possible, cut into very thin long strips (2 generous tablespoons), and both oranges juiced (⅝ cup, strained)

1 small lemon, washed zest removed with a vegetable peeler with as little white pith as possible, cut into very thin long strips (1 generous tablespoon), and lemon juiced (2 tablespoons, strained)

One 12-ounce jar red currant jam, jelly, or preserves thick enough to gel (1½ cups)

½ ounce gingerroot, peeled, trimmed, and grated with a very fine grater (1 teaspoon)

2 tablespoons Port

2 teaspoons imported Dijon mustard

Freshly ground black pepper, to taste (I like a lot)

1 teaspoon salt, or to taste

Bring a small pot of water to a boil. Add the orange and lemon zests, bring back to the boil, and cook 4 minutes. Drain the zests through a strainer and rinse with cold water. Place on paper towel to drain.

Put all remaining ingredients except salt and pepper in a small, heavy saucepan. Whisk to combine. Bring to a boil. Reduce heat to a low boil; add zests, salt, and pepper and cook for 3½ minutes, until reduced to 2 cups.

Cranberry-orange relish

MAKES 5 CUPS; SERVES 14
GENEROUSLY

THIS IS A variant on the Thanksgiving necessity, cranberry sauce that gels. Make it a day ahead so that it sets; it can be made up to three days ahead. To be honest, in my family I have several people, not all children, who prefer the clear cranberry sauce straight out of the can.

2 large juice oranges (about 8 ounces each)

Two 12-ounce packages cranberries (about 7 cups)

½ cup sugar

1 cup fresh orange juice

½ cup peeled celery, cut into ¼-inch dice

½ cup walnut pieces

Wash the oranges. Peel, seed, and cut them in quarters, holding oranges over a bowl to retain the juice. Reserve orange pieces.

In a 3-quart saucepan, mix together cranberries, sugar, the 1 cup orange juice, and the reserved juice from the quartered oranges. Bring to a boil; reduce heat and cook about 15 minutes, or until cranberries begin to burst.

Place orange pieces in a food processor and chop coarsely. Stir into cranberry mixture along with celery and walnuts. Cook, uncovered, for 5 minutes.

Remove from the heat. Stir well and allow to cool. Refrigerate, covered, in an attractive serving bowl.

dRESSINGS AND STUFFINGS

WELL, STUFF IF YOU MUST, BUT NOT AHEAD OF TIME, FOR HEALTH REASONS.
I prefer to make the same preparations as dressings that are served on the side. It's
safer, more controllable, and less soggy. Everyone at my house seems to love the crusti-
ness of the top of the dressing cooked in a pan. I not only prefer Liver-Rich Stuffing
(page 119) as a dressing—a kind of soufflé that is equally wonderful cold as a pâté—but
I also turn it, modified slightly, into Liver-Rich Dumplings (page 119), a classic
German or Austrian bobble for soup.

These dressings make good accompaniments to roasted foods other than birds.
Use them instead of potatoes with pork or veal.

On page 109 is a guide to how much stuffing goes into different birds so that the
dressings can be used in that way. If the stuffing is made ahead and refrigerated, allow
it to come to room temperature before stuffing bird. Roast as soon as bird is stuffed.

Stuffing guide

ALL GENERALIZATIONS, INCLUDING the chart that follows, are just that. The
amount of stuffing needed will vary with its wetness, compactness, and the amount
it expands in cooking. Always err on the side of too little rather than too much.
Remember, stuffed birds always take longer to cook than unstuffed ones. The chart
gives rough times.

Stuffings are usually based on some kind of starch. One of the most common is
bread in the form of crumbs or cubes, sometimes toasted. I have never figured out
the enormous amounts of money spent on commercial stuffings and bread cubes. It
must be that everybody else in the world has a better sense of how much bread they
need for dinner than I, since they don't seem to have stale bread to make into cubes
and crumbs. For those who wish to, there is a guide to making toasted dried cubes
and fresh and dried bread crumbs following the stuffing guide. Placed in an air-tight
container at room temperature, they await the cook's pleasure.

Birds can be stuffed in their main cavity and more can be tucked in under the
flap of neck skin. While in the normal course of roasting I truss only quail, I sometimes truss the legs of a bird I stuff or skewer them and wrap the skewers with
kitchen string to hold the stuffing in place both before and behind the bird. I find
this kind of closing easier to remove once the bird is roasted than the sewing-up-
with-thread method.

Skewering and wrapping to hold stuffing in place: The skewers to be used are commonly available. They are metal, five inches long, with a sharp tip and a loop of metal at the other end.

At the tail end of the bird, a line of two (quail) to four (turkey) skewers should be lined up across the opening of the cavity, piercing the skin on either side. Kitchen twine—plain white—should be looped and crisscrossed around the skewers as if lacing up a shoe. Pull slightly on the string to bring the edges of the skin closer together. Knot the string and cut off any extra.

At the neck end, if the opening is large, the same procedure should be followed as for the tail end. If the opening is small, as in a quail, the skewers should be formed into an X and the string looped and tied around them.

After the bird is roasted, cut the strings and remove the skewers by putting the thin handle of a small wooden spoon through the loop of each skewer successively and pulling it out.

BASIC STUFFING QUANTITIES

bird	*weight*		*stuffing quantity*
TURKEY	15	pounds	12 cups
DUCK	8	pounds	6–7 cups
CHICKEN or CAPON	6	pounds	5 cups
CHICKEN	5	pounds	4 cups
GAME BIRD	1½	pounds	1 cup
GAME BIRD or			
CORNISH GAME HEN	1	pound	½ cup

INCREASES IN ROASTING TIMES

For 1- to 2-pound birds, add 5 minutes to Simple Roast recipe times if birds are stuffed. Add 10 minutes to the cooking time for capon, duck, and chicken if stuffed.

See Simple Roast Turkey (page 56) for other stuffing amounts and cooking times.

BREAD
CRUMBS
AND
CUBES

FOR ALL BUT Fresh Bread Crumbs, day-old bread is preferable. If unavailable, use fresh bread. Adjust the amount of bread and the number of pans needed.

continued

FRESH BREAD CRUMBS

PULSE THE BREAD in a food processor. Use fresh crumbs as soon as possible or store in a tightly covered container for up to 1 day.

4 ounces fresh bread (5 slices with crust; 7½ slices without crust); makes 1¼ cups

DRIED BREAD CRUMBS

IF USING ITALIAN bread, cut it into pieces. Lay the bread pieces or slices in an uncovered layer and allow to dry at least overnight. In humid weather, this may take a day and a half. The bread should be completely dry. The longer the bread has dried, the finer and more uniform the crumbs and the fewer of them. Pulse the bread in a food processor. Italian bread may be grated on the smallest holes of a four-sided grater. Grating works particularly well if the bread was left over uncut and is now too hard to cut into pieces. Sieve all crumbs to get rid of overly large crumbs. Store in a brown paper—not plastic—bag.

1 pound day-old Italian bread (1 loaf), with crust; makes 4 cups
1 pound day-old sliced white bread (1 loaf), with crust; makes 3 cups

TOASTED BREAD CRUMBS

PLACE RACK ON second level from bottom of oven. Heat oven to 325°F. Use a double batch of Fresh Bread Crumbs (above). Spread the crumbs in an even layer in a 8 x 13 x 2-inch roasting pan. Bake for 7 minutes. Stir. Bake 7 minutes more. Store in a brown paper—not plastic—bag.

2½ cups Fresh Bread Crumbs; makes scant 2 cups

DRIED BREAD CUBES

PLACE RACK IN center of oven. Heat oven to 250°F. Cut the bread into ½-inch cubes. Divide the bread cubes evenly between two 18 x 13 x 2-inch roasting pans, spreading the cubes into an even layer. Bake for 1 hour, stirring from time to time. Store in a brown paper—not plastic—bag.

1 pound day-old bread (1 loaf; 20 slices), crusts trimmed, cut into ½-inch cubes; makes about 9 cups

TOASTED BREAD CUBES

PLACE RACK ON second level from bottom of oven. Heat oven to 350°F. Cut the bread into ½-inch cubes. Place the cubes in an 18 x 13 x 2-inch roasting pan. Toast for 7 minutes. Shake the pan to turn the cubes over. Toast 8 minutes more. Allow the cubes to cool. If they are not thoroughly dry, leave them in the pan until they are dry. Store in a brown paper—not plastic—bag.

1 pound day-old bread (1 loaf; 20 slices), crusts trimmed, cut into ½-inch cubes; makes 8 cups

½ pound bread, crusts trimmed, cut into ¾-inch cubes; makes 4 cups

Spiffed-up packaged dressing

MAKES 2 ½ QUARTS; SERVES 8 AS
A SIDE DISH

USUALLY I'M CREATIVE; usually I'm provident, with my own Dried Bread Cubes (page 110) on hand; but truth be told, emergencies arise. It is time to run to the store and buy one of those cellophane bags of stuffing—not bread crumbs—as nearly unseasoned as possible, and in a semi-panic, throw together some ingredients that will customize it. Confession or not is up to the cook.

¼ pound (1 stick) unsalted butter, plus small amount to butter casserole if using

2½ cups basic stock of bird being served or canned broth

1 medium onion (8 ounces), peeled and diced medium (1¼ cups)

6 stalks celery, trimmed, peeled with a vegetable peeler, and diced medium (3 cups)

½ bunch fresh flat-leaf parsley, chopped medium (½ cup)

1 tablespoon kosher salt

3 tablespoons fresh sage leaves, stacked and cut across into strips

One 16-ounce package plain bread stuffing

Freshly ground black pepper, to taste

Place rack in center of oven. Heat oven to 500°F.

Lightly butter a 2½-quart casserole.

In a medium saucepan bring the butter, stock, onion, celery, parsley, salt, and sage to a boil. Cook until the celery is translucent, 10 to 12 minutes.

Pour the dry stuffing into a large bowl. Pour all of the warm mixture from the saucepan over the stuffing. With a spatula or a large spoon mix until well combined. When cool enough, blend completely. Add pepper. Mix. Pack the stuffing into a casserole dish. Cook 30 minutes.

Dressing will stay warm at least ½ hour if covered with foil when removed from oven.

Bulgur dressing

MAKES 5 ½ QUARTS; SERVES 35 AS
A SIDE DISH

Each year at Thanksgiving, I try to come up with a new dressing as well as a tried-and-true one. Previous books of mine have been studded with them. Recently, this was stuffing-of-the-year to great acclaim, and eaten in great quantities. I almost always make too much. Feel free to halve the recipe. I made a marvelous Rich Bulgur Soup (page 113) from the leftover dressing and the turkey stock made from the carcass. It nourished all for days. I even froze some and had benefits for months to follow.

When the time comes to finally add salt and pepper, be sure to taste. The amount needed will depend highly on the kind of stock and whether it has any salt or not.

Despite the quantity, this dressing goes fairly quickly; the dark, nutty flavor of the bulgur (cracked wheat) is evoked fairly quickly, and the other ingredients are cooked separately. The dressing can be prepared ahead and baked later in half an hour. Once cooked, the dressing will keep warm for at least half an hour if covered with foil.

½ pound (2 sticks) unsalted butter, plus small amount to butter casserole

1½ pounds chicken livers, rinsed and connective tissue removed, plus turkey livers, if available , chopped fine (2¼ cups)

2 to 2¼ ounces dried mushrooms (1½ cups)

4 cups boiling water or very hot from tap

1½ medium onions (about 12 ounces), peeled and diced (1¾ cups)

½ large head garlic, cloves smashed, peeled, and minced (¼ cup)

5 cups chopped fresh white mushrooms, mixed with 1 tablespoon fresh lemon juice

3 tablespoons chopped fresh thyme leaves or 1 tablespoon dried

3 quarts Basic Chicken Stock (page 42) or canned or Basic Turkey Stock (page 60)

3 tablespoons kosher salt

2½ pounds large-grain bulgur (6 cups)

Freshly ground black pepper, to taste

In a medium sauté pan, melt ¼ pound of the butter. Add the livers and cook over medium heat just until they lose their external color, about 4 minutes. They should not harden or be brown. Remove livers from pan and reserve in a medium bowl.

Put the dried mushrooms in a microwave-safe medium bowl. Any large mushrooms should be crumbled before soaking. Pour the hot water over the mushrooms. Soak 20 minutes. Cook, uncovered, in the microwave at full power 5 minutes. Or, on the stove top, place mushrooms and soaking liquid in a small pan. Bring to a boil. Reduce heat to a simmer and cook, uncovered, 10 minutes.

With a slotted spoon, skim the mushrooms out of the broth. Reserve mushrooms in the bowl with the livers.

Strain the mushroom liquid through a sieve lined with a dampened piece of cheesecloth or a kitchen towel into a large 10-inch pot. There will be about 3 cups. Reserve.

In the sauté pan already used for the livers, melt the remaining ¼ pound butter. Add the onions and sauté over medium-low heat until transparent, 8 to 10 minutes. The onions should not brown. Add the garlic. Continue to cook until the garlic softens and is translucent, 5 to 7 minutes. Add 3 cups of the white mushrooms. Stir until mushrooms are well incorporated. Stirring occasionally, cook over medium heat until mushrooms are cooked through but not colored, 8 to 10 minutes.

Add the thyme and the reserved livers and plumped mushrooms. Cook 2 minutes over medium-low heat. Reserve.

Put the pot with the mushroom broth over medium heat. Add the stock and the remaining 2 cups of the white mushrooms. Bring to a boil. Reduce heat to a simmer and cook, uncovered, 5 minutes. Add the salt. Bring back to a boil.

Add the bulgur. Stir well. Cook, uncovered, 10 minutes in the lightly boiling broth. Remove from heat. Stir well. Leave to cool 15 minutes.

Add all the ingredients in the sauté pan to the bulgur. Mix well. Add black pepper. If making the dressing ahead of time, cover tightly and refrigerate. Bring to room temperature (about 1 hour) before baking or stuffing.

About 20 minutes before the dressing is to be baked, heat oven to 500°F. Lightly butter a 5-quart casserole. Pack the dressing into the casserole. Cook, uncovered, for 30 minutes.

Rich bulgur soup

MAKES ABOUT 6½ QUARTS; SERVES 20
AS A SIDE DISH

ONCE I MADE this with leftovers from Bulgur Dressing (page 112). I liked it so much that I decided to make a half quantity of the dressing on a bitter-cold March day just for the soup, and served it to ten people as dinner, along with lots of bread, a big salad, wine, cheese, fruit, and cookies. It made an easy, comforting party.

5 quarts Basic Turkey Stock (page 60) or canned chicken broth	⅓ cup chopped fresh tarragon (about ½ ounce)
Leftover turkey gravy, if available	Kosher salt, to taste
6 cups Bulgur Dressing (page 112)	Freshly ground black pepper, to taste

Put the stock, gravy if you have it, and dressing in a stockpot. Adjust heat to medium. Cook 30 minutes, stirring occasionally. Dressing will break up into the stock as it cooks.

When all dressing has dissolved and soup is warm throughout, add the tarragon, salt, and pepper. Serve warm.

Cranberry mint dressing

MAKES 4 ½ CUPS; SERVES 6 TO 8 AS
A SIDE DISH

I WOULD JUST as lief forgo cranberry sauce altogether. I don't really like sweet jelly with my meat. If you have a like-minded group, prepare this dressing, where cranberry flavor is provided by juice and dried cranberries, which are a better alternative to raisins. It's always pleasantly browned, but the juice can cause this to get too brown. Check and cover if need be.

1½ cups dried cranberries (4½ ounces)	2 to 3 stalks celery, peeled with vegetable peeler, cut into thirds lengthwise and sliced across into ¼-inch pieces (1 cup)
¾ cup cranberry juice	
2 tablespoons unsalted butter, plus ½ tablespoon to coat dish	¾ cup chopped walnuts
4 medium leeks, trimmed to white part only, rinsed well, cut into quarters lengthwise and sliced across into ¼-inch pieces (about 2¾ cups)	¼ cup fresh mint leaves, cut across into very thin strips
	2 teaspoons kosher salt
	Freshly ground black pepper, to taste
1 recipe Dried Bread Cubes (page 110) (about 9 cups)	

Place rack in center of oven. About 20 minutes before baking dressing, heat oven to 450°F.

In a small bowl put the cranberries to soak in the juice.

Melt the 2 tablespoons butter in a medium sauté pan. Add leeks. Cook over medium-low heat until leeks are soft, not brown.

In a large mixing bowl, put the bread cubes, leeks, celery, walnuts, mint, salt, and pepper. Mix well. Add berries and juice. Mix ingredients until well coated with the juice and the bread starts to absorb the liquid.

Rub a 2½-quart soufflé dish with butter. Pack the dressing mixture into the dish. Pat down firmly with your hands. Dressing may be made ahead up to this point and held, covered with plastic wrap, for up to 1 day in the refrigerator.

Cook for 35 minutes, checking color after 25 minutes and covering with foil if already sufficiently brown.

Sage whole-wheat dressing

MAKES 12 CUPS; SERVES ABOUT 15 AS
A SIDE DISH

THIS IS A very simple dressing with the added health of whole-wheat bread and seasonings adjusted to go with its heavier taste, not texture.

6 tablespoons unsalted butter

2 medium yellow onions (1 pound), cut in ¼-inch dice (2¼ cups)

Liver from 1 turkey or ¼ pound chicken livers, rinsed and connective tissue removed, then cut into ½-inch pieces (½ cup)

1 recipe Dried Bread Cubes (page 110), using whole-wheat bread

6 stalks celery with some leaves, peeled and cut into ¼-inch dice (2 cups)

2 tablespoons thin crosswise strips of sage leaves

2 teaspoons kosher salt

Freshly ground black pepper, to taste

1½ cups Basic Chicken Stock (page 42) or canned

Heat oven to 350°F.

Melt butter in a large frying pan. Add onions and cook over medium heat until translucent. Add liver and stir. Cook just until liver is faintly browned, about 6 minutes.

In a large bowl, stir together onion mixture, bread, celery and seasonings. Lightly fold in stock.

Bake the stuffing in a 2½- to 3-quart ungreased casserole, covered tightly with foil, for 50 minutes. After 40 minutes, remove the foil and bake, uncovered, for the remaining 10 minutes.

Lee Ann Cox's cornbread dressing

MAKES 6 CUPS; SERVES 6 TO 8 AS
A SIDE DISH

ONCE, I HAD a wonderful assistant and baker from Texas named Lee Ann Cox. When she worked for me, she developed this dressing based on her own cornbread (page 117). She kindly gave me permission to share it with you. The dressing takes almost the whole loaf. If you want to eat cornbread, warm with a stew or slathered with butter, make a double batch and place the round pans catty-corner on the baking sheet. Save one for the next day to turn into crumbs.

4 tablespoons unsalted butter

2 medium onions (1 pound), peeled and chopped (2½ cups)

4 celery stalks (6 ounces), peeled, cut in halve lengthwise, and cut across into ¼-inch pieces (1⅓ cups)

¼ cup celery leaves, finely chopped

3 cups Dried Bread crumbs (page 110), using Cornbread (page 117)

1¼ cups dried cracker crumbs (hard, dry ship's biscuits are best, but saltines will do)

½ cup Dried Bread Crumbs (page 110) made from white bread

2 large eggs if using as a stuffing, 5 large eggs if using as a dressing

2 cups Basic Turkey Stock (page 60) or canned chicken broth

½ cup hot water

4 teaspoons dried sage

1½ teaspoons kosher salt

Freshly ground black pepper, to taste

Melt butter in a large sauté pan over moderate heat. Add onions and cook until they become limp. Add celery and celery leaves and cook until onions begin to color, about 10 minutes. Remove from heat.

Combine cornbread, and cracker and bread crumbs in a large bowl. Stir in onion mixture. Whisk eggs together in a small bowl and add to crumb mixture. Stir in broth and water. Add sage, salt, and pepper and mix well.

Either fill cavity of turkey with stuffing or place in an ungreased 2-quart soufflé dish.

To cook the dressing: Heat oven to 350°F. Cover soufflé dish with a lid and bake for 45 minutes. Uncover and bake 30 minutes longer.

Cornbread

LEE ANN'S CLASSIC cornbread.

1¼ cups yellow cornmeal

½ cup all-purpose flour

4 teaspoons baking powder

1 tablespoon sugar

1 teaspoon kosher salt

1 large egg

1 cup milk

3 tablespoons vegetable oil

Preheat oven to 350°F. Position rack in center of oven. Grease a 9 x 2-inch round cake pan.

Combine dry ingredients in a small bowl. Set aside.

Whisk together the egg, milk, and oil in a medium bowl. Stir in dry ingredients.

Scrape mixture into prepared pan. Place in oven and bake for 25 minutes. Remove from oven and place on rack to cool.

Liver-rich dressing

(as a pâté, as a stuffing, and as dumplings)

MAKES 4 CUPS; SERVES 8 GENEROUSLY
AS A SIDE DISH

A VERY NICE young woman working in my kitchen refused to taste this, saying firmly, "I just don't like liver." Old-fashioned mother that I am, I insisted that she try just a taste. Much to her surprise, she liked it and took some home to share with her husband. Now, that I call success.

This dressing and all of its variations can be made with livers saved (page 20) from earlier roast birds. The recipes can be made using one kind of liver or a combination (duck, chicken, calf, or other), or livers bought from the store and allowed to soak in milk while the other preparations are being made. Since cleaning livers (page 20) reduces their volume slightly, be sure to start with enough.

The *dressing version* is so good when allowed to cool, I have served it that way several times. I usually add another teaspoon and a half of salt and extra pepper. Other good flavorings are a teaspoon of finely ground fennel or cumin or two tablespoons fresh tarragon leaves.

The **stuffing version** can be used in Cornish hens and pheasants. I wouldn't use it in a large bird; it's rich.

The **dumpling version** has no eggs and many fewer onions so as not to overwhelm the soup in which dumplings are served. It doesn't need the eggs; it is light enough. I particularly like it made with duck livers to go in duck stock.

1½ pounds livers, rinsed and connective tissue removed	4 teaspoons kosher salt
1⅓ cups finely chopped onion	12 grinds black pepper
½ cup finely chopped fresh flat-leaf parsley	6 large eggs, separated
	2½ cups Fresh Bread Crumbs (page 110)
	6 tablespoons all-purpose flour

Place rack in center of oven. Preheat oven to 375°F. Grease and lightly flour the inside of a 2½-quart soufflé dish.

Place livers, onion, parsley, salt, pepper, and egg yolks in a food processor. Process until well combined, stopping once to scrape down the sides of the bowl. Using a rubber spatula, scrape out all mixture into a medium bowl. Add the bread crumbs. Stir until well combined. Add flour. Stir until flour is completely incorporated.

Meanwhile, beat the egg whites with an electric mixer or by hand in a medium bowl until they form stiff but not dry peaks. With a rubber spatula, take up to one quarter of the whites and mix them into the liver mixture to lighten it. Carefully fold the remaining whites into the liver mixture.

Immediately pour mixture into prepared dish. Bake for 1 hour and 15 minutes total. After first 10 minutes, reduce temperature to 325°F. Dressing should be brown on the top and set. To check for doneness, insert a skewer down into the center of the dressing. When removed it should not have any blood on it. If there is blood, continue to cook for 5 more minutes.

Serve hot, right out of the oven. To serve, puncture the top with a serving spoon and fork, pull gently apart, and spoon onto warm plates. Make sure each serving has both the crusty brown exterior and the smooth insides.

To serve as a pâté: Allow dressing to cool, then unmold. Can be made up to 2 days ahead and refrigerated, tightly covered. Allow to come to room temperature for 15 minutes for best flavor.

Liver-Rich Stuffing

Make 1 recipe Liver-Rich Dressing (page 117), but do not include the eggs. If desired, from 2 to 4 cups Toasted Bread Cubes (page 110) can be added to give 1½ to 2 times the quantity and a different texture, better for larger birds. Without the Toasted Bread Cubes, the recipe makes 4 cups, enough to stuff 8 Cornish game hens or other 1-pound game birds.

Liver-Rich Dumplings

MAKES A FULL 2 CUPS, 20 TO 22 DUMPLINGS;
SERVES 4 TO 6 IN BROTH AS A FIRST COURSE

4½ slices white sandwich bread, crusts trimmed

12 ounces livers, rinsed and connective tissue removed

3 tablespoons finely chopped onion

¼ cup finely chopped fresh flat-leaf parsley

2 teaspoons kosher salt

6 grinds black pepper

3 tablespoons all-purpose flour

Place bread in a food processor. Process until it becomes fine crumbs. Transfer crumbs to a measuring cup.

Place livers, onion, parsley, salt, and pepper in a food processor. Process until well combined, stopping once to scrape down sides of bowl. Using a rubber spatula, scrape out all mixture into a medium bowl. Add 1¼ cups of the bread crumbs. Stir until well combined. Add flour. Stir until flour is completely incorporated.

Meanwhile, bring a small saucepan of water to a boil. Shape the dumplings either by pushing 1½ tablespoon quantities that are more or less round into the water (they will look a little messy), or forming them with two soups spoons into elongated ovals like quenelles. Keep spoons wet so the mixture does not stick to them. Gently place formed dumplings into lightly boiling water. Immediately lower heat so that water simmers. Cook for 5 minutes. Remove dumplings with a slotted spoon as they are cooked. Continue to make and cook dumplings until all the mixture is used.

PREVIOUS PAGE:

Roasted winter
vegetables:
acorn squash,
turnip wedges,
and carrots

LEFT:

Onions and family:
Roasted Onion Flowers,
leeks, shallots,
small onions,
Roasted and Marinated
Cippolines, and
garlic cloves

RIGHT:

Roasted Onion Soup
with Cannellini Beans

ABOVE:

From leftovers,
Lamb and Apple "Hash"
with Soft Polenta

LEFT:

A luscious Chicken
Vegetable Soup

LEFT:

Roasted
jumbo shrimp
and Lemon
Shrimp Frisée

FACING PAGE:

A favorite serving of
Roasted Monkfish Felix

RIGHT:

Monkfish Felix,
ready to roast

Roasted Veal Shoulder
with Bacon and Thyme,
served with
roasted vegetables

Roast Pork Loin in
Onion-Rhubarb Sauce,
served with roasted
asparagus

Striped Bass
with Fennel,
ready for the oven

Roasted Striped Bass
with Fennel

Red Plums with Spiced
Syrup, Pears with Asian
Glaze, and Whole
Roasted Peaches with
Ginger Syrup

FOLLOWING PAGE:

Roast Cornish Game Hens
and Jerusalem Artichokes
in Tomato-Olive Sauce

*M*EAT

"Finally," I can hear a reader sighing. It is sanctified tradition that roasting is a Sunday rite signifying a large piece of meat that is the center of Sunday dinner and appears in progressively less appealing forms through a long, bleak week. This joint, a piece of meat on a bone—usually a large section going from one bone joint to another—has often been cooked to cinders due in large part to setting it to cook before going to church and not removing it from fire or oven until after a lengthy service. One acquaintance whose father was a minister had to sit through his three morning services. The roast eaten upon returning home was always withered.

Religion is not the only cause of meat that is, to my taste, vastly overcooked. I may be able to dismiss the Irish way with meat—gray; but I must pay attention to the habits of Middle Easterners and other Mediterranean peoples who are ardent devotees of good food and still prefer their lamb at a degree of doneness that I consider unpalatable.

One of my fondest memories is of driving down a road in Greece in a more innocent time and having Easter-feasting families offer us slices of their once-a-year celebratory whole lamb as we passed. The lamb was cooked out of doors, turned for a long time on a spit over a huge bed of coals. Just outside New York, I had a larger beast done the same way by Iris Love, an archaeologist newly returned from her dig in Knidos, Turkey. Our mechoui was constantly swabbed with clean mops dipped in flavored butter and took over four hours to cook. (According to Paula Wolfert, it is spelled mechoui, but according to Claudia Roden, meshwi. Roden writes that baby lamb sacrifices are usually cooked for the festival of Eid-el-Kurban [Kibir in Egypt].)

If it is baby lamb (page 129) that is being cooked, I understand, as that is fatty meat that is always served well done. Baby goat has the same requirement. When the lamb is larger, I prefer roasting it to at most rosy and usually quite a bit closer to rare as is done in the South of France.

In Provence and in Vermont, where I can buy organic lamb, I have roasted it à la ficelle ("with a string") in a fireplace. (Except for the string this is unrelated to the recipe for boeuf à la ficelle, "beef on a string," which is poached in a strong stock.) For roasting, a length of strong cotton string is passed between the shank bone and the long tendon that attaches to it, forming a natural hanger. The string is knotted and the other ends are knotted around a nail or hook that projects into the fireplace behind the large stone that forms its top. The string is wound and unwinds slowly as the lamb leg turns before the fire, its fat and juices running into a pan—lèchefrite—placed under the meat and in front of the fire. Sometimes vegetables are placed in the lèchefrite to cook along with the meat. From time to time the string is retwisted, although if the fire is perfect, the difference in temperature between the side of the meat toward the fire and that away from it will keep the meat turning.

Through the centuries a myriad of mechanical spits have been invented to roast the meat in front of the fire. One of my great regrets was a piece of financial cowardice. Near the town of Valbonne there used to be a man who restored antique clocks and, as a corollary because they had clockwork mechanisms, he also reassembled and put in working order the great spits of former mansions and castles. He had had a previous life as an aeronautical engineer, but felt that much of what he was doing was being used for war, and so he stopped. His spits were often very ornate, with huge stones as clock weights. My daughter remembers with particular fondness one that had a little metal cage that rotated on a plane level with the hearth. It had four baskets for eggs. Each year I meant to buy one of these spits. I almost settled for a later, simpler version whose clockwork was wound up with a key. I always chickened out. When I finally thought I had enough money, he was gone.

A few visits to the huge kitchens that used these machines, that of St. Denis, outside of Paris, and Longleat, home of the Marquess of Bath, tempered my sorrow. I realized that in their vast, dungeonlike kitchens, the stone walls darkened by smoke, they did not have ovens as we do today but instead slews of red-faced (from the heat) slaveys whose job it was to tend the huge joints.

Today, one can still see outdoor vertical roasters with the meat on a number of spits lined up in front of the fire in restaurants in that country. The very best is at the restaurant La Verniaz, in the mountains behind Evian, where in the garden overlooking Lac Leman, the lake of Geneva, and surrounded by flowers they cook mainly chickens. It is also possible to buy clockwork spits in Italy and even to have them converted for American electrical systems. I have tried these and the electric rotisseries sold in this country, and I will leave the romance to others and return to my oven. The roasts take two to three times as long to cook on a rotisserie that is outside the oven, the results are uneven, and the possibility of a flare-up from dripping fat is omnipresent. Rotisseries in ovens are usable, but more work and more time-consuming than plain oven roasting. I may be giving up some romance; but I've made my choice. That is how the meats in this book are cooked. They come out richly caramelized and fragrant and provide a lot of glaze in the pan to be dissolved into rich gravies.

I want the best-tasting food with the least fuss and in the least amount of time, which means high heat in the oven. The meat does not taste steamed, as does most steam-table roast beef. Roasting is always better done at home.

Buying the meat

MEAT FOR ROASTING has never been cheap. The better the meat, the better the roast. I have included some less expensive cuts and have retested all the recipes with the most mundane quality of supermarket meat. The recipes work; but the result is infinitely better with very good meat. It is preferable to roast the best pork or lamb rather than inferior veal or beef. Save economy for stews and pot roasts, for which there are some recipes in this chapter as they use leftovers. Or begin by roasting the meat to a fine brownness in the oven instead of frying it in fat and standing around turning the meat over at the stove.

Information that is specific to a particular kind of meat will be found at the beginning of each section of the chapter, which has beef (page 131), pork (page 160), lamb (page 184), veal (page 207), and game (page 218).

Make friends with the butcher and be fussy. Even whole joints with their bones must be properly prepared; otherwise, trying to slice apart the chops of a rack of veal, lamb, or pork, or the same part of the animal on a standing rib roast, is a nightmare. The backbone, or chine, has to be either entirely cut away or trimmed and cracked so that the meat can be cut between the bones and all the way through the end of the bone to make separate pieces of meat. Look at the meat carefully when picking it up or when it is delivered and make sure that what is left of the bone can be fairly easily separated by a sharp knife.

Read about leg of lamb (pages 184–188) before going shopping. It will be much harder to carve if the butcher hasn't removed the lamb steaks (shoulder chops) that are attached to the leg by a fearsome ball joint.

Boned and rolled cuts of meat are often easier for the carver to cope with as they can be cut into fairly neat slices; but the butcher must know what is going on. This is where we are less fortunate than European cooks. There, meat will generally be found in smallish, neatly tied roasts that retain their shape when cooked. They are small and good because they are composed of individual muscles rather than a variety of different muscles corseted together with string. Whether the roast is well or badly tied, the string needs to be snipped off with shears in the kitchen before the roast is brought to the table.

Muscles contract along their fibers. If I flex my arm, the muscle pops up—yes, I still have one—and becomes rounded. Those who have cooked flank steak will have seen the same effect as the muscle reacts to the heat by contracting and becoming thick. The various muscles in a badly cut piece of meat will have fibers running in different directions. When exposed to the heat, they contract in different directions, pulling at each other and making the roast knobbly. The bone in other roasts keeps the muscles pretty much aligned.

Some meats, such as beef, are kept moist by the fat internal to the meat. Others, such as veal and venison, are very lean. Internal fat or marbling is discussed under beef (page 131). Some cuts, such as racks and loins, come with a natural covering of fat. While some should be left on, much can be pared away—preferably by the butcher—to reduce smoking and excess fat in the pan. If the meat begins to smoke due to excess fat, remove the pan from the oven and pour the fat off before continuing. Always use a clean oven (page 5) and, if possible, a vent, or have a window open.

Some meats, such as loin of venison or beef fillet, come without any fat covering. They can be barded—have thin sheets of unsalted fatback tied around them—or they can be brushed or smeared with a little fat. Some meats such as leg of lamb come with a thin membrane, called the fell, covering them. This should be removed in so far as possible, as it can smell strong when cooked.

Browning: Much of the flavor and visual attraction of roasted meat comes from its well-browned outermost layer. Almost all the meats that follow will be enticingly brown after they are roasted, except for very small ones like pork tenderloins, which will brown only lightly. There is an intriguing corollary to the observation that meats roasted at high temperatures brown beautifully: Meats for stewing or other long cooking such as pot roasting brown with significantly less hassle and less fat in the oven than on top of the stove. There are a few sample recipes in this chapter. A cook wanting to apply the technique to other recipes has only to look at pages 231–235 for basic browning times.

How much to buy: Appetites vary as does the amount of bone in a bone-in roast. Appetites for meat are not less frequent today, but are somewhat smaller. The yield from a well-done piece of meat will be less than that from a rare piece as the meat shrinks more. I have tried to give average amounts of people served for each recipe and, because leftovers are so good simply cold in a sandwich or in the numerous recipes in this chapter, extras never seem a problem. It is my style to buy a little more rather than a little less. As a general rule, I allow a half pound of boned meat before cooking for each person and three quarters of a pound of bone-in meat.

How much meat is needed is also dependent on what else is in the meal. If there are two vegetables and a sauce, a first course, a salad, and dessert, much less meat is needed and the costs can be kept down, especially if the first course is made from another day's leftovers. With a simple roast, consider an elegantly simple soup like Chicken Soup with Zing (page 46) or one of the duck soups on pages 72–73. More amply, dish up Goose Liver Mousse (page 82) or Bean Thread Noodle Salad (page 76); or ,"fishily," serve Saffron-Gold Fish Soup (page 254) or Lemon Shrimp Frisée (page 289).

Carving

THE ABILITY TO carve has been considered in the Western world the sign of a well-brought-up gentleman or lady. Leaving class-consciousness aside, it is a useful skill and requires few tools. Use a stable work surface—no teetering tables. Use a platter large enough to hold the meat while working and to hold the sliced meat unless putting it immediately onto dishes. Alternatively, have a second platter at the ready on which to put the sliced meat.

I don't like wooden cutting boards. They absorb meat odors and are hard to clean. Well and tree boards or platters, with grooves down the middle and around the edge, are virtually useless; the meat juices cannot easily be spooned up to add to the sauce or to drizzle or pour over the meat. Ceramic platters are better than silver as the silver scratches. There should be a little depth to the platter so that the juices do not spill; but the rim should not be so high that it gets in the way of the work.

A very sharp knife and a utensil to hold the meat are essential. There are carving forks that look like very large forks with somewhat bent tines. Some of these have a little piece of metal jutting out behind the tines to keep the fork stable and prevent it from going too far into the meat. There are two-tined monsters with short handles that work very well with large pieces of meat. There are even metal holders to screw over the shank bone, making an elegant handle for the piece of meat. I tend to use a clean pot holder or kitchen cloth to hold the shank bone of a ham or leg of lamb when necessary.

Boned meats can be sliced across the grain. All meats are more tender sliced that way, when it is possible. I have given carving descriptions for individual bone-in cuts when it seems necessary. Large roasts that have been allowed to sit out of the oven tented with foil for twenty minutes or so are more evenly cooked and also easier to slice. Except for whole chops or steaks such as those from a rack or a standing rib roast, roasts are generally more attractive when thinly sliced. This also tenderizes the meat.

Sauces

A ROAST COOKED at high temperature generally leaves a lovely glaze in the bottom of the pan that can easily be dissolved and dislodged once the meat has been removed and the fat poured out. Place the roasting pan on top of the stove and, over medium-high heat, deglaze by adding some liquid (amounts are given in recipes). The liquid for deglazing can be an appropriate stock, wine, crushed tomatoes, fruit juice, or even water. Holding the pan with a pot-holdered hand, scrape the bottom and sides—every bit of glaze is valuable—firmly with a wooden spoon or, in stubborn cases, with the end of a broad metal spatula. If the deglazing liquid seems watery in flavor, allow to boil for a few minutes. If it is overly intense, add a little more liquid. Salt and pepper can be added as well as chopped fresh herbs.

If the deglazing liquid is too lumpy or full of little bits of solids, pour it through a sieve into a small saucepan. Press hard on the solids, particularly if there is congealed blood. Let the sauce sit a few minutes, and skim off any remaining fat with a spoon. It helps to angle the pot or pan so that there is a thicker layer of fat on top of the liquid; the fat is easier to remove.

Bring the sauce to the table in a sauceboat or an attractive small bowl on a plate along with a small ladle. Remember, the sauce is hot and will heat a metal ladle. It is better to have some surface where the ladle can rest. Don't pour the sauce over the meat as it will be messy for carving and serving.

Even if a separate sauce is to be served with the meat, do deglaze. It cleans the pan and creates a lovely cooking liquid worth saving for adding to salad dressings, stews, pot pies, and other dishes made with leftovers.

In addition to the sauces that accompany some of the recipes, see pages 105–107, pages 292–309, and the end of this chapter for hot and cold suggestions.

Leftovers

PLEASE SEE MY general notes on The Continuous Kitchen (page 4). Suffice it to say that one of the best places to start the continuous kitchen is with roast meats. There are many recipes in this chapter for using leftovers. They usually follow all the other recipes for a specific kind of meat, such as beef, as many different kinds of leftovers of the same sort of meat can generally be used. Mix and match. On pages 222–230 I give recipes for stocks made with bones from roast meat.

These are fine collections of recipes for leftovers. They are not the dreaded remnants of days past, but rather some of my favorite foods. It will make little difference if the leftover meat is rare or well done. If no one at the original meal liked the well-done bits up around a shank bone or the crusty outside slices, this is a perfect way to use them.

If leftovers are not to be eaten or cooked immediately, they should be firmly wrapped in plastic wrap and then in aluminum foil to keep them from drying out. I usually cut the meat off the bone so that I can start a stock. I keep a supply of small stick-on labels in the kitchen along with a pen so that I can label the packed meat before it goes in the refrigerator. That way I don't have to unwrap everything to find what I want. I can even freeze the wrapped package for another week. If I want to make another meal from leftovers, I tuck them into the back of the refrigerator or they are liable to disappear in snacks.

Often, I don't fiddle with the leftovers. Sliced cold, they make wonderful sandwiches or a quick cold meal with a salad and an accompanying sauce. Do let the meat come to somewhere near room temperature. Gelid, it will not provide the best flavor.

Sandwiches can be as varied as the creative impulse. Good bread is essential. Tomatoes should be used only if they are really ripe, and then watch out for the mess. One of the mayonnaise-type sauces (pages 303–305), mustard, salsas (page 299), Tapenade (page 298), Roasted Red Pepper Spread (page 384), or Roasted Whole Red Bell Peppers (page 382) can moisten and season the pile. Think Dagwood.

Lettuces of many kinds, cheeses, and coleslaw are all possible adjuncts. Don't forget pickles, olives, roasted vegetables such as Roasted Eggplant with Green Herb Spread (page 342), one of the roasted cippolines (page 375–377), larger onions (pages 369–372), or any other leftover vegetable that doesn't have butter or need to be crisp as an accompaniment. Sounds good; let's have a picnic.

When is meat done?

THE FIRST TEMPERATURE that matters to the roaster is that of the meat when it goes into the oven. Have I ever stuck a cold piece of meat into an underheated oven? You bet. I'm often in a hurry; but the results are more even, better, when the oven is preheated to the correct temperature and the meat has been removed from the refrigerator and allowed to sit out for anywhere from a half hour to an hour to warm up.

Each cook and eater has an idea of what properly done meat is. I have already admitted to a preference for rare—underdone in British terminology—beef and lamb. By this I do not mean raw and cold, as in the "black and blue" meat served in a number of steak houses. It is equally important that veal and pork not be cooked to the point of dryness. Pork used to be a very fatty meat that required long, slow cooking and high internal temperatures when cooked. Today's pork must be handled more carefully. The porcine officials, claiming safety, recommend that pork be cooked to 165°F. I don't. Trichina, which is what they are worrying about, die at a temperature under 140°F. I cook accordingly to a juicy rose flush. Another cook can always add more time. Veal has delicate flesh unless it is really a large beef masquerading as veal (page 207).

Providing that the oven temperature is accurate and the meat is at room temperature, the recipes should result in properly cooked meat. The chart that follows on page 130 will permit the roaster to check the doneness of the meat and add more time if desired.

An *instant-read thermometer* is a nifty little invention that, when the tip is inserted into the center of the roast—not touching the bone—quickly gives an accurate reading. I say the center because roasting works from the outside in; the ends will always be more cooked. If the meat is of an odd shape or very fatty, it may be better to take two readings and average them. Remember that the meat will continue to cook after it comes out of the oven and as it sits. The juices will also circulate inside the meat a bit to even out the cooking.

I sometimes cook huge cuts, very fatty cuts, or cuts with a lot of bone to a somewhat higher temperature to allow the fat to dissolve and to make sure that the meat that is shielded by the bone is fully cooked. That, for example, is why two such different temperatures are given for veal. Veal with the bone in and with some fat cover, such as a rack, will need to be cooked to a higher temperature than totally filleted veal. As with pork, I prefer a faint flush of palest rose at the center of the meat. If the meat is stuffed, particularly with a forcemeat or a veal kidney, for example, it is necessary to cook it longer so that the bloodier meat in the center gets fully done. The stuffing will, however, keep the meat from drying out.

Baby animals such as goat and lamb are best cooked to well-done but not dry. There may be the faintest flush of pink. These young meats start out pale in color. They can be fatty—particularly the lamb—and they contain a large amount of tendon and cartilage, which softens and becomes unctuous with the longer cooking.

Game meats, such as venison and buffalo, have no internal fat to keep them moist, which is what makes them relatively healthful, but which means they toughen easily. It is always better to cook them rare, unless cooking scraggy bits or leftovers in stew or chili.

Experienced roasters know how to tell how done the meat is by touching it with an "asbestos" finger. Firm—no give—means well-done. Crusty but giving to the touch is rare; and some give, but basically resilient, is medium.

Recipes must be written for specific cuts of meat having a weight. What we buy often does not conform exactly to a recipe. Looking around a bit in the introductions to each kind of meat or using the accompanying chart should permit the cook to accommodate the actual roasting to the piece of meat at hand.

Cooking times

DIFFERENT MEATS AND different cuts have different cooking times. That's why there are recipes. I did try to find a universal rule so that I could say as I do for fish, "ten minutes per inch," or for chicken "ten minutes per pound," and then describe the exceptions. It didn't work. Timing is as much a factor of fat content, bone content, and the shape of the roast as a specific kind of meat.

The only easy rules are for boneless loin of pork or beef (the shell or strip) and venison and beef fillet. They always cook in the same amount of time since the only

	EUROPEAN RARE	RARE	MEDIUM	WELL-DONE
BEEF	125°F	135°–140°F	160°F	170°–180°F
PORK	*	140° (pinkish)	160°F (no pink)	175°F
LAMB	125°–130°F	140°F	160°F (pink)	175°F
BABY LAMB	*	*	160°F (medium well)	175°F
BABY GOAT	*	*	170°F (medium well)	180°F
VEAL	*	*	135°F	160°F
VENISON	*	120°F	*	*
BUFFALO	*	115°F	*	*

* Asterisks mean do not even try it.

way they increase in size is according to their length, which will not influence the cooking time.

If better done meat is desired, leave it to roast in ten-minute increments, taking the temperature of the meat while it is still in the oven. Compare the temperature with that in the chart (above) and make a decision. Do not cut the meat if at all possible as this will allow juices to escape.

Beef will generally take eight minutes longer to get from rare to medium and another ten to get from medium to well-done. Pork will take twenty extra minutes to get from rare to medium and another twenty to get it to well-done. Veal will take about ten extra minutes to get from rosy to totally done. Lamb will take about ten extra minutes to get from rare to medium and another fifteen to get from medium to well done.

In addition to time for roasting, time must be figured for the meat to stand afterward, except for thin cuts of meat, such as flank steak. This allows the juices and final cooking to take place as the roast sits—professionally called *collecting*. If crisp skin is desired, the meat should sit uncovered. To allow for standing time, always put the room-temperature meat in the oven fifteen minutes to a half hour before the length of time it will take to roast. If keeping the heat high is a greater consideration than a crisp crust, tent loosely with a double layer of foil.

bEEF

THERE IS NO MORE GIDDY SMELL FOR A MEAT EATER THAN A GOOD-SIZE PIECE OF BEEF ROASTING IN THE OVEN.

Great roast beef is more the result of a good butcher than brilliant cooking. This is not the time to save money or calories. Be satisfied with saving time due to tender meat and high-heat roasting. Buy the very best grade of beef that can be found and afforded. Even "prime" is not necessarily what it once was, since a much broader range of quality is allowed to be called "prime." Prime meat from famous and more expensive breeds such as black Angus and Charolais is generally more expensive than that from unnamed breeds. Today, there is also organically grown, free-range beef. It is generally leaner and it is even more important that the meat be cooked rare. Beefalo, a beef and buffalo cross, should be cooked as bison/buffalo (page 221).

While the best "prime" is to be preferred, "choice" is a reasonable alternative with the better cuts. "Good" is never good enough for roasting.

Dry-aged meat is hung in a cool place with air circulating around it until some of the water evaporates, the flavor concentrates, and the fiber breaks down. It costs more per pound since the drying means that there is less meat to sell at the end of the process than at the beginning. Dry-aged beef will be darker in color and have a more intense flavor than less aged beef. Beef is never eaten newly slaughtered, but the amount of aging will vary. Some meat is stored in cryovac packages, and it is hard to estimate the aging that goes on. Frozen beef doesn't age in a good sense; but it may get old and dried out with less of the good fat blending into the meat.

That internal fat, the *marbling*, is the sign of marvelous beef. It should show not as large streaks but rather as an all-over pattern of little dots or flecks that may run together to create the look of the veins in marble. As the meat cooks, the marbling melts into the meat, keeping it moist and succulent. If the meat is not cooked at a sufficiently high temperature, this melding of the flavor of the fat with the meat does not take place except with very prolonged cooking, during which the meat stews in its own juices and may dry out.

The flavor of good beef, roasted, is rich and round. It needs little added except salt and pepper and a glass of Burgundy or a round red from pinot noir or zinfandel grapes. Potatoes roasted along with beef for all or part of the roasting time are as traditional as Yorkshire Pudding (page 138), or they can be replaced by Melting

Potatoes (Not-on-Your-Diet) (page 395) for sinful richness, or by Roast Red New Potatoes with Garlic and Rosemary (page 393). If the need to serve more strikes, add Roasted Portobellos (page 362) and a green vegetable such as Roasted Broccoli in Lemon-Garlic Bath (page 323).

Good sauces for most cuts of hot, simply roasted beef are Horseradish Hollandaise (page 306), Béarnaise (page 307), Semi-Périgourdine (page 140), Sauté of Mushrooms (page 163), or Cumberoutlandish Sauce (page 106). Mustards are welcome with hot and cold beef. Cold beef does well with mayonnaise-type sauces, particularly Green Goddess Dressing (page 305). All of the cold sauces included between pages 292–309 would be good with meat except for the Taramasalata.

General cooking notes for beef

AS NOTED EARLIER, with all roasting, the meat must be at room temperature. On big cuts, allow a full hour or longer for it to get there. Use pans that are not much larger than the piece of meat so as to avoid burning of meat juices. Turn on a kitchen fan or open a window. If smoke begins to come from the oven, remove the pan and pour off the fat before continuing to roast. Never place the meat too high in the oven. Let it have room to breathe. Use a meat thermometer and refer to the temperature chart page 130.

Start roasting earlier than your estimate of weight or size indicates since the amount of bone and varied configurations can change cooking time radically. Because of its mass, your roast will not get cold if it waits out of the oven. It should indeed be allowed to wait at least twenty minutes before carving so that the juices can settle.

Roasted New York strip

MY FAVORITE CUT of beef for roasting has many names: New York strip, whole boneless shell, New York steak, shell steak, Delmonico steak, strip steak, and contre filet.

I was relieved to find that the great Connaught Hotel cooks, as I do, a whole shell of beef, boneless and relatively even in shape, for perfect, even cooking. This is expensive, but there are times when it is a perfect solution for festive entertaining. Once one gets the hang of it, nothing is easier. Like loin of pork and beef fillet, the timing is always the same; changes in quantity have to do with the length of the strip and not the profile of the meat.

I generally cook this at the top of the oven for better browning.

To roast potatoes in the same pan as the beef, cut enough peeled baking potatoes into eight wedges each to allow three pieces per person. Use a large enough pan so that they will fit flat around the meat. Slick them with a minimum of fat. Roast them along with the meat, turning them every fifteen minutes.

The recipe here is for a whole shell; but, as noted, the same instructions will apply to a shorter roast. Just adjust the seasonings and deglazing liquid accordingly.

One 10-pound New York strip (16-inches), trussed

1 head garlic, cloves lightly smashed and peeled, optional

3 to 4 sprigs fresh thyme, optional

Kosher salt, to taste

Freshly ground black pepper, to taste

1½ cups Basic Beef Stock (page 224), Basic Veal Stock (page 226), red wine, or a combination of two or more

2 tablespoons Basic Veal Glaze (page 227), optional

Place oven rack on second level from the top of oven, or second from the bottom if the fat cover is thick. Heat oven to 500°F.

Place strip of beef in an 18 x 12 x 2-inch roasting pan. If using, slip whole cloves of garlic between underside of meat and string. Tuck in the thyme. Slip some more garlic under the string along the top of the meat. Sprinkle the meat on all sides liberally with salt and pepper. Put into oven 1 hour before it will be served. Roast for 40 to 45 minutes.

Remove and transfer meat to a platter. Cut off strings. Remove the garlic cloves that are too blackened to use. Pour fat from pan. Put the roasting pan on top of the stove. Add stock or wine and the veal glaze, if using, and bring to a boil, scraping the bottom vigorously with a wooden spoon. Add flavorings, if using, and any juices that have collected in the platter on which the beef is resting. Let reduce by half. Taste for salt and pepper; pour into a sauceboat and serve.

Standing rib roast

NOTHING SAYS "OLDE England" quite like a standing rib roast, held upright on its bones. Some of these can get quite heroic in size; but they are nothing more than huge loin chops whose meat is rib eye steak. Mortgage the house and buy the best for a feast, whether for six, or twenty, or more (recipes follow).

Before spending all that money, there are decisions to be made. First, are the invitees food-compatible—do they all eat red meat without a whimper, even with gusto, and do they all like it pretty much the same doneness. It takes only one appalled guest treating everybody else like savages to ruin the evening. There's always better-done meat on the outside slices and, if the oven is left on, a portion can be turned to gray in short order.

Even though in restaurants I have seen ribs of beef cut from a roast come to the table with the short ribs in all their fatty glory left on and the bone resolutely attached to the meat, I usually ask the butcher to remove the short ribs, which can make a whole meal on their own (page 147). The trimmed roast is called "short."

If the butcher has done the job of removing the short ribs properly, along with trimming the chine and cracking it so that the ribs can be separated (page 124), the easiest carving method implies a guest list of Cro-Magnons. If I'm the cook, I need a strong and willing accomplice who will slice the ribs and their meat apart into sumptuous slabs. I need an accomplice because this is a large piece of meat.

Instead, when the party is elegant, I ask the butcher to cut the eye from the ribs and then tie it back into place with only a modest covering of its natural fat. That way, I can snip through the strings in the kitchen and bring the whole massive roast to the table. Once the impression is made, I remove the meat to a safe cutting surface and slice it down easily and without any hassle. The bones can be cut apart for hardy, gnawing eaters.

That is also the easiest procedure for a less formal party. However, I can proceed in a more traditional manner. I still have the short ribs removed for hoarding; but I do not have the eye cut from the bones. Instead, when the roast comes to the table, I begin to slice from an outside end as thinly as I can. When I get to a rib, I tilt the roast up and slice between the long bones—just on either side of the bone. This will let me cut a few more thin slices before I get to the next rib. Each slice has to be sliced free of the bones. This way, I serve a rib with meat on to hearty eaters, while people like me can have just thinly sliced meat. Easier is to emulate what I have the butcher do: Slide the carving knife along the rib bones toward the backbone to free the bottom of the meat and then cut down along the other bones to meet the first cut in a right angle. This frees the meat, which can be easily sliced.

The variations in the beast from which the roast comes and the ways it can be butchered make it hard to predict the weight of a particular roast. A short roast—without the short ribs—will weigh less, as will one whose fat cover has been radically excised, than an "uncensored" brute. If meat is exposed, it is a good idea to get a thin slice of fatback, unsalted, to cover it. No matter how it is trimmed, each two ribs of standing roast feeds from four to six people, depending on the size of the eye and the greed in the eyes of the eaters.

The best roasting insurance is the instant-read meat thermometer (page 128). Stick it deep into the flesh in the center of the roast, making sure not to touch the bone.

I don't smother these large pieces of meat with lots of vegetables; the plate gets too crowded. If fabulous asparagus are in season, I serve them first, in place of a salad, or on a side plate at the same time as the roast.

As a lone accompaniment, I tend to make Yorkshire pudding while the roast calms down, or I surround the uncooked roast in the pan with potatoes. I always make a simple deglazing sauce with red wine just to moisten the slices of meat and usually serve another sauce as well. Consider Béarnaise (page 307), Horseradish Hollandaise (page 306), Duxelles (page 29), or Semi-Périgourdine (page 140).

The cost of all this can be made less poisonous by thinking of the dividend meals. All the leftover beef dishes in this section, from hashes to stews to meat pies, are delicious made with roast beef. Then there are the soups and the bones—should no one have gnawed them. Simply put the bones back in the hot oven, brushed with a little melted butter mixed with Dijon mustard and sprinkled with Dried Bread Crumbs (page 110), until they are hot and crusty. This is a useful idea, as the bones from the large rib roast weigh four to five pounds—about 20 percent of the total weight of the roast.

Simple rib roast

TOTAL
ROASTING
TIME:
*see facing
page*

M Y ROAST IS rare, but not Saxon pillage. The outside slices can serve the meat eaters who like it better done. The technique and timings are simple. First, the meat is roasted for three quarters of an hour at 500°F. With the roast still in the oven, the heat is lowered to 325°F and roasted for approximately three minutes per pound. Finally, the heat is turned up to 450°F and the roasting continues for another fifteen minutes after turning up the controls.

If the consensus of friends is for the meat "bloody, bawdy," I take the three minutes a pound down to two. If they want it medium, the three minutes goes to five. For well done, heaven help them. These times presuppose the meat at room temperature and at least fifteen minutes of sitting time after the meat comes from the oven, when it will continue to cook.

Why all this fiddling with temperatures? Good beef has the highest internal percentage of fat of any meat I am liable to roast, even when it is the often excellent kind specially bred and fed to be low in fat. It is important that the meat get hot enough to have this fat melt into the meat. At the same time, I want my meat rare and not steamed, which it can become with sustained low-heat cooking. I want the meat fairly evenly cooked throughout despite its mass—the eye can be up to five inches in diameter—and the shielding of the meat by the bones. I want a nicely browned, crisp crust on the outside. The initial high-heat cooking sets the process off with a bang, rapidly creating a crust and getting the heat to the interior of the meat. The next period of lower cooking heat permits the meat to cook through without the exterior getting overdone. The final period of high-heat roasting crisps up the crust again—perfect.

Good beef is deeply flavorful. It needs little seasoning beyond copious salt and pepper. Garlic slivers can be poked between the bones and the meat and between the fat cover and the meat. I use my fingers to avoid cutting into the meat, which would allow too much of the juices to seep out.

Rib roast can be made with Yorkshire pudding, my favorite, or—if it is a relatively small roast—with its other classic accompaniment, roasted potatoes. I don't suggest the potatoes with a large roast—too many potatoes, no space in the pan. What is the point of serving a pan full of potatoes with a roast if they don't absorb the marvelous fat the meat gives off while cooking?

For the small roast, cut into quarters two and a half pounds of peeled baking or mealy boiling potatoes (see page 387 for discussion of varieties). After the roast has cooked for ten minutes, put the potato wedges in the pan, turning to coat with fat from roast. Turn them every fifteen minutes.

The roast rests while the Yorkshire pudding is cooking in the oven. Remember to make the batter at least five hours ahead so it has a chance to chill (see page 138). It is correct that the Yorkshire pudding for the smaller roast needs less cooking time—less meat, fewer guests, less pudding.

After the meat is transferred to a platter and before the cold batter is poured into the pan, I deglaze the pan to make a little moistening sauce. I generally toss in a little red wine; but other liquids such as meat stock are good as well. Some may like the less strong taste of half stock and half wine.

4½-pound short (without short ribs) standing rib roast (2 ribs) or 26-pound standing rib roast (7 ribs total)

2 to 6 cloves garlic, smashed, peeled, and slivered, optional

Kosher salt, to taste

Freshly ground black pepper, to taste

½ to 2½ cups red wine, for deglazing

1 recipe small- or large-quantity Yorkshire Pudding (page 138), optional

Place oven rack on the second level from the bottom. Heat oven to 500°F.

Place small roast in a 14 x 12 x 2-inch roasting pan, bone side down. The large roast will need an 18 x 13 x 2-inch roasting pan. Snuggle most of the garlic, if using, under the fat and spread remainder under the meat. Season well with salt and pepper. Roast for 45 minutes. With meat in oven, reduce heat to 325°F and roast another 12 minutes for the small roast. The large roast will roast for another 1 hour 15 minutes. Increase heat to 450°F and roast 15 minutes more for both sizes. Meat temperature should read 135°F on an instant-read thermometer.

Remove roast from oven. Transfer to a serving platter. Pour or spoon off excess fat, reserving about ⅛ cup fat for the small roast and ¼ cup fat for the large roast. Put pan over high heat and add wine. Deglaze pan well (page 10), scraping with a wooden spoon. Let reduce by half. Pour liquid into a small sauceboat and reserve.

TOTAL ROASTING TIME: small roast, 1 hour 12 minutes; large roast, 2 hours 15 minutes

Yorkshire pudding

TOTAL
ROASTING
TIME:
see below

A YORKSHIRE PUDDING is a sort of low popover—all hot air and crust, without sweetness. Its batter explodes upward with the same mysterious vigor as a popover from having cold batter poured into hot fat in a hot pan. Even after all these years, it always excites a gasp of admiration. It soaks up gravy and is quick and easy to prepare as long as the batter is made ahead. I usually make it the day before I need it. It will keep up to three days in a tightly closed jar in the refrigerator. I always put the batter in a jar, measuring cup, or pitcher so that it is easier to pour.

If the right pan sizes for the amount of batter are used in the correct temperature oven, a different fat (an eighth of a cup for a small quantity of batter, a quarter of a cup for large quantity) can be used as long as it doesn't burn. I recently made a very non-Yorkshire pudding using olive oil to go with a roasted fish. It was very good.

FOR SMALL QUANTITY (to go with smaller rib roast)	FOR LARGE QUANTITY (to go with large rib roast)
3 large eggs	9 large eggs
½ teaspoon kosher salt	1 tablespoon kosher salt
1 cup all-purpose flour, sifted	3 cups all-purpose flour, sifted
1 cup cool milk	3 cups cool milk
⅛ cup fat, reserved from smaller Simple Rib Roast (page 136)	¼ cup fat, reserved from large Simple Rib Roast (page 136)

Make the batter for Yorkshire pudding before roasting meat—at least 5 hours ahead—so that it has time to chill.

Put the eggs in a large bowl and beat with an electric beater or whisk for 1 minute. Add salt. Alternating the flour and the milk, add to the eggs. Beat only until all ingredients are well combined. If available, pour batter into a pitcher or large measuring cup for ease in pouring later. Cover tightly and refrigerate. Batter may be made up to 2 days ahead.

Pour reserved fat into the hot, deglazed roasting pan and place in the 450°F oven. Let heat for 3 to 4 minutes. Pour appropriate quantity of cold batter from refrigerator directly into pan. Cook 15 minutes for small quantity and 20 minutes for large quantity. Reverse pan in oven, back to front, so that pudding will rise and brown evenly. Reduce heat to 350°F. Continue to cook approximately 15 to 25 minutes for small quantity and 20 to 30 minutes for large quantity, until pudding is crusty and brown. Serve hot.

TOTAL ROASTING TIME: small quantity, 30 to 40 minutes; large quantity, 40 to 50 minutes

Roasted whole beef fillet

SERVES 12 TO 14

TOTAL
ROASTING
TIME:
20
minutes

THIS DISH BESPEAKS lavishness as it is paraded to the table by a proud cook. No one has to know how quick and easy it is to cook and cut across into neat slices. Served hot with Green Peppercorn Sauce for Duck (page 64), substituting beef stock, Béarnaise Sauce (page 307), Semi-Périgourdine Sauce (page 140), or most impressively, with Thulier Sauce (page 220). The more elegant the sauce, the fewer the vegetables. A few roasted asparagus or roasted scallions (pages 318 and 405) are plenty. If there is no separate sauce, consider a Roasted Onion Flowers (page 372) per person or Roasted Cherry Tomatoes with Basil (page 419).

The meat can be thinly sliced as an hors d'oeuvre to go on bread with a little butter and mustard or served cold at a buffet with Tarragon Mayonnaise (page 303) or a salsa (page 299). As a cold summer main course, it needs no more than a green salad, mustard, cornichons, good bread, and red wine.

I buy the meat by the inch. It cooks exactly the same way no matter the length as long as it is more than four inches long. When ordering, I usually allow about an inch and a quarter per person and an extra half inch for the two end slices. By this rule, six people will require an eight-inch piece of fillet. The muscles in a fillet all run lengthwise, so that when it is sliced across for serving it is also tenderized.

The fillet is also called the tenderloin, and it is tender. It is a long round muscle that hides behind the bones on which the shell steak and the rib roast reside. T-bone steaks have some of the shell and, on the other side of the bone, a circle of the fillet, or tenderloin. A filet mignon is a slice cut across the whole fillet to make an individual steak.

4- to 5-pound whole beef fillet (about 3 to 3½ inches in diameter, a good 18 inches long)

1 tablespoon unsalted butter, at room temperature

1 tablespoon olive oil

2 teaspoons kosher salt

¼ teaspoon freshly ground black pepper

¾ cup red wine for deglazing, optional, or 1 recipe Semi-Périgourdine Sauce (page 140)

Place oven rack on second level from bottom. Heat oven to 500°F.

Place fillet in an 18 x 12 x 2-inch roasting pan. Rub fillet with butter and oil. Sprinkle evenly with salt and pepper. Roast for 10 minutes. Turn. Roast 10 minutes more. Transfer fillet to a serving platter. Pour or spoon off excess fat. Put pan on top of stove. Add the wine or sauce and bring contents to a boil while scraping the bottom vigorously with a wooden spoon. Let reduce by half. Season with salt and pepper.

Semi-périgourdine sauce

MAKES ½ CUP

I T'S NOT WORTH making this sauce if there is no really good, gelatin-rich stock on hand. Why waste the money for a black truffle, even one in a jar or can, such as I use? This is the minimum amount of truffle for the sauce. There is never too much, just like thin or rich. A little butter can be swirled in at the end for the thickness. For variety, add a little chopped tarragon and parsley. This is the time for that truly French-style chopping—fine mincing. The goose fat is a tip-off that this sauce really did originate in the Périgord along with the black truffles; but if there is none on hand, substitute butter.

1 tablespoon Rendered Goose Fat (page 83)

2 large shallots (1 ounce), peeled and chopped very fine (2 tablespoons)

1 whole black truffle (12 grams), peeled and very thinly sliced, liquid from jar (2 teaspoons) and all peel reserved

2 tablespoons Madeira (pale or heavy) or light Port

½ cup Extra-Rich Beef Stock (page 227)

½ teaspoon tomato paste

1 tablespoon Basic Veal Glaze (page 227), optional

¼ teaspoon kosher salt

1 grind black pepper

1 tablespoon butter, optional

1 tablespoon minced parsley, optional

Melt goose fat in a small pan over low heat. When melted, add shallots and cook until very soft but not brown, about 15 minutes. Add the truffle liquid and peel, the Madeira, beef stock, tomato paste, and veal glaze, if using. Stir to mix well. Simmer over low heat for 15 minutes.

Remove sauce from heat. Using a wooden spoon, force it through a fine sieve into a bowl. Wash the pan.

Return the sauce to the clean pan and stir in the salt and pepper. Add the sliced truffle and bring to a boil. Reduce heat and simmer until reduced by a third, about 20 minutes. Turn off heat and stir in butter and parsley, if using. Spoon into a sauceboat and serve warm.

Flank steak

HERE IS ANOTHER of those basic name pickles. Flank steak is a relatively small, thin muscle with a pronounced grain the French call *bavette* or *onglet* hidden inside the whole flank, a thin cut of meat coming from that part of the belly of the beast nearest the leg. Above it is the loin. In front of it at the same level are, beginning at the front of the beast, the brisket (more later); the plate, which is an extension of the short ribs and generally used for pastrami; and the skirt, with its hanging tender or hanger steak. The confusion comes because the flank is often confused with its most common form of preparation, the London broil. Other cuts besides the flank steak are sold as and used as London broil. As the name suggests, flank steak is usually broiled or grilled.

I roast. I had the meat; I cooked the meat, and it was terrific—quicker and more tender than on the grill. What is more, as the meat roasts evenly throughout, the grain, ordinarily emphasized on the surface by the direct, intense heat of the grill, is less pronounced. The steak still needs to be properly sliced, unless it is to be tough and stringy.

To slice: Lay the meat on a large flat platter or work surface. The flatness is needed to properly get at the thin piece of meat and not have the rim of a platter interfere with the knife. Large sushi platters work well. There are juices—good—that can make a mess and get lost, so it is better to cut on something. The meat is essentially a rectangle with the grain running lengthwise. Start slicing against the grain in the thickest corner. Hold the blade of the very sharp knife very flat to the cutting surface and slice the meat thinly, with the knife at a 70-degree angle. These two anglings will give broad, thin, tender slices that increase in length as one proceeds toward the center of the rectangle. The double angling increases tenderness by maximal cutting of the fibers. Continue until reaching the opposing corner from where the cutting started. The slices will once again be short.

To roast simply, follow the instructions for the meat only in Roasted Flank Steak with Potatoes and Portobello Mushrooms (page 142). By the time the meat is browned, it is properly cooked. The roasted slices can be used in American-Chinese dishes such as beef with broccoli, in fajitas, and in sandwiches.

Roasted flank steak with potatoes and portobello mushrooms

SERVES 4

TOTAL
ROASTING
TIME:
12
minutes

Here the oven is used to turn out the steak and vegetables. The potatoes must be started as soon as the oven is cranked up. The mushrooms go in at the same time as the meat.

The meat is not marinated to tenderize it, but to add flavor. While marination seldom adds much flavor to a large or bony piece of meat or bird, it does fine here. It requires leaving the meat in the marinade for enough time, about an hour, for it to come to room temperature. It can sit out for up to four hours. The meat marinade can simply be olive oil, salt, and pepper, or it can be a second recipe's worth of the garlic marinade used for the mushrooms.

Since the meat is so thin, I take the exceptional step of briefly preheating the pan to better sear the meat.

2 pounds flank steak, trimmed of all
    surface fat

**IF NOT USING GARLIC MARINADE
FOR BEEF**
2 teaspoons kosher salt
Freshly ground black pepper, to taste

¼ cup olive oil
1 recipe Roast Portobello Mushrooms
    with Garlic Marinade (page 364),
    doubling the marinade if using for
    beef also
4 medium baking potatoes

Place one oven rack on lowest level and one rack on the next level above. Heat oven to 500°F.

Put steak in a shallow container large enough to hold it. Either sprinkle both sides with salt and pepper and coat with oil, or rub with 1 recipe of the garlic marinade.

Place mushrooms in a nonreactive container just large enough to hold them. Pour a single recipe's worth of the garlic marinade over the mushrooms, rubbing well into each one. Allow the meat and the mushrooms to stand at room temperature for at least 1 hour, turning once.

Forty minutes before roasting the steak and mushrooms, use a fork to prick the potatoes once or twice each. Place them directly on the sides of the upper rack of the oven, allowing enough room for the mushrooms, which will cook on the same rack.

Twenty minutes before roasting the steak and mushrooms, put a 14 x 12 x 2-inch roasting pan on the lower oven rack and leave to preheat for 10 minutes. Remove pan. Immediately, put the steak with all of its oil or marinade in the pan. Place on the lower oven rack, the thickest part of the steak to the rear of the oven. Place the mushrooms on the upper rack at the same time. For rare, roast the steak for 6 minutes. Turn the steak and the mushrooms. Roast 6 minutes more. Remove steak, mushrooms, and potatoes from oven. Let steak rest about 5 minutes. Slice thinly, with a sharp knife, against the grain at a 70-degree angle.

Fajitas

MAKES 36 TO 44 SLICES, DEPENDING
ON TYPE OF MEAT USED

TOTAL
ROASTING
TIME:
12
minutes

A KIDS' PARTY or mine; this is an easy, informal meal with beer for me and sodas for them. Serve on plates or with the meat slices wrapped in soft tortillas. Provide Guacamole (page 300), a salsa (page 299), thinly sliced red onions, and thinly sliced lettuce—yes, iceberg—and let everyone roll their own. If following Texas border style, use flour tortillas; but corn tortillas will have better flavor.

½ cup fresh lime juice

8 or 9 large cloves garlic, smashed, peeled, and chopped

4 serrano or jalapeño peppers, seeded and coarsely chopped, or 3 to 4 tablespoons seeded and chopped Basic Jalapeños (page 383)

2 pounds skirt or flank steak, trimmed of all surface fat

Run a blender with the lime juice, garlic, and peppers. Blend until smooth. Rub the mixture into the meat on all sides. Allow to marinate for 2 hours at room temperature or overnight in the refrigerator.

Bring meat to room temperature.

About 20 minutes before roasting the steak, place oven rack on lowest level. Preheat oven to 500°F. Put a 14 x 12 x 2-inch roasting pan in the oven and leave to preheat for 10 minutes. Put the steak in the pan, the thickest part to the rear of the oven. For rare, roast for 6 minutes. Turn. Roast 6 minutes more. Remove. Let steak rest about 5 minutes. Slice thinly with a sharp knife against the grain at a 70-degree angle. Scrape pan juices over the meat.

Brisket

A BRISKET IS a fatty piece of meat that is full-flavored and tender after prolonged cooking. It is usually either boiled or pot-roasted. Less than gentle readers may ask what it is doing in this book on roasting. The answer is that brisket is hard to brown on top of the stove, which is the almost invariable first step in cooking it. Here, it is oven browned, which saves this cook from getting spattered and burned.

The brisket may be cut into various muscles and pieces as the whole thing, boneless, can weigh fifteen pounds. The deckel, or thicker top cut (*gros bout de poitrine* in French), is usually removed today to give a neat, approximately five-pound roast.

Depending on the quality of the meat, it will have a variable amount of fat. I remove almost all of the external fat, leaving just a very thin layer on one side.

A five-pound brisket makes about twenty nice, long slices to serve at least eight normal people or six starving men. A smaller piece of about four pounds will serve six normal people. Always cut brisket against the grain. If using a brisket in your own recipe, see page 231 for Basic Browning.

Boiled brisket

Here the brisket is cooked conventionally on top of the stove after oven roasting to brown. It is the best boiled beef I know. The vegetables can be varied according to taste and season. I like to serve the very rich broth on the side in individual bowls or cups, from which guests can drink as they eat. There will still be enough broth left to make a first course with noodles (page 92) another night. Freeze any extra stock for a splendid dividend. Meat leftovers can go into Shepherd's Pie (page 154) or into sandwiches.

6-pound brisket, trimmed but not completely fat free

8 cups Basic Beef Stock (page 224) or canned chicken broth

¾ head garlic, smashed and peeled

3½ pounds small red new potatoes

1 pound baby onions

12 ounces small sugar snap peas

4 medium carrots, trimmed, peeled, and cut into 1½-inch lengths

Place rack on lowest level of oven. Heat oven to 500°F.

Place brisket, fat side down, in a 14 x 12 x 2-inch roasting pan. Roast for 30 minutes. Turn so the fat side is up. Roast 15 minutes more.

Transfer brisket to a 6-quart, heavy-bottomed pot. Pour off excess fat from roasting pan. Put pan on top of stove. Add ½ cup of the stock and bring contents to a boil while scraping the bottom vigorously with a wooden spoon. Pour over brisket. Add remaining stock and the garlic. Cover tightly and bring to a boil. Reduce heat and simmer 5 hours. As fat rises to surface of liquid, skim off. Collect fat and any liquid you may skim off with it in a tall container. Continue skimming frequently during cooking.

Meanwhile, wash potatoes. Peel onions. Leave vegetables in separate bowls of water until ready to use. Top and tail sugar snap peas and remove strings running along either side.

About 20 minutes before brisket is done, skim cooking liquid for the last time. Add potatoes, carrots, and onions to the pot. Cook at a low boil until almost tender. Add sugar snap peas and cook for 1 minute. Turn off heat. Remove meat with a fork and vegetables with a slotted spoon. Slice brisket thinly on the diagonal and serve with kosher salt, some Dijon mustard, and a bowl of cornichons. Place vegetables in a serving dish. Serve with Horseradish Sauce (page 302) and bowls of defatted broth.

TOTAL ROASTING TIME: 45 minutes plus 5 hours for boiling

Wholesome brisket with roasted vegetables

SERVES 8

TOTAL
ROASTING
TIME:
4
hours
15
minutes

THIS IS GOOD homey food. It makes two cups of succulent sauce to serve with mashed potatoes or noodles. I find that company is delighted to get this kind of food instead of something more elegant.

I'm particularly proud of the technique here which roasts both the meat and the vegetables and then combines them for prolonged slow simmering. The only time that any attention has to be paid to this is when the pans get deglazed after the initial roasting. That will take about five minutes. The rest of the cooking is carefree.

If there are any leftovers, they keep well in the refrigerator for three to four days without drying out, for snacking or sandwiches. Leftover slices are easily reheated in the remaining sauce.

4¾- to 5-pound brisket, trimmed but not completely fat free

1 head garlic, top ¼ inch sliced off

4 teaspoons olive oil

3 small onions (about 12 ounces total), peeled, root end kept intact, cut in half lengthwise, and each half cut into 3 wedges

1 pound carrots, trimmed, peeled, and cut into 3- to 4-inch pieces

½ cup water

2 cups drained and mushed Whole Plum Tomatoes (page 418), plus ¼ cup reserved roasting liquid or one 16-ounce can whole tomatoes with liquid

1 small bay leaf

Kosher salt, to taste

Freshly ground black pepper, to taste

Place one rack in the center of the oven and another in the bottom. Heat oven to 500°F.

Place brisket, fat side down, in a 14 x 12 x 2-inch roasting pan. It's best not to use a shallow pan for this, or later the juices might run over and out. Put the garlic in the pan. Drizzle with 1 teaspoon of the oil. Using your hands, rub oil onto garlic.

Put the onion wedges and carrots into a smaller, 12 x 8 x 1½-inch roasting pan. Drizzle with remaining oil. Using your hands, rub the oil over all the pieces until they are well coated. Arrange onion wedges on their sides, so that they touch carrots as little as possible.

Roast vegetables on center rack of oven for 30 minutes. Turn with a spatula. Roast 15 minutes more. Roast the brisket simultaneously on the bottom rack of the oven for 15 minutes. Turn over so fat side is up. Roast 30 minutes more.

Remove both pans from oven. Lower heat to 275°F, leaving the door ajar a minute or two to reduce temperature more quickly. Leave the brisket and garlic in the large pan and add ¼ cup of the water. The water should bubble up from the heat of the pan; if it does not, put pan on the stove over medium-high heat. With a wooden spoon, scrape around the brisket to scoop up and remove the brown bits from bottom of pan.

Put the onions and carrots into the brisket pan. Put the smaller pan on top of the stove. Add the remaining water and bring contents to a boil while scraping the bottom vigorously with a wooden spoon. Pour liquid into brisket pan.

Add roasted plum tomatoes and reserved roasting liquid or, if using canned tomatoes, stick a small knife into the opened can of tomatoes. Run it back and forth through the tomatoes and purée until only small pieces remain. Pour contents over vegetables and around brisket. Put the bay leaf into the liquid. Cover tightly with foil.

Roast on center rack of oven for 3½ hours. Remove foil, increase temperature to 500°F, and roast 15 minutes more or until brisket is nicely browned.

Remove. Sprinkle with salt and pepper. With the back of a spoon, smush the softened garlic out of each section and into the liquid. Throw the empty papers away. Transfer brisket to a platter and cover brisket with a tent of foil. Use a slotted spoon to transfer vegetables to a large serving bowl or plate. Discard the bay leaf. Pour remaining liquid into a measuring cup. Let sit long enough for the fat to rise to the surface, about 15 minutes. Skim fat off surface.

To serve, cut brisket against the grain into long thin strips. Arrange 2 to 3 slices on each plate. Spoon on some of the vegetables, and moisten everything with a generous amount of the liquid.

Short ribs

THESE ENDS OF the ribs of a standing rib roast, with their meat and fat attached, are succulent. They are common in America, hard to find in England—heaven knows why—and are called *plat de côtes couvert* in French. These long, bony pieces are often cut across into shorter bits, which is fine. The important thing is to look for pieces with a high percentage of meat to bone. The ones I like to use weigh about twelve ounces each and are a good inch and a half thick at the heaviest end.

Short ribs, like brisket, require long cooking to become meltingly tender; but they brown up in short, easy order when roasted.

Roasted short ribs with glazed garlic, fennel, and carrots

SERVES 4 TO 6

TOTAL
ROASTING
TIME:
see below

THIS IS A rich and savory dish. What seems like a small amount will satisfy even large eaters. Don't cut down on the vegetables. As it cooks the meat lets off fat, which will sink to the bottom of the pan. To serve, remove the meat and vegetables from the pan with a slotted spoon.

The forty cloves of garlic in this dish melt in your mouth or onto a waiting chunk of bread. Serve with one small boiled potato per person or with mashed potatoes. Can be made ahead and reheated.

2 short ribs (about 5½ pounds), each trimmed of some fat and cut into 6 to 7 pieces

¼ cup stock, water, or wine, for deglazing

1 tablespoon caraway seeds

1 large yellow onion (12 ounces), peeled and chopped in ¼-inch dice (2 cups)

40 whole cloves garlic, peeled (about 1 cup)

2 large fennel bulbs (14 ounces each), trimmed, stalks removed, and cut lengthwise into 8 to 9 wedges

8 carrots, trimmed, peeled, and cut in 2-inch lengths

2 teaspoons kosher salt

Freshly ground black pepper, to taste

4 to 6 boiled potatoes, to serve on the side

Place oven rack on center level. Heat oven to 500°F.

Arrange ribs in a 14 x 12 x 2-inch roasting pan. Roast for 20 minutes. Turn ribs over. Roast 25 minutes more. Reduce oven temperature to 350°F. Using a slotted spoon, transfer ribs to a large platter. Pour or spoon off excess fat. Put pan on top of stove. Add the stock or other liquid and bring contents to a boil while scraping the bottom vigorously with a wooden spoon. Add caraway seeds to liquid. Reserve.

Arrange half the onion, the garlic, fennel, and carrots in a 5-quart casserole. Add half the salt and pepper to taste. Arrange the ribs in a single layer in the casserole. Layer the remaining onion, garlic, fennel, and carrots over and around the ribs. Sprinkle with remaining salt and more pepper to taste. Pour deglazing liquid over all. Cover tightly with foil and a lid, if you have one. Cook 3 hours.

About 35 minutes before you are ready to eat, boil a pot of water and cook the potatoes for about 25 minutes, or until a sharp knife slides easily into the center of each.

TOTAL ROASTING TIME: 45 minutes at 500°F; 3 hours at 350°F

Short rib stew Mediterranean

SERVES 12

TOTAL
ROASTING
TIME:
see page 150

THIS LARGE-SCALE RECIPE makes a great party dish for a dozen people. It can easily be divided in halves or thirds. The roasting part needs to be done in three batches if making the entire amount and will cause smoke. Open the windows and turn on the exhaust fan, or go back to the long, spattering process of browning the meat on top of the stove.

22 pieces beef short ribs (about 12 ounces each, 16½ pounds total), each trimmed of some fat and cut into 3 x 5-inch pieces

Kosher salt, to taste

1½ quarts red wine

¼ cup olive oil

4 medium yellow onions (2 pounds), peeled and chopped in ¼-inch dice (4½ cups)

2 large heads garlic, smashed, peeled, and chopped

1½ cups Cognac or other brandy

4 cups Basic Veal Stock (page 226) or Basic Beef Stock (page 224)

3 medium tomatoes, cored, peeled, and coarsley chopped (2 cups)

Zest of 1 medium orange

1½ cups fresh orange juice

5 tablespoons tomato paste

2 bay leaves

½ cup Basic Veal Glaze (page 227), optional

2¾ cups drained black Niçoise olives

Kosher salt, to taste

Freshly ground black pepper, to taste

Place oven rack on center level. Heat oven to 500°F. Turn on exhaust fan.

Place about 8 ribs in roasting pan, or as many as will fit without touching. Salt the ribs. Roast for 40 minutes. Remove ribs to a cool platter. Pour or spoon off excess fat. Put pan on top of the stove. Add ¾ cup of the red wine and bring to a boil, scraping the bottom of the pan vigorously with a wooden spoon. Reserve liquid. Repeat as above until all ribs are done. Reserve all liquid and bits of meat from deglazing.

Into a large stew pot, put the olive oil and the onions. Sauté over low heat for 5 to 10 minutes. Add half of the garlic. Continue to cook until onions are transparent, another 10 minutes or so. Arrange ribs in the pot. When adding ingredients to the pot, be careful not to pick up meat and turn over. Insert your ingredients into the liquid between the bones and poke down with your spoon. The ribs become more fragile as they cook and will look nicer at the end if the meat is still on the bone.

Pour the Cognac into a small pan. Place over a medium flame and ignite the Cognac with a match. Once flame is out, pour into stew pot. Cook for 10 minutes.

continued

Add the stock, tomatoes, two thirds of the orange zest, 1 cup of the orange juice, and the remainder of the red wine. Increase heat to medium. Add tomato paste, bay leaves, and veal glaze, if you are using it. Cover. Bring mixture to a boil. Reduce heat to a simmer. Cook for 2 hours.

Stew can be held at this stage for several hours.

About 30 minutes before you are ready to serve, add the olives and the remainder of the orange zest, orange juice, and garlic. If reheating, do so thoroughly. Add salt and pepper.

TOTAL ROASTING TIME: 40 minutes to 2 hours for browning, plus 2 hours for simmering

Perfect beef stew

MAKES 4½ CUPS; SERVES 4

TOTAL
ROASTING
TIME:
*see facing
page*

THIS RECIPE USES the technique for browning stew meat on page 232. To increase the recipe, follow directions there for browning larger quantities. If canned stock is the only kind on hand, add salt with caution.

Adding the flour to the hot vegetables right after roasting cooks it just enough to make a roux to thicken the sauce.

2¼ pounds beef stew meat, cut into
    1-inch cubes

2 tablespoons olive oil

3 small yellow onions (10 to 12 ounces
    total), peeled, trimmed, and cut into
    eighths (1½ cups)

4 medium carrots (7 ounces total),
    trimmed, peeled, and cut in half
    lengthwise, then cut across into 1-inch
    pieces (1 cup)

2 ribs celery (3½ ounces total), trimmed,
    peeled with a vegetable peeler, and cut
    in half lengthwise and then across into
    1-inch pieces

1 tablespoon all-purpose flour

¼ cup water or stock

4 cloves garlic, smashed and peeled

1½ cups Basic Beef Stock (page 224)
    or canned

1 cup Cherry Tomato Purée (page 418)
    or same amount canned tomatoes
    with their juices

½ cup water

¼ cup red wine

½ bay leaf

½ teaspoon kosher salt

6 grinds black pepper

Place oven racks on the lowest and the center levels of oven. Heat the oven to 500°F.

Place the meat in a 14 x 12 x 2-inch pan. Pour 1 tablespoon of the olive oil over the meat, tossing to coat. Roast on the lowest rack for 10 minutes. Turn with a slotted spoon. Roast 10 minutes more. Turn again. Roast another 10 minutes. The meat will throw off a good deal of water, but don't worry. Once the water has evaporated, the meat will brown in the remaining fat.

When the meat is in the oven, place the onions, carrots, and celery in a 12 x 8 x 1½-inch pan. Pour the remaining tablespoon of olive oil over the vegetables, tossing to coat. After the meat has roasted 10 minutes, put the pan with vegetables on the center rack of the oven. Roast for 10 minutes. Turn. Roast another 10 minutes.

Remove both pans from the oven. Sprinkle the flour over the vegetables while they are still hot. Toss to coat. Set aside.

With a slotted spoon, move meat to a 1½- to 2-quart saucepan no wider than 7 inches in diameter. Pour or spoon off excess fat. Put pan on top of stove. Add the ¼ cup water or stock and bring contents to a boil, scraping the bottom vigorously with a wooden spoon. Pour over the meat. Add the garlic, beef stock, and cherry tomato purée or canned tomatoes to the meat. Bring to a boil. Reduce heat and simmer for ½ hour, stirring occasionally. Add the ½ cup of water. Cook another hour.

Add the vegetables to the meat. Pour the red wine into the pan in which the vegetables were cooked, using a wooden spoon to scrape up any flour that remains in the pan. Add to the meat. Add the bay leaf, salt, and pepper. Simmer 3 to 4 minutes. Remove the bay leaf. Serve with potatoes or noodles.

TOTAL ROASTING TIME: 30 minutes plus 1 hour 40 minutes for simmering

Shank

BEEF SHANK IS an underused cut. It can be cut across into thick round pieces with the bone in the middle like the osso buco from a leg of veal. The meat can be cooked separately to serve in soup or a whole piece can be braised or boiled.

Boiled short ribs and beef shank

SERVES 4, WITH 4 DIVIDEND CUPS
BROTH FOR SOUP

TOTAL
ROASTING
TIME:
*see facing
page*

IT MAY SEEM odd to find what is essentially boiled beef in a book on roasting; but a thorough browning of the meat, which is most advantageously done in a hot oven, is an easy and essential technique for many boiled beef recipes in which the meat is meant to be eaten rather than simply tossed aside after stock is made. See also Oven Browning different cuts of meat and bones (page 231–235).

Once the meat and even some of the vegetables that go in the dish have been browned in the oven, the basic techniques are the same: no salt until the dish is almost finished (otherwise too many good juices are drawn from the meat), very low heat (otherwise the meat turns into a dish rag), and thorough and repeated skimming of the broth as it cooks to avoid incorporating the heavy flavor of beef fat into the broth.

I love boiled beef hot and cold and as a ready source of leftovers for salads and jellied dishes. One of the greatest joys of making boiled meats is the soup, not only the soup that you eat with the boiled meats, but also the dividends. For more information on soups and broths, see pages 222 through 230.

The liquid that remains in the pot can keep cooking. Replace the four cups of stock fed to the eaters with four cups of water. Cook for as long as you can, up to eight hours. This long cooking time allows more of the gelatin in the bones to come out, thickening and enriching the broth. For the last half hour of cooking time, add ½ cup celery tops and leaves; leaving the celery in longer can cloud the broth.

Use leftover meat in Shepherd's Pie (page 154) or Beef Hash with Tomatoes and Fresh Spinach (page 156).

½ teaspoon vegetable oil

1-pound beef shank with bone

2 medium yellow onions (about 1 pound), peeled

6 pieces beef short ribs (7¼ ounces each, 2¾ pounds total)

12-ounce veal knuckle, trimmed of most fat, split in half (have your butcher do this)

9 cups water

3 medium carrots, trimmed, peeled, and cut into 2-inch lengths

1 bay leaf

Place rack in center of oven. Heat oven to 500°F.

Using your hands, rub the oil into both sides of the beef shank. Put shank into an 18 x 12 x 2-inch roasting pan. Put the onions in the center of the pan. Arrange the short ribs and the veal knuckle, bone sides down, in the same pan so that none of the pieces of meat touch. Do not let the meat touch the sides of the pan.

Roast for 40 minutes. Remove the veal knuckle from the pan and put in the bottom of an 8-quart stockpot. Next put the boniest pieces of the ribs into the stockpot. Add remaining ribs. Put beef shank on top.

Turn onions over in the fat that has collected in the roasting pan. Return to oven and roast 5 more minutes. Add onions to stockpot.

Put roasting pan on top of stove over medium-high heat. Add 1 cup of the water and bring contents to a boil, scraping the bottom vigorously with a wooden spoon. Cook for 5 minutes. Add to stockpot. Add remaining water.

Bring to a boil, uncovered, over medium heat. This will take about 15 minutes. Just as the bubbles begin to break the surface, skim the fat off the top of the liquid. Reduce heat to a simmer. Skim periodically.

Cook 2½ hours, adding water as needed to keep liquid barely covering the food. Take all the meat out of the broth and reserve. At this stage the meat should be very tender. Leave the veal knuckle, bones, and onions. Cook 30 minutes more. Remove veal knuckle. Add carrots and bay leaf. Cook another 30 minutes. After cooking, carrots will be soft but not mushy. Remove carrots and reserve with meat. Skim again.

At this stage, a meal for 4 people is ready. Discard the bay leaf. Ladle 4 cups of the broth from the stockpot through a sieve. Pour broth over reserved meat and carrots. Meat will easily pull apart into 4 servings. Serve with boiled potatoes or noodles.

TOTAL ROASTING TIME: 45 minutes for browning plus 3 hours and 30 minutes for boiling

Shepherd's pie *(haché parmentier)*

SERVES 6

THE ENGLISH AND the French both use up boiled meats this way. Properly made with stiff mashed potatoes and well browned, it is a heavenly, not icky, leftover. If the potatoes seem watery after boiling, let them dry out a little bit in the pan on top of the stove before mashing. They can be put through the medium disc of a food mill if that is easier than using a potato masher.

Serve with a large spoon to get some of both layers on each plate.

FOR THE MASHED POTATOES

1¼ pounds baking potatoes (2 large), peeled and cut in half

⅓ cup milk

2 to 3 tablespoons unsalted butter

2½ teaspoons kosher salt

Freshly ground black pepper, to taste

FOR THE MEAT BASE

¾ to 1 pound leftover meat from Boiled Short Ribs and Beef Shank (page 152), meat shredded, gristle and tendon removed (2 cups)

1 small to medium onion (6 ounces), peeled and chopped fine (¾ cup)

2 tablespoons Worcestershire sauce

3 tablespoons drippings from Basic Beef Stock (page 224), or other softened fat

1½ tablespoons Dried Bread Crumbs (page 110)

Twenty minutes before you are ready to cook the pie, place oven rack on center level. Heat oven to 350°F.

Make the mashed potatoes first. Cook the potatoes in boiling water for about 25 minutes, until a sharp knife inserts easily into the flesh. Meanwhile, heat the milk and butter in small saucepan. Drain potatoes. Either pass potatoes through a food mill fitted with a medium disc or return to pot and mash with a potato masher. Gradually add the warmed milk and butter, mixing well. Add salt and pepper. Reserve.

In a medium bowl, put the shredded beef. Add the onion, Worcestershire, and 1 tablespoon of the drippings. Mix well. Add 1 cup of the mashed potatoes to meat mixture. Mix well.

Grease a 9½-inch deep-dish pie plate or dish with 1 tablespoon of the fat. Put meat mixture in the dish in an even layer. Top loosely with mashed potatoes. Sprinkle the top with bread crumbs. Dab top with remaining tablespoon of fat. Cook 45 minutes, or until top is golden brown.

Basic meat pie

SERVES 4 TO 6

THIS MEAT PIE can be made with any leftover roasted meat. Leg of lamb with lamb kidneys are sensational (see Lamb and Kidney Pie, page 200). Evidently veal and veal kidneys go together and can be cooked the same way. Often the pieces of roast leftovers are a bit overdone and can be slightly tough. They will soften up nicely in this recipe; but feel free as I do to use rare leftover meat. I like it made with roast beef even though the English version usually uses inferior rump steak and gives an inferior result.

When browning meat as here on top of the stove, do not use an enameled or coated pan. It will not work.

FOR THE CRUST

1 cup all-purpose flour

1 teaspoon sugar

Pinch of kosher salt

½ cup very cold vegetable shortening

1½ to 2 tablespoons ice water

FOR THE FILLING

12 ounces leftover roast beef, cut into 1-inch cubes (3 cups)

¼ cup chopped onions

1 tablespoon unsalted butter

1 veal kidney (9 ounces), trimmed of fat, cut in half lengthwise, internal fat and veins removed (page 217–218), and sectioned into lobes

5 white mushrooms (1 ounce each), stems trimmed and wiped clean, each mushroom cut into 6 wedges (2 cups)

1 tablespoon all-purpose flour

⅔ cup Basic Beef Stock (page 224)

1 teaspoon kosher salt

1 tablespoon Worcestershire sauce

8 grinds black pepper

FOR THE GLAZE

1 egg whisked together with 1 tablespoon milk or water

Combine the flour, sugar, and salt in a large cold bowl. Add the shortening. Use two knives to cut the shortening into the flour until the mixture is in pieces the size of large peas. Sprinkle the ice water over the flour mixture ½ tablespoon at a time, tossing with a fork, until the mixture is just moist enough to hold together when pressed. Wrap the dough in plastic wrap and refrigerate at least 30 minutes.

Place rack in center of oven. Heat oven to 450°F.

In a medium skillet, brown the meat and onions over medium-high heat, about 7 minutes. Transfer to a 1-quart ovenproof dish. Melt the butter in the same skillet over medium heat. Add kidney lobes and mushrooms. Cook, stirring frequently, until no blood oozes out of kidney, about 5 minutes. Sprinkle with flour. Cook 3 minutes, stirring. Add stock; stir. Add salt, Worcestershire, and pepper. Cook 5 minutes. Add mixture to meat and onions in dish.

Roll out dough for crust to a 6-inch round. Transfer to top of dish and cover steak and kidney mixture. Using your fingers, pinch round the edges to secure crust. Brush on egg glaze. Using a sharp knife, cut a few steam vents in crust. Cook for 10 minutes. Reduce heat to 350°F. Continue to cook for 20 to 25 more minutes until crust is golden brown. Serve warm.

Beef hash with tomatoes and fresh spinach

SERVES 4 AS A MAIN COURSE

VARIOUS KINDS OF hash are traditionally made with leftover meat that has been roasted or boiled and the boiled potatoes that may have accompanied them. I like to make this hash with rare roast beef and freshly boiled potatoes. It becomes very special. However, any of the leftover beef can be used. The inclusion of tomatoes and spinach makes it a complete meal as well as a very attractive one.

After the potatoes are cooked and cubed, there should be four cups. That's what is needed if leftover potatoes are used.

Using a nonstick skillet—a great modern invention—permits the hash to be easily turned out. It is important not to turn the hash too often once all the liquid has been added, or the potatoes can get mashed, and there will be less crust. It is important to keep the heat lowish for the final cooking, or the hash can burn. I keep my nose alert. If there is any acrid smell, I immediately turn the heat even lower.

1½ pounds boiling potatoes	6 ounces fresh spinach leaves, tightly packed (2 cups)
2 tablespoons vegetable oil	
2 tablespoons unsalted butter	2 teaspoons kosher salt
1 medium onion (8 ounces), peeled and cut into ¼-inch dice (1¼ cups)	Freshly ground black pepper, to taste
	¾ cup Roasted Plum Tomato Sauce (page 419), or drained and crushed canned plum tomatoes
10 ounces leftover roast beef, cut into ½-inch cubes (1¾ cups)	

Place potatoes in a medium pot with 2 quarts water. Cover. Bring to a boil over high heat and cook until just tender, about 25 minutes. Drain and refrigerate until cold. (If you are in a hurry, the potatoes can be chilled in a water bath with lots of ice. Potatoes may be prepared up to 2 days ahead). Pull skins off potatoes and cut into ½-inch cubes.

Heat oil and butter in a 12-inch nonstick skillet over medium-high heat. Add onion and cook until translucent, about 5 minutes. Add potatoes and cook until brown, about 15 minutes. As potatoes begin to brown, use a spatula to turn mixture over occasionally, rather than stirring, so that pieces do not break up and turn to mush.

Add cubed roast beef and continue to cook about 5 minutes, folding occasionally, until any cubes with a raw or red side are all lightly browned. Add spinach, salt, and pepper and cook until spinach wilts and any extra liquid is evaporated, about 2 minutes.

Mix in ¼ cup of the tomato sauce. Cook about 2 minutes, adding remaining sauce in ¼ cup increments, cooking until liquid is absorbed. Turn heat to low and press hash into an even layer, filling the bottom of the pan like a pancake. Cook without turning or stirring until set, about 15 minutes. Remove from heat and turn out onto a round serving dish so that the crusty brown side is on top. Total cooking time is about 50 minutes.

Beef salad with horseradish dressing

MAKES ABOUT 3 CUPS; SERVES 3 AS A MAIN
COURSE, 6 AS A FIRST COURSE

THIS IS A way of using leftover roast beef if it doesn't all disappear in snatches and sandwiches. This salad can also be made with the leftover meat from making Basic Beef Stock (page 224), Boiled Brisket (page 145), or Boiled Short Ribs and Beef Shank (page 152). It is one of my standards, going all the way back to *Food for Friends.* Serve it on crisp leaves of romaine.

1½ pounds leftover roast beef, cut into ¾-inch cubes (3 cups)	1⅛ cups Basic Mayonnaise (page 303) or store-bought
2½ tablespoons finely sliced chives	Kosher salt, to taste
6 tablespoons drained prepared horseradish	Freshly ground black pepper, to taste

Place the beef and chives in a large mixing bowl.

In a separate bowl, mix the horseradish with the mayonnaise. Pour the dressing over the beef and chives, stirring to combine. Add salt and pepper.

Serve at room temperature.

Elegant Asian beef soup

MAKES ABOUT 12 CUPS;
SERVES 8 AS A LIGHT MEAL,
10 TO 12 AS A PARTY OPENER

THIS IS A takeoff from Vietnamese beef broth, pho, with dry Japanese noodles. The flavors are pleasantly complex and well balanced. The soup is good enough to start the most elegant of dinner parties. When the party is to be elegant, I do a most untraditional thing and break the noodles into pieces before cooking them. This saves the ties and favorite silk shirts of my friends. Informal, slurp.

If there are fewer leftovers, it may help to know that each portion uses a whole two-and-a-half- to three-ounce package of the noodles. If it is easier, substitute rice vermicelli, as in Beef Soup with Lemongrass and Rice Vermicelli (page 159). The noodles used here can be cooked ahead; but be sure to cover them amply with water while they sit, or they will get gummy.

8 cups Basic Beef Stock (page 224)

2 teaspoons sugar

1 whole star anise, petals separated and crushed in a mortar with pestle

7 grinds fresh black pepper

One 2-inch piece cinnamon stick

1½ pounds kuzu kiri (potato starch) thick Japanese noodles

1 bunch whole sprigs fresh cilantro, rinsed

3 tablespoons nuoc mam (fish sauce)

3 to 4 teaspoons kosher salt

Put beef stock in a medium saucepan. Add sugar, anise, 3 grinds of the pepper, and the cinnamon. Cook, covered, over low heat for 30 minutes. Strain stock through a fine sieve and return to saucepan.

Meanwhile, cook the noodles in boiling water for 8 minutes. Strain and rinse well with cold running water. Cut noodles into 3- to 4-inch pieces. Add noodles to strained stock. Add cilantro, fish sauce, salt, and remaining pepper. Cook over medium heat until warm throughout, about 4 to 5 minutes. Serve warm in individual bowls.

Beef soup with lemongrass and rice vermicelli

MAKES 10 CUPS; SERVES 8

Fabulous perfumes come from Vietnamese and other Asian soup pots. One of the best smells comes from lemongrass. Watch out. Sometimes even reputable markets will sell only the green shoots. What is wanted is the bulbous end. Better to buy overly dry lemongrass than nonaromatic stalks. If the lemongrass is dry, double the quantity and tie it in a piece of cheesecloth so that it can be removed at the end of the cooking, avoiding the hay-in-mouth feel. Here is my somewhat Western version, using leftover beef and a fabulous rich beef stock. If there is more beef on hand, it can be added.

There are many fish sauces out there. Some may be called nam pla instead of nuoc mam. It depends on the country they come from and the language spoken. The chili oil should be available in supermarkets, or make a run to an Asian market and stock up on all these basic ingredients as well as the noodles, which keep forever on the shelf.

8 cups Basic Beef Stock (page 224)

1 whole star anise, petals separated and crushed in a mortar with a pestle

One 2-inch piece cinnamon stick

Two ¼-inch slices of fresh gingerroot, peeled and cut across into thin pieces

8 ounces rice vermicelli noodles

1 root-end stalk fresh lemongrass

¾ cup leftover boiled beef from Basic Beef Stock, coarsely chopped or shredded

¼ cup nuoc mam (fish sauce)

1 teaspoon chili oil

1 teaspoon (1 to 2 small cloves) finely chopped garlic

3 to 4 teaspoons kosher salt

Scant grind fresh black pepper

2½ tablespoons fresh lime juice

3 tablespoons chopped scallions, white and green parts, for garnish

¼ cup chopped fresh cilantro, for garnish

Put beef stock in a medium saucepan. Add anise, cinnamon, and ginger. Cook, covered, over low heat for 30 minutes. Strain stock through a fine sieve and return to saucepan.

Meanwhile, soak the noodles in boiling, or very hot, water for 10 minutes. Strain and rinse with cool running water.

To prepare the lemongrass, first remove the dry husk. Trim ¼ inch off bulb-shaped end of stalk. Smash the cut end with the flat side of a large knife. Cut up the bulb in 1-inch strips. Then cut across in a small dice until there is 1 heaping tablespoon. Reserve.

Add noodles to strained stock. Add beef, fish sauce, lemongrass, chili oil, and garlic. Cook, covered, over medium heat. Once it comes to a simmer, cook for 5 minutes. Remove from heat. Add salt, pepper, and lime juice. Serve warm in individual bowls, topping each with scallion and cilantro.

pORK

PORK COMES IN TWO BASIC FASHIONS, FRESH AND PRESERVED. The preserved is either salt cured or smoked, most commonly as ham. I roast only the fresh cuts, including suckling pig.

Today's fresh pork is raised in such a way as to be much leaner than that available to our ancestors, and recipes have had to change to accommodate the leaner meat. Some cuts such as shoulder and spareribs, which are addressed later, are fatty. Whatever cut is bought, the butcher should also provide the leftover bones, which can be roasted along with the meat to enrich the gravy and be gnawed on, or roasted separately for informal food or to provide a base for a stock.

When it's boneless and without much fat, I like pork cooked at high heat until the meat registers only about 140° to 150°F, which is safe. If cook or diner cannot bear to see a trace of pink, pork can be roasted to 160°F, and I sometimes do this to assure even cooking on larger cuts; but I don't recommend it for the most desirable boneless small roasts, as the meat dries. To have safe temperatures and even cooking, it is essential that the meat be at room temperature before going into the oven. There is much less shrinkage with high-heat cooking than with older methods.

Both rack and boneless loin will take about forty-five minutes, no matter how long they are. The rack, because of bone conductivity, will reach a higher internal temperature. That is fine as both the bones and the somewhat heavier surface fat keep the meat moist.

Pork goes well with assertive flavors, spices, acids, and sweetness. It doesn't like timidity. There are various fruit accompaniments to pork here. I like pears so well that I give two versions. The Roasted Pears with Asian Glaze (page 434) that I serve with a loin can be used with any other cut. The Ginger and Fermented Black Bean Sauce (page 308) is a delight with a simple pork roast, as are the roasted cabbage recipes. For a change, use one of the dressings (aka stuffings) on pages 108–119 that are usually used with birds. If pork stock is available, it can be used in the dressing instead of bird stock. Hot roast pork goes well with duck sauces (replace duck stock or deglazing liquid with the deglazing liquid from pork or pork stock) and other cold or hot sauces on pages 292–309. For cold leftovers, consider the more flavorful, full-bodied sauces and the mayonnaise-based sauces.

Leftover roast pork loin, rack, or fresh ham can be used in all the leftover pork recipes. Roasted shoulder leftovers are probably better kept for use in hot dishes such as Pork Bolognese (page 180).

Rack

THIS IS THE pig equivalent of a standing rib roast of beef. It is much less common, but much cheaper, delicious, and a great showpiece for a dinner party. I served it to a very fancy crowd with the Sauté of Mushrooms (page 163) and an aged Côte du Rhône. It was received as a gourmet treat.

The whole racks I have been getting have ten chops and are fourteen inches long and seven inches wide, with a three-inch eye before cooking. If a smaller roast is wanted, a shorter piece should be bought. The roasting remains the same. The final internal temperature on this is higher than other pork roasts I make since the density of the bone and the unevenness of the shape can otherwise result in parts of the meat being underdone. The bone juices will keep it from drying out.

It is very important to have a good understanding with one's butcher in order to be able to serve this without a hassle.

Roast rack of pork

TOTAL
ROASTING
TIME:
45
minutes

I FIRST MADE this for Anna Tasca Lanza of Regaliali, in Sicily. Of course, I used her wine, although other nights brought out a Beaucastel. That night I served the mushroom sauté (page 163). A less expensive and equally good solution is to roast potatoes or turnips around the meat for part of the time.

To roast potatoes in the same pan as the rack, cut two and a half pounds of peeled or well-scrubbed baking potatoes into eight wedges each. Place them in the pan with the rack and cook together, turning the potatoes every fifteen minutes.

To roast turnips in the same pan as the rack, cut one pound of peeled turnips into six wedges each. After the rack has cooked for twenty minutes, place them in the pan with the rack and cook together, turning the turnips after fifteen minutes.

7¾- to 8-pound rack of pork loin, with most of the chine bone removed and rack cracked between chops for easy carving

1 bunch fresh sage (1 ounce), leaves removed; ¼ cup of the leaves rolled and cut across in thin strips to make about 3 tablespoons, about 10 whole leaves reserved or use dried (see Note)

Kosher salt, to taste

Freshly ground black pepper, to taste

½ cup red wine, for deglazing

¾ cup Basic Pork Stock (page228), for deglazing

Place rack at second level from the bottom. Heat oven to 500°F.

Between each of the chops, tuck a whole sage leaf. Sprinkle all sides with salt and pepper. Put pork, curving rib bones side down, in an 18 x 12 x 2-inch roasting pan. If the tips are left up in the air, they will overcook. Roast for 45 minutes. A meat thermometer should read 160°F or more. Remove pork to a serving platter.

Pour or spoon off any fat from the pan. Put pan on top of the stove over medium-high heat. Add the wine and stock and bring to a boil. Stir constantly with a wooden spoon, scraping to deglaze. Add the reserved sage leaves. Let liquid reduce by half. Salt and pepper, being careful to allow for possible salt in stock. Pour into a sauceboat and serve on the side. Bring rack whole to the table to allow your guests to ooh and aah. Carve at the table by slicing the chops apart.

NOTE: Be careful; dried sage is much stronger than fresh. As it should not be dominant, only rub a tiny bit of rubbed sage between the chops with your finger and use ¼ teaspoon in the sauce when substituting.

Sauté of mushrooms

WHILE I LIKE this with pork, it goes with venison and roast beef as well. It also makes a fine first course for four to six over Roasted Bread (page 367) or Hard Polenta (page 164) or as a pasta sauce. I add Soft Polenta (page 164) when serving these mushrooms with a roast.

I must confess to having originally made this with forest-gathered wild mushrooms as well as expensive purchased fresh morels and hen of the woods. This is a less expensive version, but still not cheap and just fine. See page 361 for a description of mushrooms. There are a lot of mushrooms to start with as they shrink incredibly while cooking and concentrating in taste.

As the mushrooms are moved around the hot pan, the raw ones will squeak as they hit it. Remember that the first batch of mushrooms must reduce enough so that the second batch can fit in the pan. When adding mushrooms, lift the better done ones from the bottom so that the new ones make contact with the pan—sort of like folding in egg whites. The pan will look dry; don't worry; moisture will appear like rain from a summer sky. The parsley must be fully cooked to lose its leathery texture and grassy taste. Don't throw it on at the end.

2 cups Extra-Rich Beef Stock (page 227)

1 ounce dried porcini mushrooms, broken into pieces (about ½ cup)

¼ pound (1 stick) unsalted butter

10 shallots (4 to 5 ounces), peeled and chopped fine (about 1 cup)

3 pounds button mushrooms, wiped clean, stems snapped off and finely chopped, caps cut into quarters

1 bunch fresh flat-leaf parsley, washed, leaves chopped fine (about 1 cup)

1½ pounds portobello mushrooms, wiped clean, stems snapped off and finely chopped, caps cut into pieces similar to quartered button mushrooms above

1 bunch fresh flat-leaf parsley, washed, leaves chopped fine (about 1 cup)

1 teaspoon kosher salt

½ bunch (½ ounce) fresh tarragon, leaves removed

Freshly ground black pepper, to taste

Heat 1 cup of the meat stock. Add dried porcinis. Leave to rehydrate off the heat at least 15 minutes. Strain through a very fine sieve or several layers of cheesecloth. Reserve strained liquid in a small bowl. Place porcinis in the sieve again and rinse under cool water to remove all grit. Cut into small pieces and add to reserved liquid.

continued

In a deep 12-inch-wide sauté pan, melt the butter over medium heat. Add shallots. Cook, stirring occasionally, until translucent. Add all chopped mushroom stems. Lower the heat a little and cook 20 minutes, or until the stems are very soft.

Add button mushroom caps. Using a folding motion, as if for egg whites, turn mushrooms over from the bottom until they are all moistened. Cook, turning continually, until they are very soft, not al dente, and until the mixture collapses in pan and reduces by half. Cook 20 more minutes. Add the parsley, stirring thoroughly, until evenly distributed and no longer bright green, about 1 to 2 minutes.

Add the portobello mushroom caps, using a folding motion as before to blend them in and moisten them. Cook over medium-high heat for 10 minutes. Add reserved porcinis and liquid. Rinse out bowl with a little warm water to get all of the glaze and add to pan. Add remaining 1 cup of stock.

Lower heat to prevent gelatin-rich stock from burning. Add salt, being careful to compensate for possible saltiness of stock.

The mushrooms have now cooked about 1 hour. May be reserved at this point for several hours. When ready to serve, warm over low heat, stirring occasionally. Add the tarragon. Stir to mix in. When hot, add pepper.

Polenta, soft or hard

MAKES ABOUT 6 CUPS; SERVES 6

IF MAKING HARD polenta, omit the cream and reduce the butter to four tablespoons. This way the polenta holds its shape after it has cooled, enabling it to be cleanly sliced.

Serve this with the Sauté of Mushrooms (page 163) or Lamb and Apple "Hash" (page 196), spooning either one over the polenta

Somehow, we managed to give away the credit for our birthright, cornmeal mush, to the Italians. Let's take it back and eat it.

6½ cups water	6 tablespoons melted unsalted butter for soft polenta, or 4 tablespoons melted unsalted butter for hard polenta
1 tablespoon kosher salt	
1 cup yellow cornmeal	
¾ to 1 cup heavy cream for soft polenta (omit if making hard polenta)	Freshly ground black pepper, to taste
	Kosher salt, to taste

Bring 5 cups of the water to a boil over medium-high heat in a large, heavy-bottomed pot. Add the tablespoon of salt. In a large bowl, stir the cornmeal into the remaining 1½ cups cold water. Pour into the boiling water. Stir while boiling, approximately 30 minutes. The mixture should pull away from the sides of the pan and be able to hold its shape.

For Soft Polenta: Over low heat, stir in the cream and butter. Continue to stir until the mixture is smooth and creamy. Add pepper and salt to taste. Serve immediately.

For Hard Polenta: Over low heat, stir in 2 tablespoons of the butter. Add pepper and salt to taste. Lightly grease a 7 x 4 x 2-inch loaf pan with 1 tablespoon butter. Pour polenta into pan and brush lightly with the last of the butter. Let stand until cool. Cover and refrigerate until chilled.

To serve, slice the polenta about ½ inch thick and set slices on a wire rack to dry for about 20 minutes. Grill, broil, or fry the slices until brown and crisp.

Loin

OF ALL THE pork cuts, boned and rolled loin is my favorite—the most luxurious and easiest to roast. The butcher does the boning, rolling, and tying and gives me the bones. Just as the rack is made of the ten rib chops, the loin is made of the ten center loin chops. When cut into chops, the loin has two separate muscles running on either side of the rib bones, just like a T-bone steak. There is some round tenderloin and some of the eye. The bones have the typical T shape.

I buy as much of the boned center—cut in one piece, not in chops—as I need by the inch, like yard goods, allowing three quarters to an inch of raw meat per serving, depending on how much else there is to eat. It takes about thirty minutes to come to room temperature. When the roast is cooked and shrinks slightly, I cut it into half-inch slices.

I snip off the strings in the kitchen before bringing it to the table, where the roast is easily sliced. If, while cooking, I have surrounded the pork with the bones, which will now be crisp, brown, and enticing, and the meal is informal, I give the bones to those as greedy as I. Otherwise, they go into the stockpot.

There are several recipes in this section for roast loin of pork. It's a quick and economical way to serve my family or a crowd, and the seasonings can be varied. A recipe of Herb Rub (page 293) is enough for a large loin of pork. Try rubbing cracked coriander seeds, ground cumin, and salt on the outside of the roast. Deglaze the pan with a little Basic Beef Stock (page 224). If desired, roast only with salt and pepper and follow instructions for Onion-Rhubarb Sauce (page 176), dividing ingredients in half.

All the roasted root vegetables and cabbages are perfect with pork. Cold leftovers, thinly sliced, make marvelous sandwiches with mustard, mayonnaise, and lettuce. Other leftovers can go into any of the recipes on pages 179–182.

Garlic roast pork loin

MAKES 10 GENEROUS SLICES;
SERVES 8 TO 10

TOTAL
ROASTING
TIME:
45 to 50
minutes

THIS IS THE very model of a happy recipe. Aside from my roast chicken, I would say that it has been the most used of my roasting recipes. To vary it, see the recipes that follow or the preceding introduction to pork loin. If serving with the delicious Sauerkraut Noodles (page 172), don't use the rosemary.

No noodles? Roast potatoes in the same pan as the loin. Cut two and a half pounds of peeled baking potatoes into eight wedges each, or the same amount of large, peeled boiling potatoes (see page 387 for varieties) into quarters. After the loin has cooked ten minutes, place the wedges around the loin, turning to coat with fat. Cook together, turning the potatoes every fifteen minutes. If using rosemary in the pork, sprinkle a little on the potatoes for the last few minutes of cooking.

To roast turnips in the same pan, cut one pound of peeled turnips into six wedges each. After the loin has cooked for twenty-five minutes, place them in the pan with the loin and the potatoes, if using, and cook together, turning the turnips after fifteen minutes.

Either potatoes or turnips will absorb much of the fat and possibly some of what would be used for deglazing liquid. To replace the sauce, serve with soupy Sauerkraut Noodles.

2½- to 3½-pound boned and rolled pork loin (8 to 10 inches long), bones kept, if available

4 cloves garlic, smashed, peeled, and cut lengthwise into thin slivers

A few sprigs of rosemary, optional

Kosher salt, to taste

Freshly ground black pepper, to taste

½ cup wine, for deglazing

Place rack in center of oven. Heat oven to 500°F.

With the point of a paring knife, make ½-inch slits toward the center all around the roast. Insert the garlic in the slits, accompanied by a needle of rosemary, if using. Rub roast generously with salt and pepper.

Place roast and bones, if available, in a roasting pan just large enough to hold them. Roast for 45 to 50 minutes, or until meat reaches an internal temperature of 140°F. The meat might still be slightly pink, but this is fine. Don't overcook the roast, or it will be dry and unappealing.

Remove roast and bones to a platter. Let meat rest before slicing aross, while preparing the sauce. Snip off strings. Juices will collect better in a platter than on a cutting board.

Place the pan on top of the stove over high heat. Add wine and let come to a boil. Scrape pan with wooden spoon to remove glaze that will flavor sauce. Cook until reduced by half. Serve in a sauceboat or a bowl along with the roast.

Roast pork loin with Asian glaze

SERVES 8 TO 10

TOTAL ROASTING TIME: 45 *to* 50 *minutes*

BROWN AND RICH, this roast and glaze are dependent on good ginger. Pick another recipe if it is unavailable. Good ginger will have smooth, shiny skin that is light in color and spurt juice when it is cut. Be sure to follow the glaze instructions and add the liquid to the solids in steps. This is necessary to get the ginger and garlic really smooth.

This recipe is essentially the same as the Garlic Roast Pork Loin (page 166), but with the Asian Glaze poured over the pork loin. Cook and serve with an appropriate number of Roasted Pears with Asian Glaze (page 434). Increase the Asian Glaze recipe as needed to have enough on hand for both the pears and the pork.

The bones go unused. Freeze to make stock for deglazing or for bean soup.

2½- to 3½-pound boned and rolled pork loin (8 to 10 inches long), bones reserved for Basic Pork Stock (page 228)

4 cloves garlic, smashed, peeled, and cut lengthwise into thin slivers

1 recipe Asian Glaze (page 33)

½ cup Basic Pork Stock or water, for deglazing

With the point of a paring knife, make ½-inch slits toward the center all around the roast. Insert the garlic in the slits. Place in pan just large enough to hold the meat. Pour Asian Glaze over the roast, using your hands to rub it in well. Allow to marinate at room temperature for 30 minutes.

Place rack in center of oven. Heat oven to 500°F.

Roast meat 45 to 50 minutes, or until meat reaches an internal temperature of 140°F. The meat might still be slightly pink, but this is fine. Don't overcook the roast, or it will be dry and unappealing.

Remove roast to a platter. Snip off strings. Let meat rest before slicing and while preparing the sauce. Place the pan on top of the stove over high heat. Add stock or water and let come to a boil. Scrape pan with a wooden spoon to disolve glaze. Cook until reduced by half. Serve in a sauceboat.

Roast pork loin with roasted apple compote

SERVES 6

TOTAL
ROASTING
TIME:
45 to 50
minutes

Far better than the usual apple-sauce, these apple wedges turn a rich dark brown along with the roast. They have just the right amount of bite, coupled with an innate sweetness, to be a perfect counterpoint for the pork. The cream and extra mustard are for those—often me—for whom a little too much is just enough. Much too much would be piling the plate with another vegetable—like introducing a stranger into a bridal bed.

If adding the optional ingredients, don't stir. Mix the mustard with the cream; pour over the apples, and turn the apples from the bottom in the cream. The sections are soft and fragile.

2¼-pound boned and rolled pork loin
(7 inches long), bones reserved for
Basic Pork Stock (page 228)

1 teaspoon kosher salt

1 tablespoon Dijon mustard

4 large (2 pounds) Granny Smith apples,
peeled, cored, and each cut into
8 wedges and tossed with lemon juice

⅓ cup fresh lemon juice

1 tablespoon canola or other neutral oil

½ cup heavy cream, optional

1 tablespoon Dijon mustard, optional

Place rack on second level from bottom of oven. Heat oven to 500°F.

Place loin in a 14 x 12 x 2-inch roasting pan. Rub salt all over loin. Smear mustard over top of loin. Roast for 20 minutes. Move the loin around with a wooden spatula so it won't stick. Roast 15 minutes more. Add the apples coated with lemon juice and oil, and collected juices. Spread out around the loin. Roast 10 minutes. Turn apples gently, as they are soft. Roast 10 minutes more. In total the loin should roast for 50 minutes, or until meat reaches an internal temperature of 140°F. The meat might still be slightly pink, but this is fine. Don't overcook the roast, or it will be dry and unappealing. The apples will be dark brown and will have absorbed all the good juices.

Remove loin to a platter. Snip off strings. If using cream and mustard, combine and stir carefully into apples. Let meat rest 10 to 15 minutes before slicing. Carefully remove apples with a metal spatula and place around roast. Deglaze the pan (page 10) just to clean it, as all the good bits are in the apples.

Roast pork loin in onion-rhubarb sauce

SERVES 8

TOTAL
ROASTING
TIME:
see below

EVEN THOUGH PORK is not as fatty as it once was, it still welcomes a somewhat acid sauce. Come spring and the pushing up in the garden or the arrival in the market of the first rosy stems of rhubarb, what may often seem a wintry meat is transformed into a sunny presence.

3½-pound boned and rolled pork loin (10 inches long), bones reserved for Basic Pork Stock (page 228)

2 teaspoons kosher salt

Freshly ground black pepper, to taste

1 pound onions (3 medium), peeled, halved, and thinly sliced (3 cups)

1¼ pounds rhubarb stalks, trimmed and cut on the diagonal into ⅛-inch-thick slices (3 cups)

½ cup liquid

Place rack in center of oven. Heat oven to 500°F.

Rub loin generously with salt and sprinkle with pepper.

Place in a roasting pan just large enough to hold it. Cook 50 minutes, or until meat reaches an internal temperature of 140°F. The meat might still be slightly pink, but this is fine. Don't overcook the roast, or it will be dry and unappealing.

Transfer roast to a platter. Snip off strings. Pour off all but 1½ tablespoons excess fat. Place the pan on top of the stove over medium heat. Add onions. Cook until onions are golden brown, about 10 minutes. Add rhubarb. Cook 10 minutes, until soft but not soggy, scraping pan with wooden spoon to scoop up crispy bits that will flavor sauce. Add ½ cup liquid (juices that have collected on the serving platter and/or water or cream) and stir to combine. Cook until hot throughout. Season to taste. Serve in a sauceboat or bowl with the roast.

TOTAL ROASTING TIME: 50 minutes plus 30 minutes for cooking the sauce

Roast pork loin stuffed with prunes

SERVES 6 TO 8

TOTAL
ROASTING
TIME:
40 _to_ 50
minutes

S OUTHWESTERN FRANCE IS the home of some of the world's best prunes and Armagnac, a local brandy. They go together brilliantly and lend a rich, complex flavor to pork. Cognac, or another brandy, or Port can be used instead. Be sure to use a little of the same liquor or wine when deglazing the pan.

The prunes must be soaked ahead—overnight. I court my butcher so that I can take the prunes over there and get the prunes tucked into the pocket before the loin is rolled. If this isn't possible, ask the butcher to at least cut a two-and-a-half-inch-deep pocket lengthwise through the loin; this is where the prunes go. After tucking in the prunes in a tidy line, corset the loin with string to make a neat roll.

The roast may smoke after twenty minutes; it's not burning, it's the sugar from the prunes. If vegetables are cooked in the same pan at the same time, the smoking problem will go away, and the vegetables will benefit from all those good flavors (see Note).

¼ cup Cognac, Armagnac, or Port

¾ cup pitted prunes

2½ teaspoons kosher salt

Freshly ground black pepper, to taste

1 teaspoon dried thyme

2½-pound boneless pork loin (8 inches long), unrolled, 2½-inch pocket cut across the length of the inside of the loin

FOR DEGLAZING

¼ cup Cognac, Armagnac, or Port to match the prune soaking liquid

¼ cup Basic Pork Stock (page 228) or Basic Chicken Stock (page 42) or canned

Pour ¼ cup of Cognac, Armagnac, or Port over the prunes. Cover and refrigerate overnight. Add ½ teaspoon of the salt, 4 grinds fresh pepper, and ½ teaspoon of the thyme to the prunes.

Place loin on work surface, pocket facing up. Stuff the prunes inside the pocket, so that they run along the length of the loin in a thin line. Don't let them glob up in the middle of the loin. Roll the loin and tie with kitchen string.

Rub loin generously with salt, pepper, and thyme.

Place rack in center of oven. Heat oven to 500°F.

Place loin in a roasting pan just large enough to hold it. Roast for 40 minutes, or until meat reaches an internal temperature of 140°F. The meat might still be slightly pink, but this is fine. For meat without any trace of pink, roast for 50 minutes, or until internal temperature reaches 160°F. Don't overcook the roast, or it will be dry and unappealing.

Remove roast to a platter. Snip off strings. Pour or spoon off excess fat from roasting pan. Place pan on stove over medium-high heat. Add remaining Cognac and stock, scraping pan with wooden spoon to scoop up crispy bits that will flavor sauce. Serve in a sauceboat with the roast.

NOTE: *To roast endive,* put one whole head (if the heads are large) for every two persons or one small head per person right in the roasting pan with the pork. The endive will roast as long as the loin; just turn each head every 15 minutes.

To roast carrots, peel 1½ pounds and slice into 1-inch-long and ½-inch-thick pieces. Add the carrots to the pan after the pork has cooked 20 minutes. Turn once, after 15 minutes, so they will brown nicely on both sides.

To roast turnips in the same pan, cut 1 pound of turnips into 6 wedges each. After the loin has roasted for 15 minutes, place the turnips in the pan with the loin and cook together, turning the turnips after 15 minutes.

Pork tenderloin

FOR YEARS, I ate pork tenderloin only as part of a boned and rolled loin of pork. However, in recent years I have discovered that tenderloins can be bought on their own as a long, round, skinny piece of meat—the same cut as a whole fillet of beef, but much smaller. They are tender, make neat, even slices after roasting, and are nutritionally about the equivalent of skinned chicken breast, having no fat.

Each tenderloin weighs about a pound. Some stores sell these two to a package, which is enough for a small dinner party. As many as three whole tenderloins can be cooked side by side in a single roasting pan, making enough for eight to nine. Since pork tenderloin is healthful, cooks quickly, and costs about a third as much as veal or beef fillet, it's a wonder it isn't served more often. The meat remains far moister cooked whole than cut across into medallions.

Sauerkraut noodles

MAKES 4½ TO 5 CUPS; SERVES 6 TO 8

AN ENCHANTINGLY AROMATIC dish of noodles to go with any simple pork roast. If by any chance the pork overcooked slightly and got dry, this will remedy the problem. Try making this as a medium for reheating leftover slices of roast.

5½ cups (½ pound) medium egg noodles

¼ pound (1 stick) unsalted butter

1½ teaspoons hot paprika or
    1½ tablespoons sweet paprika and
    ¼ teaspoon cayenne pepper

1 teaspoon caraway seeds

1 cup drained sauerkraut

Kosher salt, to taste

Freshly ground black pepper, to taste

Sauerkraut juice, if necessary

Boil egg noodles in salted water until cooked but firm. Drain and reserve.

Meanwhile, over low heat, melt 2 tablespoons of butter in a 12-inch skillet. Add paprika or paprika and cayenne and cook, stirring, for 1½ minutes.

Add remaining ingredients and cook until heated through and slightly swimmy. Add noodles. Add extra sauerkraut juice, if necessary.

Roasted pork tenderloins Tangiers

SERVES 6

TOTAL
ROASTING
TIME:
20
minutes

WHY TANGIERS? WELL, it sounds romantic, and the warm-tasting spices, small in quantity though they may seem, give an aroma and flavor that is distinctly reminiscent of the Middle East. Do not season the meat ahead; it will lose too much juice. Twenty minutes after the oven is hot, this easily made and simply sauced main course is ready. Rice, I think, maybe a pilaf with some raisins, would go along well.

Slice each tenderloin across into nine pieces, serving three to each eater.

1 teaspoon kosher salt

¼ teaspoon ground cinnamon

¼ teaspoon ground cardamom

8 to 10 grinds fresh black pepper

Two 1-pound pork tenderloins (each 10 inches long and 2½ inches in diameter)

2 teaspoons olive oil

½ cup Basic Pork Stock (page 228), wine, or water, for deglazing

Place rack on second level from bottom in oven. Heat oven to 500 °F.

Combine the salt, cinnamon, cardamom, and pepper in a small bowl.

Place tenderloins side by side in a 12 x 8 x 1½-inch roasting pan. Using your fingers, rub half the dry seasonings on all surfaces of one tenderloin. Smear all over with half the oil. Repeat with remaining seasonings, tenderloin, and oil. Roast for 10 minutes. Turn each tenderloin over. Roast 10 minutes more.

Transfer tenderloins to a serving platter. Pour off any fat in pan. Place over high heat. Add liquid, boil, and scrape to deglaze. Check the seasoning and add salt and pepper, if desired. Serve warm.

Shoulder

THE SHOULDER IS adjacent to the loin, and there is little reason it shouldn't make a delicious roast except that it is awkwardly bony. If the butcher bones it and ties it up neatly, it will make an excellent roast, somewhat fattier than the others. Shoulder requires a little more attention to cooking temperatures than the other pork roasts, which can pretty much be left alone. Shoulder is very fatty. Reducing the temperature reduces the smoking as does removing excess fat from the pan twice. Frankly, I just pour the fat off—not into plastic—but the fastidious can spoon. Following this technique will lead to evenly cooked, moist meat.

The shoulder is often divided into two cuts: the Boston butt, about four pounds, boned, and the picnic ham, a little over two pounds. The butt is fattier than the picnic ham. Either can be roasted on its own. Roast the butt only twenty minutes after removing the fat the first time. Roast the ham only twenty minutes after removing fat from the pan once. It should be ready; but take its temperature and add more time if needed. Oddly, these fattier cuts will still be very faintly pink at 160°F, but perfect.

Whatever size or cut, these take any of the dry seasonings of the various pork loin recipes. Choose vegetables with a strong taste and little sauce to go with this flavorful and rather moist cut, such as Roasted Rutabaga Wedges (page 403) in winter, or Honey-Glazed Turnip Wedges (page 424) in spring.

Roasted boneless pork shoulder

SERVES 8 TO 10

TOTAL
ROASTING
TIME:
2
hours
5
minutes

THE WHOLE BONELESS shoulder will make a chunky roast almost eight inches square and three inches thick. To carve it after roasting, I simply slice it across into half-inch-thick slices, which I halve across the middle for easier plating. If the butcher is really obliging, ask for the removed bones to be cut into smallish pieces. Place the bones around the meat for the final hour or so of roasting. This will be a great contribution to your deglazing sauce.

As this makes an ample amount, there may be substantial leftovers. A third of a pound of leftover meat will provide over three cups of the pasta sauce Pork Bolognese (page 180). More leftover meat makes a larger batch of sauce. Freeze some for another day.

6¼-pound boneless pork shoulder, rolled and tied, or 1 butt
Kosher salt, to taste
Freshly ground black pepper, to taste

Garlic, herbs, or other dry seasonings (see pork loin recipes, pages 165–171), optional
1½ cups water, for deglazing

Place oven rack at second level from the bottom. Heat oven to 500°F.

Season pork and place, fattiest side up, in a 14 x 12 x 2-inch roasting pan. Roast for 20 minutes. Reduce oven temperature to 450°F. Roast an additional 40 minutes. Remove excess fat from pan. Add bones, if available, to pan. Roast 45 minutes more. Remove excess fat from pan. Roast 20 minutes more, or until internal temperature reaches 160°F.

Remove roast to a platter. Snip off strings. Reserve the bones to add to Basic Pork Stock (page 228). Pour any remaining fat from the pan. Deglaze (page 10) over high heat. Boil until reduced by a third. Check seasonings and serve.

Fresh ham

SOME PEOPLE GET confused by the fact that a leg of pork is called a ham, even though it is neither brined nor smoked. Once cooked, it is a delicious cut of meat with crisp crackling skin. The leg is very large. I almost never cook a whole one. Instead, I cook a shank end—the half of the ham with the bone sticking out—as I do with a smoked ham. Smoked ham is not included here, as my favorite way of cooking it is a combination of poaching and oven baking.

Roast fresh ham with onion-rhubarb sauce

SERVES 8 TO 10; MAKES 4 CUPS SAUCE

TOTAL ROASTING TIME: see page 176

A SHANK END of ham weighs a good nine pounds. It is usually enough—depending on how much else is served, particularly at a buffet—to serve as many as fourteen. While the piece of meat is eight to nine inches wide at the broad end, it narrows rapidly toward the bone at the end. Slices should be cut by slicing at right angles to the bone and then cut so as to free the slices from the bone, which keeps them from being huge. When all the top slices are cut, the roast should be turned over and the remaining slices cut from the other side.

Before roasting, it is necessary to slash the skin—carefully, to avoid cutting the meat—so that the fat can escape. Use a very sharp knife, a mat knife such as an X-Acto, or a single-edged razor blade. Pork is often thought of as wintery and can be served with assorted root vegetables (page 379) cooked in the pan with the pork for the last forty-five minutes or so of roasting. I like to serve this in the first spring nights when the air is still chilly, but the rhubarb is in. The sauce combines rhubarb with lots of onions for sweetness to offset the tartness. It would be excellent served with Best Roast Duck (page 67), using the deglazing liquid from the duck or some duck stock instead of the pork deglazing liquid. The sauce goes as well with any other roast pork. The cream does make this sauce rich and probably calls for upping the salt slightly. It is very good and festive.

9-pound shank-end fresh ham

1 teaspoon kosher salt

Freshly ground black pepper, to taste

½ cup water, for deglazing

FOR ONION-RHUBARB SAUCE

3 tablespoons reserved fat from roasting ham

2 pounds onions, peeled and sliced thinly across into rounds (6 cups)

2½ pounds fresh rhubarb, trimmed and sliced across into ⅛-inch pieces (6 cups)

Liquid reserved from deglazing the roasting pan

½ cup water

1 teaspoon kosher salt

1 cup heavy cream, optional

Remove ham from the refrigerator. Place, fat side up, in an 18 x 13 x 2-inch roasting pan. The ham will need to sit out for 2 to 3 hours to reach room temperature. About 20 minutes before roasting the ham, place rack on second level from the bottom of the oven. Heat oven to 500°F.

Using a mat knife or a very sharp knife, carefully score the fat in a diamond pattern. Do not pierce the meat. Sprinkle ham with salt and pepper. Roast for 20 minutes. Reduce heat to 400°F. Carefully remove pan from oven and pour or spoon off fat (this reduces smoking). Reserve fat. Return ham to oven. Roast for 2 hours and 10 minutes more, or until an instant-read thermometer reaches 160° to 165°F when inserted.

Remove and transfer ham to a serving platter. Pour off all fat in pan and reserve. Place pan on top of stove over medium heat. Add the ½ cup of water. Bring to a boil and scrape bottom of pan with a wooden spoon. The liquid will turn a rich dark brown. Use as a gravy or reserve in a small bowl if making rhubarb sauce.

To make the sauce: Return pan to top of stove over medium heat. Add the 3 tablespoons of reserved fat. Add onions. Cook, stirring occasionally, about 20 minutes or until onions are limp and partially browned. Add rhubarb. Cook 10 minutes, stirring only 3 or 4 times. Do not stir too often or rhubarb pieces will lose their shape and look less attractive when served. Add reserved deglazing liquid, remaining ½ cup water, and any liquid that has collected on the serving platter. Add salt. Scrape along bottom of pan with a wooden spoon or the back of a metal spatula to deglaze. If using cream, add now. Cook another 5 minutes, tasting for salt. Serve warm with slices of ham on each plate.

TOTAL ROASTING TIME: 2 hours 30 minutes plus 30 minutes for the sauce

Barbecued racks of spareribs

SERVES 6

TOTAL
ROASTING
TIME:
12
minutes
after
poaching

While ribs are often thought of as grilled, indoors or out, I think they cook more moistly when briefly roasted in a hot oven after being blanched. They also tend to get less stringy. This is informal food and requires lots of paper napkins. Be sure that the butcher has trimmed off the bone that holds them together. Then, they can easily be cut apart with a sharp knife.

Baby back ribs are considered to be very choice. They come below the regular ribs, which extend toward the belly of the beast from the chops. I actually prefer the regular spareribs. They get crustier. Asian Glaze (page 33) can be tripled and two thirds used for blanching and the remainder used for actual glazing. Never use a glaze as a dipping sauce unless it has been thoroughly boiled after the ribs come out.

FOR THE BOILING LIQUID

6 cups water

¼ cup tomato paste

1½ medium onions (about 12 ounces), peeled and thickly sliced

3 cloves garlic, peeled and chopped medium-fine

½ teaspoon whole black peppercorns

4 whole cloves

2 tablespoons hot red pepper sauce

1 tablespoon fresh lemon juice

Two 1¼-pound racks of pork spareribs (each 7 to 9 inches long, 6 ribs per rack)

FOR THE BARBECUE GLAZE

2 tablespoons dark molasses

1 tablespoon prepared mustard

1 tablespoon cider vinegar

⅛ teaspoon hot red pepper sauce

1 teaspoon kosher salt

Place all the boiling liquid ingredients in a large saucepan. Bring to a boil and allow to simmer rapidly for 15 minutes. When the liquid is bubbling, add the ribs. Make sure they are covered with the sauce. Let the ribs simmer 45 minutes. As the liquid reduces, add water to keep it at the original level. Remove the pan from the heat and allow to cool to room temperature. Do this as much as a day ahead, and refrigerate. Return to room temperature. (*Note:* The cooking liquid may be reused. Add water to return the quantity to its original amount. Boil 5 minutes. Store in the refrigerator.)

Place 1 cup of the boiling liquid from the ribs in a small saucepan. Boil the liquid until reduced to ½ cup. Add the glaze ingredients. Stir over heat to combine thoroughly. Brush this mixture liberally over the blanched ribs before cooking them.

About 20 minutes before cooking the ribs, place rack in center of oven. Heat oven to 500°F. Place ribs in an 18 x 13 x 2-inch roasting pan and roast for 5 minutes. Turn. Roast 6 to 7 minutes more. Serve warm.

Simple pork stew

THIS STEW TAKES advantage of the ease and lack of spattering with which raw pork is browned by roasting. As with all stews made with the oven-browning technique, most of the fat can be eliminated. It is better to thicken the sauce shortly before serving with a slurry of cornstarch and water rather than to use more fat and make a roux. This means the stew can be made ahead and thickened when reheating. To double the recipe, use a two-and-a-half- to three-quart saucepan. For more on the meat cuts for stew and browning of pork, see page 232.

The rather northern Italian flavors would go well with Treviso (page 401) or Soft Polenta (page 164).

2 pounds lean pork stew meat, cut into 1½-inch cubes

1 tablespoon canola or olive oil

2 cups Basic Pork Stock (page 228) or canned chicken or beef broth

½ cup red wine

8 cloves garlic, smashed and peeled

½ bay leaf

2 tablespoons cornstarch

¼ cup water

1 teaspoon tomato paste

½ teaspoon dried rosemary

1 to 2 teaspoons kosher salt

Freshly ground black pepper, to taste

Place oven rack on bottom level of oven. Heat oven to 500°F.

Place meat in a 14 x 12 x 2-inch roasting pan. Pour oil over meat. Toss to coat well. Arrange meat in a single layer. Roast for 10 minutes. Turn with a slotted spoon. Roast 5 minutes. Turn. Roast 5 minutes more.

Remove meat from pan to a 2-quart saucepan. Pour or spoon off excess fat from roasting pan. Place roasting pan on the stove over medium-high heat. Deglaze with ½ cup of the stock, using a wooden spoon to scrape up all the crispy bits. Pour sauce into a heat-proof glass measuring cup and allow to settle for a few minutes. Skim off any remaining fat.

Pour over meat. Add remaining stock, and the red wine, garlic, and bay leaf. Bring to a boil. Reduce heat and simmer 50 minutes, stirring occasionally. If preparing up to 2 days ahead, stop at this point and refrigerate.

Return stew to a boil. Meanwhile, whisk together the cornstarch and water until smooth. Put a ladleful of hot liquid from the stew into the cornstarch and water, stir to combine, then pour the cornstarch mixture into the stew. Stir well. Reduce to a simmer. Add the tomato paste, rosemary, salt, and pepper. Cook 3 minutes, scraping the bottom of the pot with a wooden spoon to prevent the stew from burning. Check the seasoning, adding more salt and pepper if desired. Serve with steamed potatoes.

TOTAL ROASTING TIME: 20 minutes plus 55 minutes simmering

Southwestern pork confetti

MAKES 4 GENEROUS CUPS; SERVES 3

THIS IS SMASHINGLY pretty, with the green of limas or young favas, the yellow of corn niblets, the black of the beans, the red of the pepper, the brown of the meat, and the green of the herbs. What is more, it tastes good and is a quick way to use leftover roast pork. It's quick for us because we can get frozen vegetables and canned beans, which are very satisfactory in this composite dish. If using frozen vegetables, defrost them in a sieve under hot running water.

If more roast is available, it is easy to double the recipe to serve six, in which case, use a two-and-a-half- to three-quart saucepan.

½ tablespoon olive oil

1 teaspoon whole cumin seeds

1 small onion (about 3 ounces), peeled and cut into ¼-inch cubes (½ cup)

½ red bell pepper (4 ounces), seeded and chopped (½ cup)

2 cloves garlic, smashed, peeled, and coarsely chopped

1 pound cooked Roasted Boneless Pork Shoulder (page 174) or other leftover pork, cut into 1-inch cubes (2 cups)

1 jalapeño pepper, seeded, deribbed, and chopped, or 1 teaspoon seeded and chopped Basic Jalapeños (page 383)

⅔ cup water

1 cup corn niblets cut from a young ear of corn or ½ of a 10-ounce package frozen corn

¾ cup blanched baby lima beans or young fava beans, skins removed, or about ⅓ of a 10-ounce package frozen lima or fava beans

½ teaspoon dried thyme leaves

¾ cup coarsely chopped fresh cilantro

1 teaspoon kosher salt

½ cup canned black beans, rinsed well and drained, or home-cooked black beans

In a 2-quart saucepan, heat the oil over medium heat until hot. Add the cumin seed and cook for 1 minute. Add the onion, red pepper, garlic, and pork and cook for 6 minutes, stirring occasionally. Stir in the jalapeño pepper and continue to cook for 3 minutes.

Pour the water into the pan and, using a wooden spoon, scrape all of the browned bits from the bottom. Add the corn, lima beans, and thyme, stirring to combine, and cook for 3 more minutes. Stir in the cilantro and salt and continue to cook for 1 minute. Stir in the black beans and cook for 1 minute more, or until warm throughout.

Pork Bolognese

MAKES 3½ CUPS; SERVES 6 AS A FIRST
COURSE, 3 AS A MAIN COURSE

ONE EVENING I came home feeling like a little pasta for dinner. I used leftover Roasted Boneless Pork Shoulder, adapting a Bolognese sauce recipe of my own from *Food for Friends*. This is just as light and balanced among good flavors.

I used spaghettini, but linguine, buccatini, penne, or medium-size farfalle (bow ties) will do as well. Figure on two ounces of pasta per person for a first course and three ounces for a main. If cheese is the order of the day, make sure it's freshly grated and put it on the table.

½ ounce dried porcini mushrooms (about ¼ cup)

6 ounces leftover Roasted Boneless Pork Shoulder (page 174), cut into 1½-inch pieces (1 cup)

3 tablespoons olive oil

1 carrot (2 ounces), trimmed, peeled, and cut into ¼-inch dice (½ cup)

1 small onion (about 3 ounces), peeled and cut into ¼-inch dice (½ cup)

1 celery stalk, peeled with vegetable peeler and cut into ¼-inch dice (⅓ cup)

1¼ cups drained Whole Plum Tomatoes (page 418), liquid reserved, or one 33-ounce can Italian plum tomatoes, drained, liquid reserved

¼ cup red wine

1 tablespoon tomato paste

2 teaspoons kosher salt

Freshly ground black pepper, to taste

Soak the mushrooms in warm water to cover about 20 minutes, until softened. Strain mushrooms, and reserve liquid to use in a stew, soup, or pasta sauce. Rinse mushrooms under cool water to remove any remaining grit. Chop fine and reserve.

Place pieces of pork in the work bowl of a food processor. Process until all pork is ground. Reserve.

In the bottom of a medium saucepan, drizzle 1 tablespoon of the oil. Add the carrot, onion, and celery. Cook over medium heat for about 8 minutes, stirring frequently, until onion is translucent. Add mushrooms. Cook 2 to 3 minutes. Add remaining oil and pork. Cook over medium heat, stirring frequently, for 2 minutes.

Gently squish the tomatoes with your hands—don't splatter your clothes. Add to pan. Add half the reserved liquid from the tomatoes and the wine. Bring to a boil. Reduce heat to a simmer. Scrape up any browned bits from the bottom of the pan. Add tomato paste, salt, and pepper. Cook for 20 minutes.

If using right away, boil salted water and cook pasta. Drain, reserving a few tablespoons of the water. Return pasta to warm pot with reserved water. Add hot sauce. Toss. Serve warm.

Pork and potato salad

MAKES 4 CUPS

LEFTOVER PORK IS delicious cold, either whole to slice on a buffet or made into a salad, replacing the ubiquitous chicken. The best meat to use is that from the loin or rack. Under half a pound of leftovers makes eight servings for a buffet or four to six nice salads for lunch or a cold dinner with some dark greens—watercress, arugula, or mizuna—or sliced tomatoes. With its complement of vegetables, the salad looks attractive in any bowl.

3 to 4 red new potatoes (8 ounces), peeled and cut in half lengthwise, then cut across in thin slices (1½ cups)

3 tablespoons Dijon mustard

3 tablespoons Basic Mayonnaise (page 303) or store-bought

1½ tablespoons fresh lemon juice

2 teaspoons kosher salt

7 ounces leftover pork roast pieces, cut into 2½ x ½ x ¼-inch strips (1½ cups)

1 cucumber (8 ounces), peeled and cut into 2½ x ½ x ¼-inch strips (1¼ cups)

1 red bell pepper (8 ounces), both ends cut off and reserved, the pepper cut in half across the width, cored, and cut into ¼-inch strips (2 cups)

Freshly ground black pepper, to taste

In a small pan of boiling water, cook potato pieces about 10 minutes, until the tip of a knife will slide in easily. Strain and reserve in cold water.

In a medium mixing bowl, combine the mustard, mayonnaise, lemon juice, and salt. Whisk together well.

Add the pork, cucumber, and red bell pepper. Stir together until well combined. Add potatoes and black pepper. Mix gently so that potatoes do not break apart.

Transfer to a serving dish. Top with reserved petal-shaped bell pepper end pieces.

Pork and orange salad

MAKES 3 CUPS; SERVES 2 FOR LUNCH OR
4 AS A FIRST COURSE, 6 AT A BUFFET

W INTER SALADS USING leftovers can be hard to make attractive. Citrus and red seem to do the trick for this one, made with leftover pork loin or rack meat. Add the mayonnaise just before serving, or it will thin out too much.

It's a wonderful opportunity to make Three-Citrus Mayonnaise (page 304). However, if you don't want to fuss with homemade, make the dressing by combining one-half cup prepared mayonnaise, four tablespoons freshly squeezed orange juice, one tablespoon freshly squeezed lemon juice, one tablespoon prepared mustard, and freshly ground black pepper, to taste. This will make about a cup of substitute dressing, which can be combined with the other ingredients as directed below. Use the one-quarter cup of orange juice that is squeezed from the oranges' pulp after cutting out the sections to make either the Three-Citrus Mayonnaise or the doctored store-bought version.

The salad will look best when served on dark green leaves of lettuce, such as romaine or Bibb.

12 ounces leftover meat from Roast Rack of Pork (page 162), trimmed of fat and end pieces, cut into ¼ x 2-inch strips (about 2 cups)

1 red bell pepper (8 ounces), cored, seeded, deribbed, and cut into ¼ x 2-inch strips (1 cup)

½ small red onion, peeled and cut into slivers ¼-inch thick (½ cup)

2 juice oranges

¾ cup Three-Citrus Mayonnaise (page 304)

1½ tablespoons Dijon mustard

Freshly ground black pepper, to taste

Place the pork, red pepper, and red onion in a mixing bowl.

Using a serrated knife, peel the oranges until all the white membrane has been removed. Holding the orange over a small bowl to catch the juice, cut out each orange section from the white membrane on each side of it. Remove the seeds and place the sections in the mixing bowl with the pork. When all the sections have been removed, squeeze the juice out of the remaining pulp into the bowl with the rest of the juice. There will be ¼ cup juice with which to make Three-Citrus Mayonnaise or its substitute.

Combine the Three-Citrus Mayonnaise and the mustard or prepare the substitute using store-bought mayonnaise. Season to taste with the black pepper. Pour over the pork and combine thoroughly.

Suckling pig

IN ADDITION TO what we politely call pork, there are any number of pig dishes out there. I find that pig in culinary terms usually refers to a whole animal, as in Charles Lamb's "A Dissertation upon Roast Pig," in the first series of "Elia" essays. In Ecuador, I saw mammoth pigs vertically roasting in roadside stands and ate them too—they're much like barbecue. In Peru and Spain, the pigs are usually smaller suckling pigs, under twenty pounds. The Chinese are very partial to suckling pig, very intelligently preferring even smaller beasts.

The largest that I have reliably been able to get into my home oven have weighed under ten pounds. Even to achieve that, it is necessary to do some butchering; the aim is to free the rear legs slightly and bring them around so that the lower legs are vaguely parallel to the body with the trotters pointing toward the head. Any work is easy as the bones are very soft still and easily cut with a sharp, heavy knife.

Roast suckling pig

SERVES 4 TO 6

TOTAL ROASTING TIME: 1 *hour*

LIKE PEKING DUCK, these piglets are cooked primarily for their crisp skin. They cannot be carved; the flesh isn't deep enough, although very tender. Instead, pull it away with forks, or grasp with chopsticks and go. This makes it an ideal communal dish, the centerpiece of a feast, in which case, it will feed ten—many more than the yield given, which is for the number of people who will be satiated by this as a solo main course.

Make or buy ping, the Chinese pancakes usually served with duck, or provide large, firm lettuce leaves. Make scallion brushes by trimming off the root end, cutting three-inch lengths of scallion, and making numerous small incisions going toward the middle all around either end of the scallion. Drop these into cold water and the feathery ends will curl up. Drain and pile into a dish for the table. Add a little saucer or sauce dish of plum sauce per person. Put the pig in the center of the table with its garlic on a separate plate. Let people roll their own pancakes. Serve the pig as hot as possible and give out many napkins.

The pre-preparation of the pig is as Chinese as the service. Put the properly butchered pig in a pan and refrigerate, uncovered, for about twenty-four hours. Stuff with garlic. Allow to stand, uncovered, at room temperature for about two hours. The pig is roasted at a slightly lower temperature than usual to prevent smoking. It emerges from the oven very crisp and with virtually no fat in the pan. If a large oven will hold a slightly larger pig, allow an additional ten minutes per pound. I don't counsel trying a pig over twelve pounds, even if it fits in the oven.

1 suckling pig (8½ pounds), air-dried for 24 hours

Whole cloves from 7 heads of garlic (3½ cups), loose skins discarded

1 very small apple, lady or crab, optional

2 cranberries, optional

1 teaspoon olive oil plus extra for oiling foil

¾ cup water, for deglazing

Place oven rack on second level from bottom. Heat oven to 475°F.

Prepare the pig for cooking. Use a large knife to cut off the tail. Starting just below the tail, cut between the rear legs, splitting the legs apart. Stuff the cavity with the garlic cloves. Smush the pig, front and rear legs splayed out, into an 18 x 13 x 2-inch roasting pan. If desired, cram a lady apple into the pig's mouth, and/or remove the eyeballs and replace them with a cranberry in each socket. Rub the teaspoon of oil onto the pig, reserving enough to lightly oil three 5 x 5-inch pieces of tin foil. Loosely cover the ears and snout with the oiled foil to prevent them from burning.

Place in oven tail end first. Roast for 1 hour.

Remove pig as well as any garlic cloves that have fallen out from the cavity to a serving platter. While the meat rests, place pan on stove over medium heat and deglaze pan with the water (page 10), using a wooden spoon to scrape up any glaze. Pour pan juices into a glass measuring cup. Allow to settle for 5 minutes, then remove grease that rises to the top. Serve in a sauceboat on the side.

lAMB

I LOVE ROASTED LAMB ALL BROWN AND CRUSTY ON THE OUTSIDE, ALL RARE, RED, AND JUICY ON THE INSIDE. I make roast leg of lamb so often that I sometimes think its garlicky perfume has taken over the entire house. It makes my life easy because I can pop it in a hot oven when my guests walk in the door. It will be done when I need it and not cold or overdone. Lamb is the traditional meat to serve with Bordeaux along with some little, dried white (navy) or fresh green (haricot) beans, simmered with stock until they glisten and are flecked with herbs and traces of more garlic.

Almost any vegetable recipe given in this book can be served with lamb, from artichokes to sunchokes, from tomatoes to potatoes.

I find the deglazing liquid to be sauce enough. Those with more ambition can browse through the list of sauces on pages 292–309 for a selection. Mustard is a good friend to lamb, cold or hot, as are cornichons and pickled onions or walnuts.

Depending on the part of the world they come from, eaters will have differing ideas about doneness. There is no compromise about lamb. Irish friends will not eat lamb at my house. I serve it rare; they eat it only gray. Having seen the glorious flocks in Ireland, I have to assume that the Irish are letting lamb get over-the-hill or using lamb that is really destined to provide wool. The French idea of rare— *seignant*—will be a lot rarer than that of most Americans, who tend more toward pink. Please see page 130 for internal lamb temperatures as measured with an instant-read thermometer. Cook the lamb for times given in the recipes. If more time is needed, add it in ten-minute increments.

Some people seem not to like lamb. It is eaten much less in the United States than in Europe or Asia. I think that is because we not only tend to overcook lamb, we also tend to forget to remind the butcher to remove the fell, the thin outer membrane, like a thin sheet of vellum, over the muscles. If the fell is not removed, the lamb will smell unpleasantly strong. It can be removed by prying up an edge with the point of a sharp knife and then ripping it off like a Band-Aid.

While chump chops and mutton have their proponents, I am unable to buy this past-lamb meat. Consequently, it is not in this book. At the other end of the spectrum, I can buy from time to time baby lamb, which is very small and pale in color. See pages 202–207 for information and recipes; but don't look if squeamish about cutting up a whole animal.

Those who are accustomed to French or English lamb will be used to aged lamb, whereas in America lamb is sold very fresh. To get the aged taste, place the lamb, loosely covered, on a rack over a pan into which it can drip for two days in the refrigerator. The taste of lamb will also vary with the place it grazes. Salt marsh lamb, such as Devon lamb, has a vaguely salty taste like the famous French pré-salé. New Zealand lamb tends to come in cryovac and to be slightly aged and a little smaller in size than most domestic lamb. Lamb from the Colorado mountains used to be very famous and is still very good.

There is one notable omission from what I feel is a very complete array of roasted lamb recipes: crown roast of lamb. I think it is an abomination. Stuffed, as used to be common, with a forcemeat, the lamb is invariably overcooked before the forcemeat is cooked through. If anyone is unable to resist this preparation of two racks, forced backward into a circle, their rib bones sticking in the air, I recommend that it be cooked as the Deviled Rack of Lamb (page 192) and then the open center filled with cooked vegetables. Be warned that it will be messy to carve with the vegetables spilling out.

All of the lamb in this chapter is seasoned with some dry seasonings or a dryish mixture, then deglazed after roasting and served with a deglazing sauce. The Herb Rub (page 293) and the Rosemary Rub (page 205) go well on all cuts to be roasted. Deglazing liquids can be Basic Lamb Stock (page 229), fruit juices, or my favorite, red wine. Simply roasted lamb requires no sauce; but there is an English tradition of Mint Sauce (page 188), and some people like semisweet sauces like Cumberoutlandish Sauce (page 106) or Something like Bigarade Duck Sauce (page 65), replacing the duck elements with the same of lamb.

There are a number of recipes that I think are really excellent for leftover lamb. It is good in sandwiches and salads and reheats well. There can never be too much lamb.

Simple roast leg of lamb

WHOLE LEG SERVES 8 TO 10; SHORT LEG
SERVES 6 TO 8

TOTAL
ROASTING
TIME:
see page 188

HEREWITH THE RULE that gets the lamb roasted. Further on in this section are recipes for variously butchered lamb legs. The recipes can be adapted by following this guideline. The seasonings and deglazing suggestions for one can be applied to another.

Legs of lamb will vary in weight, depending on how they are trimmed and whether they are boned or not; most should serve eight people. If I have more people to serve, I prefer to find two very small legs rather than a larger one.

A whole untrimmed leg of lamb weighs eight to ten pounds. Ask the butcher to trim the leg, remove the fell, and cut through to the bone—not through the bone—to partially separate the steaks or chops after the joint. This will facilitate both seasoning and eating. The whole leg, trimmed, will weigh six to seven pounds. A whole leg of lamb boned, rolled, and tied will weigh four and a half to five pounds.

A short leg of lamb is simply a whole leg with the steaks or chops after the joint removed. A short leg, trimmed, with bone weighs five to six pounds. The same short leg boned, rolled, and tied weighs three and a quarter to four pounds.

There are basically two ways to carve a leg of lamb that has its bone in. Depending on which carving method is used, there will be either slices that each have rare centers and better done rims or a variety of slices accommodating preferences for rare through well-done. For both methods, it is best to grab the shank bone with the hand that doesn't hold the knife. There used to be wonderful silver bone holders. I don't have one and tend to use a clean kitchen towel to grab with.

To achieve portions that are all equally cooked, hold the knife perpendicular to the bone (with the leg in front of you and the bone parallel to the table) and carve toward the bone.

By carving parallel to the bone instead, there will be better done slices from the first cuts and rarer slices closer to the bone. Equally tasty are the slices carved from below the bone after the top is carved. These are almost always carved parallel to the bone.

Boned and rolled short or whole legs of lamb must have their strings removed after roasting. They are then usually cut across into slices as thin as possible. They will give rarer centers in a rim of better-done meat.

One oddity of roasting shows up very clearly in the following list: a boned leg takes longer to cook than one with its bone in, which is inevitably heavier. The bone acts to spread the heat through the meat. Meat against meat cooks less quickly than meat against bone. Choose the roasting time according to the leg being used.

Variations in the deglazing liquid will provide variations in sauce. Consider, in addition to those given in the recipes that follow, bourbon, vermouth, orange juice, pomegranate juice, passion fruit juice, or Calvados and cream.

1 trimmed whole leg of lamb (6 to 7¾ pounds) steaks or chops after joint separated from one another but not detached, or

1 trimmed whole leg of lamb, boned, rolled, and tied (4 to 5 pounds), or

1 trimmed short leg of lamb (5½ pounds), or

1 trimmed short leg of lamb boned, rolled, and tied (3¾ to 4 pounds)

Kosher salt, to taste

Freshly ground black pepper, to taste

1 to 2 cups Basic Lamb Stock (page 229), water, or wine, for deglazing

Place oven rack on second level from the bottom. Heat oven to 500°F.

Season the lamb with salt and pepper. Place the lamb in an 18 x 13 x 2-inch roasting pan.

For whole leg of lamb with bone, roast for 1 hour. For boneless whole leg, roast 1 hour 10 minutes. For short leg with bone, roast at 500°F for 10 minutes. Reduce heat to

425°F. Roast another 35 minutes. For short leg boned, rolled, and tied, roast at 500°F for 10 minutes. Reduce heat to 425°F. Roast 40 minutes more.

Remove to a platter. Snip off strings. Pour or spoon off excess fat. Put pan on top of stove. Add the liquid and bring contents to a boil while scraping the bottom vigorously with a wooden spoon. Let reduce by half. Add any juices that have collected around the lamb to the sauce. Serve on the side in a sauceboat.

TOTAL ROASTING TIME: whole leg with bone, 1 hour; whole leg boned, rolled, and tied, 1 hour 10 minutes; short leg with bone, 45 minutes; short leg boned, rolled, and tied, 50 minutes

Mint sauce

MAKES 1 SCANT CUP

THIS IS THE classic English sauce for lamb—not mint jelly, which is poisonously green and far too sweet. The sauce can be used as soon as made; but if allowed to sit several hours, though less handsomely green, it will have a rounder flavor. There are always trade-offs. The sauce is intense, and the single cup should be enough for a leg of lamb.

1 large bunch (4 ounces) fresh mint without much stem, leaves removed, washed, patted dry, and finely chopped (1 cup)

⅓ cup boiling water
1 tablespoon sugar
⅓ cup cider vinegar
¼ teaspoon kosher salt

Place mint in a small container. Add ⅓ cup boiling water and stir in the sugar. Let stand until cool to the touch, about 15 minutes. Stir in the cider vinegar and salt. Serve immediately or reserve for later use.

Roast leg of lamb with herb rub

SERVES 8 TO 12

TOTAL
ROASTING
TIME:
1
hour

THIS IS ONE of my favorite ways to prepare lamb. A simple variant is to insert the garlic slivers and then to sprinkle the outside of the leg copiously with kosher salt, freshly ground black pepper, and rosemary.

I often surround the leg with roasted potatoes, sometimes sprinkling them with more Herb Rub or salt, pepper, and rosemary. To do so, cut two pounds new potatoes in half or in quarters, or cut two and a half pounds of baking potatoes into eight wedges each. After the lamb has cooked for fifteen minutes, add potatoes to pan, rolling them around in any fat in the bottom of the pan. Turn potatoes every fifteen minutes. You might add a handful of whole unpeeled garlic cloves at the same time as the potatoes.

The recipe below is for a whole leg of lamb with the chops still attached to the roast. A short leg, which is what I ordinarily prepare, will take only forty-five minutes (at two different temperatures; see pages 186–188), and the potatoes go in with the lamb. They will need to be lightly slicked with oil as the lamb fat will not have started to melt.

A whole boned and rolled leg, which is easily carved across into slices, takes an hour and ten minutes. Given the longer cooking time, I usually cut the potatoes only into quarters and add them to the pan fifteen minutes after the roast goes in the oven.

1 recipe Herb Rub (page 293)
7½- to 7¾-pound leg of lamb, steaks or chops beyond the joint separated but not detached

2 heads garlic, separated into cloves; 1 head smashed, peeled, and cloves cut into slivers; or 1 to 4 whole heads optional
1 cup red wine, for deglazing

Place oven rack on second level from the bottom. Heat oven to 500°F.

Make the herb rub, reserving 2 cloves of garlic. Cut reserved garlic into slivers.

Place the lamb in an 18 x 13 x 2-inch roasting pan. With a small sharp knife, make small ½-inch slits toward the center of the leg. Place a sliver of garlic in each of the slits. Massage the herb rub into the roast on all sides, making sure to rub it into all the nooks and crannies, especially in between the chops, which the butcher should have separated, at one end of the leg. Turn the leg so that its rounder side is facing up in the pan. Roast for 1 hour. If using garlic, throw in a handful of unpeeled whole cloves 30 minutes before the lamb is done, or slice ½ inch off the stem end of one or more whole heads and place in the roasting pan with the lamb.

continued

Remove the lamb to a platter. Let rest 10 minutes before carving.

Pour or spoon off any fat from the roasting pan. Place the pan over high heat. Pour in the wine and any juices that have collected in the platter. Bring to a boil, scraping constantly with a wooden spoon to scrape up any glaze that may have stuck to the pan. Degrease. Serve as a sauce for the lamb.

Roast leg of lamb with orange juice, red onions, and mint

SERVES 6 TO 8

TOTAL
ROASTING
TIME:
45
minutes

I HAD A FRIEND who loved my lamb; but she had friends who didn't permit any wine in their food. What to do? I suggested changing friends. She didn't, so I came up with this recipe instead.

There will be pits in the olives unless an eager cook pits them by squeezing each olive at the pointy end to force the pit out through the stem end. A knife works also. I like rice or Soft Polenta (page 164) with this.

2 medium red onions (about 1 pound), peeled and thinly sliced across
2 juice oranges, skin on, scrubbed and thinly sliced across
1 trimmed short leg of lamb (5½ pounds)
1 tablespoon dried mint

Kosher salt, to taste
Freshly ground black pepper, to taste
½ cup drained black Niçoise olives
½ cup fresh orange juice
½ cup Basic Lamb Stock (page 229)

Place oven rack on second level from bottom. Heat oven to 500°F.

In a roasting pan just large enough to hold the lamb, make a layer of onion rings to fit just under the lamb. Top onion rings with half of the orange slices. Coat lamb with mint, salt, and pepper. Cover with remaining orange slices. Roast lamb for 10 minutes. Reduce heat to 425°F. Roast 35 minutes more.

Remove lamb to a platter. Over high heat on top of the stove, add remaining ingredients to onions and oranges. Cook, scraping the bottom of the pan with a wooden spoon until mixture is hot. Turn off heat. With a slotted spoon, remove onions, oranges, and olives to a vegetable dish. Skim liquid in pan of any fat; add more salt and pepper if desired. Place sauce in a gravy boat or bowl.

Serve each person with some sliced lamb and some of the onion concoction, and pass the sauce.

Roast saddle of lamb

Saddle of lamb, the loin chops on both sides in one roast, is perhaps the most luxurious of lamb roasts. Don't buy it for heavy feeders or if you want chops. What makes a saddle so fabulous is the way it is carved. The meat is cut on the diagonal in lengthwise strips from either side of the backbone. Start by making an incision down one side of the backbone until the knife hits the ribs. Then hold the knife fairly flat to the top surface of the meat—at a twenty-degree angle to it—with the back of the knife parallel to the backbone. Start cutting slices as thinly as possible until all the meat is off the bone. The first slice will have a crisp covering of fat. The last slice will be a long, thin wedge. Turn the saddle around and repeat on the other side. After this meat is served, turn the saddle upside down; cut any strings tying the flaps together and slice the little strips of meat across.

Some experts say that a saddle will serve four to six people. I prefer to make two saddles for six to eight. As many as three saddles can be roasted side by side in a large pan. Allow five minutes extra cooking time.

Be careful not to order a loin. Some butchers construe a saddle to be what I would call a baron, both rear legs and the saddle. A baron will not fit in my oven unless the lamb is a baby (page 204).

As an alternative to the mint in this recipe, consider Herb Rub (page 293), which makes enough for two saddles. Although in this recipe the flavor comes from dried mint—better for roasting—I have served Mint Sauce (page 188) made with fresh mint and mixed with the deglazing liquid from the roast. Since there is not an overwhelming quantity of meat, this is a good place for Melting Potatoes (Not-on-Your-Diet) (page 395). Don't crowd the plate with vegetables. The slices take up space. Instead, follow the main course with a green salad.

6- to 7-pound saddle of lamb	Freshly ground black pepper, to taste
1 teaspoon dried mint, optional	½ cup red wine, for deglazing
1 tablespoon kosher salt	

Place oven rack on center level. Heat oven to 500°F.

Rub lamb all over with mint, salt, and pepper. Put in a roasting pan just large enough to hold meat, flap side down.

Roast for 25 minutes for medium-rare, 20 minutes for rare. Remove from oven and transfer lamb to a platter. Let rest 10 minutes before carving.

continued

Pour or spoon off any fat from the roasting pan. Place over high heat and pour in the wine. Stir constantly, scraping the bottom of the pan with a wooden spoon until the meat glaze and wine are completely combined. Pour into a sauceboat.

The only tricky part comes at the table. Maybe you can palm it off onto a self-proclaimed master carver. If not, approach the meat with a longish, sharp, thin carving knife. Make slices that are parallel to the bone but at a sharp diagonal, as close to parallel to the table as possible. Put two rosy rare slices on each plate, and pour a puddle of sauce over the slices. When all the meat is carved from one side of the top, reverse the platter and continue carving the second top side. If people want seconds, turn the saddle over; cut the two flaps free and carve them across in small rounds.

Deviled rack of lamb

SERVES 6 TO 8

TOTAL
ROASTING
TIME:
20
minutes

EVEN THOSE WHO are not ordinarily fond of lamb will happily eat a rack in a restaurant. Racks are the rib chops, all seven from one side of a lamb in a single piece. One rack generally serves two people, but if the rest of the meal is large, or two racks are being made, the odd chops can serve an extra friend or two. Make sure the butcher removes the chine and cracks between the ribs so that the rack can easily be cut into chops at the table.

I don't like my rack Frenched, although it is considered more elegant. Frenching means that aside from the eye of the chop, the bone next to the chop, and a thin rim of fat around the chop, all the meat and fat covering the bones is removed. It is over those naked bones that the Victorian conceit of paper frills (hiding nakedness had a high priority, as did not touching the food with one's fingers) are sometimes placed. I prefer to have the chop bones in all their crisped splendor, with thin strips of meat to tear with my teeth. Even the most prissy condone eating rib chops with one's fingers.

No matter how the rack is butchered, it will take about twenty minutes on the center rack of a 500°F oven (unless the lamb is more dowager than maiden) to achieve a pleasant rare pinkness. Up to four racks can be fitted into a pan at one time by placing pairs of racks so that their meat is toward the edge of the pan and the bones face toward the center. If Frenched, the bones can be interlaced. If un-Frenched, they can overlap. In this way, four racks can be put in one large pan.

A simple solution is to coat four racks with a recipe of Herb Rub (page 293), or a double recipe of Rosemary Rub (page 205).

If there is a chop left over, I usually eat it for breakfast, cold. I do not recommend reheating these tender little bits; they toughen.

As a rack comes from the fore part of the lamb (kosher), I give a mildly spicy version, in which matzoh crumbs can be used instead of cracker crumbs at Passover. The cracker crumbs I really prefer come from ship's biscuits—hard—but saltines are probably more widely available. It is also perfectly possible to use three quarters of a cup of Dried Bread Crumbs (page 110).

2 racks of lamb (2 to 2½ pounds each, 7 to 8 chops per rack), most of the chine bone removed and rack cracked between chops for easy carving

2 tablespoons vegetable oil

4 teaspoons coarse-grained mustard

1 teaspoon dried rosemary, crushed

½ teaspoon kosher salt

½ teaspoon freshly ground black pepper

¾ cup cracker crumbs (6 to 8 saltines), finely ground with a rolling pin, or matzoh or Dried Bread Crumbs (page 110)

Place oven rack on center level. Heat oven to 500°F.

Place racks in a 14 x 12 x 2-inch roasting pan.

Whisk together remaining ingredients except the cracker or bread crumbs in a small bowl. Coat both sides of the racks with the mixture. Pat on a layer of crumbs.

Roast for 20 minutes for rare. Let stand 5 minutes before carving.

Simple roasted boneless lamb shoulder

SERVES 8 OR A FAMILY'S WORTH
PLUS LEFTOVERS

TOTAL
ROASTING
TIME:
see page 194

THE OTHER POSSIBLE front-end kosher roast is the shoulder. This was pointed out to me by my friend Corby Kummer. He is braver than I, being happy to roast the meat with its bones and then carve around them. I find the bones particularly difficult and get my butcher to bone and roll the meat for me.

It is very difficult to get a good reading of this roast from a thermometer because of the fat and gristle. Instead, follow the timings and don't be upset if this cut gets slightly beyond medium. That internal fat will keep it moist. As that fat oozes out, it will also make the oven smoke unless the temperature is turned down. Season as any other lamb roast.

continued

Lamb shoulder makes a good family meal with mashed potatoes and is sumptuous for leftovers. For myself, I deglaze the pan with wine. If there will be children at the table, it is safer to deglaze the pan with lamb broth or chicken broth.

The boned and rolled roast is about ten inches long and four and a half inches in diameter at the widest part.

3¼-pound boneless lamb shoulder, rolled and tied	Freshly ground black pepper, to taste
Kosher salt, to taste	½ cup red wine, Basic Lamb Stock (page 229), or canned chicken broth, for deglazing

Place oven rack on second level from the bottom. Heat oven to 500°F.

Place lamb shoulder, fattiest side up, in a 12 x 8 x 1½-inch roasting pan. Sprinkle with salt and pepper. Roast for 45 minutes. Pour or spoon off fat from pan. Reduce oven temperature to 450°F. For rare, roast 20 minutes more, or until internal temperature reaches 140°F. For medium, 30 minutes more, or until 160°F. For well-done, roast 45 minutes more, or until internal temperature reaches 175°F.

Transfer lamb to a serving platter. Snip off strings. Pour or spoon off excess fat. Put pan on top of stove. Add the liquid and bring contents to a boil, while scraping the bottom vigorously with a wooden spoon. Let reduce by half. Serve on the side in a sauceboat.

TOTAL ROASTING TIME: rare, 1 hour 5 minutes; medium, 1 hour 15 minutes; well-done, 1 hour 30 minutes

Wintery lamb stew

MAKES 5½ CUPS; SERVES 4 TO 5

TOTAL
ROASTING
TIME:
*see facing
page*

LAMB MAKES WONDERFUL, inexpensive stew. This recipe uses the basic lamb-browning technique on page 234 which can easily be applied to other stews. I used boned lamb, but it is possible to use bone-in meat, hacked up; but there will be less actual meat for people to eat.

I like this stew fairly thick to eat with spoons, but if it is being served over rice or noodles, the cornstarch could be halved.

4 tablespoons unsalted butter

2 to 3 very small onions (6 ounces), trimmed and peeled

3 pounds lamb neck and shoulder pieces, cut into 1½-inch pieces

1½ cups red wine

½ cup water

3 to 4 cloves garlic, smashed, peeled, and cut in half

1⅔ cups Basic Lamb Stock (page 229) or one 14-ounce can chicken broth

2 tablespoons Basic Veal Glaze (page 226), optional

1 bay leaf

2 tablespoons chopped fresh flat-leaf parsley

1 pound parsnips, trimmed, peeled, and cut into 1-inch pieces (1½ cups)

One 1-pound celery root, trimmed, peeled, and cut into ½-inch pieces (1 cup)

6 ounces baby carrots, trimmed and peeled

¼ cup cornstarch

1 tablespoon anchovy paste

2 tablespoons chopped fresh sage

2 tablespoons kosher salt

Freshly ground black pepper, to taste

Place rack in center of oven. Heat oven to 500°F.

Place an 18 x 12 x 2-inch roasting pan on top of the stove over medium heat. Add the butter and let it melt. Add the onions and lamb. Stir to coat pieces with butter.

Roast in oven 15 minutes. Turn by either shaking pan vigorously or sliding out rack and using a spoon or tongs. Roast another 15 minutes. Slide out rack and remove pieces of lamb to a large stew pot or stockpot. Roast onions 15 minutes more. They will be nicely browned. Remove them to pot with lamb.

Pour or spoon off excess fat. Place pan over medium-high heat and add ½ cup of the red wine and the water. Bring to a boil. Hold pan securely with one hand. Scrape bottom of pan with a wooden spoon until all the crisp bits of food and glaze are unstuck. Pour contents into stew pot.

Add garlic, stock, veal glaze, if using, and the remainder of the red wine. Cover. Slowly bring to a simmer; this will take about 15 minutes. Simmer 1 hour. Skim carefully. It helps if the pot is tilted a little. Add the bay leaf, parsley, parsnips, celery root, and carrots. Cover. Return to a simmer. Skim again. Cook 20 minutes.

Make a slurry by pouring some of the hot broth into the cornstarch. Mix well. Stirring constantly, pour back into pot. Add anchovy paste and sage. Stirring again, bring to a boil. Cook 3 to 5 minutes, or until the cornstarch has dissolved. Add salt and pepper. Discard the bay leaf. Serve.

TOTAL ROASTING TIME: 45 minutes plus 1 hour 55 minutes stove-top cooking

Lamb and apple "hash" with soft polenta

MAKES 2 CUPS "HASH";
SERVES 2 TO 4 AS A MAIN COURSE,
4 TO 6 AS A FIRST COURSE

THIS IS NOT a true American or English hash that sticks together to make a cake when sautéed. Instead, it takes its name from the French word *hacher*, to cut up. The meat is indeed cut into small pieces and makes what is almost a rich sauce. I like it over Soft Polenta and serve it as a first course, much in the style of a pasta course. Speaking of which, this would make a fine pasta sauce for broad noodles like papardelle. Would grated Parmesan be too much? I don't know.

Be careful. The liquid boils off almost immediately when this is prepared, and the combination of the rich gelatin it leaves and the sugar in the apples makes this burn easily. I use a nonstick pan to make life easier. Cooking this in a flat pan as if it were truly a hash, coupled with the caramelizing sugar from the apples, gives it a glorious golden brown color.

2 tablespoons unsalted butter

1 medium onion (8 ounces), peeled and cut into ¼-inch dice (1¼ cups)

¼ teaspoon ground cinnamon

⅛ teaspoon ground nutmeg

½ teaspoon paprika

½ teaspoon ground cumin

Pinch of cayenne

1 tablespoon kosher salt

6 grinds black pepper

1 teaspoon finely chopped fresh thyme leaves

12 ounces leftover meat from Simple Roast Leg of Lamb (page 186), lamb shanks (page 197), or Simple Roasted Boneless Lamb Shoulder (page 193), cut into ¼-inch cubes (2 cups)

2 Granny Smith apples (7 ounces each), peeled, cored, and cut into ½-inch cubes

2 teaspoons freshly squeezed lemon juice

½ cup Basic Lamb Stock (page 229) or canned chicken broth

1 recipe Soft Polenta (page 164)

In a 10-inch nonstick skillet, melt 1 tablespoon of the butter over low heat. Add the onion, stirring occasionally. When onion begins to brown, add cinnamon, nutmeg, paprika, cumin, cayenne, salt, pepper, thyme, and the last tablespoon of butter, cooking until thyme is wilted. This takes 10 minutes. All of the onion should be brown.

Add the lamb and the apples. Increase heat to high. Cook until apples begin to brown, 5 to 10 minutes, occasionally scooping up sections as they brown and turning over with a spatula.

Add the lemon juice and ¼ cup of the stock. Boil 2 minutes, until liquid is evaporated. Do not stir anymore. Reduce heat to low.

Use the spatula to spread the mixture out evenly in the pan. Press down to compact. Increase heat slightly to medium. Cook 15 minutes. Scoop up in large pieces with spatula and turn oven. Pour the last ¼ cup of stock into the pan, and press down once more. Cook over medium heat for 15 minutes.

Serve over soft polenta.

Oven-braised lamb shanks with white beans

SERVES 4 TO 12

TOTAL
ROASTING
TIME:
see page 198

LAMB SHANKS HAVE wonderful meat. After oven-roasting to brown, they need long, slow cooking to break down the gelatinous material that, when properly cooked, makes them so sexy.

Lamb shank is the last joint of the leg. The most important thing about it is that it has become hard to find. Lamb shanks are "in" in trendy restaurants. However, a butcher can order them if given advance notice. In order to get enough lamb shanks for repeated testing, I used meat from an ordinary supermarket and a fancy butcher. There was no difference in the timing or in the delicious result. The size and weight vary; but average weight is one pound three ounces each. The timing won't change much with different sizes. Four shanks fit comfortably in a medium pan when placed lengthwise with the fat part of one resting next to the bone end of another.

This dish needs to be started the night before it cooks, unless the cook quick-soaks the beans (see Note). The lamb shanks can be browned the day before or while the beans are quick-soaking.

This recipe provides a lot of beans—about fourteen cups cooked—in proportion to the meat. It is not a mistake. I like to eat the beans just garnished with the meat. That accounts for the odd amount of servings given. If a whole shank is to be served to each eater, then there are only four portions; but if the shanks are fished out and the meat stripped from the bones, there will be anywhere from eight to twelve portions.

I happily eat any leftover beans the next day. Less avid souls can add a cup and a half of lamb or chicken stock for each cup of leftover beans and make a robust soup.

continued

Four 1¼-pound lamb shanks, trimmed
   of extra fat

2 small onions (about 3 ounces each),
   peeled

6 medium cloves garlic, peeled

1 cup water

Two 1-pound bags dried white beans, such
   as Great Northern or navy, soaked
   overnight in enough water to cover by
   2 inches

1 bouquet garni (tied with kitchen string):
   one 2-inch sprig fresh rosemary, five
   2-inch sprigs fresh oregano, six 2-inch
   sprigs fresh thyme, ½ bay leaf

3 cups Cherry Tomato Purée (page 418)
   or Plum Tomato Purée (page 418),
   or 3 cups canned whole tomatoes with
   juices

1 cup red wine

2 cups Basic Chicken Stock (page 42)
   or canned

2 teaspoons kosher salt

Place rack in center of oven. Heat oven to 500°F.

Place shanks in a 14 x 12 x 2-inch roasting pan so that they do not touch one another. Roast for 20 minutes. Remove from oven. Use tongs to turn shanks and add whole onions to the pan, turning to coat with fat. Return to oven, rotating pan so that the end that was in the back of the oven is now in the front of the oven. Roast another 10 minutes. Add the garlic cloves. Roast 10 minutes more. Shanks will be crusty and brown. Reduce oven temperature to 375°F.

Remove shanks, onions, and garlic to a plate. Pour or spoon off fat from pan, reserving 2 tablespoons. Place the pan on top of the stove over high heat. Add 1 cup water and let it come to a boil. Scrape pan with a wooden spoon to deglaze all browned matter. Reserve liquid.

Using the reserved fat, grease the bottom and sides of a 10½-inch-wide (7-quart) stainless steel, enameled cast iron or tin-lined copper casserole with a tightly fitting lid. Place half of the beans in the greased pot. Add onions, garlic, shanks, and the bouquet garni in an even layer and top with the rest of the beans. Add tomato purée, wine, stock, and reserved deglazing liquid. Cover and bring to a boil over high heat. Cook in oven for 2 hours. Remove from oven. This dish can be prepared to this point a day ahead of time. Be sure to return to room temperature (about 1 hour) before continuing with recipe.

Sprinkle with salt and work salt down into mixture by wiggling a wooden spoon into it in various places. Return to 375°F oven, uncovered, and cook 20 minutes, or until warm throughout, adding more liquid as necessary.

TOTAL ROASTING TIME: 40 minutes plus 2 hours 20 minutes for braising

NOTE: *To quick-soak beans:* Bring the beans to a boil, amply cover with water, and simmer 15 minutes before covering. Turn off the heat and let the beans sit for an hour before draining them.

Mulligatawny soup

MAKES 8 CUPS; SERVES 8 AS
A MAIN COURSE

THE RETURNING COLONELS of the Raj brought back and bowdlerized the fondly remembered recipes of India. Often this soup was made with beef. I like it better with the emphatic flavors of lamb or mutton. The ingredients list looks endless; but the instructions are mercifully short.

This soup is very rich, and a cup was enough even for me. I adored it—and ate all of it up on a succession of days. Two to three tablespoons of chopped leaf coriander (cilantro) can be added at the end if the guests are sure to like it. It adds a nice flavor to the brew.

2 tablespoons unsalted butter

1½ tablespoons curry powder, preferably Madras

2 cloves garlic, smashed, peeled, and chopped fine

¼ teaspoon ground nutmeg

⅛ teaspoon ground cloves

1 small onion (about 3 ounces), peeled and cut into ¼-inch dice (½ cup)

1 large carrot, trimmed, peeled, and cut into ¼-inch dice (½ cup)

1 stalk celery, stripped with vegetable peeler and cut into ¼-inch dice (¼ cup)

½ green bell pepper, halved, seeded, deribbed, and cut into ¼-inch dice (½ cup)

5 cups Basic Lamb Stock (page 229) or canned chicken broth

3 cups Whole Plum Tomatoes (page 418), Plum Tomato Purée (page 418), or two 14-ounce cans Italian plum tomatoes, seeded, chopped, and drained

½ cup pearl barley

2 teaspoons kosher salt

1 apple, peeled, cored, chopped into ¼-inch dice, and tossed with 1 teaspoon fresh lemon juice

2 tablespoons chopped fresh flat-leaf parsley

8 ounces leftover lamb shanks (page 197) or Simple Roasted Boneless Lamb Shoulder (page 193), cut into ¼-inch dice (1 cup)

1½ tablespoons fresh lemon juice

Melt the butter in a 2-quart saucepan. Add the curry, garlic, nutmeg, and cloves. Cook over low heat for 2 minutes, stirring occasionally. Add the onion, carrot, celery, and pepper. Cover and cook for 2 minutes. Add stock, tomatoes, barley, and salt. Cover and bring to a boil. Reduce to a simmer. Cook 50 minutes. Add apple, parsley, lamb, and lemon juice. Cook just until warm throughout, about 10 minutes. Serve warm.

Lamb and kidney pie

SERVES 4 TO 6

THIS IS A version of my favorite, steak and kidney pie. I like it possibly better. It uses the best kidneys—lamb kidneys—which seems appropriate. I may also be fond of it because well-done end pieces work best. That's usually what's left from my lamb roasts.

Do not use a nonstick pan for the browning; it won't work. Feel free to add a quarter of a pound of mushrooms, cut into one-inch pieces

FOR THE CRUST

1 cup all-purpose flour

1 teaspoon sugar

Pinch of kosher salt

½ cup very cold vegetable shortening

1½ to 2 tablespoons ice water

FOR THE FILLING

2 medium carrots, trimmed, peeled, and cut into 1-inch lengths (2 cups)

1 tablespoon unsalted butter, plus 1 teaspoon, optional

12 ounces leftover meat from Simple Roasted Boneless Lamb Shoulder (page 193) or Simple Roast Leg of Lamb (page 186), cut into 1-inch cubes (3 cups)

¼ cup chopped onion

2 lamb kidneys (2 ounces each), cut in half lengthwise, trimmed of fat and blood vessels snipped out, and cut into 1-inch pieces

2 tablespoons all-purpose flour

1⅓ cups Basic Beef Stock (page 224)

1 teaspoon kosher salt

1½ tablespoons Worcestershire sauce

8 grinds black pepper

4 ounces white button mushrooms, wiped clean, stems trimmed, cut in 1-inch pieces, optional

1 cup shelled peas, defrosted if frozen

FOR THE GLAZE

1 large egg whisked together with 1 tablespoon milk or water

Make the crust first as it must chill. Combine the flour, sugar, and salt in a large, cold bowl. Add the shortening. Use two knives to cut the shortening into the flour until the mixture is in pieces the size of large peas. Sprinkle the ice water over the flour mixture, ½ tablespoon at time, tossing with a fork, until the mixture is just moist enough to hold together when pressed. Wrap the dough in plastic wrap and refrigerate at least 30 minutes.

Place rack in center of oven. Heat oven to 450°F.

Bring a small pot of water to a boil. Add the carrots. Cook 4 to 5 minutes, until tender when pierced with a knife. Drain and reserve.

Put ½ tablespoon butter in a medium skillet, brown the meat and onion over medium-high heat, about 8 minutes. Transfer to a 1-quart ovenproof dish. Melt another ½ tablespoon butter in the same skillet over medium heat. Add kidneys and carrots. Cook, stirring frequently, until no blood oozes out of kidneys, about 5 minutes. Sprinkle with flour. Cook 3 minutes, stirring. Add stock, using a wooden spoon to scrape up any glaze on the bottom. Add salt, Worcestershire, and pepper. Cook 5 minutes. Add mixture to meat and onions in dish. If using mushrooms, cook over medium heat for five minutes in an extra teaspoon of butter and add to meat. Stir peas into meat mixture.

Roll out dough for crust to a 6-inch round. Transfer to top of dish and cover meat mixture. Using your fingers, pinch round the edges to secure crust. Brush on egg glaze. Using a sharp knife, cut a few steam vents in crust. Cook 10 minutes. Reduce heat to 350°F and continue to cook for 20 to 25 more minutes until crust is golden brown. Serve warm.

Lamb soup with lentils

MAKES 7 GENEROUS CUPS; SERVES 6 TO 7
AS A HEARTY FIRST COURSE,
4 TO 5 AS A MEAL

THIS IS JUST the kind of hearty soup I like to turn into a meal. Speaking of posh! I made this with leftover baby lamb sometime during the many days I was testing those recipes. Of course, it does just as well with any leftover roasted lamb.

This uses almost no meat, a half cup. The real leftover is the lamb stock made from a supply of bones. It will not taste the same with another stock; but try chicken or pork if a rampant desire to try this recipe hits.

2 tablespoons olive oil

1 medium onion (8 ounces), peeled and chopped in ¼-inch dice (1¼ cup)

3 cloves garlic, smashed, peeled, and minced

1 bunch (8 ounces) broccoli di rape, tough stem ends discarded and the remainder cut into 1-inch lengths (4 cups, loosely packed)

1 cup lentils

6 cups Basic Lamb Stock (page 229)

8 ounces leftover lamb meat, cut into ¼-inch cubes

2 to 3 teaspoons kosher salt

Freshly ground black pepper, to taste

In a 2-quart saucepan with a heavy bottom, heat the oil over medium heat. Cook the onion until limp, about 6 minutes. Add the garlic and cook for an additional minute. Add the broccoli di rape and cook until limp, about 3 minutes. Stir in the lentils and add the stock. Cover. Bring to a boil and reduce to a simmer. Cook until the lentils are soft, about 30 minutes. Add the lamb, salt, and pepper. Mix well. Heat until warm throughout.

Baby lamb and goat

THIS IS THE place to stop reading if the very thought of cutting up a whole animal, let alone a baby animal, makes the head reel, the stomach quake. If proper baby animals weighing under thirteen pounds are available, as they are in the Southwest, California, Florida, Cuba, Mexico, Spain, Portugal, and Italy, they can be roasted in the oven like Roast Suckling Pig (page 183), but without the air drying.

The small goat is called *capretto* in Italian and *cabretto* in Spanish. The lamb (properly milk fed with white flesh and weighing around eight pounds) is called *abbacchio* in Italian and *corderito* in Spanish. The Italians happily oven roast with potatoes—usually halved lengthwise—surrounding the animals and sprinkled with lemon juice, olive oil, and rosemary. Spanish-speakers are more apt to spit roast or cook over a smoking pit, butterflied and suspended.

As a disadvantaged New Yorker, I was unable to get really small animals to roast. It was only by calling on Tony May and his chef Theo Schoenegger of the restaurant San Domenico in New York that I could get still young but larger ones—around twenty to twenty-five pounds—to test. Being around fifty inches long, they were too big to go into my oven. This is not a cause for despair. The meat is still delicious but requires more work to prepare it for roasting. It was butcher or nothing. Fortunately, I had previously butchered ordinary lambs, and they are a lot more difficult. The baby animals have soft bones. In some communities it may be possible to order just the parts needed.

The hardest part of butchering emotionally and physically is cutting off the head and neck. The dividend is having over three pounds of lamb or two and a half pounds of goat that is bony and gelatinous to boil up for stock with other bits that need removing, such as the ends of the legs and the tail. The kidneys, which are large, could be used in Lamb and Kidney Pie (page 200), and the heart can be added to the stock. The rest of the animal must be cut up with a large sharp knife into roasting-size pieces that will fit in the oven.

Baby lamb and goat are always well cooked, not rare. They will be moist and the skin crisp with no hint of pink.

Butchering a lamb or goat

DO THIS THE day before roasting. As pieces for the roasting come off the carcass, wrap them in plastic wrap. Those not being used for the party should be rewrapped in foil and frozen.

Remove the end joints of all legs by twisting them and severing the tendon with a sharp knife. Reach inside the body cavity and remove all innards. If kidneys are still attached, separate them from the body with a sharp knife.

To remove the head: Lay the lamb or goat on a clean cutting board. With a very sharp knife, free the meat from the bone at the point where the neck meets the body of the animal. Removing the meat makes it easier to get at the bone. When bare bone is exposed, sever the head and neck from the body with a cleaver or sharp knife.

To remove the two rear legs: Split the animal in half just above the saddle—double loin—and below the ribs. This will be easier if the butcher is taller, younger, and heavier than I, or any one of these. Put the beast on its belly. Take the knife and make an incision all around the center of the animal, following the swellings that indicate the divisions of the muscles—in fact, the waist. Cut in until reaching bone. Hold the ends of both back legs in one hand. Put your other forearm on the back of the animal just above the waist. Lift the legs while pressing with the forearm. There should be a sharp crack. With the knife, free all around the cracked backbone and wiggle the knife in to free the two halves. A small sharp knife may be needed at this juncture to get into the bone intersections, or a cleaver can be smacked through the remaining bone.

Put stock on to cook with head, innards, and odds and ends of bones amply covered by water. Allow to cook nine to sixteen hours. Bring individual cuts to room temperature, about one hour, before proceeding with the following recipes.

There will now be two halves of an animal. The rear half is the baron, which can be roasted whole if it fits into the oven. The lamb baron will weigh about nine pounds, the goat, around seven. If it's too big, proceed to separate the saddle from the legs. Make an incision between the top of the legs and the saddle. Repeat the lifting and pressure routine once again to crack the backbone. Again, use a smaller sharp knife or a cleaver to separate the saddle fully. It will weigh about a pound and a half.

To separate the legs: Remove any excess fat between them. Pull one leg away from the other. With the knife circle the haunch, being careful to get as close to the bone as possible so as not to lose any meat. This makes it possible to find the joint. Force the leg outward to expose the joint fully, and cut through it with a knife to remove the leg. Repeat the procedure with the other leg. This will give you two whole legs. For *short legs*, remove the chops and any bone above the joint. Each short rear leg is over two pounds. The trimmed-off pieces can be used for *stew*.

The front half weighs about nine pounds and contains two *racks* of two pounds each. Release the meat from either side of the backbone by cutting and scraping the meat away from the bone as one would to remove the breasts of a chicken. Turn the rib cage over so the backbone is flat against the table. Using one elbow as a brace against a side of the rib cage, push down on the other side of the ribs to remove them from the spine. When they crack, repeat the procedure on the other side.

Turn over the rib cage again so as to look directly at the spine. Use a sharp knife to separate any fat, cartilage, or meat holding the racks to the spine.

Either cook the two *forelegs*, weighing five pounds together, as a piece, or separate them as was done with the rear legs to get two two-and-a-half-pound legs

Roast baron of baby goat or lamb

SERVES 8

TOTAL
ROASTING
TIME:
see below

THIS IS A handsome presentation at the table, and the deglazing sauce is particularly good. The internal temperature when done averages 170°F—not pink, well done but tender, with addictively good golden, crisp skin. The goat will not smoke. The lamb may.

To carve, make diagonal slices through the skin into the meat so that each portion contains some skin and some meat. Otherwise, a piggy friend such as I will steal all the skin.

7½-pound baron of baby goat or 9-pound baron of baby lamb

Triple recipe Rosemary Rub (page 205)

1½ cups Baby Goat or Lamb Stock (page 229), other meat stock such as veal or chicken or water, plus ¾ cup stock or water, for deglazing

9 cloves garlic, smashed and peeled

Kosher salt, to taste

Freshly ground black pepper, to taste

Place oven rack on second level from bottom. Heat oven to 500°F.

Place baron in a 18 x 13 x 2-inch roasting pan. Use your fingers to massage rosemary rub into meat. Roast for 30 minutes.

Meanwhile, pour 1½ cups of the stock into a blender. Add garlic. Blend until smooth and frothy. Reserve.

Reduce temperature to 375°F. Cook for 15 minutes. Add stock and garlic mixture to pan and cook another 25 minutes for goat and 30 for lamb. Transfer meat to a serving platter. Pour or spoon off excess fat from pan. The goat will have almost none. Put pan on top of stove. Add the remaining ¾ cup stock and bring the contents to a boil while scraping vigorously with a wooden spoon. Let reduce by half. Pour into a heat-proof measuring cup; allow to settle; remove any fat that rises to the surface. Correct the seasoning with salt and pepper.

TOTAL ROASTING TIME: baby goat, 1 hour 10 minutes; baby lamb, 1 hour 15 minutes

Rosemary rub

THIS IS A GOOD, all-purpose rub for lamb of any kind or baby goat before roasting. Alternatively, for the goat, use a very intense sauce, such as the Barbecue Glaze (page 177).

1 tablespoon fresh lemon juice

1 scant tablespoon olive oil

½ teaspoon dried rosemary

½ teaspoon kosher salt

Freshly ground black pepper, to taste

In a small bowl, combine the lemon juice, olive oil, rosemary, salt, and pepper. Scrape down the sides of the bowl and use as desired.

Roast saddle of baby lamb or goat

SERVES 2 TO 3

TOTAL ROASTING TIME: 35 minutes

AFTER THE SADDLE is roasted, cut the meat from the bone and then cut crosswise into serving pieces.

1 recipe Rosemary Rub (above)

1 saddle of baby lamb or goat (1½ pounds), flaps wrapped around and under saddle and tied

1 cup Baby Goat or Lamb Stock (page 229), other meat stock, such as veal or chicken, or water

3 cloves garlic, smashed and peeled

Kosher salt, to taste

Freshly ground black pepper, to taste

Place oven rack on second level from bottom. Heat oven to 500°F.

Use your fingers to massage rosemary rub into meat. Place saddle in a 12 x 8 x 1½-inch roasting pan. Roast for 20 minutes. Meanwhile, pour ½ cup of the stock into a blender. Add the garlic, blend until smooth and frothy. Reserve. Reduce oven temperature to 375°F. Pour lamb stock and garlic mixture into pan. Roast 15 minutes, or until internal temperature reaches 160°F.

Remove meat to platter. Pour or spoon off excess fat from pan. Put pan on top of stove. Add the remaining ½ cup of stock and bring contents to a boil while scraping the bottom vigorously with a wooden spoon. Let reduce by half. Pour into a heat-proof measuring cup. Allow to settle for 5 minutes, then remove any fat that rises to the surface. Correct the seasoning with salt and pepper.

Roast rack of baby lamb or goat, whole or Frenched

SERVES 2 TO 3

TOTAL ROASTING TIME: *see below*

Bотн racks can be cooked at the same time to serve four to six when the ribs are cut apart.

1 recipe Rosemary Rub (page 205)

1 rack of baby lamb or goat (2 pounds whole, 14 ounces Frenched; see page 192)

1 cup Baby Goat or Lamb Stock (page 229), other meat stock such as veal or chicken, or water

3 cloves garlic, peeled and smashed

Kosher salt, to taste

Freshly ground black pepper, to taste

Place oven rack on second level from bottom. Heat oven to 500°F.

Massage rosemary rub into meat. Pour ½ cup of the stock into a blender. Add the garlic. Blend until smooth and frothy. Reserve.

For a whole rack: Place in a 14 x 12 x 2-inch roasting pan. Roast for 20 minutes. Reduce oven temperature to 375°F. Roast an additional 10 minutes. Pour stock and garlic mixture into pan. Roast 15 minutes more, or until internal temperature reaches 160°F.

For a Frenched rack: Wrap foil around the exposed ribs. Place in a 14 x 12 x 2-inch roasting pan. Roast for 20 minutes. Reduce oven temperature to 375°F. Pour stock and garlic mixture into pan. Roast 15 minutes more, or until internal temperature reaches 160°F. Remove foil from ribs.

Remove meat to platter. Pour or spoon off excess fat from pan. Place pan on top of stove. Add the remaining ½ cup stock and bring contents to a boil while scraping vigorously with a wooden spoon. Let reduce by half. Pour into a heat-proof measuring cup. Allow to settle for 5 minutes, then remove fat that rises to the top. Correct the seasoning with salt and pepper.

Carve the meat. Serve with pan juices.

TOTAL ROASTING TIME: whole rack, 45 minutes; Frenched rack, 35 minutes

Roasted short hind leg or foreleg of baby lamb or goat

SERVES 4 TO 5

CARVE THE ROASTED leg in lengthwise slices.

1 recipe Rosemary Rub (page 205)

1 short hind leg or foreleg of baby lamb or goat, trimmed (2½ pounds)

3 cloves garlic, smashed and peeled

1 cup Baby Goat or Lamb Stock (page 229), other meat stock such as veal or chicken, or water

Kosher salt, to taste

Freshly ground black pepper, to taste

Place oven rack on second level from bottom. Heat oven to 500°F.

Massage rub into meat. Place the leg in a 14 x 12 x 2-inch roasting pan. Roast for 20 minutes. Meanwhile, in a blender, blend together garlic and ½ cup of the lamb stock until smooth and frothy. Reduce oven temperature to 375°F. Roast an additional 10 minutes. Pour stock and garlic mixture into pan. Roast 15 minutes more, or until internal temperature reaches 160°F.

Remove meat to platter. Let stand 10 minutes. While the meat rests, pour off excess fat from pan. Place pan on top of stove. Add the remaining ½ cup of stock and bring contents to a boil while scraping the bottom vigorously with a spoon. Let reduce by half. Pour liquid into a heat-proof measuring cup. Allow to settle, then remove any fat that rises to the surface. Correct the seasoning with the salt and pepper.

VEAL

GOOD VEAL IS EXPENSIVE AND HARD TO FIND, WHICH IS WHY THIS IS A SHORT SECTION OF THE BOOK.

Veal has to be very good, or there is little point in roasting it. It will be dry and tough. The best of all possible worlds is a tender cut of a tender animal. Otherwise, it is better to poach or braise the meat, which is one of the reasons that, although I have included Tonnato Sauce on page 285, I don't give a real recipe for vittello tonnato; the veal for that is better off poached. If you cannot resist, use thinly sliced roast veal leftovers. Veal rack and loin will be pretty satisfactory, even if the market isn't the world's best. Veal breast will be all gristle no matter where it is bought and should be baked at low temperature or braised. Veal shoulder can be very good if the source is excellent. Otherwise, it is just like the breast.

We were all once conditioned to believe that only the very pearliest and whitest of veal was good, no matter how huge it might be. We know a little more today and have more options. The very choicest veal is bob veal, about a week old, mother fed, and weighing about fifty pounds. This is the meat—organic, of course—that I get in Vermont and in France at very special restaurants like Michel Guérard's. Other meat—usually male—can be called veal until it is twenty-six weeks old; but it will weigh as much as four hundred pounds and will be white and tender only because it is fed on formula and not permitted to be active.

Someplace in between comes two kinds of veal. Both are about sixteen weeks old and in the area of three hundred pounds. One kind, called "nature veal," is fed on formula after being taken from the mother at a week old. The calf is not permitted to eat anything other than the formula. The flesh is barely pink, and the fat very white. European veal will be of the "nature veal" persuasion. When a calf eats solid food along with mother's milk, its flesh darkens. This is the other kind of young, but not tiny, veal. To me it has more flavor; but it can be firmer.

My friend Jaimie Nicoll from Summerfield Farm, in Virginia, grows veal of this second kind. One of the advantages of the veal that has been permitted to rove and eat is that it is not so pumped up with chemicals. In various parts of the country, it is possible to get organic meat raised on organic feed. It will never be pearly; but the cook is doing a little bit for the planet and the health of those fed.

If you are lucky enough to have available young fresh free-range veal, keep the cooking simple.

Veal is lean and not marbled; the older it gets, the more surface fat it will have. Sometimes, this fat is removed entirely. I like to pare the fat down, leaving just the merest coating over the meat to keep the meat moist as it roasts. If there is no fat, the very thinnest slice of unsalted fatback or bacon can be placed over the meat for the same purpose. If the oven begins to smoke, remove the fat with tongs.

Veal does very well with sauces. It has just enough flavor to support a full-bodied sauce without competing with it. Try Champagne Sauce (page 44), Tarragon-Wine Sauce (page 31), Cumberoutlandish Sauce (page 106), and Béarnaise Sauce (page 307), substituting Basic Veal Stock (page 226) for other stocks where applicable.

Good vegetables with veal are endive, fennel, onions, and tomatoes. Rice goes well with the more elegant sauces.

Veal is too expensive to plan on having lots of leftovers. It also is too delicate to reheat well. If there are more leftovers than will be served with Tonnato Sauce as a first course or as a sandwich filling, make Simple Veal Salad (page 216). Leftover veal can also be substituted in Lamb and Kidney Pie (page 200). There it really is protected and doesn't get overcooked.

Roasted veal loin

SERVES 6 TO 8

TOTAL
ROASTING
TIME:
45
minutes

THIS IS AN elegant dinner party main course. Expensive and good. Boned and rolled loin of veal is a tender cut. It does not need prolonged cooking, nor should it be well done. Two loins can be roasted in the same large pan, leaving space between the loins and the edge of the pan. Two loins will give off more from their fat cover than one. This can smoke. Pour or spoon off the fat when reducing the heat.

A boned and rolled loin (as discussed on page 165) is made up of two separate muscles and may have a natural fat coating or not. A double loin often served in restaurants is four muscles—two from each animal—rolled together. A double loin will take forty minutes at 500°F and forty-five minutes at 325°F.

All loins should be allowed to rest after roasting. They can then be sliced fairly thinly across. If the pan is being deglazed—no vegetables—use a liquid that goes with the sauce or vegetable being served. Champagne Sauce (page 44) would call for a similar white wine or Champagne and a vegetable such as Sauté of Mushrooms (page 163), Basic Asparagus (page 318), Normandy Cabbage (page 330), or Mahogany Roasted Endives (page 351).

A single loin can be roasted with potatoes or carrots or a combination of the two. Cut two pounds of peeled baking potatoes into eight wedges each. Put the potatoes, slicked with a tiny bit of oil (canola or olive), in the pan around the loin and cook as directed, turning the potatoes every fifteen minutes.

Carrots companion well with roast as well. Peel and trim one pound of carrots. After the loin has cooked ten minutes, put them in the pan with the loin, coating with fat in the pan. After reducing the heat, add one quarter cup of liquid to the pan. Turn carrots after ten minutes.

3½-pound boned and rolled loin of veal (9 inches long), with natural fat cover trimmed to very thin

6 to 8 fresh sage leaves

1½ teaspoons kosher salt

Freshly ground black pepper, to taste

½ cup water, Basic Veal Stock (page 226), or wine, for deglazing

Place oven rack on second level from bottom. Heat oven to 500°F.

Put the veal in the center of a 14 x 12 x 2-inch roasting pan. From each end of roast, push sage leaves between the muscles. Use the handle of a wooden spoon to make sure to push enough in. Sprinkle all sides with salt and pepper. Roast for 25 minutes with the thicker end toward the back of the oven. Lower heat to 375°F. Roast 20 minutes more. The veal is done when the internal temperature at the thicker end reads 135°F on a meat thermometer. Remove to a platter, cut off string, and allow to rest for 15 minutes.

Meanwhile, pour or spoon off excess fat from the pan. Put pan on top of stove over medium-high heat. Add liquid and bring to a boil. Scrape the bottom of the pan with a wooden spoon to get up all the glaze. Let liquid boil for 2 minutes. Pour into a sauceboat and serve on the side.

Roasted double veal loin stuffed with veal kidney

SERVES 8 TO 9 GENEROUSLY

TOTAL
ROASTING
TIME:

1
hour

40
minutes

THIS RECIPE IS derived from one of James Beard's. He loved the dish. He was a big man, and perhaps this mammoth roast appealed to him. I find that it doesn't slice nicely; it comes apart. I would rather roast the veal kidney (page 217) on its own and serve neat slices along with slices of a single rolled veal loin. In that case, triple the sauce from the kidney recipe to serve with both the kidney and the loin.

This is a classic dish of which I am none too fond. The kidney is split in half lengthwise and encircled by the two loins, tied together. It takes two loins because otherwise there isn't enough meat to go all around the kidney. With all this meat, it is doubly important that it be at room temperature before roasting. I have stuffed it by making a lengthwise pocket in a single loin as in the Roast Pork Loin Stuffed with Prunes (page 170).

Veal with kidney wants more assertive seasonings than veal on its own.

1 double boneless loin of veal (7 inches long), with natural fat cover trimmed to very thin, rolled and tied around a 9-ounce veal kidney (5½ pounds total)

1 tablespoon unsalted butter, softened

3 to 4 teaspoons kosher salt

Freshly ground black pepper, to taste

2 teaspoons chopped fresh rosemary or 2 tablespoons chopped fresh thyme leaves, or 1 tablespoon herbes de Provence, optional

1 cup water, stock, or wine, for deglazing

Place oven rack in second shelf from bottom. Heat oven to 500°F.

Put the veal in the center of a 14 x 12 x 2-inch roasting pan. Rub butter all over veal. Sprinkle all sides with salt, pepper, and herbs, if using. Roast for 40 minutes with the thicker end toward the back of the oven. Lower heat to 325°F. Roast 1 hour more, until internal temperature reaches 165°F. Kidney should be fully cooked but may be slightly rosy.

Remove to a platter, cut off string, and allow to rest for 15 minutes.

Meanwhile, pour or spoon off excess fat from the pan. Place pan on top of stove over medium-high heat. Add liquid and bring to a boil. Scrape the bottom of the pan with a wooden spoon to get up all the glaze. Let liquid boil for 2 minutes. Pour into a sauceboat and serve on the side.

Roasted rack of veal

TOTAL
ROASTING
TIME:
1
hour
20
minutes

A RACK OF veal is an extraordinarily impressive piece of meat, with ten full rib chops standing in a row. To make sure that it can be carved, see page 192 for instructions for the butcher.

Veal goes brilliantly with sage, which is what I use here. It would be equally happy with fresh tarragon. Use a good third of a cup and make Tarragon-Wine Sauce (page 31), using the deglazing liquid.

7½-pound rack of veal, with most of the
    chine bone removed and rack cracked
    between chops for easy carving
10 to 20 large fresh sage leaves

Kosher salt, to taste
Freshly ground black pepper, to taste
1 cup red wine, Basic Veal Stock (page
    226), or other liquid, for deglazing

Place oven rack in second shelf from bottom. Heat oven to 500°F.

Put the veal, curved sides of the bones down, in the center of an 18 x 12 x 2-inch roasting pan. Between each chop tuck a few sage leaves. Sprinkle all sides with salt and pepper. Roast for 40 minutes. Lower heat to 300°F. Roast 40 minutes more. The veal is done when the internal temperature reads 160°F on a meat thermometer. You can turn oven off, leaving veal inside; the temperature will hold for several hours.

When ready to serve, remove veal to a platter. Pour or spoon off excess fat. Put pan on top of stove over medium-high heat. Add liquid and bring to a boil. Scrape the bottom of the pan with a wooden spoon to get up all the glaze. Let liquid reduce by half. Pour into a sauceboat and serve on the side.

Roasted veal shoulder with bacon and thyme

SERVES 10 TO 12

TOTAL
ROASTING
TIME:
1
hour
30
minutes

DON'T BOTHER TO roast this cut unless the meat is absolutely first-rate. A good butcher is the best guarantee. The supermarket rarely suffices. Even at good butchers, this is a fairly reasonably priced cut.

To roast potatoes in the same pan with the shoulder, use a larger pan so they will fit. Cut two and a half pounds baking potatoes into eight wedges each. After the shoulder has cooked for thirty minutes, put the potatoes in the same pan, turning to coat with the fat in the pan. Cook as directed, turning the potatoes every fifteen minutes.

To roast carrots in the same pan, use a larger pan so they will fit. Peel and trim two pounds of carrots. After the shoulder has cooked fork forty minutes, put them in the pan, tossing them to coat with the fat in the pan. After ten minutes, add one quarter cup of liquid to the pan. Turn carrots after twenty minutes.

1 teaspoon kosher salt

Freshly ground black pepper, to taste

5¾-pound boned and rolled veal shoulder, very good quality

12 ounces smoky bacon, cut into 6⅛ x ¼-inch strips, any rind removed and served (6 strips)

2 tablespoons chopped fresh thyme leaves

Place rack in center of oven. Heat oven to 500°F.

Salt and pepper the veal. Lay 3 bacon strips in the middle of a 12 x 8 x 2-inch roasting pan. Sprinkle with 1 tablespoon of the thyme.

Place veal on top of bacon. Sprinkle with remaining thyme. Cover with 3 bacon strips. Sprinkle any rind on top. Roast for 30 minutes. Reduce heat to 300°F. Roast 60 minutes more. Allow to cool slightly. Best when thinly sliced.

Veal stew

MAKES 4 CUPS; SERVES 4 TO 6

TOTAL
ROASTING
TIME:
see facing page

V EAL AND FENNEL have a special affinity brought to the fore in this darkly brown stew and pointed up with the aroma and acid of lemon. Veal stew is one way to get the flavor without the cost. Here, I use the oven-browning technique, page 234. Many veal stews are white. White stews require a completely different technique with no browning.

If canned broth or cubes are used, reduce the salt. Serve over noodles or rice.

2 pounds veal stew meat, cut into
    1½-inch cubes

1 tablespoon canola oil

2 cups Basic Veal Stock (page 226) or
    canned beef broth

1 medium fennel bulb (1¼ pounds),
    fronds removed, fibrous outer layer of
    bulb removed with a vegetable peeler,
    quartered lengthwise, and sliced into
    long thin strips (3¼ cups)

2 bunches scallions, roots removed, white
    parts cut into 2-inch lengths and green
    parts thinly sliced across on the bias
    (scant 1 cup), kept separate

Three 1-inch strips lemon zest

3 tablespoons cornstarch

¼ cup water

5 teaspoons kosher salt

Generous amount freshly ground black
    pepper, to taste

2 tablespoons fresh lemon juice

Place rack on lowest level of oven. Heat the oven to 500°F.

Place the meat in a 14 x 12 x 2-inch roasting pan. Pour the canola oil over the meat, tossing to coat. Roast for 10 minutes. Turn with a slotted spoon. Roast another 5 minutes. Turn. Roast 3 minutes more.

Transfer meat to a 3-quart saucepan. Pour or spoon off any excess fat from the roasting pan. Place pan on the stove over medium-high heat. Deglaze with ½ cup of the stock, using a wooden spoon to scrape up all the glaze. Pour into a heat-proof measuring cup and allow to settle for a few minutes. Skim off any remaining fat. Pour over meat. Add fennel and remaining stock to saucepan. Bring to a boil. Reduce heat and simmer 14 minutes, stirring occasionally.

Add the scallion whites and lemon zest. Bring to a boil. Reduce to a simmer. Cook 3 minutes. If preparing ahead, stop at this point and refrigerate. Can be made 2 days ahead. When ready to eat, return stew to saucepan, bring to a boil, reduce to a simmer, and continue.

Whisk together the cornstarch and water until a smooth slurry forms. Ladle cup of liquid from the pot into the slurry. Stir and add to the stew. Stir well. Bring to a boil.

Reduce to a simmer. Add the scallion greens. Cook 3 minutes, scraping the bottom of the pot with a wooden spoon to prevent the stew from burning. Add salt and pepper. Cook 2 more minutes. Stir in the lemon juice. Remove from heat and allow to rest 5 minutes before serving with noodles or rice.

TOTAL ROASTING TIME: 18 minutes plus stove-top cooking

Whole roasted calf's liver

SERVES 15 TO 20

TOTAL
ROASTING
TIME:
30
minutes

THE TEXTURE OF the cooked meat is like velvet (not "buttah"). This makes excellent party fare, once it is certain, of course, that everyone is up for liver. Liver is rich, so it feeds even more than you might imagine. Serve with fresh leaf spinach in butter, and mashed potatoes.

Whole calf's livers vary in weight. Try to buy a small one. Kosher calf's livers are paler in color and lighter in taste than ordinary ones. They are well worth hunting out. They run between seven and eight pounds. Ordinary calf's livers can be in the same weight class; but can be much larger. Don't despair. Calf's livers cook as do fish, by thickness. Ten minutes per inch will give rare liver—my favorite. Medium-rare will take about twelve minutes per inch. Any better done is a crime and probably accounts for the vast dislike in which calf's livers are held by much of the population.

It is essential that that thin membrane, like transparent surgical gloves, on the outside of the liver be stripped off by cook or butcher.

A little sweetness goes well with calf's livers and can be supplied by either Madeira or raspberry vinegar. If using raspberry vinegar, consider serving Basic Beets (page 319) and sprinkling the cooked, sliced beets with a little extra vinegar, salt, and pepper. The sauce for this dish is put through the blender to thoroughly purée the blood-rich liver juices with the rest of the liquid. This will thicken the sauce and make it seem creamy. Be careful when reheating the sauce; it can easily get grainy.

7-pound whole calf's liver (preferably kosher, 15 inches long and 2½ inches at thickest point), outer skin and major veins removed by butcher

2 teaspoons kosher salt

8 grinds black pepper

4 tablespoons unsalted butter

½ cup Madeira or raspberry vinegar

½ cup water

Place rack in center of oven. Preheat oven to 500°F.

continued

Place liver flat on work surface. Sprinkle half of the salt and pepper on one side of the liver. Turn and repeat. Use a roasting pan large enough so that liver can lie flat. Gently melt butter in roasting pan on top of stove. Remove pan from heat and swirl to coat with butter. Quickly turn liver in butter to coat both sides. Pat liver into a flattish layer with smooth side up. Place in oven with thicker part of liver to rear. Roast for 10 minutes. Shake pan so liver doesn't stick. Use a pastry brush to sop up all the pan juices and brush on top of liver. Roast another 10 minutes. Brush with juices. Roast 10 minutes more.

Remove liver to a serving platter. Pour or spoon off excess fat from pan. Place roasting pan over medium-high heat. Add Madeira and water, scraping up any brown glaze and pale blood with a wooden spoon. Let reduce by half. Pour liquid into a blender and process until smooth. Pour liquid into a small saucepan and heat over very low heat for 5 to 7 minutes. Add more salt and pepper, to taste. Serve in a sauceboat on the side.

Slice liver, starting in one corner, on the diagonal, at a sharp angle to get large, ¼-inch-thick slices.

Simple veal salad

MAKES 2 ½ CUPS; SERVES 2 TO 4

THIS SIMPLE SALAD allows the veal to express itself. More flavor, and the veal is swamped.

I use the smallest red-skinned new potatoes I can find for maximum color. For a little green and more flavor, sprinkle the bowl of salad or individual servings with finely cut or snipped chives.

8 ounces leftover Roasted Veal Loin (page 209), cut into ¼-inch dice (1⅓ cups)	½ teaspoon kosher salt
½ cup sour cream	8 ounces red-skinned new potatoes, steamed or microwaved whole, refreshed in cold water, each cut into 8 pieces
1 tablespoon fresh lime juice	

Combine all ingredients in a medium bowl. Serve on a bed of green lettuce leaves.

Roasted veal kidneys with Calvados and horseradish

SERVES 3 TO 4

TOTAL
ROASTING
TIME:
20
minutes

KIDNEYS ARE A special taste, not for everyone. In this country they are for fewer palates than in many other countries. I figure that the most fellow kidney eaters I am likely to gather is three to four, hence the size of this recipe. Kidney lovers may also be the type of cooks who don't mind some smoke in the kitchen. Let it be known now that this recipe does create smoke from the fat bouncing around in the oven. Turn on the exhaust fan, open a window; but please do not write me a letter complaining about the smoke as if it were a surprise. Enjoy the flavor. Also, be sure to open the oven door fully so as not to slosh hot spattering fat when removing the kidneys from the oven. Use oven mitts.

Kidneys cook better when completely encased in a fat layer. If there is not enough fat attached to the kidneys, buy sheets of fatback to wrap around them.

Veal kidneys are hard to come by. Not many butchers carry them. Do not use frozen kidneys. Kidneys used to be readily available, inexpensive, and came in their own hard shell of fat—the cleanest fat in the animal's body. I threw them on a grill or roasted them with only their natural fat, which got deliciously browned and crisp. If luck provides such a kidney, go for it. Otherwise follow this recipe, which uses two sheets of unsalted fatback, each measuring about six inches square, as a substitute. Whole kidneys used to be served one per person. That may be a bit much in our less heroic times as each kidney weighs eight to ten ounces without fat, about a pound and a half with fat. Some kidneys may weigh thirteen ounces without fat. Due to their shape, they cook in the same time as smaller ones. Today, I assume that each kidney serves one and a half to two guests.

2 whole veal kidneys (approximately 1½ pounds each)

2 sheets unsalted fatback, each 6 inches square, if no fat on kidneys

Kosher salt, to taste

Freshly ground black pepper, to taste

FOR THE SAUCE

2 tablespoons Calvados

½ cup apple cider

1 tablespoon fresh lemon juice

¼ cup freshly grated horseradish or ⅓ cup drained prepared horseradish

½ cup heavy cream

¾ teaspoon kosher salt

⅛ teaspoon freshly ground black pepper

2 to 3 teaspoons white vinegar

2 tablespoons chopped fresh flat-leaf parsley

Place rack on second level from the bottom of the oven. Heat oven to 500°F.

continued

Kidneys may come attached to a thick cradle of fat that separates easily. Place them on cutting board, fat facing toward you. Holding knife blade parallel to cutting surface, cut fat in half lengthwise, trying to make two layers of fat. Gently pull kidneys away from fat so as to make them easier to clean; you may need a knife to sever the fat where it attaches to the kidney's center.

Turn kidneys so that internal pockets of fat face toward you. Cut in half lengthwise through fat. Use kitchen scissors to remove interior fat and veins by snipping around the fat's outer edge, being careful not to separate the lobes. If the kidneys come without fat, simply cut in half lengthwise and trim.

For kidneys in their own fat: When the 4 halves are trimmed, put them back together to resemble 2 whole kidneys. Salt and pepper each. Either return each to its cradle of fat or if you are using fatback, use 1 piece for each whole kidney. Place 1 piece fatback on the work space, lay kidney on lengthwise, and cover with remaining piece. Wrap up edges like a little package and tie with kitchen string. Salt and pepper the outside of the package. Repeat with second kidney.

Place in a medium roasting pan that is at least 1 inch deep to hold the hot fat when it melts; there will be a lot of it. Roast for 20 minutes. The fat should be very brown and crinkly, and the kidneys rare to rose-colored.

Make the sauce separately while the kidneys are cooking. Over low heat, warm the Calvados in a small pan. Carefully light with a match and wait until flames die down. Pour into an 8-inch sauté pan.

Add the cider, lemon juice, and 2 tablespoons of the horseradish to the pan. Cook over medium heat until reduced by about half. Add the cream and cook until about 1 cup of liquid remains. Add salt and pepper. Add the remaining horseradish. Adjust the seasoning with salt, pepper, vinegar, and parsley.

Place several layers of paper towel on a plate. Using tongs or a slotted spatula, place kidneys on the plate. Paper towels will absorb any remaining fat. Remove kitchen string from kidneys. Serve the kidneys whole or, separate the halves, placing each, rounded side up, on a plate. The fat can be removed; but I like it the way it is with thin crispy layers of fat. Pass the sauce on the side.

*g*AME

I MEAN FOUR-FOOTED GAME. For birds, see page 88. For sauces to go with game, see page 105.

This is not a large section since it is hard to get game of good enough quality for roasting.

Venison

I LIKE VENISON, deer meat. The inexpensive cuts are perfect for stews and the inevitable chili, fine comfort food for casual dining; but that is not the province of this book. What is needed for a party is a boneless loin of venison (see below), also known as a boneless shell of venison. Venison is healthful because it has no internal fat. That means that it is palatable only rare.

Fresh domestic venison can be sold only to restaurants or eaten by the hunter. Unless the cook is a hunter or has friends who are, the venison available is farm venison, unless it's imported. The farm venison is paler in taste than the truly wild; but it is still excellent. Try to avoid frozen. Fresh meat that is shipped in Cryovac is perfectly acceptable.

Roasted boneless loin of venison

SERVES 8 TO 10

TOTAL
ROASTING
TIME:
15
minutes

THIS IS ANOTHER of those meats that is bought by the inch. I usually allow two half-inch-thick slices per person. Therefore I order an inch per person and add a half inch for the end pieces. Don't be alarmed if there is what looks to be a tough membrane running along one side. This is the silverskin. It doesn't need to be removed. It will mostly disappear during cooking. If it doesn't, it is no problem to slice the meat across and slide the knife over the silverskin to remove the slice.

I like to cut the slices on the diagonal to make oval slices, which I find more attractive on the plate. Two loins can be roasted side by side in the same pan. Simply double the ingredients. For a large party of twenty-four to thirty guests, I cook three whole loins and triple the ingredients. As the loins are often longer than my largest pan, I cut off the extra—I don't want the loins to touch the rim of the pan—and assemble the pieces as if they were an extra loin.

This dish really needs the butter, or the meat will not brown. Figure on a tablespoon of butter per loin. If the loin at hand weighs less and is therefore less thick than the ones I call for, figure the timing at three and a half minutes per half inch of thickness.

The sauce given here is a variant of Thulier Sauce, the creation of the master chef Thulier at L'Ostau de Beaumanière. The very rich sauce will be better with a somewhat sweet Port. It will keep until the foie gras is stirred in. The foie gras enriches and binds the sauce in the same way that swirling butter into a hot sauce does. It is important that the foie gras not melt entirely or it will make splotches or a layer of fat. Green Peppercorn Sauce for Duck (page 64) with Rich Beef Stock (page 225) replacing the duck stock, and Cognac, the deglazing liquid, would make a nice alternative to Thulier Sauce.

1 tablespoon unsalted butter, at room temperature, plus small amount for pan

3¾-pound boneless loin venison

Kosher salt, to taste

Freshly ground black pepper, to taste

½ cup white wine

⅓ tube (2 teaspoons) anchovy paste

FOR THE THULIER SAUCE

2 tablespoons unsalted butter

2⅔ ounces shallots, peeled and chopped medium-fine (¼ cup)

⅓ bunch fresh flat-leaf parsley, washed, leaves chopped medium-fine (¼ cup)

¼ cup ruby Port

2 tablespoons plus 2 teaspoons Basic Veal Glaze (page 227) or store-bought

1⅔ ounces canned whole foie gras or fresh, mashed with a fork until smooth

1 teaspoon tomato paste, from tube if possible

Kosher salt, to taste

Freshly ground black pepper, to taste

Place rack in center of oven. Heat oven to 500°F.

Smear a small amount of butter inside of an 18 x 13 x 2-inch roasting pan so that venison won't stick. Place loin in roasting pan. Make sure entire loin fits inside of pan. If not, cut to fit, sticking cut pieces together to cook. Smear loin with a tablespoon of butter. Salt and pepper. Roast for 15 minutes.

Remove the venison to a platter. Put the roasting pan on top of the stove over medium-high heat. Pour the white wine into the pan and bring to a boil. Keep at high heat. Scrape bottom and sides of pan with a wooden spoon to loosen tasty bits of meat and fat. Whisk in the anchovy paste. Cook 5 minutes. Reserve deglazing liquid in small bowl.

To make the sauce: In an 8-inch sauté pan, melt the butter over low heat. Add the shallots and simmer until translucent. Add the parsley. Continue to cook over low heat until mixture is thoroughly cooked and rather dry.

Add the Port, veal glaze, and reserved deglazing liquid to the herb reduction. Mix well. Bring to a boil. Cook until reduced by half. Reduce heat to low.

Whisk in the foie gras. Add the tomato paste. Whisk to mix. Heat just until warm. Add salt and pepper.

bison (buffalo)

BISON, THE AMERICAN BUFFALO ON THE NICKEL, HAD BEEN VIRTUALLY ELIMINATED FROM THE AMERICAN PLAINS. Now it is being farmed and provides a somewhat sweet, fat-free red meat.

Roast bison (buffalo) loin

SERVES 10

TOTAL
ROASTING
TIME:
20 _to_ 22
minutes

BISON NEEDS TO be cooked unbelievably rare to stay juicy and tender. Look for a final temperature of 100°F to 115°F. Slice the meat very thinly. It's a rich treat.

2 tablespoons kosher salt

1 tablespoon freshly ground black pepper

½ boneless bison loin (4¾ to 5 pounds, 9 x 9 x 2 inches), outer layer of fat removed, tail kept intact

½ cup red wine, for deglazing

Place oven rack on center level. Heat oven to 500°F.

Rub salt and pepper into meat. Place in a 14 x 12 x 2-inch roasting pan. Roast 20 to 22 minutes, or until internal temperature reaches 110°F to 115°F.

Remove meat to a serving platter. Pour or spoon off excess fat from pan. Place pan on stove over medium-high heat. Add the red wine, using a wooden spoon to scrape the bottom of the pan. Let reduce by half. Pour pan juices into a heat-proof measuring cup. Allow to settle for 5 minutes. Pour into the sauce any juices that have collected in the serving platter. Slice meat very thinly. Serve sauce on the side in a sauceboat.

MEAT STOCKS AND GLAZES

Meat stocks are still the basis of the best in cooking—pure or turned into glazes (see page 227). Vegetables or seasonings can always be added later in customized versions for each recipe, avoiding the risk of clouding, spoilage, or too great a concentration of salt. To turn two quarts of stock into a flavored clear soup, chop one small onion, one small clove garlic, one small or half a large carrot, one tomato, one stalk of celery, and four sprigs of parsley. Cook the chopped vegetables and herbs in a tablespoon of butter over low heat for twenty minutes. Pour into the stock. Simmer twenty minutes. Put through a fine sieve. Taste; add salt and pepper; serve hot. A few noodles cooked on the side or a few cooked julienned vegetables make these clear soups festive.

Stocks should be made in stockpots whenever possible. I have a huge pot and make multiples of the recipes. Choose pots made from nonreactive materials so as not to discolor the stocks, especially if they contain wine, vinegar, tomatoes, or something else acidic. Stockpots are significantly higher than they are wide. The stock keeps circulating over the bones and/or flesh as it cooks.

The solids in the stock should always be covered with liquid by at least two inches. The liquid may be water, wine, or deglazing liquids from roasting. Choose one that is sympathetic to the bones. Always begin by bringing the stock to a boil. Skim off any impurities. Reduce the heat to a simmer so that the stock barely breaks a bubble from time to time. This will keep fat from being bound into the stock by the gelatin that is being extracted from the bones. It will also keep the stock clearer, as will as much skimming during the course of the cooking as there is time for.

The bone gelatin is one of the chief virtues of good stock, giving the stock a smooth, rounded, velvety finish. Immature bones have more gelatin than those from older animals. That is why a veal knuckle is often added to the makings for stocks of other flavors.

Bone stocks need to cook for a long time in order to extract all this gelatin. Twelve hours is about standard for me; twenty-four is not too much. Top off the water from time to time by adding cold water, which will force fat to the top. While the stock is cooking, cover it with an otoshi-buta (page 11) or a lid set ajar to minimize evaporation. If the pot is fully covered, it is impossible to see what is happening and to properly control the heat.

If the bones of previously roasted meat are not being used, it is a good idea to roast bones before simmering to intensify their flavor and, where desired, to deepen the color of the stock through the caramelization of the bone surface. Burned bone is not desirable. It can be smelled. What is wanted is a nice, dark brown color. If vegetables are being included in stocks, they are frequently roasted before using. See tomatoes, carrots, and onions in the Vegetables and Some Fruits chapter.

Stocks with a roasted base are not for every use. They may be too rich and flavorful, too dark in color. Sometimes a light chicken stock (page 42) is desired for Chinese cooking or in oyster soup. The Fish and Seafood chapter has many fish stocks.

The amount of stock made will vary with the pot, the heat, and the length of time that the cooking is allowed to go on. The quantity can be adjusted by further cooking for the purpose of reduction or adding water. Be very careful when reducing gelatin-rich stocks or indeed making them. The gelatin can burn if the heat gets too high.

After stocks are cooked they should be strained (depending on the amount of solids) through a sieve or a colander that has been lined with a double layer of cheesecloth or a dish towel that has been wrung out in cold water. This will make the stock clearer. Either skim off fat immediately or refrigerate and remove fat after it hardens.

If the stocks are made to use later, divide them among eight-ounce freezer containers. Once frozen, they can be unmolded and wrapped in aluminum foil. Replace in the freezer, labeled with what kind they are and the date made. When I remember, I like to keep a dated stock inventory on the freezer door. Frozen stock will keep for about six months.

Unless started with a previously made and seasoned stock, these stocks have no added salt or pepper. If substituting canned broth or bouillon cubes for them in a recipe, be very careful when adding salt.

Basic beef stock

MAKES 1½ QUARTS; SERVES 6

TOTAL
ROASTING
TIME:
see below

Bᴇᴇꜰ ʙʀᴏᴛʜ ᴏᴜᴛ of a can or stock cubes are foul and to be avoided. It is better to substitute canned chicken broth if home-made supplies are depleted.

Beef gives good flavor to stock but lacks gelatin. Add a veal bone for texture. The meat from making the stock is a good meal as long as it isn't boiled to dishrag status. Slice very thin and serve with some of the broth and any bones with marrow still in them. A little horseradish or very coarse salt would be good. Remember, this stock has been cooked with vegetables. If not using broth immediately, refrigerate and then skim when it is cold. Otherwise, because of the vegetables, the stock can go sour and spoil.

Beef stock makes fabulous soups. See recipes, pages 158–159.

1 pound beef shank bones, split at butcher	1 medium tomato (8 ounces)
1¾ pounds veal bones, split at butcher	½ cup water or wine, for deglazing
1 medium onion (8 ounces), peeled and cut in half	2¼-pound piece of meat from beef shin (leave in 1 piece)

Place rack in center of oven. Heat oven to 500°F.

Arrange bones and onion in a 14 x 12 x 2-inch roasting pan. Roast for 25 minutes. Turn and add tomato. Roast 20 minutes more.

Remove and transfer bones and vegetables with a slotted spoon to a stockpot. Pour or spoon off excess fat from pan. Put pan over high heat, add liquid, and scrape up any glaze with a wooden spoon. Let reduce by half. Pour deglazing liquid into stockpot. Add water to cover bones by 2 inches. Cover pot and bring to a boil. Reduce heat to a high simmer, with lid slightly ajar, and let cook for 9 to 16 hours. Skim any scum that rises to the top, and periodically check the water level. Add cold water from time to time.

Three hours before using, add the beef shin meat to the stockpot. Add water to cover. Cover and bring to a boil. Reduce heat to a simmer. After 3 hours the beef should be nicely poached, but not at all stringy. Remove beef to a platter.

Line a colander with a damp dish towel and strain soup through it. Skim off fat or skim after refrigerating.

TOTAL ROASTING TIME: 45 minutes plus stove-top cooking

Rich beef stock

THIS DOUBLE-RICH STOCK is an enrichment of Basic Beef Stock and starts with it. I use the bones and plate scrapings from Standing Rib Roast of Beef to make a deliciously rich stock.

All bones and scraps from Simple Rib Roast (page 136) (7 bones, 4⅓ pounds total), cut into individual pieces

9 cups water, plus 1 cup water, for deglazing

2 cups Basic Beef Stock (page 224)

Place rack in center of oven. Heat oven to 500°F.

Put all bones and scraps, bone sides down, in a roasting pan. Roast for 30 minutes. Turn. Cook 20 minutes more. Do not burn. This extra roasting gives the stock a rich flavor.

Put bones and scraps in a tall and narrow stockpot. Add the 9 cups of water and the stock to cover bones by 2 inches. Cover and bring to a boil.

While water is coming to a boil, pour or spoon off excess fat from the roasting pan. Put the pan on top of the stove over high heat. Add the 1 cup water and bring to a boil, stirring constantly to scrape up all the brown bits from the bottom of the pan. Add to stockpot.

Reduce heat so that the liquid is simmering. Using a metal spoon, skim off the scum that rises to the top. The more you skim, the clearer the stock will be. Cook 9 to 16 hours (9 is sufficient, 16 is ideal), checking water level every 2 hours, topping off as needed to keep bones covered. To prevent evaporation as much as possible, find a lid that fits inside the pot and put it directly onto the surface of the stock.

Strain. Remove fat. Freeze or refrigerate.

TOTAL ROASTING TIME: 50 minutes plus stove-top cooking

Basic veal stock

TOTAL
ROASTING
TIME:
see below

Veal stock is used primarily as a sauce base or to enrich sauces, stews, and soups. Good chefs plop dabs of veal stock or its reduction, veal glaze, into this and that for that restaurant finish. It will keep at least six months in your freezer. Label and divide up into half- and whole-cup containers. Make multiple quantities if the bones are available.

5 pounds veal knuckles, split at butcher

4 small onions (about 12 ounces total), peeled or not

1 cup stock or water, for deglazing

2 quarts water or Basic Beef Stock (page 224) or any combination thereof

Place rack in center of oven. Heat oven to 500°F.

Put the veal bones and onions in a medium or large roasting pan. Roast for 20 minutes. Shake pan. Roast 25 minutes more.

Put the roasted veal bones and onions into a stockpot. Pour or spoon off any excess fat. Deglaze pan (page 10) with 1 cup liquid. Pour liquid into stockpot. Add remaining water or stock. Cover and bring to a boil. Reduce heat to a simmer. Cook 9 to 16 hours, skimming occasionally, adding water as needed to keep bones covered by 2 inches. When bones are falling apart or you have cooked the stock as long as possible, remove and let cool.

Skim and pour through a fine sieve. Divide stock into tightly sealed plastic containers, label, and freeze until needed.

TOTAL ROASTING TIME: 45 minutes plus stove-top cooking

Basic veal glaze

ALL MEAT GLAZES are modeled on this one. Reduce carefully so as not to burn it. The taste is not exactly that of veal stock. This is more caramelized. It takes up much less room in the freezer than the stock from which it comes. If I have made a vast vat of Basic Veal Stock, I multiply this recipe.

1 quart Basic Veal Stock (page 226)

Pour stock into a 2-quart saucepan and bring to a boil. Lower the heat and let simmer until the stock is deep brown and syrupy. It may be necessary to transfer the contents to a smaller pot as it reduces. Be careful not to let it burn.

Let cool, divide into containers, label, and refrigerate or freeze until needed.

Extra-rich beef stock

MAKES 1¾ QUARTS

THE SECRET TO this extra richness is the glaze. After a few hours of cooking, there is a bonus of soft, delicious beef to nibble on. Try it with some horseradish. Save some beef to put back in the broth for a hearty soup, or cut cubes into smaller pieces and toss with a mustard-horseradish vinaigrette and serve with warm new potatoes for a simple supper.

1½ pounds veal bones, split at butcher
1¾ pounds chuck beef, cut into 2- to 3-inch pieces

2 cups Basic Veal Glaze (page 227)
7 to 8 cups water, or to cover by 2 inches

In a stockpot put the bones, beef, glaze, and water. Cover and bring to a boil. Reduce heat to low, so that the liquid is just simmering. With a metal spoon, skim off the scum that rises to the surface. The more you skim, the clearer the stock will be.

Cook 9 to 16 hours, checking the water level after 1, topping off as needed to keep bones covered. After about 3, remove the meat. It should not be in the dishrag stage, but soft and edible. Continue to cook the stock until the bones are very brittle and falling apart. Nine hours is generally a minimum for this; 16 hours is better.

Strain. Remove fat. Freeze or refrigerate.

Basic pork stock

MAKES 5 CUPS

TOTAL
ROASTING
TIME:
see below

THE BONES AND plate scrapings from Roast Rack of Pork make a surprisingly rich stock for deglazing, bean soups, and pork stews. Pork stock is virtually cheating, it is so easy.

All bones and scraps from Roast Rack of
    Pork (page 162)

2½ quarts water or to cover by 2 inches

½ cup red wine or other liquid,
    for deglazing

Place rack in center of oven. Heat oven to 500°F.

Put all bones and scraps in a small or medium roasting pan. Roast for 10 minutes. Turn. Roast 10 minutes more. This extra roasting gives the stock an even richer flavor.

Put bones and scraps in a stockpot. Add water to cover by 2 inches. Cover and bring to a boil.

While water is coming to a boil, put the roasting pan on top of the stove over high heat. Deglaze pan (page 10) with the wine or other liquid. Add to stockpot. Reduce heat so that the liquid is simmering. Using a metal spoon, skim off the scum that rises to the top. Cook 9 to 16 hours (9 is sufficient, 16 is even better); replenish water as needed.

Strain, skim, label,and refrigerate or freeze.

TOTAL ROASTING TIME: 20 minutes plus stove-top cooking

Basic lamb stock

MAKES 3 TO 4 QUARTS

Lᴀᴍʙ ʙᴏɴᴇꜱ ᴀʟꜱᴏ provide a lot of flavor easily.

All bones and scraps from raw
    or roasted saddle, rack, or leg of lamb
    or baby lamb

Cold water to cover by 2 inches

Break up carcass or separate bones to fit in stockpot. Cover with water by 2 inches. Cover and bring to a boil. Reduce heat to a simmer. Skim well. Use an otoshi-buta (page 11), if available, to hold bones down in liquid, or a lid left slightly ajar. Replenish water as needed. Cook for 9 to 16 hours. Skim occasionally.

Strain. Cool and skim again. Divide stock into tightly sealed plastic containers, label, and freeze until needed.

Baby goat or lamb stock

MAKES 3 TO 4 QUARTS

Bᴀʙʏ ᴀɴɪᴍᴀʟꜱ' ʙᴏɴᴇꜱ are rich in gelatin; these are no exception. The stock is surprisingly flavorful.

Head, neck, and leg ends trimmed when
    butchering (page 202) an uncooked
    baby goat or lamb, heart and kidney
    cleaned, or all bones and scraps from
    any roasted baby goat or lamb
    (pages 204–207)

3 to 4 quarts water or to cover by 2 inches

Break up and separate bones to fit in stockpot. Add scraps. Cover with water. Cover and bring to a boil. Reduce heat to a simmer. Skim well. Use an otoshi-buta (page 11), if available, to hold bones down in liquid, or a lid left slightly ajar. Replenish water as needed. Cook for 8 to 12 hours. Skim occasionally.

Strain. Cool and skim again. Divide into containers, label, and refrigerate or freeze.

Extra-rich roasted triple stock or soup

MAKES 1½ QUARTS

TOTAL
ROASTING
TIME:
chicken,
60
*minutes
plus*

THIS IS ABOUT as good as stock gets. It has a chicken in it to include as part of the soup or separately (or use the carcass from a roast chicken) and veal knuckles and beef stock for a balance of flavors and gelatin. The canned chicken broth is an insurance policy in these days of anemic chickens; but it is easily replaced by water. If the oven is large, the chicken can be roasted at the same time as the bones. If not, roasting time will increase to 1 hour and 45 minutes.

5 pounds veal knuckles, split at butcher

2 small onions (about 6 ounces)

1 quart Basic Beef Stock (page 224)

5½-pound chicken, wing tips cut off and reserved with giblets

One 14-ounce can chicken broth

2 cups water, with more as needed to keep ingredients covered

Place rack in center of oven. Heat oven to 500°F.

Put the veal bones and onions in a 12 x 8 x 1½-inch roasting pan. Roast for 20 minutes. Shake pan. Roast 25 minutes more.

Put the roasted veal bones and onions into a stockpot. Pour or spoon any fat off the roasting pan. Deglaze pan (page 10) with 1 cup of the beef stock. Pour deglazed liquid into stockpot.

Put chicken in a small roasting pan. Move rack to lower third of oven. Roast for 1 hour, moving the chicken around with a wooden spatula to keep it from sticking after the first 10 minutes.

Meanwhile add remaining beef stock, chicken stock, wing tips, and giblets to the stockpot. Cover and bring to a boil. Reduce heat to a simmer. Cook, skimming occasionally, while chicken roasts.

Remove chicken and let cool enough to handle. Remove skin and throw away. Remove meat. Reserve for use in one of the recipes using chicken leftovers (page 34) or for use later in this rich broth.

Break up chicken carcass and add to stock. With skimming spoon, poke bones down into the liquid. If there is not enough liquid to cover all the bones, add water to cover by 2 inches. Continue to cook 9 to 16 hours, skimming occasionally as scum rises to the surface, and adding water as needed to keep liquid covering bones.

When bones are falling apart, remove from heat. Pour through a fine sieve. Let cool and skim again. Reserve to be used later or add chicken meat to eat now for the richest chicken soup of life.

OVEN BROWNING

Anybody who has followed me this far in the book will realize that I am very proud of my technique for the oven browning of meats that are to be cooked further in liquid in soups, stews, and braises such as pot roasts.

It uses a lot less fat than stove-top browning. The pan surface is larger, so that more can be done at a time. Less attention needs to be paid while the meat cooks. There is less spattering to potentially burn the cook. Best of all, it is controllable. When I say to brown meat, I know exactly what the cook's result will be. So does the cook.

Beef

BASIC
BROWNING,
BRISKET

6-pound brisket, trimmed but not completely fat-free; serves 8 to 10 as a main course

Place oven rack on bottom level. Heat oven to 500°F.

Place brisket, fat side down, in a 14 x 12 x 2-inch roasting pan. Roast for 30 minutes. Turn so the fat side is up. Roast 15 minutes more.

Remove brisket to a platter. Pour or spoon off excess fat from roasting pan. Place on top of stove. Add ½ cup liquid and bring contents to a boil, scraping the bottom vigorously with a wooden spoon. Let reduce by half. Pour into a heat-proof measuring cup. Allow to settle for 5 minutes. Remove any fat that rises to the top. Add to the sauce any juices that have collected around the brisket.

TOTAL ROASTING TIME: 45 minutes

BASIC
BROWNING,
SHORT
RIBS

2 short ribs, about 5½ pounds total; serves 4 to 6 as a main course

Place rack in center of oven. Heat oven to 500°F.

Cut short ribs into individual rib pieces and trim some of the fat. Place in a 14 x 12 x 2-inch roasting pan. Roast for 25 minutes. Turn ribs over. Roast 20 minutes more. Remove ribs to any dish large enough to hold them. Pour excess fat from roasting pan. Place pan on stove.

Add ¼ cup liquid and bring contents to a boil, scraping vigorously with a wooden spoon. Let reduce by half. Pour into a heat-proof measuring cup. Allow to settle for 5 minutes. Remove any fat that rises to the top. Pour into the sauce any juices that have collected around the short ribs.

TOTAL ROASTING TIME: 45 minutes

CHUCK AND SHIN are probably the least expensive and best cuts for stewing. Their somewhat open texture, marbling of fat, full flavor, and fibrousness that becomes gelatinous makes them ideal for these preparations.

Beef emits a lot of liquid during browning. Don't use a jelly roll pan. Use something deep enough to hold the liquid, which evaporates by the end of the cooking. After testing all rack positions, I found the lowest position to be the best.

The meat is cut into one-inch cubes. Each piece weighs about an ounce, so there will be about sixteen to a pound. A small pan holds a pound and a half, about twenty-four pieces; a medium pan holds three pounds six ounces, about fifty-four pieces; a large pan holds five pounds, about eighty pieces.

1½ pounds beef stew meat, cut into 1-inch cubes; makes 2⅔ cups cooked meat

Place oven rack on lowest level. Heat oven to 500°F.

Cut beef stew meat into 1-inch cubes. Place in a 12 x 8 x 1½-inch roasting pan. Slick meat and pan with 1 tablespoon fat. Roast for 10 minutes. Turn with a slotted spoon. Roast another 10 minutes. Turn again. Roast 10 minutes more.

Remove meat from pan. Pour or spoon off excess fat from roasting pan. Put pan on top of stove. Add ¼ cup liquid and bring contents to a boil, scraping the bottom vigorously with a wooden spoon. Let reduce by half. Pour into a heat-proof measuring cup. Allow to settle for 5 minutes. Remove any fat that rises to the top. Pour into the sauce any juices that have collected around the meat.

TOTAL ROASTING TIME: 30 minutes

Pork

FOR STEW, USE boned shoulder or leg. Don't waste the expensive cuts.

Pork, like beef, emits a lot of liquid during browning. Don't use a jelly roll pan. Use something deep enough to hold the liquid, which evaporates by the end of the cooking. After testing all rack positions, I found the lowest position to be the best.

The meat is cut into one-inch cubes. Each piece weighs about an ounce, so there will be about sixteen to a pound. A small pan holds a pound and a half, about twenty-four pieces; a medium pan holds three pounds six ounces, about fifty-four pieces; a large pan holds five pounds, about eighty pieces.

When the meat is cooked, there will be some fat remaining in the pan, which needs to be discarded.

1½ pounds pork stew meat, cut into 1-inch cubes (24 cubes, about 1 ounce each); makes 2⅔ cups cooked meat

Place oven rack on lowest level. Heat oven to 500°F.

Cut pork stew meat into 1-inch cubes. Place meat in a 12 x 8 x 1½-inch roasting pan. Slick meat and pan with 1 tablespoon fat. Roast for 10 minutes. Turn with a slotted spoon. Roast another 10 minutes. Turn again. Roast 10 minutes more.

Remove meat to platter. Pour or spoon off excess fat from roasting pan. Put pan on top of stove. Add ¼ cup liquid and bring contents to a boil, scraping the bottom vigorously with a wooden spoon. Let reduce by half. Pour into a heat-proof measuring cup. Allow to settle for 5 minutes. Remove any fat that rises to the top. Pour into the sauce any juices that have collected around the meat.

TOTAL ROASTING TIME: 30 minutes

Lamb

LAMB BROWNS VERY well in the oven and perfumes the kitchen. It has enough fat so as not to require any extra. Use inexpensive cuts for soups, stews, or braising. Neck and shoulder, boned or hacked through the bone, both do well, as do shanks.

BASIC
BROWNING,
LAMB
SHANKS

THE AVERAGE WEIGHT is one pound, three ounces. Six shanks fit comfortably in a large pan when placed lengthwise with the bone end of one shank next to the round end of another. Four fit comfortably in a medium pan when arranged similarly. Two fit comfortably in a small pan when placed similarly.

Two 1¼-pound lamb shanks, trimmed of extra fat; serves 2

Place rack in center of oven. Heat oven to 500°F.

Place shanks in a 12 x 8 x 1½-inch roasting pan. Roast for 20 minutes. Remove from oven and turn with tongs. Cook 20 minutes more. Shanks will be crusty and brown.

Remove shanks. Pour or spoon off excess fat from pan. Put pan on top of stove. Add ⅓ cup liquid and bring contents to a boil, scraping the bottom vigorously with a wooden spoon. Let reduce by half. Pour into a heat-proof measuring cup. Allow to settle for 5 minutes. Remove any fat that rises to the top. Pour into the sauce any juices that have collected around the stew meat.

TOTAL ROASTING TIME: 40 minutes

BASIC
BROWNING,
LAMB
SHOULDER
AND NECK
PIECES

THE NUMBER OF pieces used here is very rough, as it will depend on the presence or absence of bone and the cut of lamb. All lamb will leave fat, which needs to be discarded as it is too strongly flavored to use.

3 pounds lamb shoulder and neck pieces (about 20 pieces), trimmed; serves 4 to 5 as a main-course stew

Place rack in center of oven. Heat oven to 500°F.

Place lamb pieces in a 18 x 13 x 2-inch roasting pan. Roast for 15 minutes. Turn pieces with tongs or a spoon. Roast 15 minutes more. Pieces will be crusty and brown.

Remove pieces. Pour or spoon off excess fat from pan. Put pan on top of stove. Add 1 cup liquid and bring contents to a boil, scraping vigorously with a wooden spoon. Let reduce by half. Pour into a heat-proof measuring cup. Allow to settle for 5 minutes. Remove any fat that rises to the top. Pour into the sauce any juices that have collected around the lamb pieces.

TOTAL ROASTING TIME: 30 minutes

Veal

BASIC
BROWNING,
VEAL STEW
MEAT

THIS IS A good way to get maximum veal for the buck, as less expensive cuts such as boned shoulder, neck, and breast work perfectly well. Veal shrinks a great deal in browning, and I recommend the slightly larger cube size of an inch and a half.

The larger size and the lack of internal fat means fewer cubes to the pound. A pound of veal will make about nine pieces (about an ounce and three quarters each). A small pan holds a pound; a medium pan holds two pounds.

Veal emits more water and less fat than do the same size cubes of pork. Even though the cubes are larger, the veal takes two minutes less to brown than does pork. There is very little fat left at the end.

This is very good for brown stews. It is not for blanquettes, fricassees, and other white stews.

2 pounds veal stew meat, cut into 1½-inch cubes (18 cubes, about 1¾ to 2 ounces each); makes 3 cups cooked meat

Place oven rack on lowest level. Heat oven to 500°F.

Cut meat into 1½-inch cubes. Place meat in a 14 x 12 x 2-inch roasting pan. Slick meat and pan with 1 tablespoon fat. Roast for 10 minutes. Turn with a slotted spoon. Roast another 5 minutes. Turn again. Roast 3 more minutes.

Remove meat from pan. Pour or spoon off excess fat. Put pan on top of stove. Add ½ cup liquid and bring contents to a boil, scraping the bottom vigorously with a wooden spoon. Let reduce by half. Pour sauce into a heat-proof measuring cup, allow to settle for 5 minutes, and skim off any remaining fat. Pour into the sauce any juices that have collected around the stew meat.

TOTAL ROASTING TIME: 18 minutes

fISH

and some shellfish

The oceans, rivers, and lakes of the world provide one of our richest, most various, and best-tasting foods. As long as we do not poison the waters or become greedy about their treasures we will have wonderful fish and seafood. It is a shame that many do so little with them except in restaurants, especially as fish are low in calories and generally healthful.

Roasting is an easy way to cook fish. It is reliable; the timing is virtually foolproof and there is very little smell of cooking fish in the kitchen. The texture in most cases will be very similar to that of poached fish; and there is no messing with a lot of water or court bouillon and the fish does not get watery or give up any of its good flavors to the poaching liquid. While I have cooked many fish—happily—in a microwave oven, it is hard to cook a really large fish that way.

The one cardinal rule of roasting fish—as with any other cooking technique—is that the fish be fresh and vibrant. Many Chinese and the Japanese, great aficionados of fish, will not buy a fish unless it is swimming, or at least quivering, which certainly assures that it is relatively local. We should not be astonished. We have long known that lobster must be bought alive and active.

For most of us, checking for freshness in fish means seeing that the skin is taut. If the head is on, the gills should be of a clear red color, not brown, and the eyes should bulge out slightly and be clear rather than opaque. In all whole fish and fillets other than tuna, swordfish, and shark, the flesh should be pearly and semi-translucent rather then drab, flat, and opaque. Tuna, swordfish, and shark flesh will never be translucent; but should be moist-looking and rather shiny. (There is one exception; but it doesn't really relate to roasted fish. Connoisseurs of sushi often like their tuna to have some age on it, much as we age beef or the French age lamb.) It is particularly important to know about the flesh, as many people buy fillets and steaks rather than whole fish. Fish should never have a strong odor. A briny whiff is perfectly fine.

Once the market is checked for what is in season and what appeals, simply pick a way of preparing the fish that is equally attractive. The recipes in this book are meant to be guidelines. The fish on hand may be of a different weight or size or of a different type altogether. Many fish for which no recipes are given are also excellent for roasting. The breams and John Dory are outstanding, as are the larger freshwater fish such as large mouth bass, small mouth bass, and channel catfish. White fish must be cooked fairly briefly due to the softness of their flesh. It may even be that fish are not available in the form described. A whole fish may not be there to be bought or may be too daunting. All is not lost; check Roasting a Fish: Whole Fish, Double Fillets, or Single Fillets and proceed accordingly. The basic rules for roasting fish are very simple.

Fish with skin will become brown and crisp. Without skin, there won't be much of that brown crispness. With or without skins, butter will provide more browning than oil. Fish without bones need slightly more roasting time than those with. All timings—in the interest of safety—are for completely cooked fish. This means fish that is cooked through—not rare. However, the fish remains moist and tender. If rare, undercooked fish is preferred, reduce the timings by about one minute per inch of thickness. As with all roasts, the fish should be at room temperature before going in the oven to ensure even cooking. Usually, by the time the fish skin is scored and/or has marinated for a while, it will be ready to cook.

There is little special equipment that is needed for roasting fish, assuming that the kitchen already has a large roasting pan. Most useful is a pair of large spatulas of the kind used by short-order burger cooks. Pancake turners can be substituted; but the "serious" ones are stronger and longer. A pair of them can lift any fish that will fit in the oven and go onto a platter. Needle-nosed pliers or strong tweezers are helpful for removing the small pin bones that even good fish stores often leave in fillets.

Different kinds of fish can be substituted for those given in the recipes, depending on seasonal or other availability. Knowing the names and species of your local fish is important. What is "black cod" on the West Coast of America is called "sable" on the East Coast. The fish is not a cod at all. To complicate matters, many West Coast fish with an assortment of names, such as "redfish," are actually cods. On the Atlantic coast and in the Gulf a wide variety of fish with red skins are called "redfish"; they are not red snapper no matter what anyone says.

When choosing a whole fish, look for one that is relatively thick compared to its length. The cooked fish will give nicer, moister portions.

One benefit of roasting a large fish is leftovers. A little cool fish arrayed on a bed of greens with a light sauce makes a first course for the most gala of meals. A little more makes a main course on a hot day. Try one of the sauces on pages 292-309 or Roasted Plum Tomato Sauce (page 419).

If energy, ambition, and leftovers allow, use recipes I've included throughout the chapter for salads, soups, and fish cakes. Cooked fish doesn't reheat very well; but in these new, unrecognizable disguises the pre-prepared fish is a blessing rather than a liability. If we think of cooking as the use of one food as a building block for another, we can see how many of the world's best dishes evolved and why keeping the kitchen going on a regular basis is not mind-boggling but pleasant and easy.

A nice thing to do when roasting fish is to roast a vegetable along with it. For example, a three-inch-thick fish will normally take thirty minutes to cook. It could be surrounded with new potatoes, which also take thirty minutes. Add a minimum of fat to the potatoes as the pan will already have fat from the fish. Just season with salt and pepper or choose seasonings that complement the fish dish. If the potatoes take longer than the fish, it may be better to cook them in a separate pan. Put them on a rack lower than the one with the fish. Don't put them above the fish, as this will change its cooking time.

As I have grown more and more comfortable with roasting, I have done more and more of this companion roasting. It requires almost no attention, and the oven is hot, in any case.

Roasting a fish

Whole fish: It may mean talking to somebody where you normally shop or locating a fish store; but nothing makes a more gala presentation or a moister, more succulent main course than a whole fish. Fish may be roasted in steaks and thick fillets; but by far the best result, except for tuna, swordfish, and double fillets (page 272), will come from roasting a whole fish.

The amount of fish needed depends on the fish. Different fish have different ratios of bone and head to flesh. Recipe suggestions for quantity are based on the norms for that kind of fish. If substituting a different kind of fish, look at recipes for that fish to estimate how much is needed. When ordering, describe as follows to ensure that you receive the fish correctly dressed: "x pound(s) of fish, scaled and cleaned, gills removed, head and tail on."

The fish must be at room temperature for the cooking times in this chapter to be correct. Once removed from the refrigerator, the fish takes about an hour to reach room temperature. This is a good time to marinate the fish if called for in the recipe.

If the size of the fish available requires a different cooking time than that in the recipe, either remove the fish at the end of its cooking time and return the vegetables to the oven or add the vegetables to the pan when the fish has cooked for the additional time it requires.

Cleaning and preparing the whole fish: If the fish comes with skin on, run palm of hand along the fish toward the head, against the direction in which the scales lie. This will reveal whether the fish man has left scales on the fish, which is particularly common around the head. If there are scales, a vigorous rubbing with fingernails or the edge of a sharp knife should remove them.

Wash the interior of the fish, including the inside of the head, extremely well with cold running water to remove any traces of blood while scraping the point of a sharp knife down both sides of the spine to free any blood that is hidden behind the membrane.

With a large kitchen knife, cut two, three, or four parallel diagonal slashes into each side of the fish, depending on the size of the fish and the number of portions to be served. The slashes make the fish lie flat, even when cooked, and make portions easy to remove from the bones.

Roasting the whole fish: Put the fish in the smallest pan that will hold it comfortably. Placing it on the diagonal will give more room for larger fish. If the head and tail jut out slightly over the rim of the pan, that is perfectly okay.

Roast two or more smaller fish at one time as long as they can be placed in the pan next to each other lying flat. Placing them head to tail will generally give more room. Since the timing is based on the thickness of any one fish, more fish in the pan will not alter the cooking time.

Rub the fat or marinade into the sides, slits, and internal cavity of the fish for maximum flavor, moistness, and even cooking.

With the exception of soft-fleshed fish such as bluefish, shad, and mackerel, which require shorter than standard roasting times, or the very firm-fleshed fish such as monkfish, which require longer roasting times (see the Index for recipes), the thickness of the fish determines the time in the oven. To measure the thickness of a whole fish, place it flat on a cutting board. Using a ruler held perpendicular to the cutting board, measure the fish at the thickest point—usually slightly behind the gills. Cook the fish ten minutes for each inch of thickness. For example, if the fish is two and a quarter inches thick, it will need to cook for twenty-two and a half minutes. If the fish is being cooked with other ingredients, such as a stuffing, or if there is a thick layer of food under the fish, increase the cooking time.

Testing for doneness: The fish is cooked when a knife inserted through its thickest point toward the backbone reveals flesh that is opaque, not translucent. The fish may or may not flake, depending on the kind.

Serving the whole fish: The slashes cut in the fish before cooking make the fish easy to serve. Lift the fish, by section, between the slashes. When all the fish on the first side is served, lift up the bone from the tail end and put it to one side. Serve the remaining fish. Don't discard the head or bones. They are the makings for another day's soup.

If the fish is to be served with a sauce, even a deglazing sauce, put the sauce in a bowl or sauceboat, spooning it on each portion. This makes the fish easier to serve. Bones and bits of skin have a nasty way of getting into other things on the platter. Serve vegetables and garnishes separately too.

Double fillets: If a whole fish is hard to get or makes the cook squeamish, proceed the same way with two matching large fillets. This will make saucing and serving easier.

Ask the store to cut and fillet a center piece—a chunk through the bones and the skin. This will result in two matching fillets, which can be requested skin-on or skin-off. If even this is not available, choose two fillets that closely match each other in size and shape. If two fillets are not enough to make the number of servings desired, get four all of the same size.

Turn the fillets skin side down. If the fillets are skinless, the skin side will be the shinier, smoother side. A hand run firmly along the surface of the fillet will reveal if there are any pin bones, which even a good market may leave in. Using needle-nosed pliers or large tweezers, pull out the pin bones.

Place the fillets one on top of another, skin sides out, so that the thicker side of one fillet is on top of the thinner side of the other. This should provide a rough rectangle of fish of even thickness. Fold any protruding pieces over and tuck them in between the two fillets to ensure even cooking. Follow the general rule for determining cooking time, ten minutes per inch of thickness, making sure to measure the thickness of the fillets after you have sandwiched them together. However, if a thick stuffing is placed between the fillets, they will require a longer cooking time of about two minutes for each half inch of vegetables and herbs or five minutes for each half inch of a fish or seafood forcemeat.

Single fillets: Single thickish fillets of fish such as cod (page 271) can be roasted satisfactorily. Remove any pin bones and proceed with the recipe.

Stuffings

SOME OF THE dressings, sauces, or vegetables in this book can be used as stuffings for whole fish; they can also be put between the double fillets before cooking. Try Mushroom Purée (page 29), Bulgur Dressing (page 112), Roasted Plum Tomato Sauce (page 419), Green Herb Spread (page 295), or Hidden Depths Eggplant sauce (page 343). A simpler preparation might include a flavored butter or vegetable such as Basic Whole Red Bell Peppers (page 382). For sauces, try Jalapeño-Lime Sauce (page 302) or Ginger and Fermented Black Bean Sauce (page 308).

Basic fish stock

A WHOLE ROASTED fish provides me—once the guests have left—with the makings of fish stock. I carefully save all the good bits of leftover fish in the refrigerator. I put the head and bones in a sieve, rinse them well, break them up into smaller pieces, and put them in a pot with liquid to cover. The liquid can be water, white or red wine, or a fortified wine like vermouth in various quantities and combinations—usually two parts water to one part wine. Like other stocks, fish stock should be cooked in a pot taller than it is wide so less liquid is needed and it is rotated over the bones more often as it cooks. I add no vegetables or seasonings of any kind, leaving those for the soup. Vegetables can cloud the stock or go bad.

Any time I can get fish bones, heads, or, joyously, a cod collar (a big chunk of bone and gelatin), I make fish stock the same way. I segregate stock made from oily fish such as salmon to use only in soups and other dishes based on those fish.

I cook fish stock a long time, a satisfactory habit as long as I am not using the flat frames of flounder and sole, which give a bitter stock if cooked longer than twenty minutes—forty at the outside. Since these are not fish I roast anyhow, the problem does not arise.

I top the simmering liquid with an otoshi-buta (page 11). Just enough heat escapes to keep the stock from boiling up, and too much reduction is avoided. Alternatively, I set a lid on the pot so that it is ajar.

I have written this basic recipe for a small amount of bones and liquid. If making more, do not increase the liquid proportionately. I've included extra liquid to keep the stock from boiling dry. If it seems to be getting too dry, add some cold water. Incidentally, a Crock-Pot™ will keep the stock simmering without any worries about leaving the stove on. The microwave oven makes short work of fish stock.

3 pounds fish heads and bones, other than those of flat fish, fresh or from a previously roasted fish

2 quarts liquid

If not using fish heads and bones from previously roasted fish, wash very well to eliminate all traces of blood and cut out the nasty-tasting oil-rich gills with scissors. Put the fish heads and bones in a stockpot and cover with the liquid. Place the pot over high heat, cover, and bring to a boil. Skim off the scum that rises to the top. Lower the heat and simmer the stock 4 to 6 hours, or until approximately 4 cups of broth remain, skimming as necessary. Refrigerate for 2 to 3 days or freeze for up to 6 months.

Divine fish chowder

MAKES 5 CUPS; SERVES 4

I ONCE KNEW a woman named Divine. She was not a John Waters star but a follower of Father Divine and took his name in homage. She made one fine fish chowder. I never equaled it until recently. I made a chowder using leftovers from Roasted Double Fillet of Cod (page 272). I inadvertently overcooked the potatoes; there it was. Any leftover fish can be used, say salmon. If you have salmon bones and a head, make a stock from them. With a green salad, this is a warming family meal for a winter night. It is elegant enough to open a company meal.

1 medium onion (8 ounces), peeled and chopped fine (1¼ cup)

2 tablespoons unsalted butter, or bacon grease if using optional lardoons

1 tablespoon all-purpose flour

1 cup Basic Fish Stock (page 243)

2 cups whole milk

1 cup heavy cream

1 medium floury potato (8 ounces), such as Idaho, peeled and cut into ¼-inch dice (1½ cups)

2 teaspoons kosher salt

6 to 8 grinds black pepper

2½ cups flaked leftover roasted fish

Hot red pepper sauce, to taste, optional

2½ ounces bacon lardoons, from 2 strips bacon cut into ¼-inch dice and roasted (Basic Lardoons, page 392), optional

Put the onion and butter or bacon grease into a medium saucepan. Cook over medium heat for 10 minutes, or until onions are translucent. Sprinkle flour evenly over onions and stir until well combined. Add stock, 1 cup of the milk, and cream, stirring until smooth. Add potatoes, salt, and pepper. Cover and bring to a boil over high heat. Reduce heat to medium and cook for 35 minutes, or until potatoes are very soft.

Add fish, stirring gently and thoroughly along the bottom of the pan so mixture will not stick. Add remaining cup of milk or as much as necessary to make a pleasantly creamy texture. Heat until warm throughout. Add more salt and pepper if needed and a touch of hot red pepper sauce if wanted. Top each portion with lardoons, if using.

FIRM-FLESHED FISH

The fish in this first group are all pleasantly firm and easy to handle. They can be roasted according to the basic rule of ten minutes an inch at 500°F.

Salmon

SALMON IS PROBABLY THE FISH MOST OFTEN SERVED WHOLE AND THERE-FORE THE MOST READILY AVAILABLE. There are many different fish—such as char and trout—masquerading under the single name "salmon." While the recipes given for the different fish are fairly interchangeable, and salmon can be substituted in most of the other recipes calling for a whole fish, it is worthwhile knowing the differences between the flavors, yields, and textures to know how much boned fish can actually be served after filleting a given weight of cooked "salmon." The yield can go from as little as a third of the weight of the whole raw fish with a king salmon to as much as four fifths with a coho salmon; that's a big difference.

Pacific salmon such as king, Chinook, and the redder-fleshed sockeye are generally softer and fattier than Atlantic salmon—also more fattening. From time to time, I have eaten Pacific albinos with very pale flesh. They are superb.

Save leftover flesh and bones. These treasures can be used in Everyday Fish Cakes (page 250), Sesame-Ginger Salmon Salad (page 248), Best Cod Hash (page 274), Dilled Salmon Orzo Soup (page 249), or Divine Fish Chowder (page 244). A lovely jelly forms on leftover salmon in the refrigerator. Put it in the Dilled Salmon Orzo Soup or use it to enrich other dishes.

Roasted Atlantic salmon

SERVES 6 AS A MAIN COURSE

TOTAL
ROASTING
TIME:
see page 246

A PACIFIC SALMON can be substituted. When I was lucky enough one spring to get a line-caught (wild) Atlantic salmon, I had a true if expensive delicacy. This is a good, basic recipe for any large fish. Increase or decrease sauce ingredients, depending on the size of the fish. A half cup of chopped fresh dill or mint can be added to the roasting pan when making the deglazing sauce. If the idea appeals, cook two tablespoons to a quarter cup of finely chopped shallots in the wine before using it. For a richer sauce, stir in a quarter cup of heavy cream or two tablespoons of butter after the sauce is reduced and cook just until hot. The butter should barely dissolve.

Basic Asparagus (page 318) or steamed peas are traditional vegetables with salmon. The vegetable can be cooked on another rack while the fish roasts. Don't use a very strong-tasting vegetable; it will overwhelm the fish.

4-pound scaled, gutted, and cleaned (gills removed) Atlantic salmon (2¼ inches at thickest point), head and tail on, interior cavity well washed to remove any blood

2 tablespoons olive oil

2 tablespoons fresh lemon juice

2 tablespoons kosher salt

Freshly ground black pepper, to taste

½ to ¾ cup white wine

OPTIONAL INGREDIENTS

¼ cup heavy cream

1 tablespoon unsalted butter

½ cup fresh tarragon leaves, coarsely chopped dill, or finely sliced lovage, lemon balm, or mint

Remove the fish from refrigerator. With a large kitchen knife, cut 3 parallel diagonal slashes into each side of the fish. Cut about 1 to 1½-inches into the flesh. Place the fish on a diagonal in an 18 x 13 x 2-inch roasting pan. If part of the fish head and/or tail hangs over the corners, that is fine. Rub the olive oil and lemon juice into both sides of the fish, including the slashes, and into the interior. Sprinkle both sides with salt and pepper. It will take about 1 hour for the marinating fish to come to room temperature.

About 20 minutes before cooking the fish, place rack in center of oven. Heat oven to 500°F.

Roast for about 22 minutes. Using two very large spatulas, remove fish to serving platter.

Put the roasting pan on top of the stove. Add the white wine and bring contents to a boil while scraping the bottom vigorously with a wooden spoon. Let reduce by half. Add cream or butter and/or herbs, if using. Season to taste. Serve on the side in a sauceboat.

TOTAL ROASTING TIME: 22 minutes (10 minutes per inch of thickness)

Roasted coho salmon

Wᴴɪʟᴇ ᴛʜɪs ɪs a good basic recipe for these most elegant of fish, it really soars when served with Gingered Cucumbers (page 336), which can be cooked in the same oven with the fish for about the same time. One coho will serve four. Use half the amount of other ingredients and make a half recipe of cucumbers using a small pan.

Three 2-pound scaled, gutted, and
   cleaned (gills removed) coho salmon
   (each 2 inches at thickest point), head
   and tail on, interior cavity well washed
   to remove any blood
1 tablespoon kosher salt
1 tablespoon unsalted butter

1 bunch (1 ounce) fresh mint, leaves
   chopped and stems reserved
½ cup white wine
Freshly ground black pepper, to taste
½ cup water
One 8-ounce container nonfat yogurt
   (¾ cup)

With a large kitchen knife, cut 3 parallel diagonal slashes into each side of each fish, slicing about ½ to 1 inch into the flesh. Sprinkle fish on both sides with salt.

Use ½ tablespoon of the butter to grease an 18 x 13 x 2-inch roasting pan. Be sure to butter the sides of the pan so that the fish will not stick.

Place all 3 fish in the pan. Outer 2 fish should be placed with backbones toward the edges of the pan. If there is room, do not let fish touch each other or sides of pan. Stuff mouths and body cavities with mint stems.

Sprinkle with ¼ cup of the white wine. Put tiny dabs of remaining butter in each visible slit and inside the heads. Lightly but evenly grind black pepper over the fish.

Place rack in center of oven. If making Gingered Cucumbers (page 336) at the same time, place a second rack in the bottom of the oven. Roast cucumbers as in that recipe. Heat oven to 500°F.

Roast for 20 minutes. Using a large spatula, remove to a platter. Place pan on top of stove. Add the remaining white wine and the water and bring contents to a boil while scraping the bottom vigorously with a wooden spoon. Let reduce by half. Reduce heat to a simmer and stir in the chopped mint.

Reduce heat to lowest possible. Add the yogurt. Cook, stirring, until barely warm. Spoon over fish or pour sauce over cucumbers in a separate bowl.

TOTAL ROASTING TIME: 20 minutes (10 minutes per inch of thickness)

Salmon stock

MAKES 2¼ CUPS

HEADS AND BONES left over from roasted salmon can make a more than usually intense stock that gels with a pale golden salmon color. There will be just enough for a loving pair to share Dilled Salmon Orzo Soup (page 249) or eight to enjoy a double quantity of Divine Fish Chowder (page 244) using leftover salmon as the fish.

Frame, head, skin, and small bones from 4-pound Roasted Atlantic Salmon (page 245)

½ cup white wine

4 cups water

Put all fish remnants in a stockpot. Add the wine and 3½ cups of the water. Bring to a boil. Reduce heat to a simmer. Cook for 2 hours, skimming the froth off the top with a metal spoon every 30 to 45 minutes. After 1½ hours, add the remaining ½ cup water.

Strain through a very fine sieve. Reserve for the soup chowder or refrigerate.

Sesame-ginger salmon salad

MAKES 2 CUPS; SERVES 4 AS A FIRST COURSE, 2 AS A MAIN COURSE

THIS PRETTY AND simple salad can be multiplied as many times as there are leftovers.

2 cups of 1-inch fish pieces from leftover roasted salmon

3 teaspoons sesame oil

2 tablespoons soy sauce, preferably tamari

2 tablespoons rice wine vinegar

2 tablespoons chopped fresh cilantro

2 tablespoons chopped scallions, white and green parts

½ teaspoon grated fresh gingerroot

2 to 3 grinds black pepper

1 head endive

Place salmon pieces in a medium bowl. The pieces do not need to be the same size.

In a small bowl, whisk together remaining ingredients except the endive.

Pour the liquid over salmon pieces. Toss gently with your hands until all pieces are covered. Serve on a bed of endive.

Dilled salmon orzo soup

MAKES 2 CUPS; SERVES 2 AS A
FIRST COURSE

IF THERE IS more stock, make more soup for a first-course company dinner.

1½ cups Salmon Stock (page 248)

2 tablespoons small dice of celery stalk, peeled first with a vegetable peeler

1 tablespoon chopped scallions, white and green parts

1 tablespoon chopped fresh dill

¾ cup of ½-inch fish pieces from leftover roasted salmon

½ cup cooked orzo

¼ teaspoon kosher salt

1 to 2 grinds black pepper

Put the salmon stock and celery into a small saucepan. Bring to a boil. Reduce heat to a simmer and cook about 5 minutes. Add the scallions, half the dill, and the bits and pieces of salmon and simmer another 5 minutes. Add the orzo, stirring well, and simmer until heated throughout. Add salt and pepper. Serve, sprinkled with remaining dill.

Richie Rich fish cakes

MAKES 2 FISH CAKES; SERVES 2

THESE ARE A little sloppy to handle because of all the cream; but for sublime richness, they are worth the fiddling. The recipe serves only two as a main course. These are based on leftovers. If there is more fish, allow a half cup per person. I have made these with salmon and cod. Both were fine. I wouldn't use a dry fish, such as swordfish, or a strong one, such as bluefish.

These cakes form a nice crisp crust and truly don't need a sauce or—fortune forbid—ketchup. Just add a salad of small leaves for a good main course.

18 saltine or other crackers

1 cup flaked leftover roasted fish

1½ tablespoons finely diced celery

1½ tablespoons finely diced onion

½ teaspoon kosher salt

3 grinds black pepper

⅓ cup heavy cream

½ tablespoon unsalted butter

Crush crackers with a heavy rolling pin until in very fine crumbs (about ¾ cup).

continued

Place all ingredients except crumbs and butter in a medium bowl. Smush together until well combined. Sprinkle the crumbs evenly on the work surface. Divide fish mixture in half. Form each half into a cake about 4 inches in diameter and ¾ inch thick. Plop each cake down onto crumbs. Pat crumbs all over so that all exposed surfaces are covered.

Melt butter in a small, nonstick skillet just large enough to hold the two cakes. With a pancake turner or large spatula, gently transfer crumb-covered cakes to skillet. Cook over medium heat for 6 minutes. Turn with a spatula and cook for 6 minutes more. Surfaces should be nicely browned; if they start to get too brown, reduce heat.

Everyday fish cakes

SERVES 4 ADULTS, 8 CHILDREN

THESE CAN BE made with leftover salmon or another fish, such as cod. Children who like fish sticks will like these in smaller sizes, but not with the jalapeños. Adults like them a lot better served with the peppers and Tartar Sauce (page 305). Make two batches of two cakes at a time. Serve one each as a main course.

25 saltine or other crackers	10 grinds black pepper
3 cups flaked leftover roasted fish	2 eggs, lightly beaten
3 tablespoons peeled and finely chopped celery	1 teaspoon seeded, deribbed, and chopped Basic Jalapeños (page 383), optional
3 tablespoons finely chopped onion	
¾ teaspoon kosher salt	¼ cup (½ stick) unsalted butter

Crush crackers with a heavy rolling pin until in fine crumbs, about 1 cup. Place in a layer on a sheet pan or on a work surface.

Combine remaining ingredients except for butter. Divide fish mixture into 4 equal parts (8 for children). Form each part into a cake about 3½ inches in diameter and ¾ inch thick. Plop each cake down onto crumbs. Pat crumbs all over so that all exposed surfaces are covered.

Melt half the butter in a small nonstick skillet just large enough to hold 2 cakes. With a pancake turner or large spatula, gently transfer 2 crumb-covered cakes to skillet. Four of the child-size cakes cook at a time. Cook over medium heat for 6 minutes. Turn with a spatula and cook for 6 minutes more. Surfaces should be nicely browned; if they start to get too brown, reduce heat. Repeat with remaining butter and fish cakes.

Striped bass

Striped bass is one of the world's greatest eating fish, with semifirm, moist, very white flesh that has a slightly sweet, nonoily taste. Not all fish sold as bass are true striped bass, particularly because striped bass are now being farmed and are often cross-bred with other fish. Wild striped bass that have been line-caught are infinitely better than farm-raised and are usually larger. Farm-raised fish will generally weigh about two and a half to three pounds and be about two and a half inches thick.

When deciding what size fish to buy, allow about eight ounces (half a pound) of boned flesh per person for a main course, or four ounces for a first course. Since approximately a third of the weight of a whole striped bass is head and bones (I don't call them waste since they make fabulous stock; see page 243), buy three pounds of fish for four main-course servings.

Grouper, sea bass, black bass, large- and small-mouth freshwater bass, red snapper, the mullets, John Dory, orange roughy, and the breams can be substituted in any of the striped bass recipes. On the Pacific coast, use rockfish.

It would be a shame to waste striped bass leftovers on dishes in which its subtle flavor and texture get lost, except perhaps for Richie Rich Fish Cakes (page 250). Instead, serve leftovers with a sauce chosen from pages 292–309.

Roasted striped bass with fennel

SERVES 6 TO 8 AS A MAIN COURSE

TOTAL ROASTING TIME: *see page 252*

Dried stalks of the herb fennel flame on open fires in the South of France when loup de mer (sea bass) is grilled; the flavor of fennel seems to go naturally with striped bass. Here, the fennel is Florence fennel served as a vegetable.

I had a fabulous wild bass when I made this; but the recipe is easy to adapt for smaller farm-raised striped bass. Substitute two of the largest ones available. Put them side by side, head to tail, in a roasting pan. If using the two farm-raised bass, put another rack in the oven under the rack where the bass will go. Put the fennel in a second, medium-sized roasting pan and set it in the oven ten minutes before starting the fish.

continued

6-pound scaled, gutted, and cleaned (gills
    removed) striped bass (3 inches at thick-
    est point) or two 3-pound farm-raised
    striped bass, head and tail on, interior
    cavity well washed to remove any blood
½ cup olive oil

½ cup fresh lemon juice
2 tablespoons kosher salt
10 to 15 grinds black pepper
4 large fennel bulbs (10 ounces each,
    2½ pounds total), with some stalk
    and fronds

Remove the fish from refrigerator. With a large kitchen knife, cut 3 parallel diagonal slashes into each side of the fish. Cut about 1 to 1½ inches into the flesh. Prepare an 18 x 13 x 2-inch roasting pan by rubbing about ¼ cup of the olive oil all over it with your hands. Place the fish in the pan on a diagonal. If part of the fish head and/or tail hangs over the corners, that is fine.

Rub 2 tablespoons of the olive oil, 2 tablespoons of the lemon juice, and 1 tablespoon of the salt into sides of the fish, including the slashes, and into the internal cavity. This is enough liquid so that a thin film will be visible. Grind some pepper into the cavity.

It will take about 1 hour for the marinating fish to come to room temperature. Meanwhile, rinse off your hands and prepare the fennel. Cut off stalks and fronds. With a large knife, coarsely cut up the stalks. Stuff as many pieces as will fit into the fish head and body cavity. Reserve the fronds. Trim a thin slice from the root end of bulbs to clean, but leave bulbs in 1 piece. With a vegetable peeler, remove dark areas and coarse string from outside of bulbs. Cut each bulb lengthwise through leaves and stem ends to make wedges, about 8 to 10 per bulb.

Make a layer of fennel wedges around fish. Spoon over them the remaining olive oil and all but a few teaspoons of the lemon juice. Sprinkle the wedges with the remaining salt and the pepper.

From time to time, tilt the roasting pan to collect some of the juices in a corner and spoon over fish and fennel.

About 20 minutes before roasting the fish and fennel, or if cooking separately, before roasting the fennel, place rack in center of oven. Heat oven to 500°F. Roast for 35 minutes.

Using 2 very large spatulas, remove fish to serving platter. Either surround fish on platter with fennel and pour pan juices and remaining lemon juice over all, or place fennel and pan juices in a separate serving bowl, which will make it easier to bone the fish, and pour remaining lemon juice over fish. Coarsely chop reserved fennel fronds. Sprinkle over fish and fennel platter or, if using separate serving bowl for fennel, divide evenly between the fish and fennel.

TOTAL ROASTING TIME: 35 minutes (10 minutes per inch of thickness)

Striped bass Provençal salad

MAKES 5 CUPS; SERVES 6 AS
A FIRST COURSE

A BEAUTIFUL, LARGE, roasted striped bass may provide a reasonable amount of leftovers. The same will be true when one farm-raised striper isn't enough for everybody and two are cooked. Choose a less assertive olive oil with this to let the bass sing through.

1½ tablespoons tarragon vinegar

2 teaspoons anchovy paste mixed with
1 tablespoon warm water

3 tablespoons olive oil

2 heads endive plus 1 more head endive, escarole, or other lettuce for garnishing plates

3½ cups leftover pieces of roasted striped bass

2 tablespoons whole fresh tarragon leaves, roughly cut

½ cup walnut pieces

2 tablespoons drained and rinsed capers

Kosher salt, to taste

Freshly ground black pepper, to taste

In a small bowl, whisk together the tarragon vinegar with the thinned anchovy paste. Add olive oil and whisk until smooth.

Cut 2 of the heads of endive on the diagonal into shreds (1½ cups). Put all remaining ingredients except the head lettuce for garnish into the serving bowl. Drizzle oil and vinegar mixture over all. Blend gently with your hands until well mixed. Do not mix too vigorously or the fish will break into too many bitty pieces. You don't want it to look like tunafish salad.

To serve, place a few leaves of your chosen lettuce on each plate and spoon about ¾ cup of fish salad on top. Serve cool or at room temperature. Can be made an hour ahead, covered with plastic wrap, and put into the refrigerator to cool.

Saffron-gold fish soup

SERVES 4 AS A FIRST COURSE

THIS VERY ELEGANT soup looks best in equally elegant two-handled cream soup bowls. The head and bones used for the stock are always left over from a dinner; I throw them into a pot as soon as I clear the table and get the stock going. I often have some white wine left over that was served with the fish—one halcyon night it was Champagne—and I use it in the soup. If a fresh bottle of white needs to be started, it can be served later along with the soup. If there isn't enough fish left over—allow about an ounce and a half per person—it is an easy matter to poach a little fish in the soup at the end of the cooking time. Any white-fleshed fish or a little salmon will do. Truly the whole soup would be good made entirely with salmon stock and salmon leftovers.

This soup is so elegant that the stock needs to be carefully strained and skimmed to remove any floating fat.

FOR THE STOCK

Frame, head, skin, and small bones from one 6-pound or two 3-pound roasted striped bass or salmon

1½ cups white wine

5 quarts water or 4 cups Basic Fish Stock (page 243)

FOR THE SOUP

One ½-gram vial stem saffron

3 stalks celery, peeled with a vegetable peeler, cut lengthwise into 2 x ⅛-inch pieces (1 cup)

Four 1½-ounce pieces of leftover roasted striped bass

Kosher salt, to taste

Freshly ground black pepper, to taste

To prepare the stock: Combine all ingredients in a 9-inch-diameter stockpot. Bring to a boil, uncovered. (This takes about 35 minutes.) Skim and reduce heat to a low boil. Cook for 2 hours, skimming about every 30 minutes.

To strain the stock, dampen either a double layer of cheesecloth or a clean kitchen towel. Wring out water. Place a strainer in a clean pot. Line the strainer with the dampened cloth. Carefully pour the stock through the strainer. Remove strainer and cloth. When cool enough to touch, wring out cloth over pot to get all the juices out. Discard cheesecloth. (If using a kitchen towel, be sure and rinse it in cold water and then throw it in with the next load of laundry. If it sits too long, it becomes stiff and hard to clean.)

To prepare the soup: Place the 4 cups of fish stock in a 6-quart saucepan. Add the saffron. Simmer for 20 minutes. Add the remaining ingredients. Heat just until warm throughout.

To serve, place a piece of fish in the bottom of each soup bowl. Ladle about 1 cup of the soup and celery over the fish, until the bowl is almost full but not too full to carry.

SEA BASS AND BLACK BASS

MANY OF US ARE FAMILIAR WITH SEA BASS WITHOUT KNOWING IT IF WE HAVE ORDERED A WHOLE FISH IN A CHINESE RESTAURANT. It is one of the favorite fish of the Chinese, particularly for its succulent cheeks. Sea bass is somewhat flakier than striped bass, but it is a fine substitute in any recipe calling for striped bass—unlike black bass, which has a stronger flavor. Sea bass is good in Divine Fish Chowder (page 244), Richie Rich Fish Cakes (page 249), and Everyday Fish Cakes (page 250).

Sea bass are generally not huge fish and so are perfect for a small group. If serving more than four and a larger sea bass is not available, cook two fish in the same pan at the same time. The fish tend to run about three pounds, but they have only twice as much flesh as bone. They are relatively short and thick for their weight, and the rule of ten minutes an inch for the cooking time still holds. Stock made from the head and bones of sea bass is elegant; but if the sea bass has been made with the Chinese flavorings, rinse the stock fixings well before proceeding.

Black bass look very much like sea bass and are of the same family, along with the striped bass. Black bass, as their name suggests, are quite a bit darker of skin than the sea bass, while striped bass have visible stripes running lengthwise down their skin. Black bass are eaten more along the southern part of the Atlantic coast of the United States, while sea bass are eaten in the north and all along the Atlantic coast of Europe.

Black bass have a stronger flavor and slightly coarser flesh than sea bass. Stock made with its head and bones is really quite strong-tasting and should not be used for a clear soup such as the striped bass stock (page 254). It is fine in a tomato- or wine-based fish soup or stew.

Black bass can be used in both of the following recipes, which have strong flavors. In general, choose strongly flavored preparations for black bass. Depending on the length of the fish, it can have anywhere from a two-to-one flesh-to-bone ratio to a three-to-one ratio. There is more flesh proportionately on the bigger fish.

Black bass with roasted plum tomato sauce and basil

SERVES 6 AS A MAIN COURSE,
WITH 2½ CUPS SAUCE

TOTAL
ROASTING
TIME:
see below

THIS IS A felicitous pairing of fish with a slightly assertive flavor and a good strong sauce. After the fish comes out of the oven, remove it to a platter while finishing the sauce. Tent the fish with aluminum foil to keep it warm if there will be a delay in serving the fish. The fish will give up about a half cup of liquid as it sits. Add it to the sauce. There is too much sauce for the fish alone; but in very non-Italian fashion, I like to serve spaghettini as a side dish, and I mix most of the sauce into that, leaving just a little to top the fish.

This is one time that the usually miserly idea that a pound of pasta will feed six or more is absolutely correct.

3¾-pound scaled, gutted, and cleaned (gills removed) black bass (3 inches at thickest point), head and tail on, interior cavity well washed to remove any blood

1 tablespoon plus 1 teaspoon olive oil

½ cup basil leaves, plus 10 leaves with 1 inch of stem, washed

4 cloves garlic, smashed and peeled

2 cups Roasted Plum Tomato Sauce (page 419) or 2 cups drained canned plum tomatoes, coarsely chopped

¼ cup red wine

Place rack in center of oven. Heat oven to 500°F.

With a large kitchen knife, cut 3 parallel diagonal slashes into each side of the fish, slicing about 1 to 1½ inches into the flesh. Place the fish on a diagonal in an 18 x 13 x 2-inch roasting pan. If part of the fish head and/or tail hangs over the corners, that is fine.

Rub 2 teaspoons olive oil into one side of the fish, including the slits. Turn the fish over and repeat. Stuff the cavity with ½ cup of the basil, all of the garlic, and ½ cup of the tomato sauce. Place the remaining 10 basil leaves underneath the fish.

Roast for 30 minutes, or slightly less if you prefer. Using 2 very large spatulas, remove fish to a serving platter, but do not remove the basil that was under the fish. Put the roasting pan on top of the stove. Add red wine and bring contents to a boil, scraping the bottom vigorously with a wooden spoon. Cook for 2 minutes. Add the remaining tomato sauce and stir to combine thoroughly. Stir in the basil, tomato sauce, and garlic from the fish's cavity and any liquid that has collected on the serving platter.

TOTAL ROASTING TIME: 30 minutes (10 minutes per inch of thickness)

Roasted sea bass with fermented black beans

TOTAL
ROASTING
TIME:
see below

THE DELIGHTFULLY AROMATIC seasonings are typical in Chinese steamed fish dishes. Fermented black beans—salty little nuggets that keep on the shelf virtually forever—lend a little mystery.

I tried this dish with both sea bass and a larger black bass. I preferred it with the sea bass; I give quantities for both. The quantity given first for each ingredient is for smaller sea bass. The quantity in parentheses is for black bass or a larger sea bass.

2½-pound scaled, gutted, and cleaned (gills removed) sea bass (2½ inches at thickest point), head and tail on, interior cavity well washed to remove any blood, or 3¾-pound scaled, gutted, and cleaned (gills removed) black bass (3 inches at thickest point), head and tail on, interior cavity well washed to remove any blood

1 tablespoon sesame oil (1 tablespoon plus 1 teaspoon)

2 tablespoons tamari soy sauce (2 tablespoons plus 2 teaspoons)

2½ ounces fresh gingerroot, peeled, trimmed, and cut into ⅛-inch-thick coin-shaped slices (3¼ ounces)

1½ cups loosely packed fresh cilantro with stems (2 cups)

1 tablespoon fermented black beans (1 tablespoon plus 1 teaspoon)

¼ cup rice wine vinegar (⅔ cup)

3 tablespoons water (¼ cup)

Place rack in center of oven. Heat oven to 500°F.

With a large kitchen knife, cut 3 parallel diagonal slashes into each side of the fish, slicing about 1 to 1½ inches into the flesh. Place the fish on a diagonal in an 18 x 13 x 2-inch roasting pan. If part of the fish head and/or tail hangs over the corners, that is fine.

Rub half the sesame oil and ½ tablespoon of the tamari into 1 side of the fish, including the slits. Turn the fish over and repeat. Stuff the cavity with two thirds of the ginger, and one third of the cilantro and beans. Place remaining ginger slices underneath the fish.

Roast for 25 minutes (30 minutes for the larger fish), or slightly less if you prefer. Using 2 very large spatulas, remove fish to a serving platter, but do not remove the ginger that was under the fish. Put the roasting pan on top of the stove. Add remaining tamari and cilantro, plus the vinegar and water, and bring to a boil, scraping the bottom vigorously with a wooden spoon. Cook for 3 minutes. Stir in cilantro, ginger, and fermented black beans from the fish's cavity and any liquid that has collected on the serving platter. Pour sauce over fish, spooning solids on top of the fish.

TOTAL ROASTING TIME: 25 to 30 minutes (10 minutes per inch of thickness)

Black bass aspic

SERVES 2 AS A MAIN COURSE,
4 AS A FIRST COURSE

ANY SAUCE LEFT over from Black Bass with Roasted Plum Tomato Sauce and Basil will make a good aspic owing to the gelatinous nature of the fish and the deglazing liquid added to the sauce once the fish is roasted. The aspic makes an attractive luncheon dish or first course if some of the leftover fish is combined with it and allowed to set up in the refrigerator overnight. The proportions for this dish are a third of a cup of sauce to a scant half cup of fish.

⅔ cup leftover sauce from Black Bass with Roasted Plum Tomato Sauce and Basil (page 256)

2 tablespoons water

¾ to 1 cup leftover fish from Black Bass with Roasted Plum Tomato Sauce and Basil

Place sauce and water in a small bowl. Heat in microwave for 30 seconds, just to soften sauce. If there is no microwave, put the sauce and water in a small saucepan and gently heat over a low flame. Mix well. Tear fish into small pieces. Mix into tomato sauce. Rinse a metal bowl or mold with ice-cold water. Pour out, but do not dry bowl. Fill with fish mixture, pressing down firmly. Cover with plastic wrap. Refrigerate for 4 to 6 hours. To unmold, dip metal bowl briefly in hot water. Invert onto a serving dish.

*r*ED SNAPPER

KEEPING FISH STRAIGHT: RED SNAPPER, A SUPERB EAST COAST FISH, IS NOT A BREAM; IT JUST LOOKS LIKE ONE. There is a bream with red skin, highly esteemed in France, that is called *dorade*. The Pacific also yields breams that are highly esteemed in Japan. In the same family as the red sea bream, but not the red snapper, is the sheep's head, after which Brooklyn's Sheepshead Bay got its name. Aside from my sort of bookish interest, these relationships interest me because the snapper shares what is to me a far more important characteristic with members of other families: the bass, the bream, and the grouper. They are all compact, meaning that the flesh is medium-firm and not stretched out in a flat layer, but bunched together toward the center of the fish, making for easier and better cooking. They all roast well and make wonderful stock, and can be cooked in the ways given here.

Watch out on the Pacific coast for fish that are supposed to be local and are called "red snapper." They are a form of rockfish.

Roasted red snapper with tarragon

SERVES 6 AS A MAIN COURSE

TOTAL
ROASTING
TIME:
see below

I'M SORRY TO be so imprecise about the tarragon, but I made this when the tarragon outside my kitchen door in Vermont was going crazy and had to be cut back ruthlessly, so I used a lot of tarragon to stuff the fish. When tarragon is expensive, just make sure you have the half cup for the sauce and use any extra sprigs in the cavity. Tarragon and snapper seem to have a special affinity for each other.

Half the weight of each whole snapper is bone and head. Snapper has a very thick spine and so requires a little extra cooking time.

5 ½- to 6-pound scaled, gutted, and cleaned (gills removed) red snapper (3 inches at thickest point), head and tail on, interior cavity well washed to remove any blood

⅓ cup fresh lemon juice

⅓ cup olive oil

2 tablespoons kosher salt

2 tablespoons freshly ground black pepper

1 large bunch (1 ounce) fresh tarragon sprigs; remove leaves to equal ½ cup, loosely packed, for the sauce

1 cup water or white wine, for deglazing

With a large kitchen knife, cut 3 parallel diagonal slashes into each side of the fish. Cut about 1 to 1½ inches into the flesh, cutting from one edge to the other. Snapper is quite fibrous and will marinate and cook better when carefully cut. Put your hand in each slit to make sure the cut goes through to the bone. Place the fish on a diagonal in an 18 x 13 x 2-inch roasting pan.

Rub lemon juice, olive oil, and salt and pepper into sides of the fish, including the slits, and into the internal cavity. Cram the sprigs of tarragon into the clean cavity. Fit in as many as possible, but do not let them hang out, or they may burn. Marinate at room temperature for 1 hour.

About 20 minutes before roasting, place rack in center of oven. Heat oven to 500°F. Roast for 35 minutes.

Using 2 very large spatulas, remove fish to serving platter. Put the roasting pan on top of the stove. Add the water or wine and bring contents to a boil, scraping the bottom vigorously with a wooden spoon. Let reduce by half. Stir in the ½ cup tarragon leaves. Serve on the side in a sauceboat. Serve with steamed small new potatoes.

TOTAL ROASTING TIME: 35 minutes (10 minutes per inch of thickness)

Red snapper potato salad

MAKES 4 CUPS; SERVES 4 AS
A FIRST COURSE

THE LAST TIME I made this, I happened to have a few steamed mussels left over, which I threw in at the end with the hard-boiled eggs. It was wonderful.

2 cups leftover pieces Roasted Red
    Snapper with Tarragon (page 259)

7 to 8 small white new potatoes
    (1 pound), steamed or boiled with skin
    on and cut into quarters (1¼ cups); if
    only larger potatoes available, cut into
    1-inch pieces

3 tomatoes (8 ounces each, 1½ pounds
    total), cored and cut into 1-inch pieces

1 Kirby cucumber (the kind for pickles)
    or 2 ordinary cucumbers, ends
    removed, quartered lengthwise, and
    cut across into ½-inch slices

¼ cup fresh apple mint leaves, or
    2 tablespoons fresh mint leaves,
    stacked and cut across into thin strips

½ cup Basic Mayonnaise (page 303) or
    store-bought

1 to 2 tablespoons fresh lemon juice

3 large hard-boiled eggs, peeled

Put the snapper, potatoes, tomatoes, cucumber, and mint into a medium bowl. Add the mayonnaise and lemon juice. Using your hands or a spoon, toss gently until all ingredients are coated. It is nicer if the fish stays in chunks, so do not mix vigorously. Cut the eggs into quarters and add. Gently mix again. Serve on a bed of mixed greens if you like.

gROUPER

GROUPERS TEND TO BE LARGE AND ARE GOOD FOR A PARTY, ESPECIALLY SINCE ONLY A FOURTH OF THE WEIGHT IS BONE. The flesh is white and clean-tasting. The head and bones make an equally clean-tasting stock. Grouper can be substituted in the bass and snapper recipes. Use stock and leftover meat in Divine Fish Chowder (page 244), either of the fish cakes (pages 249–250), or Best Cod Hash (page 274). Any leftover meat goes well with Three-Citrus Mayonnaise (page 304), or use it as a substitute for bass in Striped Bass Provençal Salad (page 253).

Roasted grouper with green beans and mushrooms in tomato sauce

TOTAL
ROASTING
TIME:
see page 262

SERVES 6 AS A MAIN COURSE

SERVE A BOWL of rice to go on the side of this Southern favorite fish. The rice will absorb the copious sauce provided by the tomatoes and mushrooms. I like to serve the steamy onions over the rice as well. The onions cook inside the fish so that they will not burn. They won't brown, either. If cooked onions don't seem appealing in the salad, omit them.

Many canned tomatoes are very salty. If you are using them, wait until the dish is finished cooking before adding salt. Taste and add salt as desired. If using roasted plum tomatoes, add two teaspoons of salt.

5- to 6-pound scaled, gutted, and cleaned (gills removed) grouper (3 inches at thickest point), head and tail on, interior cavity well washed to remove any blood

¼ cup olive oil

1 small onion (3 ounces), peeled and halved, then thinly sliced across (1 cup)

¾ pound green beans, ends trimmed, then snapped in half (6 cups)

¾ pound white mushrooms, trimmed, wiped clean, and thinly sliced across (4 cups)

2½ cups Whole Plum Tomatoes (page 418), peeled, coarsely chopped, and drained, plus ¼ cup of the liquid they give off or water, or one 28-ounce can whole tomatoes, drained, coarsely chopped, with ¼ cup juice reserved

3 tablespoons red wine vinegar

3 tablespoons thinly sliced fresh sage leaves

Freshly ground black pepper, to taste

2 teaspoons kosher salt, or less if using canned tomatoes

Place rack on second level from the bottom in oven. Heat oven to 500°F.

With a large kitchen knife, cut 3 parallel diagonal slashes into each side of the fish. Slice about 1 to 1½ inches into the flesh, cutting from one edge to the other. Place fish on the diagonal in an 18 x 13 x 2-inch roasting pan. Rub 1 tablespoon of the olive oil onto both sides of the fish. Stuff the onions in the cavity.

Place green beans and mushrooms in a medium bowl. Pour the remaining 3 tablespoons of olive oil over the vegetables and toss to lightly coat. Try not to break up the mushrooms.

Spread the beans and mushrooms around the fish in the pan. Roast for 25 minutes. Meanwhile, place the tomatoes in a medium bowl. Add the vinegar, sage, and black pepper, and salt. Remove roasting pan with fish from oven. Pour the tomato mixture over the vegetables. Pour reserved liquid over fish. Roast 10 minutes more.

Using 2 very large spatulas, remove fish to a large serving platter. If the vegetables are to be served on the same platter, place fish with backbone toward one long edge of platter and vegetables all along the other side. Alternatively, serve vegetables in a separate dish, leaving the fish on a platter for easier boning.

TOTAL ROASTING TIME: 35 minutes (10 minutes per inch of thickness)

SOFT-FLESHED FISH

The following group of fish has notably softer flesh than the preceeding one. Often the flesh is darker in color as well. These fish can, at worst, become mushy and too strongly flavored with overcooking; therefore the timings are different from the basic rule. Each fish is given a basic recipe and cooking time of its own because in this group the timing varies from fish to fish.

*b*LUEFISH

BLUEFISH RUN IN THE ATLANTIC IN SUMMER AND EARLY FALL. The best way to have impeccable bluefish is to know or be a fisherman and eat the fish very fresh. Left to sit, the darkish, somewhat oily flesh can become unpleasantly strong. I find that the smaller bluefish are better for roasting. Large ones are marvelous for marinating raw in a dry cure like gravlax. They also smoke beautifully.

The complementary seasonings to bluefish are acids such as lemon juice and vinegar; strong, sharp-tasting herbs such as fennel and dill; and mustard. Oddly enough, this does not mean that bluefish likes hot peppers. Bluefish run in the summer and are an easy way to use summer flavors, fresh herbs, and other light flavors, to full advantage.

Bluefish have a relatively heavy weight of bone and head, which means that a whole fish will serve fewer people than the unwary cook might think. For example, an already gutted, scaled, and cleaned bluefish that weighs two pounds serves only two people. The fish need only roast for eight minutes per inch. Overcooked, they get mushy.

Summertime roasted bluefish

I LIKE TO glaze and refrigerate the fish in the morning and take it out to come to room temperature when I get home. The glaze for this doesn't get too strong, even if it is on the fish for several hours. Since small bluefish take only around a quarter of an hour to roast, I can slip the pan into the oven just before everybody is ready to eat.

Two 2-pound scaled, gutted, and cleaned (gills removed) bluefish (2 inches at thickest point and 18 to 20 inches top to tail), head and tail on, interior cavity well washed to remove any blood
2½ ounces fresh gingerroot, peeled and chopped medium-fine
¼ cup fresh lime juice

1 tablespoon olive oil
1 teaspoon kosher salt
½ cup loosely packed basil leaves, plus a few extra, for garnishing
1½ cups Basic Fish Stock (page 243), water, or wine, for deglazing
Freshly ground black pepper, to taste

With a large kitchen knife, cut 3 parallel diagonal slashes into each side of each fish, slicing about 1 to 1½ inches into the flesh, down to the bone. Place fish on a diagonal in an 18 x 13 x 2-inch roasting pan. If part of the fish head and/or tail hangs over the corners, that is fine.

Put 1½ ounces of the ginger and half the lime juice in a blender. Blend until a smooth purée. Scrape down sides of blender with a rubber spatula. Add remaining lime juice, oil, and salt. Blend until smooth. Pour purée over fish in pan. Using your hands, rub purée down deep into each slit and all over each fish. Combine the ½ cup basil leaves and remaining ginger. Put half the mixture into the clean stomach cavity of each fish. Smush in as much as possible. As long as the basil leaves are tucked in they will not burn. Leave to marinate and come to room temperature, about 45 minutes to 1 hour.

About 20 minutes before roasting the fish, place rack in center of oven. Heat oven to 500°F. Roast for 16 minutes.

Using 2 very large spatulas, remove fish to serving platter. Put pan on top of stove. Add liquid and bring to a boil while scraping vigorously with a wooden spoon. Let reduce by half. Reduce heat to a simmer. Add pepper. Pour sauce over fish on platter, or serve separately in a sauceboat. Garnish with remaining basil leaves.

TOTAL ROASTING TIME: 16 minutes (8 minutes per inch of thickness)

Simple roast bluefish

TOTAL
ROASTING
TIME:
see below

2-pound scaled, gutted, and cleaned (gills removed) bluefish (2 inches at thickest point and 18 to 20 inches top to tail), head and tail on, interior cavity well washed to remove any blood

1 tablespoon olive oil
Kosher salt, to taste
Freshly ground black pepper, to taste
1½ cups Basic Fish Stock (page 243), water, or wine, for deglazing

Place oven rack on second level from bottom. Heat oven to 500°F.

With a large kitchen knife, cut 3 parallel diagonal slashes into each side of the fish, slicing about 1 to 1½ inches into the flesh, down to the bone. Place fish on a diagonal in an 18 x 13 x 2-inch roasting pan. Using your hands, rub the oil into the fish, working it into the slits and inside the cavity. Sprinkle with salt and pepper.

Roast for 16 minutes. Using 2 very large spatulas, remove fish to a large serving platter. Put pan on top of stove. Add the stock or water and bring contents to a boil while scraping the bottom vigorously with a wooden spoon. Let reduce by half. Serve on the side in a sauceboat.

TOTAL ROASTING TIME: 16 minutes (8 minutes per inch of thickness)

Mackerel

THERE IS A LARGE FAMILY OF MACKEREL. In Europe, they are often served lightly pickled with onions, wine vinegar, and coriander seeds. The best mackerel I have ever eaten was at Myrtle Allen's Ballymaloe House in Shanagarry, County Cork, Ireland. It was a couple of hours out of the ocean and lightly smoked. To my surprise, mackerel roasts brilliantly, becoming neither mushy nor too strongly flavored. Again, the mackerel must be very fresh. Of the varied mackerel family, those most commonly available in the market—from smallest to largest—are New England (Atlantic) mackerel, Spanish mackerel, and king mackerel. They do not vary wildly in taste nor in thickness, but can get very long, as with large king mackerel. Spanish mackerel have attractive yellowish spots on the skin. The mackerel are related to the tunas.

Simple roast mackerel

2½-POUND MACKEREL SERVES 6 AS A
MAIN COURSE; 5-POUND MACKEREL SERVES
8 AS A MAIN COURSE

TOTAL
ROASTING
TIME:
see below

Mackerel vary widely in size. I have roasted several, from a two-and-a-half-pound Spanish mackerel to a five-pound king mackerel. The roasting time is figured neither by length nor weight. It is still a function of thickness. However, the roasting time is nine minutes per inch rather than the standard ten minutes. The fish will be done when it just separates freely from the bone.

2½- to 5-pound scaled, gutted, and cleaned (gills removed) mackerel (2 to 2½ inches at thickest point), head and tail on, interior cavity well washed to remove any blood

1 to 2 tablespoons canola or other neutral oil

Kosher salt, to taste

Freshly ground black pepper, to taste

½ cup Basic Fish Stock (page 243), water, wine, for deglazing

Place rack in center of oven. Heat oven to 500°F.

With a large kitchen knife, cut 2 to 3 parallel slashes, depending on the length of the fish, into each side of the fish, slicing about 1 to 1½ inches into the flesh, down to the bone. Place fish on a diagonal in a 18 x 13 x 2-inch roasting pan. Using your hands, rub the oil into the fish, working it into the slits and inside the cavity. Sprinkle with salt and pepper. Cook for 20 to 25 minutes, depending upon the thickness of the fish.

Using 2 very large spatulas, remove fish to a large serving platter. Put pan on top of stove. Add the liquid and bring contents to a boil while scraping the bottom vigorously with a wooden spoon. Let reduce by half. Serve on the side in a sauceboat.

TOTAL ROASTING TIME: 18 minutes (9 minutes per inch of thickness)

Spanish mackerel on the verge of Vergé

SERVES 6 AS A MAIN COURSE

TOTAL
ROASTING
TIME:
see facing
page

ONE OF MY favorite fish dishes is made by Roger Vergé at his restaurant, Moulin de Mougins, in France. It is a sumptuous affair of a whole loup de mer (sea bass) in a red wine and foie gras sauce. I have raped that dish to create a simpler foie gras–less version that goes very well with mackerel. Try it on bass if you like. There is an ample amount, over a tablespoon, of full-flavored sauce per portion. If you want to follow Vergé more closely, be posh to the limit and stir in foie gras puréed in a mortar instead of the butter. Never boil these sauces; they will separate.

Do not put pepper or salt on the fish. It will get enough from the tomato paste in the sauce. The skin lifts off easily from the mackerel, and the sauce seems to me to be more voluptuous right on top of the flesh, rather than on the skin. This cup of sauce is heaven with flesh of any kind.

2½-pound scaled, gutted, and cleaned (gills removed) Spanish mackerel (2 inches at thickest point), head and tail on, interior cavity well washed to remove any blood

1 tablespoon canola or other neutral oil

VERGE OF VERGÉ SAUCE

1½ cups red wine

1 bay leaf

3 cloves garlic, unpeeled

2 tablespoons tomato paste

½ cup Basic Fish Stock (page 243), or same stock as fish being sauced

2 tablespoons unsalted butter, cut into bits

Place rack in center of oven. Heat oven to 500°F.

With a large kitchen knife, cut 3 parallel diagonal slashes into each side of the fish, slicing about 1 inch into the flesh. Place the fish on a diagonal in an 18 x 13 x 2-inch roasting pan. If part of the fish head and/or tail hangs over the corners, that is fine. Rub oil all over both sides of the fish and into the slits. Roast for 18 minutes.

For the sauce: Meanwhile, combine the remaining ingredients, except for the butter, in a small saucepan. Cover and bring to a boil. Reduce to a simmer and cook for 15 minutes. Strain and reserve.

Using 2 very large spatulas, remove fish to serving platter. Put roasting pan on top of stove. Add reserved sauce and bring to a boil while scraping bottom vigorously with a wooden spoon. Lower heat to a simmer and reduce by half.

Remove boiling sauce to a small bowl. Immediately, stir in bits of butter, mixing until they just disappear; they should not truly melt. The butter acts as a smoothing, soothing binder for the sauce. Pour sauce over fish on platter, or serve separately in a sauceboat.

TOTAL ROASTING TIME: 18 minutes (9 minutes per inch of thickness)

King mackerel with jalapeño-lime sauce

SERVES 8 AS A MAIN COURSE

TOTAL
ROASTING
TIME:
see page 268

KING MACKEREL ARE large, handsome fish. If the one at hand is a little larger than the oven, do not worry. Place the fish on a diagonal in the pan and shove it in the oven. The oven door and back may push up the tail and toothy grin a bit, but it will work out.

5-pound scaled, gutted, and cleaned (gills removed) king mackerel (2½ inches at thickest point), head and tail on, interior cavity well washed to remove any blood

2 tablespoons canola or other neutral oil

1 tablespoon fresh lime juice

FOR THE SAUCE

½ cup fresh lime juice

2 tablespoons seeded, deribbed, and chopped Basic Jalapeños (page 383)

½ teaspoon kosher salt

Scant ¼ teaspoon freshly ground black pepper

½ cup canola or other neutral oil

½ bottle dark beer, such as Dos Equis, for deglazing

½ cup water, for deglazing

With a large kitchen knife, cut 4 parallel diagonal slashes into each side of the fish, slicing about 1 inch into the flesh. Place the fish on a diagonal in an 18 x 13 x 2-inch roasting pan. The head and tail will hang over the pan. Rub the oil and lime juice into both sides of the fish, including the slits and internal cavities. It will take at least 1 hour for the marinating fish to come to room temperature.

To prepare the sauce: Place the lime juice, jalapeños, salt, and pepper in the blender. Blend until a smooth purée. Add 1 tablespoon of the oil and blend. Slowly add remaining oil until mixture is well combined and thick. Using a rubber spatula, scrape out all the sauce into a serving bowl. Cover with plastic wrap and refrigerate until 20 minutes before ready to use.

About 20 minutes before roasting the fish, place rack in center of oven. Heat oven to 500°F. Roast for 23 minutes.

Using 1 or 2 large spatulas, remove fish to a serving platter. Place pan on top of stove.

continued

Add beer and water and bring to a boil while scraping the bottom vigorously with a wooden spoon. Let reduce by half. Season to taste with salt and pepper. Serve on the side in a sauceboat.

To serve, make a lateral cut down the center of the fish where there is a row of bones. Peel off skin. Flesh will detach easily in sections from the bone. Scoop 2 tablespoons of jalapeño sauce onto each plate with fish.

TOTAL ROASTING TIME: 23 minutes (9 minutes per inch of thickness)

*f*RESH SARDINES

SARDINES ARE A SOFT-FLESHED FISH. Fresh and whole, they are alien to most Americans. Canned and salty, they make many run for cover. Rich in fats that are wonderful for you, sardines require less fat in the pan. Add these warm or cool to antipasto. They make a good companion to Basic Treviso (page 401). Serve them on their own with a touch of salt, a grind of fresh pepper, and a little lemon juice or vinegar. Do not serve them with a sauce because there are many bones for eaters to remove. Choose your company carefully for these bony delicacies. Any leftover flesh can be added to Roasted Plum Tomato Sauce (page 419), along with a few plumped raisins, and used as a sauce for pasta.

Simple fresh sardines

SERVES 3 TO 4 AS A FIRST COURSE

TOTAL ROASTING TIME: *see below*

1 pound gutted whole sardines (approximately 10, about ¾ inch at thickest point, about 6 inches long tip to tail), heads and tails on, interior cavities well washed to remove any blood

2 teaspoons olive oil

Kosher salt, to taste

Freshly ground black pepper, to taste

Place rack in center of oven. Heat oven to 500°F.

Place sardines in a 14 x 12 x 2-inch roasting pan. Slick sardines and pan with oil. Sprinkle with salt and pepper. Roast for 3 minutes. Turn. Roast 3 minutes more.

TOTAL ROASTING TIME: 6 minutes (8 minutes per inch of thickness)

Roasted sardines and tomatoes with basil

SERVES 6 TO 8 AS A FIRST COURSE

IF YOU ARE lucky enough to get your hands on some fresh sardines, roasting is an easy way to enjoy them. They work particularly well for a large number of people. These are not as crisp as grilled sardines, but roasting them is very good if a quantity is wanted for a first course. Sardines have lots of little bones that can drive one crazy. Serving them with something flat and simple like the roasted tomatoes keeps eating within the realm of the possible as eaters pick out the bones. Don't add a soft bed of lettuce to this or you will be sinking, with all those teeny bones, into a morass.

2½ pounds tomatoes (10 ounces each), cored and cut across into ½-inch slices

3 tablespoons olive oil

24 gutted whole sardines (each ¾ inch at thickest point, about 6 inches long tip to tail), heads and tails on, cleaned, interior cavities well washed to remove any blood

FOR THE VINAIGRETTE

1 clove garlic, smashed, peeled, and mushed to a paste in a mortar with a pestle

3 tablespoons fresh lemon juice

Liquid from the roasted tomato pan

¼ teaspoon kosher salt

Freshly ground black pepper, to taste

½ cup fresh basil leaves, stacked and cut across into thin strips, 1 tablespoon reserved

Place 1 rack in center of oven and another on the next lowest level. Heat oven to 500°F.

Arrange tomato slices in an 18 x 13 x 2-inch roasting pan. Drizzle 2 tablespoons of the olive oil over them. Turn slices in oil so both sides are coated. Roast on lower rack for 8 minutes. Meanwhile, arrange the sardines in an 18 x 13 x 2-inch roasting pan. Drizzle with remaining oil and turn sardines over in the oil.

Turn over the tomatoes in the oven with a spatula or fork. Place the sardines in the oven on the center rack. Roast 3 minutes. Turn the sardines. Roast 3 more minutes.

Make the vinaigrette by combining all the ingredients in a small bowl.

To serve, arrange the tomato slices on a large serving platter. Arrange sardines on the diagonal on top of tomatoes. Top each sardine with a bit of reserved basil. Drizzle vinaigrette over all. Allow to sit 10 to 15 minutes so flavors combine. Serve at room temperature.

ORDINARY FILLETS OF FISH

Whole fish may be unavailable or may seem daunting to handle, with all of their bones, their eyes staring from their heads, or—as in the case of monkfish—may simply be inappropriate. Sometimes whole fish are just too big—a tuna or a swordfish, for example, or even a large cod. When it comes time to serve, sometimes it is pleasanter to cut nice even slices from fillets rather than wrestle with a large fish and its bones. There are many possibilities for boned fish. Of course, buying fillets means giving up the makings of stock.

The simplest solution is the kind of single fillet available in most markets, often in the guise of a "sole" or a flounder. The basic cod recipes that follow are prototypes for roasting single fillets and two fillets sandwiched together, called "double fillets" (see pages 241 and 242). For a full description of how to match double fillets, see the Simple Double Cod Fillet (page 272). It doesn't pay to try to roast very small fillets. Basically, fillets are timed by thickness, as are most other fish. To find out the cooking time for the fillet of your choice, look up the fish in the Whole Fish section. Tuna (page 286), swordfish (page 283), monkfish (page 279), and shad (page 276) are special and delightful cases.

C O D

TRUE COD ARE AN ALMOST ENTIRELY ATLANTIC FISH. There is a lookalike relative, a Pacific cod, that is called "true cod" to differentiate it from all the cod wannabes. It is not as firm or fine as Atlantic cod. Watch out for so-called rock cod, fished in the Pacific. They may be perfectly fine and can even be roasted in ways similar to cod, but they are really different kinds of rockfish, whose skin may vary from red—no, those are definitely not red snapper—to gray and brownish. Their flesh is somewhat softer than that of cod.

Cod have a mild, juicy, pearly white flesh and can be huge fish, weighing up to ninety pounds. In the United States, smaller cod up to about twenty inches long are called scrod. Cod—air-dried, salted, smoked, and fresh—has been a major item in European and European-American trade for centuries. It is no accident that we have a Cape Cod and a cod hangs in wooden effigy in the Massachusetts State House.

Close relatives of the cod are haddock (which smokes and dries well but does not take to salting), hake, and ling. The last is truly confusing as there is a Pacific fish called "ling cod"—a euphemism for greenling—that is totally unrelated to cod. Cobia, found in the Gulf of Mexico and all the way down South America, is also called "ling." Throw yourself on the mercy of the fish store.

For roasting, cod is best cooked as a large skinless fillet(s) from a whole fish. When roasted, the result is pure white, flaky, moist pieces of flesh. To make fish stock without having leftover heads and bones from roasted fish, try a cod collar or a head. Also considered choice bits of the cod, but almost impossible to buy on their own, are the cheeks, tongue, and liver.

I include two versions of basic roasted cod, one for a single fillet and one for roasting two center-cut fillets. Either single or double, cod fillets follow the standard cooking time for fish: ten minutes per inch of thickness.

Never hesitate to roast more cod than you need for a single meal. Leftovers are a treasure in Divine Fish Chowder (page 244), both kinds of fish cakes (pages 249 and 250), and Best Cod Hash (page 274).

Simple single cod fillet

SERVES 4 AS A MAIN COURSE

TOTAL
ROASTING
TIME:
see below

U SE SALT AND PEPPER on roasted cod fillets if desired. See pages 292–309 for sauces, cold and hot, that go with this most adaptable of fish, including leftovers.

1¾- to 2-pound cod fillet (1¾ inches at thickest point)

1 tablespoon olive oil

Place rack in center of oven. Heat oven to 500°F.

Place fillet in a 14 x 12 x 2-inch roasting pan. Rub fillet and pan with oil. Roast, skin side up, for 17 minutes. Transfer to a serving platter. Serve warm.

TOTAL ROASTING TIME: 17 minutes (10 minutes per inch of thickness)

Simple double cod fillet

TOTAL
ROASTING
TIME:
see below

IF YOU ARE set on serving fish for a crowd, and if you cannot get your hands on or are not comfortable working with a whole fish, two matching large fillets, skin on or off, are a good alternative.

Order a 9-inch-long center cut of cod, filleted, skin on or off as you prefer, fillets left whole. An easy way to vary the basic double fillet is to put a layer of chopped herbs, about an eighth of an inch thick, and some salt and pepper between the two fillets.

See pages 292–309 for sauces, cold and hot, that go with this most adaptable of fish. If using herbs in the fish, choose a sauce that goes well. If dill is between the fillets, use Dilled Lemon Oil (page 294). If using basil, consider Roasted Plum Tomato Sauce (page 419) or Tapenade (page 298); when roasting cod with coriander, try one of the salsas on page 299.

2 center-cut matching cod fillets (about 1½ pounds each), about 9 inches long, skin on or off

1½ tablespoons olive oil

Place rack in center of oven. Heat oven to 500°F.

Place the fillets flat and skin side down on your work surface. Run your fingers over the thickest and widest part of the fillets to detect the row of small pin bones running down the center of the fillets. Use fish pliers or household needle-nose pliers to pull out the bones, being careful not to tear the flesh.

Place the fillets one on top of the other, skin sides out, the widest end of the top fillet over the narrowest end of the bottom fillet. Fold any protruding pieces over and tuck them between the 2 fillets to ensure even cooking.

Holding a ruler perpendicular to your work surface and next to the fillets, measure the thickness of the fillets at the thickest point after you have sandwiched them together. Calculate 10 minutes of cooking time per inch of thickness. However, if placing stuffing in between the fillets, they will require a longer cooking time (see page 242).

Slick half of the olive oil over the pan. Place the fish in the pan and rub remaining oil over exposed areas of fish. Roast according to timing rule described above. After removing fillets from oven, allow to rest for 2 to 3 minutes; they will continue cooking. Using 2 large spatulas, transfer to a serving platter.

TOTAL ROASTING TIME: 10 minutes per inch of thickness

Roasted cod with Pacific Rim glaze

TOTAL
ROASTING
TIME:
see page 274

SERVES 4 AS A MAIN COURSE

THIS IS A good recipe for early spring, when the ginger rhizomes are more likely to be plump and juicy. It is easy to tell good fresh gingerroot in the market. It will not have fibrous, hairy bits jutting out aggressively. The skin will be fairly pale in color and smooth, with the normal rings around the ginger being fairly flat. It will not be wrinkled, nor will there be new nubbins of growth starting up. Good fresh ginger has more juice and a more balanced flavor than old, and it will purée more smoothly to make the paste needed in this recipe. All the liquid for the glaze isn't added at once. If it is all added along with the garlic and ginger, little pieces of them will bounce around unpuréed.

The recipe may easily be doubled to feed eight by laying one large cod fillet next to the other in a large pan. Don't use this recipe with Basic Double Cod Fillets; not enough of the spicy zing gets into the fish. Serve with rice to sop up all the delicious juices.

PACIFIC RIM GLAZE

4 to 5 cloves garlic, smashed, peeled, and cut into medium pieces

2 ounces fresh gingerroot, peeled, cut across the grain into thin slices, and cut into medium pieces

1 fresh jalapeño pepper (about ½ ounce), cut in half, seeded, deribbed, and cut into medium pieces, or 1 teaspoon chopped Basic Jalapeños (page 383)

2 tablespoons soy sauce, preferably tamari

2 tablespoons mirin

3 tablespoons dark corn syrup

¼ cup rice wine vinegar

FOR THE FISH

1 tablespoon olive oil

1¾- to 2-pound cod fillet (1¾ inches at thickest point)

¾ cup Basic Fish Stock (page 243), water, or wine, for deglazing

½ bunch (¾ ounces) fresh cilantro, washed well, leaves removed from about half the stems, others left in sprigs

Place rack in center of oven. Heat oven to 500°F.

To make the glaze: Put garlic, ginger, and jalapeño in a blender. Add the soy sauce and mirin. Blend until a smooth purée, scraping down the sides of the blender with a rubber spatula as needed. Add corn syrup and vinegar. Blend again until smooth. Using the spatula, scrape into a small bowl and reserve.

Pour olive oil into an 18 x 12 x 2-inch roasting pan. Rub the oil all over the bottom of the pan and up the sides. Put the fillet in the pan. Pour half the glaze over the fillet. Rub thoroughly into fillet. Turn fillet over and pour on remaining glaze. Rub in. Arrange fillet in pan with the side that was attached to the skin facing up. Fillet should not touch sides of pan if possible; place on the diagonal if needed.

Roast for 17 minutes, checking after 12 to see if there is liquid left in pan and adding ⅓ cup warm water if pan is dry.

Using 2 very large spatulas, remove fillet to serving platter. Put the roasting pan on top of the stove over medium-high heat. Add ¾ cup deglazing liquid to the pan. As it begins to bubble, scrape the bottom of the pan with a wooden spoon. Scrape up all the dark crispy bits. Let liquid reduce by half. Use as a sauce with the fish.

Pour sauce over fish on serving platter. Decorate top of fish with cilantro leaves. Arrange sprigs around sides of platter.

TOTAL ROASTING TIME: 17 minutes (10 minutes per inch of thickness)

Best cod hash

SERVES 4 TO 6

SOMEHOW HASH HAS gotten itself a bad name and even extended its infamy to certain lowish restaurants denigrated as hash houses. Hash is indeed usually made with leftovers—last night's roast and last night's boiled potatoes. I love hash enough that I would even cook the ingredients from scratch. Fortunately, I usually do have the leftovers from a roast, in this case, cod. In earlier times cod was little attended to, it was so prolific, and was often served boiled. That's not a good idea because the fish absorbs too much water. Cod hash was probably the kind of fish hash most commonly made.

This hash can be made with almost any leftover fish in this book; but it is scrumptious made with roasted cod. If there are a lot of people, then a poached egg per person for topping will assure that even six people will have plenty to eat. Ketchup is a possibility.

1 pound floury potatoes, such as Idaho, halved

2 tablespoons canola or other neutral oil

2 tablespoons unsalted butter

1 small onion (about 3 ounces), peeled and cut into ¼-inch dice (½ cup)

2 to 3 stalks celery, peeled with vegetable peeler, cut into thirds lengthwise, then across into ¼-inch dice (⅓ cup)

½ medium red bell pepper, seeded, deribbed, and cut into ¼-inch dice (½ cup)

⅓ cup milk

1 egg

2½ to 3 teaspoons kosher salt

1 to 2 pinches of cayenne pepper

Scant ¼ teaspoon ground black pepper

2 cups flaked leftover roasted cod

Place potatoes in medium pot with 2 quarts of water. Cover and bring to a boil over high heat and cook until tender, about 25 minutes. Drain and let cool. Peel and cut into ½-inch dice (about 3 cups). Set aside.

Heat oil and butter in a 12-inch nonstick skillet over medium-high heat. Add onion and cook until translucent, about 5 minutes.

Add potatoes and cook until brown, about 15 minutes. As potatoes begin to brown, use a pancake turner to scoop up mixture and turn over occasionally, rather than stirring, so that pieces do not break up and turn to mush. Add celery and bell pepper. Cook for 5 minutes, until wilted.

Meanwhile, combine milk, egg, salt, cayenne, and pepper. Pour over potato mixture. Add cod and scoop with pancake turner to fold into mixture. Press hash into an even layer filling the bottom of the pan like a pancake. Lower heat to medium-low and cook without turning or stirring hash until set, about 15 minutes. Remove from heat and turn out onto a round serving dish so that crusty brown side is on top.

Cod stock

MAKES 10 CUPS

THERE ARE NO heads and bones for this stock from fillets; but ask the store that cut the fillets to save the head and bones. They were paid for. If that doesn't work, buy a cod head or collar and proceed. Cod stock has a good neutral flavor and can be used in Divine Fish Chowder (page 244).

Frame, skin, head, tail and all bones from filleting cod for roasted cod fillet	Water to cover
	1 to 2 cups white wine, optional

In a stockpot, put all the fish parts, water, and wine, if using. Cover and bring to a boil. Reduce heat to low. Using a metal spoon, skim off the scum that rises to the surface. The more you skim, the clearer the soup. Cook a minimum of 8 hours and up to 12 hours, checking water level periodically and topping off as needed to keep bones covered. The cartilage in the bones should begin to disintegrate, and the bones will fall apart. This means all the goodness is now in your liquid, and no longer in the bones.

Strain the stock and put it into the narrowest container it will fit in. Let cool. Put in the refrigerator overnight so that the sediment will settle. Spoon off any fat. Remove from refrigerator and carefully ladle out the clear part of the stock. Be careful at the bottom to avoid the cloudy part full of sediment; it can be bitter.

Label and keep stock in plastic containers with tightly fitting lids. Will keep in freezer for up to 6 months.

UNUSUAL FILLETS OF FISH

Next, I turn to a group of fish that are not normally thought of as providing fillets, nor of being roasted. Yet they were some of the most exciting dishes I made for this book—centerpieces for any party. All will require a little cooperation from the store. I find that good ones welcome the challenge. All of these fish have textures and timing requirements that differ from those of standard fish.

Shad is flat and has rather soft flesh and needs to cook less. It doesn't reheat, and its only use cold is as part of a mixed hors d'oeuvre or antipasto instead of sardines, whose oil-rich texture is similar.

Monkfish requires longer cooking than any other fish that I tried. It has a sweet, nutty flavor and is excellent cold to use as one might use lobster in a salad. Its cartilage, skin, and head make excellent soups and stocks.

Swordfish may have been the biggest winner, its impressive bulk resembling roast veal. It is cooked according to my basic timing rule. Leftovers are best used cold because the flesh can become slightly powdery when reheated; but a microwave oven will warm a single slice with its sauce.

Tuna is glorious when just cooked; but it is a good idea to try and roast just what you will need because leftovers turn rather dry and crumbly on the tongue. This didn't stop all the people who worked with me when I tested tuna from asking if they could take some home. They didn't complain the next day.

SHAD

WHEN FRESH SHAD IS AVAILABLE, REST ASSURED THAT A GLIMMER OF SPRING IS IMMINENT, EVEN IF IT HAS REACHED ONLY FLORIDA BEFORE NORTHERNERS LIKE MYSELF HAVE SHOVELED THE DRIVEWAY FOR THE LAST TIME.

Shad is one of that odd group of fish that seems to have its home address printed into its genes. After being born in the shallows of some river, shad move in a school out to sea, where they remain for five years before migrating one fine spring day back to the banks of their birth. Historically, shad have been netted in the rivers as they make their way up from the sea. They are not as delectable as they are when they come downriver after they have spawned. Recently, I have noted a disquieting tendency among fishermen to net the fish when they are still at sea, it being claimed that they will thus be less tired and fatter. I wonder what the long-term effect will be of taking shad before they move into spawning waters.

Everybody who has fished, cooked, or written about shad is aware of the perils of its bones. Boning it, in the kitchen or at table, is not a job for me to take on. I am grateful that there are still professionals who know how to fillet the fish because its flavor is unctuous and subtle. The fillets are an oddity unto themselves. They actually come as whole fish whose bones have been removed, leaving them with many pockets.

Shad are relatively inexpensive. Their flesh is every bit as good as their roe.

Simple roasted shad

SERVES 4 TO 6 AS A MAIN COURSE

TOTAL
ROASTING
TIME:
see below

I ALWAYS USE butter for shad; but the butter avoiders can use a neutral oil like canola. Avoid olive oil and mixed oils such as "salad oil." Don't worry if shad is a little pink along where the spine would have been. It shouldn't be raw. Peek and replace in oven if need be. Shad easily overcooks. Remove from pan as soon as cooked. There isn't much fat here, and with time the skin will stick.

1½ teaspoons unsalted butter
2-pound filleted whole shad with skin on (1¾ inches at thickest point), head and tail removed

Kosher salt, to taste
Freshly ground black pepper, to taste
Lemon wedges for serving

Place oven rack on second level from bottom. Heat oven to 500°F.

Smear a small amount of the butter into the center of a 12 x 8 x 1½-inch roasting pan. Place fillet in center of pan, on top of butter. Open out shad to expose boned inside. Dab teeny pieces of butter down the center of the fillet. Sprinkle with salt and pepper. Fold shad back up to resemble a whole fish. Roast for 12 minutes. Remove to platter. Serve warm with lemon wedges.

TOTAL ROASTING TIME: 12 minutes (7 minutes per inch of thickness)

Roasted shad with fennel

N<small>EW FRESH BULB</small> fennel arrives in spring, as if heralding the shad. They go well together. The stuffing is light, and it slows down the roasting time only a few minutes. If you have a source of fresh sorrel, cut the leaves into thin strips across the veins and use them to stuff the fish instead of fennel. Tumble the cooked sorrel into the pan after you remove the fish and deglaze the pan with a little water. This is a classically French and Native American combination. Reputedly, the acidity of the sorrel softens the shad bones. I don't hold with that, but the flavors are lovely.

Either way, with fennel or sorrel, serve an acidic white wine such as a Muscadet.

1½ teaspoons unsalted butter

2-pound filleted whole shad with skin on (2 inches at thickest point), head and tail removed, or 2 individual shad fillets

2 to 3 tablespoons fresh lemon juice

Kosher salt, to taste

Freshly ground black pepper, to taste

1 whole fennel bulb (1 pound), trimmed, peeled with a vegetable peeler, and bulb cut into fine strips (about 1 cup), with fronds chopped medium and reserved

Place oven rack on second level from bottom. Heat oven to 500°F.

Smear a small amount of the butter into the center of a 12 x 8 x 1½-inch roasting pan or other pan that just fits the fillet. Place fillet in center of pan, on top of butter. Fold out flaps of fillet so that fillet is flat in pan. Dab teeny pieces of butter down the center of the fillet. Sprinkle down the center with a small amount of lemon juice and then with salt and pepper. Pile up about three quarters of the fennel strips on top of the butter. Fold over fillet flaps to cover the fennel. Top with remaining fennel strips. Sprinkle with remaining lemon juice, dabs of butter, salt, and pepper.

Roast for 14 minutes. Remove to platter. Sprinkle with reserved fennel fronds. Serve right away.

TOTAL ROASTING TIME: 14 minutes (7 minutes per inch of thickness)

$\mathcal{M}$ONKFISH

MONKFISH IS ONE OF THE UGLIEST CREATURES YOU WILL EVER EAT. In France, the shopkeepers love to say they do not show the head to their customers, lest they run screaming from the store. Yet its European cousins, the French lotte and Venetian coda di rospo, are prized as cooking fish whose firm, sweet flesh resembles lobster and has infamously been substituted for it in high-priced dishes.

Monkfish can be divine or dire, depending on how it is cooked. Like sweetbreads, it requires a very long cooking time or it will be chewy, about twice as long as other roasted fish. One compensation is that the tail fillets have absolutely no bones whatsoever.

Most stores or fishmongers do not ever have the whole hideous fish, which Alan Davidson very appropriately lists among the "uncouth fish." Monkfish have huge heads and long "tails," which are the pieces always sold as fillets. Technically, a whole fillet is actually half of an entire monkfish tail. You now know more than many a purveyor—several I have dealt with in New York, at even the finest shops, had no clue that each tail yields two fillets. Make sure that the store skins the pieces thoroughly.

Simple roasted monkfish

SERVES 4 TO 6 AS A FIRST COURSE, 2 TO 4 AS A MAIN COURSE, DEPENDING ON SIZE

TOTAL ROASTING TIME: *see below*

SINCE MONKFISH MUST cook thoroughly, I take its temperature as I would that of a piece of meat. The internal temperature should be 160°F. Be sure to allow enough time for the cooking. Monkfish takes twenty-five to thirty minutes per inch of thickness—at least two and a half to three times as long as most other fish. Two tail fillets may be cooked next to each other, but not touching, to increase the number of servings.

1½- to 2-pound skinned monkfish fillet from half a tail (2½ inches at thickest point)

2 tablespoons olive oil

Kosher salt, to taste

Freshly ground black pepper, to taste

Place rack in center of oven. Heat oven to 500°F.

Place fillet, dark side down, in a 14 x 12 x 2-inch roasting pan. Rub olive oil over fish and pan. Sprinkle with salt and pepper. Roast for 25 to 30 minutes per inch of thickness. Fish should have an internal temperature of 160°F when done.

TOTAL ROASTING TIME: 1 hour to 1 hour 15 minutes (25 to 30 minutes per inch of thickness)

Roasted monkfish Felix

TOTAL
ROASTING
TIME:
*see facing
page*

For many years, my first dinner after the plane to Nice was at one of the outdoor tables at Felix, in the Old Port of Antibes. Felix would bring whole fish to the table and ask what kind he should cook. This is where I saw my first whole monkfish, to which I was almost equally as drawn and repelled by as the revolting-looking chapon, a gray relative of the reddish rascasse, famous as an ingredient for bouillabaisse. I ate the monkfish with pleasure.

My favorite way of having both these beautiful-tasting ugly fish prepared at Felix was in the oven with potatoes, tomatoes, and lemons. This is my homage to that dish.

The timing is a bit tricky. The problem is getting the potatoes, which should be waxy (see page 387) so they don't fall apart, cooked through by the time the fish is done. For this reason I have given two versions of the recipe. The first is for one small fillet and the second, for two larger ones, follows. Don't be tempted to use smaller pans than those indicated or the vegetables will not cook through.

This is one dish in which the vegetables and the fish can and should be served together. Pour any excess juices into a sauceboat or bowl. There are no bones to get you in trouble when you cut the fish to serve it. Cut the fillets across into slices. Surround each slice on a plate with its fair share of vegetables and cooking liquid. If you want this as a first course, cut the fillets into one-inch-wide pieces. For a main course, cut each fillet into three pieces. The lemons are edible.

¼ cup plus 1 tablespoon olive oil

2 lemons, very thinly sliced, seeds removed (about 1 cup)

1 medium onion (8 ounces), peeled and thinly sliced (1¼ cup)

1 pound firm waxy potatoes, such as banana fingerlings or red bliss, peeled and thinly sliced lengthwise (2½ cups)

4 sprigs fresh thyme

2 tomatoes (about 1 pound), cored, stemmed, and cut across into ¼-inch slices

½ cup Roasted Plum Tomato Sauce (page 419), diluted with ¼ cup water, or ½ cup drained canned plum tomatoes, plus ¼ cup reserved juice

1½ teaspoons kosher salt

1½-pound skinned monkfish fillet from ½ tail

Freshly ground black pepper, to taste

Place rack in center of oven. Preheat oven to 500°F.

Spread the ¼ cup olive oil evenly over a 14 x 12 x 2-inch roasting pan. Make 1 thin vertical strip of lemon slices in the center of the pan. Around the lemons, arrange layers of the onion, potatoes, and thyme sprigs, in that order, ending with a layer of tomato slices. The layers should cover the entire surface of the pan, even if some layers are sparser then others. Push the layers down evenly into the pan so they don't hump up in sections. Pour tomato sauce evenly over all the vegetables and the lemon slices.

Salt the fish on both sides. Place fish, dark side down, lengthwise on top of the tomato sauce. Grind black pepper over the fish. Drizzle fish and vegetables with the remaining tablespoon of olive oil.

Roast for 1 hour, or until internal temperature is 160°F. Checking the temperature will ensure the proper texture for the fish. If necessary, roast 10 to 15 minutes more.

Remove the fish to a platter. Remove vegetables—including any crisp bits—with a slotted spoon and surround the fish. If there are abundant cooking juices, which will depend on the quality of the vegetables, you may want to pour them into a sauceboat or pitcher. Otherwise, pour them over the fish.

TOTAL ROASTING TIME: 1 hour to 1 hour 15 minutes (25 to 30 minutes per inch of thickness)

Monkfish Felix for a crowd

SERVES 10 AS A FIRST COURSE,
6 AS A MAIN COURSE

TOTAL
ROASTING
TIME:
see page 282

WHEN COOKING THE monkfish for a main course at a party, buy the largest tail pieces available.

7 tablespoons olive oil

3 lemons, very thinly sliced, seeds removed (about 2¾ cups)

3 medium onions (about 1½ pounds), peeled and thinly sliced (3¾ cups)

1¼ pounds firm, waxy potatoes, such as banana fingerlings or red bliss, peeled and thinly sliced lengthwise (2¾ cups)

8 to 10 sprigs fresh thyme

3 tomatoes (about 1½ pounds), cored, stemmed, and cut horizontally across into ¼-inch slices

1 cup Roasted Plum Tomato Sauce (page 419), diluted with ¼ cup water, or 1 cup drained canned plum tomatoes, plus ¼ cup reserved juice

1 tablespoon kosher salt

Two 2- to 2½-pound skinned monkfish fillets from 1 tail

Freshly ground black pepper, to taste

Place rack in center of oven. Preheat oven to 500°F.

Spread ¼ cup of the olive oil evenly over an 18 x 13 x 2-inch roasting pan. Make 2 thin parallel strips of lemon slices lengthwise in the pan. Around the lemon slices, arrange layers of the onions, potatoes, and thyme sprigs, in that order, ending with a layer of tomato slices. The layers should cover the entire surface of the pan, even if some layers are sparser than others. Push the layers down evenly into the pan so they don't hump up in sections. Pour tomato sauce evenly over all the vegetables and the lemon slices.

Salt the fish on both sides. Place the two fillets dark sides down lengthwise on top of the tomato sauce, next to but not touching each other or the sides of the pan. Grind black pepper over the fish. Drizzle fish and vegetables with the remaining olive oil.

Roast for 1 hour, or until internal temperature is 160°F. Checking the temperature will ensure the proper texture for the fish. If necessary, roast for 10 to 15 more minutes.

Remove fish to a platter. Remove vegetables—including any crisp bits—with a slotted spoon and surround the fish. If there are abundant cooking juices, which will depend on the quality of the vegetables, you may want to pour them into a sauceboat or pitcher. Otherwise, pour them over the fish.

TOTAL ROASTING TIME: 1 hour to 1 hour 15 minutes (25 to 30 minutes per inch of thickness)

Rich monkfish stock

MAKES 4 CUPS

THE SECRET TO making this rich, flavorful stock is the long cooking time. (Less time will yield more stock with less taste.) Reduce a large amount of stock at a vigorous boil until there are just four cups. The stock is wonderfully gelatinous and mild in flavor. All of it can be used—even the sediment has no bitterness. Use this as the base of any fish soup, for instance, Divine Fish Chowder (page 244), using leftover monkfish instead of the cod. The stock makes a marvelous aspic.

Ask the fish shop to save the skin and cartilage from monkfish tails to make the stock. If there is a head, bravo. Usually all these pieces are thrown away, so they won't mind.

1¾ pounds cartilage and skin from 2 monkfish tails

3 cups white wine

2 cups water, plus more as needed

Put all ingredients together in a stockpot. Cover and bring to a boil. Reduce heat to a simmer. Skim the scum off the top of the liquid. Cook, uncovered, at least 6 to 8 hours, or up to 12 if you have time. Check periodically to see that fish parts are covered by liquid. Top off with water as needed, and continue skimming any scum that has collected on the surface. Reduce by boiling if need be.

Strain through a fine sieve, lined with damp cheesecloth. Let cool. Will keep, frozen, for about 6 months, refrigerated about 3 days.

Piquant saffron monkfish soup

MAKES ABOUT 5 CUPS; SERVES 4
AS A FIRST COURSE

THIS RECIPE MAY easily be multiplied to increase the number of first courses for more guests. The fish and vegetables are leftovers from Roasted Monkfish Felix.

4 cups Rich Monkfish Stock (page 282)

One ½-gram vial stem saffron

1 cup of ½-inch fish pieces from leftover Roasted Monkfish Felix (page 280),

1 cup leftover vegetables from Roasted Monkfish Felix, lemons discarded

6 to 8 drops hot red pepper sauce or to taste

Kosher salt, to taste

Freshly ground black pepper, to taste

Put the stock and saffron in a medium saucepan. Bring to a boil, covered, then reduce heat to medium and cook 10 minutes. Add the fish, vegetables, and hot sauce. Return to a boil, covered. Reduce heat to a simmer. Heat just until warm throughout. Add salt and pepper. Serve in individual bowls, dividing the fish and vegetables evenly into the broth.

As-good-as-meat roasted swordfish

SERVES 12 AS A MAIN COURSE

TOTAL
ROASTING
TIME:
see page 284

THIS MAY BE my candidate for the book's most exciting recipe. It requires a thick slice cut across the whole swordfish fillet. The slab is then seasoned as if it were a rack of lamb and roasted. It is sensational looking when it comes from the oven. Carefully—it's hot—pull off the long strip of skin from the back of the fillet. Bring the fish to the table in all its glory and slice it across into half-inch-thick slices. The sauce can be poured over the fish or served on the side.

Swordfish is expensive—about the same price per pound as loin of veal, but there is less shrinkage. It feeds almost twice as many people as the same weight of veal. Also, good swordfish is more readily available than really fabulous veal.

Serve this with Roasted Cherry Tomatoes with Basil (page 419), a potato of your choice, and a robust red wine. If making mashed potatoes, serve some of the sauce on top of them—there will be about a cup and a half of sauce.

To measure the fillet for thickness, lay it on its side. Use the basic timing rule of ten minutes per inch of thickness, which will yield flesh that is barely pink in the center and moist throughout; if all-white flesh is preferred, cook five minutes longer.

When ordering swordfish, ask for a three-and-a-quarter-inch-thick piece of whole swordfish fillet with the skin on. This will normally be taken from half a fish. There will be a V-shaped section of dark meat running through the center. The fillet will measure about thirteen inches wide by four inches high and weigh in the neighborhood of five and a quarter pounds. Because the fillet is so dense, allow a good hour and fifteen minutes for it to come to room temperature.

The herb mixture is very good on lamb as well as swordfish. Don't make it in a food processor unless it is a very small one. Food processors will not sufficiently grind the mixture. A blender or an electric spice or coffee mill is fine.

2 cloves garlic, smashed and peeled	1 recipe Herb Rub (page 293)
5¼-pound piece of whole swordfish fillet (3¾ inches at thickest point), skin on	½ cup water, for deglazing
	¾ cup drained Niçoise olives, optional

Place rack in center of oven. Heat oven to 500°F.

Cut the garlic into thin slivers. Use the point of a small knife to make small incisions in all sides except the skin side of the fillet. Insert the garlic slivers into the incisions, as if larding a leg of lamb.

Place fish in a 12 x 8 x 1½-inch roasting pan, skin side facing out toward one side of the pan. Spoon half the herb mixture over the fillet. Rub thickly over all surfaces except the skin side. Turn fillet over and spoon on remaining herb mixture. Rub in. Arrange fillet in pan so that it touches sides of pan as little as possible; place on the diagonal if necessary.

Roast for 37 minutes. Using 2 very large spatulas, remove fillet to serving platter, again with the skin side facing out toward one side. Peel off the skin with fingers, using a knife if necessary to loosen it from the flesh. Slice fillet across into ½-inch-thick slices.

Put the roasting pan on top of the stove over medium-high heat. Add the water to the pan. Scrape the bottom of the pan with a wooden spoon, loosening all the dark, crisp bits. Add to the pan the liquid that has collected in the bottom of the serving platter. Bring sauce to a boil. If using the olives, reduce heat to a simmer, add olives, and heat through until just warm. Use as a sauce with the fish.

TOTAL ROASTING TIME: 37 minutes (10 minutes per inch of thickness)

Swordfish tonnato

MAKES 1½ CUPS SAUCE

ANY LEFTOVER ROASTED swordfish makes a superb cold dish with a dollop of that rich concoction, tonnato sauce, which the Italians use on leftover roast veal and which many of us put on thin, cold slices of roasted turkey. I would never use freshly cooked tuna in this sauce, any more than I would personally put it in a salade Niçoise. The texture just isn't right.

Serve the leftover slices of As-Good-as-Meat Roasted Swordfish (page 283). If there were olives in the original sauce and they haven't all been eaten, use a few to top each slice of sauced fish. Otherwise, the tonnato sauce can be topped with extra capers and olives, finely chopped parsley, or nothing at all. The sauce is enough for four to six people. Make the whole amount even if there isn't enough leftover fish. Serve the dividend on boiled potatoes or in a roast meat sandwich.

FOR THE TONNATO SAUCE

One 6½-ounce can water-packed tuna, drained

2 anchovy fillets

1½ tablespoons drained and rinsed capers, plus extra for garnish, optional

⅔ cup Basic Mayonnaise (page 303) or store-bought

1½ tablespoons olive oil

1½ tablespoons fresh lemon juice

2 tablespoons finely chopped fresh flat-leaf parsley, plus extra for garnish, optional

Kosher salt, to taste

Niçoise olives for garnish, optional

Gently wipe off each slice of roasted swordfish to remove herb coating. Reserve fish.

Place tuna, anchovies, and capers in a food processor and process until smooth. Add mayonnaise and process again until smooth. With the machine running, add oil in a thin stream.

Add lemon juice, parsley, and salt. Process briefly to mix. Taste and add more lemon juice or salt if desired. Refrigerate, tightly covered.

To serve, arrange 1 to 2 slices per person on a plate and top each with 3 tablespoons of the sauce. Dot with capers, olives, and/or parsley, if using.

Roasted and glazed tuna

SERVES 4 TO 5 AS A MAIN COURSE

TOTAL
ROASTING
TIME:
see below

WHEN ORDERING THE tuna, ask for a three-inch-thick piece of whole tuna fillet, without skin. This will normally be taken from a quarter section of a fish and resemble a triangular-shaped wedge measuring five and a half to seven and a half inches per side and weighing two and a half to three pounds. Measure the thickness of the tuna fillet by laying it on its side—no point sticking in the air. Pat the flesh slightly to get as even a thickness as possible. If the piece of fish varies very much in thickness, time the cooking by the thinner edge and then check whether the fish is done by inserting a knife into the interior. The flesh will be barely pink in the center; if completely opaque flesh is wanted, cook five minutes longer. For rare tuna, cook five minutes less. Avoid overcooking.

1 tablespoon canola or other neutral oil
2 tablespoons Chinese soy sauce without
    molasses, or tamari soy sauce

2½- to 3-pound piece whole tuna
    fillet (3 inches at thinnest point),
    skin removed

Place rack in center of oven. Heat oven to 500°F.

In a small bowl, combine the oil and soy sauce, stirring well. Reserve.

Place fish in a 12 x 8 x 1½-inch roasting pan, skin side facing out towards one side of the pan. (Do not place the fillet in the pan so that the point of the triangle is sticking up in the air.) Pour half the marinade over the fillet and rub into all surfaces of the fillet except the skin side. Treat as if it were a piece of Japanese Kobe beef, massaging gently. Turn fillet over and pour on remaining marinade. Massage in. Arrange fillet so that skin side is facing out toward one side of the pan, touching the sides of pan as little as possible. Marinate 1 hour 15 minutes at room temperature, massaging marinade into fillet from time to time.

Roast for 30 minutes. Using 2 very large spatulas, remove fillet to serving platter, again with the skin side facing out toward one side. Slice fillet across the grain into 1-inch-thick slices.

TOTAL ROASTING TIME: 30 minutes (10 minutes per inch of thickness)

ROASTED SHELLFISH

To be hideously honest, there are just not many shellfish that are better roasted than they are cooked other ways. I give those candidates in this brief section.

SHRIMP

SHRIMP ARE WIDELY AVAILABLE AND EXTREMELY POPULAR. The only ones worth roasting are the jumbos, about an ounce and a half each, or twelve to the pound. Deveining, taking out the dark strip down the back of the shrimp, under the shell, is a matter of preference. No one will be poisoned if it's left in.

Shrimp can be roasted whole in the shell or peeled; but the very best way is to butterfly them, leaving the shell on. Remove any legs or feelers. Lay the shrimp flat on a work surface. With a sharp knife held parallel to the work surface, cut them in half lengthwise right up to the tail, leaving them attached at the tail and the tail on. Do not cut all the way through. Open up the shrimp so the two shell sides are down. That is a butterflied shrimp.

More fish can be roasted in larger pans. They should just fit in.

Simple jumbo shrimp

SERVES 8 AS A FIRST COURSE

TOTAL
ROASTING
TIME:
5
minutes

About 24 jumbo shrimp in the shell
    (about 1½ ounces each, 2¾ pounds
    total, 4½ to 6 inches long), butterflied

3 tablespoons olive oil

Kosher salt, to taste

Freshly ground black pepper, to taste

Place rack in center of oven. Heat oven to 500°F.

Place shrimp in an 18 x 13 x 2-inch roasting pan. Rub shrimp with olive oil. Sprinkle with salt and pepper. Roast, flesh side down, for 2½ minutes. Turn. Roast for 2½ minutes more.

Spicy roasted shrimp

Basic ROASTED SHRIMP are given a Southwestern turn with a spicy lime marinade. I serve them on their own as a first course, with the pan juices apportioned between them. The hungry can add rice, and also beans, and guacamole. This quantity will serve three for a quick main course with the three side dishes.

FOR THE MARINADE

2 tablespoons fresh lime juice

3 tablespoons olive oil

½ teaspoon seeded, deribbed, and chopped Basic Jalapeños (page 383)

1 clove garlic, smashed, peeled, and chopped fine

Kosher salt, to taste

Freshly ground black pepper, to taste

24 jumbo shrimp (1½ ounces each, 2¾ pounds total, 4½ to 6 inches long), in the shell, butterflied

Whisk together marinade. Place shrimp, shell side down, in an 18 x 13 x 2-inch roasting pan. Pour marinade over shrimp and set aside for 1 hour, turning over once.

About 20 minutes before roasting, place rack in center of oven. Heat oven to 500°F. Arrange shrimp, flesh side down, in the pan. Roast for 2½ minutes. Turn shrimp over. Roast 2½ minutes more. Pour pan juices over shrimp and serve warm or at room temperature.

Lemon shrimp frisée

TOTAL
ROASTING
TIME:
see below

SERVES 8 AS A FIRST COURSE

Sʜʀɪᴍᴘ SALAD IS too often a mass of pink, heavy with mayonnaise. Lemon Shrimp Frisée is another kind of recipe; it's shrimp with salad. To feed eight as a first course (or eat lots yourself), make about three pounds of Simple Jumbo Shrimp (page 287), using olive oil as the fat. The salad will serve four as a cool main course and can be easily doubled; but the greens need not be doubled.

"Frisée" refers to the French name for chicory—the paler the color, the tenderer and better. It is also an allusion to the frizzled leeks.

1 small leek, trimmed, cleaned, and cut across into ¼-inch-thick slices

2 tablespoons olive oil

FOR THE SCALLION VINAIGRETTE

2 cloves garlic, smashed and peeled

1 teaspoon kosher salt

1½ tablespoons red wine vinegar

¼ cup olive oil

1 bunch scallions, trimmed, white and pale green parts cut across into 2-inch lengths, then lengthwise into thin strips (about 1 cup)

1 large head chicory, washed, dried, trimmed and torn into pieces

3 endives, trimmed and cut across into thirds, then lengthwise into thin strips (about 4 cups)

1 recipe Simple Jumbo Shrimp (page 287), peeled

8 ¼-inch-wide strips lemon zest from 1 fresh lemon, sliced lengthwise very thin

Freshly ground black pepper, to taste

Place rack in center of oven. Heat oven to 500°F. Arrange leek slices in a 12 x 8 x 2-inch roasting pan. Drizzle with oil. Toss until well mixed. Roast for 6 minutes. Turn. Roast 6 minutes more. Remove and reserve.

To make the vinaigrette: Using a mortar and pestle, pound the garlic with the salt into a paste. Transfer to a small bowl. Add vinegar. Mix well. Whisk in oil a little at a time. Add scallions. Blend well. Put the chicory and endive in a large bowl. Add vinaigrette. Toss until all greens are well coated.

To serve, divide greens among 8 plates. Put 3 shrimp on each plate. Top with a bit of roasted leek, then a strip of lemon zest. Sprinkle with black pepper.

TOTAL ROASTING TIME: leeks, 12 minutes; shrimp, 5 minutes

SCALLOPS

DON'T TRY ROASTING BAY SCALLOPS, OR THOSE WITH A DIAMETER LESS THAN 1¼ INCHES. There is just not enough flesh to sustain the high heat. Melting butter on top of the stove gives a head start to a nice beurre noisette (nut-colored butter) for roasting the scallops.

A large pan holds as many as sixty large sea scallops, which is expensive, but good for a blow-out party. A single roasted scallop on a slightly larger round of toast spread with Tapenade (page 298) makes a gala canapé. Serve three scallops on a bed of endive and top with Three-Citrus Mayonnaise (page 304) for a first course, hot or cold, or place the scallops in a puddle of one of the sauces on pages 292–309.

Simple roasted scallops

SERVES 6 AS A FIRST COURSE

TOTAL ROASTING TIME: 5 *minutes*

A 12 x 8 x 1½-INCH roasting pan will hold twenty-four scallops, an 18 x 13 x 2-inch pan as many as sixty.

2 tablespoons unsalted butter or olive oil

24 large sea scallops (1¼ pounds, about 1¼ to 2 inches wide)

Place rack in center of oven. Heat oven to 500°F.

If using butter, melt first in a 12 x 8 x 1½-inch roasting pan on top of stove. Place scallops in pan. Rub butter or olive oil over each scallop. Roast for 5 minutes. Scallops should be opaque but not too firm or they will be tough.

OYSTERS AND CLAMS

I LIKE OYSTERS AND CLAMS RAW. However, there are many people who like hot oysters and clams. Roasting heats and opens them. Once they are hot, slip a little bit of butter on top of the meat and add a grind a bit of pepper or sprinkle on a few drops of hot red pepper sauce. A pleasant variation is to top each with some Horseradish Hollandaise Sauce (page 306). Cooking them cannot protect against disease unless someone wants to eat rubber bands.

Simple roasted oysters or clams

SERVES 4

TOTAL
ROASTING
TIME:
10
minutes

16 large oysters, in the shell, well
    scrubbed, or 2 pounds littleneck clams
    (16 to 20)

¼ pound (1 stick) unsalted butter, optional

Fresh lemon juice, optional

Freshly ground black pepper, optional

Place rack in center of oven. Heat oven to 450°F.

Place oysters or clams curved side down in a roasting pan so that as they open the juices do not spill out. Roast for 10 minutes, or until shells open to about ½ inch; they don't have to gape. Remove from roasting pan with large spoon.

Pry shells completely open. If using butter, top each oyster with about ½ tablespoon and each clam with about 1 teaspoon, and sprinkle with a little lemon juice and pepper.

Sauces, glazes, and marinades

Many of the recipes in this section can be used on foods other than fish. Some are what we commonly think of as sauces. In roasting, we often also want glazes and marinades—wet and dry—that flavor the food or become part of the sauce when the roasting pan is deglazed. A very high proportion of the hot sauces for roasted foods is based on deglazing the savory residue in the pan after the roasted food is removed. The cold sauces are often used to transform leftovers.

Deglazing sauces are gravies with fancier names. I seldom thicken gravies. If a thicker gravy is wanted, for each cup of gravy, add a tablespoon of cornstarch dissolved in two tablespoons of cold water to form a thick paste. It is usually best to stir a little of the hot liquid into the cornstarch paste before adding it to the pan so that the gravy doesn't have lumps. Alternatively, leave some fat in the roasting pan, place it on top of the stove over medium heat, and stir into it a tablespoon of flour for each cup of finished gravy. Cook flour about three minutes before adding the liquid.

Deglazing sauces are generally made by putting the roasting pan, emptied of the roasted food and any superfluous fat, on top of the stove and adding liquid while scraping vigorously with a wooden spoon until all the roasting residue is dissolved. Use medium to high heat. This also cleans the roasting pan. The deglazing liquid can be reduced by boiling after all the glaze at the bottom of the pan has been dissolved.

The liquid may be water, wine, fruit juices, coffee (for red-eye gravy), or stock. If I have been good and followed my own counsel, I will have stock on hand in the refrigerator or the freezer made with the bones and, in the case of fish, heads of foods I have roasted.

This section starts with the lone dry marinade. It goes on to the wet marinades and the closely related glazes and then cold and hot sauces. Marinades should be used as directed in recipes or rubbed on fish or meats to permeate them with flavor as they come to room temperature, or as long as four hours ahead. There is no sanitary problem as the foods will be thoroughly cooked.

Most of the ingredients are generally available. They may not all be sitting on your shelf now; but it is a good idea to buy a selection because they can provide depth of seasoning and spontaneous changes in flavor. Fresh ingredients such as citrus fruits, tomatoes, herbs, and ginger do have to be bought as the need arises, or like garlic, from time to time.

Herb rub

MAKES ⅜ CUP

THIS SIMPLE HERB mixture is delicious on As-Good-as-Meat Roasted Swordfish (page 283) and a wide variety of foods and is almost a classic on rack of lamb. I have used it on other fish with great success. The recipe makes enough for a large fish, a large loin of pork or a leg, or two saddles or four racks of lamb.

12 cloves garlic, smashed and peeled

1 tablespoon dried oregano, preferably Greek

¼ teaspoon dried rosemary

1 tablespoon dried thyme

2 tablespoons kosher salt

2 teaspoons freshly ground black pepper

¼ cup olive oil

Cut garlic into medium pieces. Place in blender along with the oregano, rosemary, thyme, salt, pepper, and olive oil. Blend until a smooth purée. Scrape down sides of blender with a rubber spatula and, using the spatula, scrape into a small bowl. Reserve and use as directed in recipes.

Balsamic marinade

MAKES ½ CUP

TRY THIS ON game birds or a loin of pork and on fish. The flavor goes well with Italianate vegetables such as cippolines (page 375), Basic Whole Red Bell Peppers (page 382), or Roasted Broccoli with Lemon-Garlic Bath (page 323).

4 cloves garlic, smashed and peeled

2 teaspoons kosher salt

Freshly ground black pepper, to taste

¼ cup balsamic vinegar

¼ cup olive oil

In a mortar with a pestle, or on a cutting board with a knife, smash the garlic with the salt and pepper until it is a smooth paste. Put the vinegar in a small bowl. Whisk in the paste until it is smooth and whisk in olive oil until smooth.

Tandoori wet rub

MAKES ½ CUP

This salacious-sounding rub for chicken or fish is intense. The scant half cup will deal with two chickens, a whole fish, or a short leg of lamb.

1 tablespoon unsalted butter

3⅓ cups ¼-inch- diced onion

6 cloves garlic, smashed, peeled, and sliced across

1 teaspoon ground cardamom

1 teaspoon chili powder

¾ teaspoon turmeric

½ teaspoon ground cumin

½ teaspoon mace

¼ teaspoon mustard powder

⅛ teaspoon ground cinnamon

⅛ teaspoon freshly grated nutmeg

Freshly ground black pepper, to taste

2 teaspoons kosher salt

1 tablespoon fresh lime juice

3 tablespoons nonfat yogurt

Put the butter in a medium saucepan. Melt over low heat. Add all remaining ingredients except the lime juice and yogurt. Cook over low heat until onions and garlic are translucent but not brown, about 10 minutes. Scrape contents into a blender. Add lime juice and yogurt. Blend until well combined.

Dilled lemon oil

MAKES ¼ CUP

This intense marinade is sufficient for a medium-size whole fish, eight to ten zucchini, or a capon.

½ tablespoon fresh lemon juice

1 bunch (1½ ounces) fresh dill, thick end of stems removed

3 tablespoons olive oil

1½ teaspoons kosher salt

Freshly ground black pepper, to taste

Put the ingredients in a blender. Whirl until smooth. Using a rubber spatula, scrape out into a small bowl.

Mint bath marinade

MAKES ⅔ CUP

THIS IS GOOD for vegetables, a four- to five-pound whole fish, or a large chicken.

¼ cup fresh lemon juice

¼ cup olive oil

¼ cup packed fresh mint leaves, chopped medium-fine

1 teaspoon kosher salt

Freshly ground black pepper, to taste

Combine all the ingredients in a small bowl.

Green herb spread

MAKES ½ CUP

THIS HERBAL MIXTURE is so rich and thick it almost looks like a green mayonnaise. Serve it on any cold roasted leftover, even eggplant slices.

4 to 5 cloves garlic, smashed, peeled, and chopped medium

1 tablespoon fresh lemon juice

4 to 5 tablespoons olive oil

½ bunch (½ ounce) fresh thyme, leaves picked off stems

½ bunch (¼ ounce) fresh oregano, leaves picked off stems

1 teaspoon kosher salt

Freshly ground black pepper, to taste

In the blender, put the garlic, lemon juice, and 2 tablespoons of the oil. Blend until smooth, stopping to scrape the sides once or twice with a rubber spatula. Add remaining oil, thyme, oregano, salt, and pepper. Blend until smooth, scraping once or twice. Reserve.

Riviera sauce

MAKES ¾ CUP

THIS SAUCE IS perfect served hot with a four-pound chicken, a three-pound whole fish, or, doubled, over a short leg of lamb.

¾ cup white wine vinegar

⅔ cup golden raisins

One ½-gram vial stem saffron

3 tablespoons tomato paste

Freshly ground black pepper, to taste

Combine all ingredients in a small pan. Bring to a boil over medium heat, and reduce to a simmer. Cook for 15 minutes.

Orange-cumin glaze

MAKES ½ CUP

FRESH-TASTING WITH A hint of the Mediterranean, this is good on two whole chickens, a large turkey, or a large fish. Try it on vegetables such as sweet potato slices (page 398) or portobello mushrooms (page 362). Two other good glazes are Asian Glaze (page 33) and Pacific Rim Glaze (page 273). Glazes are meant to be brushed on foods to be roasted. Don't use too much.

5 tablespoons canola or other neutral oil

1½ to 2 teaspoons ground cumin

½ teaspoon kosher salt

¼ cup fresh orange juice

Freshly ground black pepper, to taste

Combine all ingredients in a small bowl.

Simple light vinaigrette

MAKES 1 CUP

THE HARDEST THING to tell someone how to make is a simple vinaigrette because vinegars, oils, and even the lemon juice that may be substituted for the vinegar vary so widely in flavor. The best recommendation I can give is to taste the ingredients and add the acid to the oil slowly, along with small amounts of salt. Salt and acid make each other more intense. Don't make the mistake of going for a killer olive oil and an expensive balsamic vinegar together. They will destroy each other. Rice wine vinegar is mild. Malt vinegar is sharp so use it with an oil other than olive. Cider vinegar is fine with either mild olive oil or peanut oil. Lemon juice and fruity red wine vinegar go well with the mighty killer oils.

Two teaspoons of prepared mustard or a half teaspoon of mustard powder can be added for a slight mustardy flavor and more stability or emulsification.

Scandinavians, Germans, and their descendants usually add a little sugar, which is good in a vinaigrette made with red wine vinegar and some chopped dill to serve over beets.

¼ cup red wine vinegar (or other acid)
1½ teaspoons kosher salt
2 grinds black pepper

4 teaspoons minced fresh dill (or other fresh herb)
¾ cup olive oil

Place vinegar in a medium bowl. Add salt, pepper, and dill. While whisking, slowly pour oil into vinegar, stopping now and then to whisk more vigorously to fully incorporate the ingredients.

Sesame-cilantro vinaigrette

MAKES ABOUT ½ CUP

T HE WARM FLAVORS of this vinaigrette are good with endive and other bitter greens and with fish and lamb salads.

3 teaspoons sesame oil

2 tablespoons soy sauce, preferably tamari

2 tablespoons rice wine vinegar

2 tablespoons chopped fresh cilantro

2 tablespoons chopped scallions, white and green parts

½ teaspoon grated fresh gingerroot

2 to 3 grinds black pepper

In a small bowl, whisk together all the ingredients.

Tapenade

MAKES 1 CUP

T HIS SOUTH-OF-FRANCE classic goes with leftover roasted fish and any other cold roasted leftover.

1 cup drained oil-cured black olives, about ¾ cup pitted

¼ cup tightly packed fresh basil leaves

6 oil-packed anchovy fillets, drained

1 tablespoon fresh lemon juice

1 clove garlic, smashed, peeled, and thinly sliced

½ small dried red chile pepper or ¼ teaspoon dried red pepper flakes

2 tablespoons drained and rinsed capers

¼ cup olive oil

Combine all ingredients except the olive oil in a food processor and process, scraping down the sides once or twice with a rubber spatula, until coarsely chopped. While the motor runs, add the oil slowly and process a few seconds until the mixture is a smooth purée. Check the seasonings and adjust if necessary. Store, covered, in the refrigerator for at least 24 hours and up to 4 weeks. Bring to room temperature before serving.

Papaya salsa

MAKES 2 CUPS

THIS SMASHING SAUCE must be put together at the last minute or the papaya will turn it mushy. Chop everything ahead and combine before using. The recipe calls for half of a one-pound papaya. I just eat the other half or double the recipe.

About ½ ripe papaya (8 ounces), peeled and cut into ½-inch cubes (1 cup)

1 medium tomato (8 ounces), cored and cut into ½-inch cubes (1 cup)

⅓ cup thinly sliced scallions, white and green parts

2 tablespoons fresh lemon juice

1 teaspoon kosher salt

¼ to ½ teaspoon cayenne pepper

1 teaspoon ground cumin

2 teaspoons canola or other neutral oil

Combine first five ingredients in a medium bowl. Place the cayenne, cumin, and oil in a small skillet. Heat over a low flame, stirring, until just warmed throughout. Remove from heat. Scoop part of papaya mixture into skillet. Swirl around and with a rubber spatula, scrape all out into bowl with remaining papaya and tomato mixture. Mix well to incorporate the spices.

Jalapeño-mango salsa

MAKES 1 CUP

A SWEET RATHER THAN hot salsa that keeps well in the refrigerator and is good with most roasted leftovers.

1 ripe mango (14 ounces), peeled and cut into ¼-inch dice (1 cup)

1 teaspoon seeded, deribbed, and chopped Basic Jalapeños (page 383) or more, to taste

2 tablespoons chopped red onion

1 clove garlic, smashed, peeled, and chopped very fine

⅛ teaspoon kosher salt

1½ tablespoons fresh lime juice

2 tightly packed tablespoons chopped fresh cilantro

Combine all ingredients in a medium bowl. Mix gently to combine.

Guacamole

MAKES 2 ¼ CUPS

SO MUCH GREEN glop masquerades under this name that I hesitate to recommend it; but with really ripe dark-skinned Haas avocados that have been mashed, not puréed, I think it is worth rescuing. This version, straight from my book *Party Food*, is pleasant, mild, and fresh. If you or your guests like things hotter, add more peppers. If you cannot bear to serve anything this unadorned, stir in a tablespoon of grated onion and two tablespoons of chopped coriander.

Don't add tomato to the guacamole. Tomato makes it watery. Consider making one of the salsas (pages 299) and serving it with the guacamole. If you cannot find fresh hot peppers, substitute a third of a green bell pepper and hot red pepper sauce, to taste. Do not use dried peppers or pepper flakes. The guacamole will keep for the length of a party because of the amount of lime juice and garlic.

If you are multiplying the recipe several times, purée the flavoring mixture in the blender.

1 tablespoon kosher salt

5 cloves garlic, smashed and peeled

3 small fresh hot peppers such as jalapeños, stemmed, halved, seeded, and deribbed, or 3 teaspoons seeded and chopped Basic Jalapeños (page 383)

5 tablespoons fresh lime juice

3 large (1½ pounds) ripe Haas avocados

Sprinkle salt over garlic cloves and mince very fine, pressing the garlic into the salt with the flat of the knife from time to time until it forms a paste. Add the peppers to the garlic paste and mince again, pressing on the peppers, salt, and garlic mixture to make a fine paste that retains all the pepper juices. Scrape into a small bowl, stir in 2 tablespoons of the lime juice, and set aside.

Just before serving, cut avocados in half lengthwise. Remove the pits and scoop the meat from the skins with a teaspoon. In a nonreactive serving bowl, mash the avocados with a fork. Stir in garlic mixture and remaining lime juice.

Taramasalata

MAKES 2 CUPS

THIS GREEK MAYONNAISE made from fish roe is as good on cold vegetables and fish as it is as a dip or on Roasted Bread (page 367). Traditionally, taramasalata is made with carp or cod roe that has been preserved with salt. This tarama can be bought in jars, as can a prepared taramasalata. Since packaged tarama is often terribly salty, I prefer to start with salmon roe (caviar), which can be fresh or from a jar. It is generally less salty. If it is the right season of the year and there is a very good fish store, you may be able to get really fresh—unsalted—fish roe, which will make an even better dish.

This recipe makes a very thick sauce. For a thinner one, make it in a food processor and add about a quarter of a cup more oil; or make the sauce as directed below and whisk in some heavy (whipping) cream.

Don't use the greenest, heaviest-tasting olive oil for this or nobody will be able to taste the fish roe. Serve with toasted sections of pita bread.

7 cloves garlic, smashed and peeled

1¼ cups salmon roe (caviar)

1 ounce crustless Italian bread, broken into chunks

¼ cup fresh lemon juice

1 cup olive oil

In a blender, purée the garlic. Add the roe, bread chunks, and lemon juice and start blending. Dribble in the olive oil in a very thin stream; by the time the oil is completely incorporated, the mixture will be smooth and very thick. Stop the blender from time to time in order to scrape down the sides and break any air bubble that forms over the blades. You can tell if that is happening when the blender begins making an empty whirring noise.

If not using immediately, refrigerate, covered. It will last at least 1 week. Bring to room temperature before serving.

Jalapeño-lime sauce

MAKES 1 CUP

CONSIDER USING THIS sauce with leftovers from roasted rich, oily fleshed fish, duck, and goose.

½ cup fresh lime juice

2 tablespoons seeded and chopped
   Basic Jalapeños (page 383)

½ teaspoon kosher salt

Scant ¼ teaspoon freshly ground black
   pepper

½ cup canola or other neutral oil

Place the lime juice, jalapeños, salt, and pepper in the blender. Blend until a smooth purée. Add 1 tablespoon of the oil and blend again. Slowly add remaining oil until mixture is well combined and thick. Using a rubber spatula, scrape out all the sauce into a serving bowl. Cover with plastic wrap and refrigerate until 20 minutes before ready to use.

Horseradish sauce

MAKES 1 CUP

THIS COLD SAUCE is often served with smoked fish and is also good with the richer cold leftovers of roasted fish, lamb, or beef.

½ cup heavy cream

2 tablespoons horseradish purée (see
   Horseradish Hollandaise Sauce,
   page 306) or

1½ tablespoons drained prepared horseradish, finely chopped and mixed with
   1 teaspoon white wine vinegar and 1
   teaspoon heavy cream

Whip the cream until it forms soft peaks. Fold in the horseradish purée or its substitute. Serve.

Basic mayonnaise

MAKES 1 CUP

THOSE WHO WORRY about the health risk of eating raw eggs shouldn't make mayonnaise. Substitute the bottled stuff. Deglazing juices, tomato paste or purée, anchovy paste, mustard, or herbs can be added.

2 egg yolks	½ cup vegetable oil
2 teaspoons fresh lemon juice	Kosher salt, to taste
½ cup olive oil	Freshly ground black pepper, to taste

Place yolks and lemon juice in a food processor and process until well blended. While the machine is running, add oils in a thin stream and process until thoroughly incorporated and mixture is smooth. Season with salt and pepper.

Tarragon mayonnaise

MAKES 1 CUP

THIS SAUCE IS sublime with cold fish, chicken, or capon. A little Pernod can be added for a deeper flavor to accompany shellfish.

3 egg yolks	½ cup canola or other neutral oil
2 teaspoons fresh lemon juice	¼ cup finely chopped fresh tarragon
2 tablespoons tarragon vinegar	½ teaspoon kosher salt
½ cup mild-flavored olive oil	Freshly ground black pepper, to taste

Place yolks and lemon juice in a food processor and pulse until combined. Add vinegar and pulse again until combined. With the machine running, pour in the olive and canola oils in a steady stream. Stop and scrape down sides of work bowl with a rubber spatula. Add tarragon, salt, and pepper. Process for 2 to 3 minutes, until well combined and greenish in color.

Three-citrus mayonnaise

MAKES 4 CUPS

USING WHOLE EGGS makes this a frothy sauce almost like a sabayon, but cold and more stable. Refrigerate and use as needed. Start with a mild olive oil or the citrus flavors will be overwhelmed. For a substitute, if this is too much fuss, see Pork and Orange Salad (page 182).

5 tablespoons fresh orange juice
4 teaspoons fresh lemon juice
2 tablespoons fresh grapefruit juice
2 eggs
1 teaspoon kosher salt

1 cup canola or other neutral oil
1½ cups olive oil
1½ teaspoons finely chopped orange zest
1¾ teaspoons finely chopped lemon zest
1¾ teaspoons finely chopped
    grapefruit zest

Combine the 3 juices in a measuring cup. Place the eggs, half the juice, and salt in a food processor and process for 1 minute. With the machine running, gradually add the oils. As mixture thickens, slowly add remaining juice. Scrape out mayonnaise into a medium bowl. Stir in zests. Cover tightly with plastic wrap and refrigerate overnight.

Minty mayonnaise

MAKES ¾ CUP

GOOD WITH COLD fish, good with cold chicken, good with cold lamb. Use a few mint sprigs for garnish.

¼ cup fresh lime juice
2 teaspoons ground cumin
½ cup Basic Mayonnaise (page 303)
    or store-bought

1 teaspoon kosher salt
Freshly ground black pepper, to taste
1 bunch (1 ounce) fresh mint, washed,
    leaves removed, and finely chopped

In a medium bowl, whisk together the lime juice, cumin, mayonnaise, salt, and pepper. Add mint and blend well.

Tartar sauce

MAKES 2 CUPS

THIS IS THE great American standard for fried fish and seafood as well as fish cakes. The recipe can be easily multiplied and will keep refrigerated for at least one week.

2 cups Basic Mayonnaise (page 303) or store-bought

2 tablespoons white wine vinegar

3 sweet gherkins, minced

6 tablespoons drained and rinsed capers

Combine all ingredients in a small bowl. Refrigerate, covered, until cold.

Green goddess dressing

MAKES 2¼ CUPS

ANYBODY WHO HAS read James Beard or Helen Brown will be familiar with this San Francisco dressing, traditionally served with cold crabmeat. I have used it in chicken and shrimp salads, as well as with leftover fish, chicken, and turkey. It is addictive.

1 cup Basic Mayonnaise (page 303) or store-bought

1 cup sour cream

One 2-ounce can anchovies, drained and chopped

1 tablespoon fresh lemon juice

3 tablespoons tarragon vinegar

2 teaspoons chopped fresh tarragon leaves

3 tablespoons chopped fresh chives

½ cup chopped fresh flat-leaf parsley

½ teaspoon kosher salt

Freshly ground black pepper, to taste

Combine all ingredients in a food processor and process until smooth. Chill.

Horseradish Hollandaise sauce

MAKES 1 ⅔ CUPS

THE PROPORTION OF butter to eggs gives this sauce an airy, fluffy texture that is heavenly with simply roasted fish, beef, and chicken. You will have about two tablespoons of horseradish purée left over. Cover tightly, refrigerate, and save to make Horseradish Sauce (page 302).

½ pound (2 sticks) unsalted butter

FOR THE HORSERADISH PURÉE
¼ cup drained prepared horseradish
1 tablespoon white wine vinegar

1 tablespoon heavy cream
2 egg yolks
1 tablespoon water
½ teaspoon kosher salt

Melt the butter in a small saucepan over medium heat. Keep warm.

To make the horseradish purée: Place the horseradish, vinegar, and cream in a blender. Purée until smooth, stopping from time to time to scrape down the sides with a rubber spatula. Scrape into a bowl and reserve.

Place the egg yolks in a slightly larger non-reactive saucepan. Whisk in the water and the salt. Place over medium-low heat. Slowly pour the warm butter into the egg yolks, whisking constantly. After all the butter has been incorporated, continue whisking approximately 3 to 5 more minutes over the heat, until the sauce is light and fluffy and has almost doubled in volume. Remove from heat and continue whisking until the sauce is skin temperature.

Whisk in the reserved horseradish purée. Serve immediately.

Béarnaise sauce

MAKES 2 CUPS

WHILE THIS SAUCE is a classic accompaniment to beef, I like it as well on salmon, tuna, and swordfish.

The proportion of eggs to butter gives this sauce a mayonnaise-like texture that jiggles when moved, like a lightly set custard.

1 pound (4 sticks) unsalted butter

5 tablespoons finely chopped fresh tarragon leaves

3 tablespoons finely chopped fresh flat-leaf parsley

2 tablespoons finely minced shallots

¼ cup tarragon vinegar

3 egg yolks

½ teaspoon kosher salt

Melt the butter in a small saucepan. Keep warm.

Place 4 tablespoons of the tarragon, 2 tablespoons of the parsley, the shallots, and tarragon vinegar in a small non-reactive saucepan. Simmer over medium heat until solids soften and vinegar reduces by half. Strain through a fine sieve. Reserve liquid. Discard solids.

Whisk together the egg yolks and salt in a slightly larger non-reactive saucepan. Whisk in the reduced vinegar and place over medium-low heat. Slowly pour the melted butter into the egg yolk mixture, whisking constantly. When all the butter is incorporated, continue whisking over the heat until the sauce has thickened, about 3 minutes. Remove from heat. Continue whisking until cool to the touch. Stir in the remaining tablespoons of parsley and tarragon. Serve immediately.

Ginger and fermented black bean sauce

MAKES 1½ CUPS

ALTHOUGH THIS SAUCE is served hot over roasted fish, lamb, or pork, it can be allowed to cool and used with leftovers. If you can find Chinese black soy sauce with molasses, use it instead of tamari and omit the sugar.

2½ ounces fresh gingerroot, peeled, trimmed, and cut into ⅛-inch-thick slices (½ cup)

¼ cup sesame oil

¼ cup tamari soy sauce

2 teaspoons sugar, optional

¾ cup water

¼ cup fermented black beans

½ bunch loosely packed fresh coriander leaves with 3 inches of stem (¾ cup)

Place ginger and oil in a blender. Blend until smooth, stopping once to scrape down sides with a rubber spatula. Add soy sauce and sugar, unless the soy with molasses has been found. Blend until smooth. Pour contents of blender into a small saucepan. Pour water into blender and blend. This helps remove all ginger residue. Pour water into saucepan with ginger and soy sauce mixture. Bring to a boil. Reduce heat to a high simmer and cook for 5 minutes. Add beans and coriander. Cook 2 minutes more. Remove from heat.

Tomato-olive sauce

MAKES 2 CUPS

GOOD WITH ROASTED birds or fish, this sauce can also be used to heat up leftovers. I have simmered it with lamb. Olives can be pitted if preferred.

2 tablespoons olive oil

1 tablespoon red wine

About 2 tomatoes (¾ pound, 6 ounces each), cored and chopped into large pieces (2 cups)

¼ cup drained medium green olives

Kosher salt, to taste

Freshly ground black pepper, to taste

In a small non-reactive saucepan, combine the oil, wine, and tomatoes and cook 1 minute over high heat. Add olives and cook 2 more minutes. Season with salt and pepper. Serve warm.

Other sauces, glazes, and marinades

$\mathcal{V}$EGETABLES

and some fruits

I must admit I have never been really clear about the distinction between fruits and vegetables. I have decided to call everything I normally serve with a main course a "vegetable." At the end of this chapter is a small selection of what in my simple-minded way I automatically think of as fruits. There is some small confusion inherent in the reality that some vegetables are combined to make first or main courses and some of the fruits can be seasoned to serve alongside the main course. If the order of vegetables and fruits isn't self-evident, check the Index.

Vegetables may not leap to the mind when thinking of roasting even though stock and soup recipes routinely call for roasted onions and tomatoes. Roasting is, however, one of the best ways of cooking many vegetables to intensify and bring out their flavors. In most instances it is preferable to grilling which, while attractive, does not cook the vegetables thoroughly. The technique requires for flavor and to avoid sticking the use of some fat. It can be olive oil, butter, canola or another vegetable oil, or, in many of the most succulent recipes, the fat from a meat being roasted. Animal fats, butter, and meat drippings will brown the vegetables more intensely.

In this chapter, I try to tell which vegetables are suitable for roasting, techniques for cooking and cutting them, and how they can be served. As with all roasting, the best ingredients give the best results. I believe in buying from local sources in season and buying organic vegetables whenever possible.

Roasted vegetables have many uses. We tend to think of vegetables as accompaniments to other foods. However, roasting is a no-fuss way to thoroughly brown vegetables—see roasted Chopped Onions (page 371)—before adding them to a dish such as a stew, either at the start or the end of the cooking. An assortment of well-cooked vegetables is welcome as a main course, and roasted vegetables, lightly sauced or well combined, make one of the most appealing first courses. They can be simply and attractively presented on a plate, or fancily on some puff pastry; but one of my favorite ways is to make one piece of Roasted Bread (page 367) per person and put a portion of vegetables on top. Sprinkling with some relevant finely chopped herbs, a few small sprigs of an herb like chervil, or topping with a thin slice of Parmesan, roasted pepper, prosciutto, or an anchovy can finish it off splendidly.

Roasted vegetables can also be made into salads, soups, and pasta sauces. Many of those recipes are in this chapter, as well as recipes for using leftover roasted vegetables.

Basic roasting instructions for each vegetable permit you to cook just as much of a vegetable as you want to serve. If one simply adds salt and pepper to most of the vegetables cooked according to these basic instructions, they make good vegetable accompaniments or first courses. By noting the *basic timings* given for each vegetable, you can often roast vegetables—such as potatoes—surrounding the meat or fish you are preparing. Or you may want to roast them in a separate pan on another rack. Check both items from time to time—the reflected heat from the added pan may hasten the browning.

Oddly enough, the vegetables most commonly called roasted—peppers—are seldom roasted at all. They are usually charred over a burner or under the broiler. A little experimentation has proved to me that true roasting is in fact easier and more even. This method is under Peppers; most vegetables in this chapter are listed alphabetically.

Vegetables roasted in their skins, such as tomatoes for stock and potatoes, will have more vitamins and more flavor even though they may have less unctuousness and subtlety than peeled ones. When using storage vegetables in winter, be aware of differences in flavor and tenderness due to age. With the exception of parsnips, which actually gain sweetness if they are left in the ground until after first frost, most of the root vegetables that roast so well will, like turnips, become stronger in flavor, less sweet, and more fibrous as the winter continues.

Aside from vegetables such as tomatoes, the best vegetables for roasting tend to be the root vegetables; the members of the *Allium* family, such as onions, leeks, and shallots; the salad vegetables such as the chicories—radicchio and endive—and fennel. Give this simple method a try and enjoy unexpectedly rich flavors with little work or fussing over a hot pot of sputtering fat.

Vegetables should always be in a single layer in the roasting pan unless otherwise noted. Choose a pan accordingly, or use two pans on two racks, switching them halfway through the roasting time. Do not increase the quantity given for a specific pan size. The vegetables will not brown properly or have as rich a flavor.

As I mentioned, most vegetables need a film of fat: olive or canola oil, butter, or drippings from a roasted meat (such as goose, chicken or duck fat) to brown well. Since you don't want a puddle of fat but a mere sufficiency, the best method is to add vegetables and fat to the pan and roll the pieces of vegetable in the fat with your hands, so as to lightly coat the inside of the pan as well as the vegetables. Throughout this book, this is called *slicking*.

The unexpected hors d'oeuvre platter

UNEXPECTED MIGHT BE what goes onto this last-minute platter, plate, or bowl, but it refers equally to that friend or group of people who show up unannounced. To feed them, some of the long-keeping, ready-in-the-refrigerator recipes in this chapter are key. They save me from that mad dash and scramble for a decent accompaniment with drinks. (Of course, one can even plan on using any combination of these for an upcoming party. We weren't all Girl or Boy Scouts, but that trusty "Be prepared" motto can come in handy.)

Pull out a combination of "keepers," made when time allows, and scoop into attractive dishes. Bread can be bought fresh, labeled, and frozen. Pull out as much as is needed, wrap in microwave-safe paper towel, and zap for two minutes. All of the following will keep for up to two weeks, tightly wrapped, in the refrigerator, except for the cippolines, which keep indefinitely. A nice assortment might be Roasted Cippolines Riviera (page 377), roasted red peppers in Balsamic Marinade (page 293), Roasted Red Pepper Spread (page 384), and Sort-of-Italian Eggplant Caviar (page 348). Add recipes from other chapters, such as the Goose Liver Mousse (page 82).

Vegetable medley platters

A BOON FOR vegetarians, roasted vegetables work equally well for any healthy, responsible eater today. They aren't boring but filled with bursts of flavor and texture. For a vegetable platter, choose two or more, allowing enough for a small serving of each vegetable per person as a first or side course and more items and larger portions for a vegetarian main course. Keep in mind the colors, textures, and flavors of each dish so as to have a pleasing assortment. Almost any of the recipes in this chapter are usable. In spring, consider Roasted Sliced Fennel Bulb (page 352), Roasted, Then Braised Scallions (page 406), Roasted Cherry Tomatoes with Basil (page 419), and Roast New Potatoes with Dill (page 394). In winter, substitute Warm Winter Red Cabbage with Dill (page 328), roasted Whole Parsnips (page 378) or Crispy Creamy Roasted Jerusalems (page 415), and roasted eggplant slices (page 340).

Combining vegetables to roast

IT'S NICE TO know that many of the vegetables listed separately in this chapter can actually be combined in the same pan and roasted all at once to save not only time, but pan cleaning and oven space, with the bonus of interesting flavor combinations. I often rummage through the refrigerator and the vegetable bin and use up what's on hand. Wild Turkey with Roasted Vegetables resulted from one of these forages (page 94). Dry herbs and seasonings can be stirred into the vegetables along with the fat before roasting. It is better to add fresh herbs for only the last ten to fifteen minutes of the roasting time. After roasting, a small amount of vinegar, stock, fruit juice, cream, yogurt, or butter can be added to make a moister assemblage. Prepared seasonings such as Worcestershire sauce or hot red pepper sauce can also be stirred in.

Remember that vegetables shrink as they roast, and it is important to start with more than are needed. If roasting mainly vegetables that require thirty minutes of cooking, add quicker-cooking vegetables such as mushrooms and peppers for the last fifteen minutes; there will be enough space in the pan.

4 cups of vegetables will fill a small pan (12 x 8 x 1½ inches)

8 cups of vegetables will fill a medium pan (14 x 12 x 2 inches)

12 cups of vegetables will fill a large pan (18 x 13 x 2 inches)

A general rule is that no more than a few teaspoons of fat will be needed for a small pan and at most two tablespoons of fat for a large pan.

Match up vegetables whose cooking times are the same. Peel the vegetables except for small new potatoes. Cut the vegetables into relatively even pieces. Turn them halfway through the cooking time.

Here are some vegetables grouped by their cooking times to get started:

30 MINUTES

Beets, small	Parsnips
Cherry tomatoes	Potato wedges
Fennel	Shallots, whole large
Garlic, heads, or cloves, peeled or not	Sweet potato wedges
Leek whites, cut into 1-inch pieces	Turnip wedges
Onions, small, slices, wedges	Zucchini, halves or halves cut into 2-inch lengths

20 MINUTES

Shallots, whole medium	Treviso
Tomatoes	Zucchini, chunks

15 MINUTES

Bell peppers, cut into 1- to 2-inch squares	Jerusalem artichokes
Broccoli	Mushrooms
Italian frying peppers	

*A*RTICHOKES

ARTICHOKES ARE A KIND OF THISTLE. When grown in a mild climate—I have grown them in Vermont, but it is an unnatural act involving burying the plants just before frost under a bushel basket and immuring them in dirt—those that escape and go to seed develop a beautiful purple bristle shaped like an old-fashioned shaving brush. What we eat is the flower of this plant before the thistle top emerges or, in the case of baby artichokes, before it truly forms in the shape of a choke.

The choke, what the French call *foin* ("hay"), is the immature bristle that lies, pale cream color, on top of the heart or base of the artichoke and under the leaves. It can literally choke. If there is any doubt as to its immaturity, it should be scraped out with a knife or a spoon. The leaves, whose rich goodness we skim off with our teeth, are actually the petals.

There are a number of related plants in the artichoke family. In some, leaves are rounded with rather sharp spines at the tip. These are the globe artichokes, and I have not found them suitable for roasting. Others may have a more pointed shape and may be green or flushed with violet. For roasting, these need to be small. There should be no choke or else it should be so small that when the artichoke is halved or quartered lengthwise the little bit at the bottom can be cut out with a spoon or a knife.

BASIC
BABY
ARTICHOKES

1 pound baby artichokes with immature chokes (6 to 7, about 2½ to 3 ounces each); serves 3 to 4 as a side dish

Cut baby artichokes in half lengthwise. Rub with lemon juice. Use smallest pan that will hold artichokes comfortably in a single layer. Pour ¼ cup fresh lemon juice in pan. Place artichoke halves in pan, cut side down. Slick halves with 1 tablespoon fat. Roast on center rack of 500°F oven for 20 minutes. Remove. Add ¾ cup water or stock. Cover tightly with foil. Roast 15 to 20 minutes more.

TOTAL ROASTING TIME: 35 to 40 minutes

Roasted baby artichokes with garlic

TOTAL
ROASTING
TIME:
40 *to* 45
minutes

T RY TO BUY small artichokes that are fairly uniform in size so they will roast evenly. If you have a choice, buy the ones with longer stems; they look prettier arranged on a platter for serving and the stems are good to eat. Use a roasting pan that is flat on the bottom and just large enough to hold the halved vegetables, otherwise the liquid will sink to the center of the pan and the artichokes will not cook evenly. A large pan, 18 x 13 x 2-inches, holds thirty halves, packed in. A medium pan, 14 x 12 x 2-inches, holds twenty-two halves. The garlic cloves cook right along with the artichokes, flavoring them and becoming delightfully creamy. Be sure to add at least one clove garlic per guest. These artichokes are best served as a first course. They combine well with roasted peppers (page 382).

½ cup fresh lemon juice

15 baby artichokes (2½ to 3 ounces each), rinsed well if sandy

2 tablespoons olive oil

2 teaspoons kosher salt

10 to 12 cloves garlic, unpeeled

1½ cups Basic Chicken Stock (page 42) or canned

Freshly ground black pepper, to taste

Place rack in center of oven. Heat oven to 500°F.

Pour the lemon juice into an 18 x 13 x 2-inch roasting pan.

Prepare 1 artichoke at a time so they won't turn black once cut. Pull off the bottom row of leaves and discard. Use a small knife to trim and peel the stalk. Using kitchen scissors, cut the prickly tips off each leaf. Using a large knife, cut artichoke in half lengthwise and immediately put halves, cut side down, in pan with lemon juice. Using a small knife, cut the small choke out of each half and discard. Return artichoke to lemon juice. Continue until all artichokes are prepared. Brush each half with a small amount of the olive oil. Arrange in 6 tightly packed rows in pan. Sprinkle with salt and snuggle garlic between artichokes. Roast 20 minutes. Remove from oven. Add stock and cover tightly with foil. Roast 20 to 25 minutes more. Sprinkle with pepper. Serve warm from the oven, or prepare ahead and serve at room temperature.

*a*SPARAGUS

WHEN THE GREEN ASPARAGUS OF SPRING COME OUT OF THE OVEN, THEY ARE VERY GREEN AND SLIGHTLY CRUNCHY, WITHOUT EVER BEING TIED IN BUNCHES OR SLOPPING AROUND IN WATER. Add a sauce if desired; but I like to eat these as is, out of hand, sprinkled with half a teaspoon kosher salt and the juice of half a lemon. White asparagus are too fibrous for this treatment.

BASIC ASPARAGUS

THIS TIMING IS for pencil-thin or medium asparagus. When multiplying the recipe to use as many asparagus as pan will hold, add oil a little at a time. The asparagus don't need to be drowned. It is better to get an intense flavor from just a film of the very best olive oil. Too much can be overly assertive.

10 ounces pencil asparagus (36, about ⅜ inch wide); serves 4 to 5 as a first course

1 pound medium asparagus (16 to 18, about ⅝ inch wide); serves 3 to 4 as a first course

Some friends tease me; but I peel asparagus. You don't have to.

To peel: Place on the work surface and run a vegetable peeler down all sides of the asparagus from just under the tip to the end.

To roast: Snap ends off. Use smallest pan that will hold asparagus comfortably. Slick asparagus and pan with 1½ teaspoons olive oil. Roast in the center of a 500°F oven for 6 minutes. Turn and roast for 5 minutes more.

TOTAL ROASTING TIME: 11 minutes

Aubergines: see Eggplants

bEETS

FOR BEET LOVERS—BEETS ARE VEGETABLES THAT ARE USUALLY HATED OR ADORED—ROASTING WILL INCREASE PLEASURE. The flavor of beets varies with age and size more than almost any other vegetable. Very young ones, such as those I pull from my garden in Vermont, can be eaten with their well-scrubbed skins left on after roasting. The tops—greens—of such spring and summer beets should be saved for simple sautéing.

As they get older, beets are less sweet and the skin less pleasant. It will need to be removed after roasting. It's best to peel beets as soon as they are cool enough to touch, otherwise the skin sort of sticks on. After peeling, unless you are happy to have burgundy-toned fingers, wash hands immediately with a mildly abrasive powder. Alternatively, wear gloves while peeling.

The huge beets sold as "roasted" in European markets are really baked like potatoes in their skins at about 325°F until they can be easily pierced with a small sharp knife.

If preparing the beets ahead, put a little vinegar or oil on them to keep them from drying out after cooking. Vinegar will also keep the color vivid, undarkened. One disadvantage of roasting is that beets are less vibrant in color than they would be boiled or steamed.

Roasted beets can be served as a simple vegetable with salt, pepper, perhaps a bit of butter or mild oil, and the optional addition of a little vinegar, dill or dill seed, or even cream or yogurt and celery seed. The warm, peeled beets can be sliced and tossed with Simple Light Vinaigrette (page 297) to serve as a salad or as part of a vegetable-medley first course.

BASIC BEETS

1 pound whole beets (4 to 5, about 3 to 5 ounces each); serves 1 to 2 as a side dish

Trim stems to ½ inch. Rinse well. Use smallest pan that will hold beets comfortably. Slick beets and pan with ¾ teaspoon fat. Roast on center rack of 500°F oven for 30 to 40 minutes, depending on size of beets. When beets are just cool enough to touch, slip off skins if removing.

TOTAL ROASTING TIME: 30 to 40 minutes

Whole roasted beets

TOTAL
ROASTING
TIME:
30 *to* 40
minutes

SMALLER BEETS WORK best for roasting whole. Try to find beets from three to five ounces each, up to three inches in diameter. These roasted beets are a perfect addition to a vegetable medley platter. A small pan will hold about eighteen pieces, which will require very little oil. It doesn't matter if the beets touch in the pan.

1 tablespoon canola oil

18 beets (3 to 5 ounces each, 4 pounds total), cleaned and stems trimmed to ½ inch

OPTIONAL INGREDIENTS

2 tablespoons unsalted butter, salt and pepper, 2 tablespoons chopped dill or

¼ cup heavy or sour cream, salt and pepper, and 2 teaspoons celery seed or

⅓ cup orange juice, 1 teaspoon lemon juice, salt and pepper, and some grated orange zest or

¼ cup red wine vinegar, salt and pepper, and 2 tablespoons tomato paste or

⅓ to ½ cup vinaigrette or

½ cup sour cream or yogurt, salt and pepper, and 2 teaspoons dill seeds

Place rack in center of oven. Heat oven to 500°F. Pour the oil into a 12 x 8 x 1½-inch roasting pan. Using your hands, rub the oil all over the pan and all over each beet. Arrange beets to fit in pan. Roast for 15 minutes. Shake pan vigorously to move beets around. Roast for 15 minutes more. The beets are done when the tip of a sharp knife will slip easily into them but they are still firm. Larger beets, up to 5 ounces, should roast for 10 more minutes.

Remove. Let beets cool enough to touch. Peel. Serve at room temperature as is, or reheat with a combination of the optional ingredients.

Beet-pink salad

MAKES 5 CUPS; SERVES 6 TO 8 AS
A SIDE DISH OR A FIRST COURSE

THIS CRUNCHY PINK salad is good with a whole roasted fish (page 240), served at room temperature or as part of a first course. As a first course, it goes wonderfully with smoked or salted fish such as herring and canned fish like sardines. If made ahead—up to three days—remove from the refrigerator a half hour before serving.

1 recipe Whole Roasted Beets (page 320), beets cut in half lengthwise, then sliced across into ⅛-inch-thick pieces

9 to 10 stalks celery (1 small head), peeled with a vegetable peeler and cut on the diagonal into ⅛-inch-thick pieces

1 small red onion (4 ounces), peeled and cut in half lengthwise, then sliced across into ⅛-inch-thick pieces

¼ cup fresh lemon juice

½ bunch (¾ ounce) fresh dill, stems removed and fronds coarsely chopped (about ¼ cup)

1 teaspoon kosher salt

Freshly ground black pepper, to taste

2 tablespoons canola or other neutral oil

Put beets, celery, and onion in a medium bowl. In a smaller bowl, combine the remaining ingredients. Pour dill mixture over beet combination. Mix with a spoon until all ingredients are well coated and combined. Serve slightly chilled but not cold.

Crunchy beet borscht

MAKES 2½ QUARTS; SERVES 8 TO 10

THIS SIMPLE WINTER soup works on the modular plan of cooking. Make it from scratch or use up leftovers of Beet-Pink Salad by adding one and two thirds cups of stock to each cup of leftover salad and a fifth of each of the other ingredients listed below. Each cup of leftover salad will make enough soup for two people.

continued

1 recipe Beet-Pink Salad (page 321)

2 quarts Basic Chicken Stock (page 42) or canned

¼ cup plain distilled white vinegar

2 tablespoons sugar

1 tablespoon kosher salt, or less if using canned broth

Freshly ground black pepper, to taste

One ½-pint container sour cream, for topping

¼ cup fresh dill, coarsely chopped, for topping

Combine the salad, stock, vinegar, sugar, salt, and pepper in a large saucepan or stock-pot. Heat, stirring occasionally, until hot throughout. Serve in individual bowls. Top each bowlful with 1 to 2 tablespoons of sour cream and a sprinkling of dill.

bROCCOLI

THERE ARE MANY GOOD WAYS TO COOK BROCCOLI: STEAMING, STIR-FRYING, BOILING, FRYING, AND MICROWAVING. Broccoli can be cooked in whole branches or with the stems and florets separated.

Broccoli is rarely roasted; but if the stems are well peeled and the whole branches are sliced lengthwise through the stem and florets into pieces with a width of no more than two to two and a half inches at the floret end, the resulting oil-slicked strips roast brilliantly in fifteen minutes. They turn a toasty brown and are good on their own or as an ingredient in other recipes.

BASIC
BROCCOLI

CONSIDER A MILD vinegar, such as rice wine or balsamic, as an alternative to water or stock as the liquid.

1 pound broccoli (1 head), sliced; serves 2 to 4 as a side dish

Peel broccoli stems well and cut whole head lengthwise into strips, each being no wider at the floret than 2 inches. Use smallest pan that will hold broccoli slices comfortably. Slick slices and pan with 3 to 4 tablespoons fat. Add ¼ cup liquid. Roast on lowest rack of 500°F oven for 15 minutes. If some pieces are thicker than 2 inches, they will take longer.

TOTAL ROASTING TIME: 15 minutes

Roasted broccoli with lemon-garlic bath

SERVES 2 TO 4 AS A FIRST COURSE,
4 AS A SIDE DISH

TOTAL
ROASTING
TIME:
15 *to* 25
minutes

B E SURE TO peel the entire length of the broccoli stem well or there will be woody patches due to uneven cooking. This dish can be made four to eight hours ahead and loosely covered with foil. Serve tepid as a first course or with room-temperature lamb or fish. Reheat or serve immediately as a side dish with Simplest Roasted Chicken (page 23) or a simple roasted fish (pages 245–269).

1 head broccoli (about 1 pound)

2 cloves garlic, smashed and peeled

1 teaspoon kosher salt

Freshly ground black pepper, to taste

¼ cup fresh lemon juice

¼ cup olive oil

Strip the whole length of the stem well with a vegetable peeler; cut lengthwise into 9 to 10 pieces (roughly 2-inch-wide strips at the floret end).

Place rack on lowest level of oven. Heat oven to 500°F.

Arrange pieces of broccoli in a 14 x 12 x 2-inch roasting pan. It is okay if they are close together.

In a mortar with a pestle or on a cutting board with the back of a knife, smash the garlic with the salt and pepper until it is a smooth paste. Put the lemon juice in a small bowl. Whisk in the garlic paste. Continue to whisk until smooth. Whisk in the olive oil until smooth. Pour the mixture evenly over the broccoli. Turn broccoli in mixture until all sides are coated.

Roast for 7 minutes. Turn. Roast for 8 minutes more. Broccoli is done when the stalk is easily pierced with the tip of a sharp knife. Thinner pieces will cook more quickly. Remove them and, for those pieces not yet done, roast 5 to 10 more minutes.

May be served warm from the oven, or made ahead and served at room temperature. The broccoli may also be made ahead and reheated in a 500°F oven for about 7 minutes.

Roasted broccoli spaghettini

SERVES 6 AS A FIRST COURSE,
4 AS A MAIN COURSE

TOTAL
ROASTING
TIME:
15
minutes

THIS QUICK-AND-EASY pasta sauce starts in the roasting pan. Have a chunk of Parmesan—well wrapped—in the refrigerator, and grate just what is needed. Buying pre-grated cheese in those plastic containers, even at the fanciest food shop, is not worth the time, effort, or money. At least, avoid commercial cardboard containers.

1 recipe Roasted Broccoli with Lemon-Garlic Bath (page 323)

1 pound spaghettini

½ cup freshly grated Parmesan cheese

2 tablespoons olive oil

Kosher salt, to taste

Freshly ground black pepper, to taste

½ teaspoon red pepper flakes, optional

Follow the Roasted Broccoli with Lemon-Garlic Bath recipe as indicated, but cut the broccoli strips into 2-inch-long pieces before roasting.

While broccoli is roasting, bring a pot of salted water to a boil. Cook pasta and drain, reserving 3 to 4 tablespoons of the cooking water in the bottom of the pot. Return pasta to pot. Toss with cheese to melt slightly. Add olive oil and scrape broccoli into pot. Toss pasta and broccoli together over low heat. Add salt and pepper to taste and red pepper flakes, if desired.

CABBAGES

ROASTING CABBAGE BRINGS A WARM, GOLDEN FLAVOR TO A VEGETABLE OFTEN NEGLECTED AS A POSSIBLE SIDE DISH EXCEPT WHEN THINLY SLICED IN COLESLAW. Cabbage can be roasted ahead and then briefly reheated while other dishes roast in the oven, or can be used in other cabbage recipes in this chapter. All start with roasted Basic Green Cabbage or Basic Red Cabbage.

There are many different kinds of cabbage. Ordinary green cabbage, Savoy cabbage, and red cabbage all roast well. Savoy is the kind with crinkly leaves and is especially tender and mildly flavored. I like it very much. The basic preparation is the same as that for green cabbage, and it can be used in any of the recipes that call for roasted green cabbage. Napa cabbage does not roast well. It becomes unpleasantly dry. I would have thought that wedges of cabbage would roast well. They don't; the cooking is too uneven. Braise them instead, or cut the cabbage into ½-inch-thick slices.

There is an odd law of diminishing returns with cabbage. While six cups of raw slices will make three cups roasted according to the basic technique, twelve cups of raw slices does not make six cups cooked. Start with about nineteen cups of red cabbage slices or twenty-two cups of green cabbage slices to make six cups cooked. This is not as overwhelming as it seems because a one-pound head of green cabbage will make six cups of raw slices and a two-pound head of the heavier red cabbage will make over ten cups of raw slices.

Because the basic roasted cabbage reduces further when it is cooked again in the following recipes, each recipe based on one head of cabbage will serve three. If you want to serve six, double the amount of roasted basic cabbage prepared.

All cabbages should be well cored, cut into quarters, and then across into half-inch-wide strips. The larger amounts of strips for doubled recipes will make a thicker layer. That is fine.

BASIC
GREEN
CABBAGE

SIMPLY ROASTED, GREEN or Savoy cabbages are delicious with pork chops, roast pork, or a rich fish such as salmon. The strips can be tossed with caraway seeds. Green or Savoy roasted cabbage works well in Mildly Cardamom Cabbage (page 326), Normandy Cabbage (page 330), Asian-Flavored Roasted Cabbage (page 329), and Hungarian Roasted Cabbage (page 327). Roasted cabbage is delicious served with cod.

This recipe can easily be multiplied. The cooking time will remain the same but you need to start with three and a half heads raw to double the cooked quantity. Very tricky.

Toss with bacon drippings, chicken or goose fat if you have any, or melted butter or olive oil.

One 2-pound head green cabbage, sliced; serves 6 as a side dish
(makes 3 cups cooked)

Quarter, core, and cut the cabbage into ½-inch-wide strips (6 cups). Place cabbage strips, roughly in an even layer, in a large pan. Slick cabbage and pan with 3 tablespoons fat. The fat will not coat each and every piece of cabbage. That is fine. Roast in upper level of 500°F oven for 15 minutes. Toss and turn strips. They will still be very moist, particularly in the center of the pan. Be sure to scoop up center pieces and redistribute them around pan for even cooking. Roast 15 minutes more. Cabbage should be less moist, with about half the pieces beginning to brown nicely at the end of the roasting.

TOTAL ROASTING TIME: 30 minutes

BASIC
RED
CABBAGE

EVEN THE MOST simply roasted red cabbage should have some vinegar (red wine, cider, or malt) tossed in after cooking to keep the color radiant. Unlike green cabbage, when quantities change so do cooking times. If doubling the recipe, increase the cooking time to one hour and toss the cabbage after each fifteen minutes. It makes twice as much cooked cabbage. This basic cabbage recipe is transformed into a festive dish in Warm Winter Red Cabbage with Dill (page 328).

One 2-pound head red cabbage, sliced; serves 8 as a side dish (makes 4 cups cooked)

Quarter, core, and cut the cabbage into ½-inch-wide strips (10 cups). Place cabbage strips, roughly in an even layer, in a large pan. Slick cabbage and pan with 3 tablespoons fat. The fat will not coat each and every piece of cabbage. That is fine. Roast in upper level of 500°F oven for 15 minutes. Toss and turn strips. They will still be very moist, particularly in the center of the pan. Be sure to scoop up center pieces and redistribute them around pan for even cooking. Roast for 15 minutes more. Cabbage should be less moist, with about half the pieces beginning to brown nicely at the end of the cooking. Toss with 2 tablespoons vinegar.

TOTAL ROASTING TIME: 30 minutes

Mildly cardamom cabbage

MAKES 1½ CUPS; SERVES 3 AS A SIDE DISH

TOTAL
ROASTING
TIME:
30
minutes

THE SWEET TASTE of cabbage comes through with these mild Indian seasonings, and they leave my mouth feeling very fresh. Goes with any simply roasted bird or fish. To double, see roasted Basic Green Cabbage (page 325).

1 head green cabbage (2 pounds),
   quartered, cored, and cut across
   into ½-inch-wide strips (6 cups)

3 tablespoons unsalted butter, melted

1 teaspoon kosher salt

¼ cup white wine

3 tablespoons heavy cream

Seeds from 4 cardamom pods

Place rack in upper level of oven. Heat oven to 500°F.

Put the cabbage and butter in a 14 x 12 x 2-inch roasting pan. Toss the pieces until lightly coated. The butter will not coat each piece of cabbage.

Roast for 15 minutes. Remove pan from oven. Use a spatula to toss and turn pieces. They will still be very moist, particularly in the center of the pan. Be sure to scoop up center pieces and redistribute them around pan for even cooking. Roast for 15 minutes more. About half the pieces will be nicely browned. Sprinkle with salt. May be held at this stage for up to 24 hours.

Combine wine, cream, and cardamom in a small bowl. Place the roasting pan with the cabbage over medium heat. Pour in wine mixture. Stirring with a wooden spoon, deglaze the pan, turning the pan from time to time to dissolve all the brown glaze at the bottom of the pan. Cook 5 minutes, until hot.

Hungarian roasted cabbage

MAKES 1½ CUPS; SERVES 3 AS
A SIDE DISH

TOTAL
ROASTING
TIME:
30
minutes

THIS IS PERFECTION with Simplest Roast Chicken (page 23) or a Roasted Rack of Veal (page 212). To increase quantities, see roasted Basic Green Cabbage (page 325).

1 head green cabbage (2 pounds),
   quartered, cored, and cut across
   into ½-inch-wide strips (6 cups)

3 tablespoons unsalted butter, melted

1 teaspoon kosher salt

¼ cup white wine

2 teaspoons mild paprika

2 teaspoons caraway seed

¼ cup sour cream

Place rack in upper level of oven. Heat oven to 500°F.

Put the cabbage and butter in a 14 x 12 x 2-inch roasting pan. Toss the pieces until lightly coated. The butter will not coat each piece of cabbage.

Roast 15 minutes. Remove from oven. Use a spatula to toss and turn pieces well. They will still be very moist, particularly in the center of the pan. Be sure to scoop up center pieces and redistribute them around pan for even cooking. Roast 15 minutes more. About half the pieces will be nicely browned. Sprinkle with salt. May be held at this stage for up to 24 hours.

While cabbage is roasting, combine remaining ingredients in a small bowl. Reserve. Place the roasting pan over medium-low heat. Pour on reserved ingredients. Stir with a wooden spoon and deglaze pan, turning pan from time to time to dissolve all the brown glaze on bottom of the pan. Do not let boil or sour cream will curdle. Cook 5 minutes, until warm throughout.

Warm winter red cabbage with dill

MAKES 4 CUPS; SERVES 8 AS A SIDE DISH

TOTAL
ROASTING
TIME:
30
minutes

THE ACIDS KEEP the cabbage an inviting warm red color. This cries out to be paired up with a Roast Fresh Ham with Onion-Rhubarb Sauce (page 175) or Garlic Roast Pork Loin (page 166). In a second oven, cook this dish for the last 30 minutes a Simple Roast Goose (page 78) cooks.

1 head red cabbage (2 pounds), quartered, cored, and sliced across into ½-inch-wide strips (10 cups)

1 medium red onion (6 ounces), peeled, halved, and thinly sliced across (1½ cups)

3 tablespoons goose fat, melted lard, or unsalted butter

1½ teaspoons kosher salt

2 tablespoons red wine vinegar

¼ cup red wine

2 tablespoons tomato paste

1 teaspoon dill seeds

¼ cup Basic Goose Stock (page 80), Basic Beef Stock (page 224), or Basic Chicken Stock (page 42) or canned

1 tablespoon sugar

4 grinds black pepper

Place rack in upper level of oven. Heat oven to 500°F.

Put the cabbage, onion, and fat in an 18 x 13 x 2-inch roasting pan. Toss the onions and cabbage until lightly coated with the fat.

Roast 15 minutes and remove from oven. Use a spatula to toss and turn the pieces well. The cabbage will still be very moist, particularly in the center of the pan. Be sure to scoop up center pieces and redistribute them around pan for even roasting. Roast 15 minutes more. About half the pieces will be nicely browned. Sprinkle with salt. May be held at this stage for up to 24 hours.

Combine remaining ingredients in a small bowl. Reserve. Place the roasting pan over medium heat. Pour on reserved ingredients. Stir with a wooden spoon and deglaze pan, turning pan from time to time to dissolve all the brown glaze at the bottom of the pan. Cook 5 minutes, until most of liquid has been absorbed.

Asian-flavored roasted cabbage

MAKES 1½ CUPS; SERVES 3
AS A SIDE DISH

TOTAL
ROASTING
TIME:
30
minutes

THE SHRINKING WORLD has been a great boon to those of us who like to vary the flavors in our food. What used to be exotica are now standards in most kitchens. In this recipe the warm flavor of roasted cabbage is reinforced by the warm taste of brown sesame oil and tamari, just as the cabbage's sweetness is emphasized by the mirin. The contrast of the vinegar and the hot pepper sauce balances everything. I have served this to acclaim with simply roasted fish (pages 245–269).

To increase the quantity, see roasted Basic Green Cabbage (page 325).

1 head green cabbage (2 pounds),
   quartered, cored, and cut across
   into ½-inch-wide strips (6 cups)
3 tablespoons canola or other neutral oil
1 teaspoon kosher salt
1 teaspoon sesame oil

¼ cup mirin
2 tablespoons rice wine vinegar
2 teaspoons tamari soy sauce or Japanese
   soy sauce
4 to 6 drops hot red pepper sauce or
   ¼ teaspoon red pepper oil

Place rack in upper level of oven. Heat oven to 500°F.

Put the cabbage and canola oil in a 14 x 12 x 2-inch roasting pan. Using your hands, toss the pieces until lightly coated. The oil will not coat each piece of cabbage.

Roast 15 minutes and remove from oven. Use a spatula to toss and turn pieces well. They will still be very moist, particularly in the center of the pan. Be sure to scoop up center pieces and redistribute them around pan for even cooking. Roast 15 minutes more. About half the pieces will be nicely browned. Sprinkle with salt. May be held at this stage for up to 24 hours.

Meanwhile, combine remaining ingredients in a small bowl. Reserve. Place the roasting pan over medium heat. Pour on reserved ingredients. Stir with a wooden spoon and deglaze pan, turning pan from time to time to dissolve all the brown glaze at the bottom of the pan. Cook 5 minutes, until warm.

Normandy cabbage

MAKES 6 CUPS; SERVES 10 TO 12
AS A SIDE DISH

CREAM AND APPLES are the hall-marks of the cooking of Normandy. Their inclusion in this recipe bulks up the collapsed cabbage. In a substantial meal, say Roast Goose with Turnips (page 79) with the cabbage as a side dish, it will serve ten to twelve people. It is rich.

TOTAL ROASTING TIME: 30 minutes

2 Granny Smith apples (6 to 8 ounces each), peeled, cored, halved, and cut into ¼-inch-thick slices (3½ cups)

½ cup fresh lemon juice

¼ pound (1 stick) unsalted butter

1 large onion (12 ounces), peeled, halved, and cut across into ¼-inch-thick slices (4 cups)

3 pounds green cabbage, quartered, cored, and cut across into ½-inch-wide strips (13 cups)

⅓ cup apple juice or cider

3 tablespoons Calvados or applejack

2 tablespoons drained prepared horseradish

2 tablespoons apple cider vinegar

1 teaspoon kosher salt

¼ cup heavy cream

5 grinds black pepper

Toss apple slices with 6 tablespoons of the lemon juice. Reserve.

Place rack in upper level of oven. Heat oven to 500°F.

Melt butter in an 18 x 13 x 2-inch roasting pan on top of stove. Remove. Add apple slices. Using a spatula, toss gently to keep slices intact, until each is well coated. Add onion, tossing, then cabbage. Toss again. Roast in oven for 15 minutes. Toss and turn pieces. Put pan in oven and roast for 15 minutes more.

Meanwhile, combine apple juice or cider, Calvados, horseradish, vinegar, salt, and cream in a small bowl. Reserve. Place the roasting pan over medium heat. Pour on reserved ingredients. Stir with a wooden spoon and deglaze pan, turning pan from time to time to dissolve all the brown glaze on bottom of pan. Cook 5 minutes, until liquid has reduced by half. Remove from heat. Add remaining 2 tablespoons lemon juice. Sprinkle with pepper. Stir to coat well.

CARROTS

CARROTS ARE SO COMMON IN THE KITCHEN, SO USEFUL, THAT WE TEND TO THINK OF THEM AS A SINGLE FLAVOR. In a more thoughtful mode, we can see that carrots come in many colors and degrees of sweetness, fibrousness, percentage of core—the usually lighter part down the middle—and age, thickness, and bitterness of skin. They range from the hideous, bitter giants known as chefs' specials, which are useful mainly because there is less peeling and preparation involved, to tender and sweet baby carrots with pale greens still attached, which often need no peeling, only scrubbing.

Remove the tops as soon as the carrots are home, which keeps the carrots moister. It is better to buy carrots with attached tops as the freshness of the tops will be a good indication of the freshness of the carrots. Usually, the greens are thrown out. Only the youngest greens are useful as a vegetable or in soups and even they require two blanchings in boiling salted water before they can be used for cooking. Carrots that are hairy are not fresh. Don't buy them.

We are used to seeing carrots that are, no matter what their size, orange and pointy. Carrots were originally white and were bred to be orange to make them more appealing. The added color also increased their vitamin A content—that beta carotene we hear so much about. In various parts of the world, carrots may range from almost purple through red to orange. There are ball-shaped carrots like the Planet, short conical carrots like the Chantenay, and carrots that are almost straight like the Nantes. Most of the differences in shape have to do with gardening conditions. However, it is a shame the Nantes types of carrot are not grown more in America. Since they are straight and smooth, they are easier to cut into even pieces without waste, and they have less core.

Roasting carrots is only one of many good cooking methods. The advantages are the added sweetness from browning—caramelizing—the outsides and the added intensity of flavor as some water is eliminated from the carrots instead of more being added. This is not a technique for bitter carrots.

BASIC
CARROTS

CARROTS ARE EXCELLENT simply roasted, with butter as the fat or olive or canola oil. Butter browns them more darkly. Liquids to use with carrots can range from orange, lemon, or apple juice to stocks or even water. Do not use milk or cream as it will burn in this small quantity. Do not put pepper on the carrots at the beginning of the roasting as it will turn acrid with the prolonged cooking time. Do add some salt. Other seasonings that may be added—but not all together—are a pinch of cayenne or somewhat more ground cumin, coriander seeds, or celery seeds.

WHOLE CARROTS

1 pound whole carrots (6 to 7, about 2½ ounces each); serves 3 to 4 as a side dish

Wash, trim, and peel whole carrots. Use smallest pan that will hold carrots comfortably in a single layer. Slick carrots and pan with 1 tablespoon fat. Roast on second level from the bottom of a 500°F oven for 10 minutes. Reduce oven heat to 325°F. Add ¼ cup liquid. Roast 20 minutes. Turn. Roast for 20 minutes more.

TOTAL ROASTING TIME: 50 minutes

SLICED CARROTS

1 pound carrots cut in ½-inch-thick slices; serves 4 to 5 as a side dish
  (makes 3 cups cooked)

Wash, trim, and peel carrots. Cut across into ½-inch-thick slices. Place carrot slices in smallest pan that will hold them comfortably in a single layer. Slick carrots and pan with 1 tablespoon fat. Roast on second level from the bottom of a 500°F oven for 15 minutes. Turn. Add ¼ cup liquid. Roast for 10 minutes more.

TOTAL ROASTING TIME: 25 minutes

NOTE: See Roasted Vegetable Combination (page 379) and Balsamic Vegetable Trio (page 380) for using carrots in other dishes.

Carrots pot roast style

MAKES 2½ CUPS; SERVES 4 AS A SIDE DISH

TOTAL
ROASTING
TIME:
50 *to* 60
minutes

THERE ARE SOME vegetables that reward one with special flavors and melting textures when cooked for a prolonged time. Carrots are one. I find that I always eat more than my share of the carrots from the pot roast. Here is a way of making these delicious carrots on their own to serve with less fatty meats. Note that only the first step is truly roasting; the rest—still in the oven —is braising.

Even more so than is the case with all other roasting recipes, it is important to use the right pan for this one. The pieces of carrots must cover the entire bottom of the pan.

If they don't, there can be a lot of smoke. The recipe can always be increased to make the number of carrot pieces that will fill the pan. See how that relates to the amount of carrots in the recipe and adjust the other ingredients proportionately. The roasting time will not change.

I would always make more rather than less as people like these a lot. Leftovers are good to have cold as a first course or vegetarian lunch on another day. I prefer to spend a little more time on this dish and use plum tomatoes that I have roasted myself. Canned can easily be substituted.

FOR ROASTING FRESH PLUM
TOMATOES

4 fresh plum tomatoes

½ tablespoon olive oil

½ teaspoon kosher salt or
   1 cup drained canned tomatoes, if not
   roasting fresh ones

6 to 7 medium carrots (1 pound),
   trimmed, peeled, and cut across into
   3- or 4-inch pieces (3½ cups)

1 tablespoon olive oil

6 cloves garlic, smashed and peeled

½ bunch fresh mint (½ ounce), chopped
   (¼ cup)

3 slices lemon, seeds removed, plus
   reserved juice from rest of lemon
   (about 1 tablespoon)

¼ teaspoon ground cumin

½ teaspoon anise seed

1 tablespoon sugar

1 teaspoon kosher salt

Freshly ground black pepper, to taste

If roasting fresh tomatoes (and not using canned): Place 1 rack in center of oven for tomatoes and another rack on next level down for carrots. Heat oven to 500°F.

Place tomatoes in smallest roasting pan that will hold them comfortably. Drizzle with oil. Rub each until lightly coated. Sprinkle with salt.

Place carrots in a 12 x 8 x 1½-inch roasting pan. Drizzle with the oil. Rub carrots and pan with oil.

Roast both tomatoes and carrots 10 minutes. Shake the pan with the tomatoes to move them around, and use a spatula to turn the carrots. Roast for 10 minutes more.

Remove pans from oven and turn heat down to 325°F. Add all other ingredients except the reserved lemon juice, and the black pepper, and the canned tomatoes, if using, to the carrots. Slip skins off of roasted tomatoes.

Whichever tomatoes are being used, coarsely chop them and dump all tomatoes and pan juices—not juices from the can—over and around carrots. Mix well. Cover tightly with aluminum foil. Roast 15 minutes. Turn carrots and stir mixture. Roast for 15 minutes more. Carrots should be very soft at this stage. If they are not, roast for 5 to 10 more minutes. Remove. Add lemon juice, black pepper, and more salt to taste. May be served hot or at room temperature.

Bright carrot slices

MAKES 4 CUPS; SERVES 6 TO 8
AS A SIDE DISH

TOTAL
ROASTING
TIME:
25
minutes

Fresh gingerroot and lemon juice give a light, bright taste to the roasted carrots. Not all the carrot slices will turn a dark color, but a good number will be lightly browned.

2 tablespoons unsalted butter, melted

12 to 13 medium carrots (2 pounds), trimmed, peeled, and cut across into ½-inch slices (6 cups)

FOR THE GLAZE

¼ cup fresh orange juice

2 tablespoons fresh lemon juice

2 tablespoons sugar

1 teaspoon freshly grated gingerroot

½ teaspoon kosher salt

⅛ teaspoon ground cumin

Place rack on second level from the bottom of oven. Heat oven to 500°F.

Put melted butter and carrot slices in a 14 x 12 x 2-inch roasting pan. Toss until slices are lightly coated. Arrange slices in pan so that they touch as little as possible. Roast 15 minutes.

Meanwhile, in a small bowl, combine ingredients for the glaze. Reserve.

Remove pan from oven. Pour glaze mixture over carrots. Using a spatula, turn slices over in the liquid. Roast 10 more minutes. Carrots should be easy to pierce with the tip of a sharp knife but still firm.

Chicory: see Endives

Cippolines: see Onions

Courgettes: see Zucchini

Cucumbers

The oddest thing I have chosen to roast is cucumbers—odd not in themselves, but odd to think of roasting. More oddly still, they roast well. For everyday eating raw, I prefer Kirbys—the sort of cucumbers, when they are in their very short season, from which pickles are usually made. Kirbys are bumpy, crunchy, and have no shine. The ordinary cucumbers that litter our markets are shiny and way too large and have overgrown seeds that need to be removed before cooking. Additionally, their shine comes from wax. Those cucumbers need to be peeled before eating.

The best cucumber for roasting is the variously named hothouse, English, and tea cucumber. Long, narrow and straight, it is usually unwaxed but may come shrink-wrapped in a glove of plastic. Use a knife to peel off the plastic. This sort of cucumber should have no true seeds but rather a sort of honeycomb texture in the center, where the seeds would have been tucked in a normal cucumber.

BASIC
CUCUMBERS

1 pound (1 large) hothouse or English cucumber, peeled, quartered, and cut into 1¾-inch lengths; serves 2 as a side dish

Peel, trim, and quarter cucumber. Cut into 1¾-inch lengths (under 2 cups). Place cucumber pieces in smallest pan that will hold them comfortably in a single layer. Slick cucumbers and pan with 1 teaspoon fat. Roast in lowest level of 500°F oven for 5 minutes. Turn. Add ½ teaspoon kosher salt. Roast for 20 minutes more. At end of roasting, stir in ⅓ cup stock, sour cream, or yogurt. Add 2 teaspoons chopped fresh dill or fresh mint (optional).

TOTAL ROASTING TIME: 25 minutes

Gingered cucumbers

MAKES 9 CUPS; SERVES 6 TO 8
AS A SIDE DISH

TOTAL
ROASTING
TIME:
25
minutes

I HAVE ALWAYS loved cucumbers as a poached vegetable and in sorbet as well as in their more normal habitats of salads and cold soups. I find them particularly appealing with fish. Just as I was beginning to think about fish recipes for this book, a dinner party came along, and in a fit of folly, I decided to try cucumbers as a vegetable to cook at the same time as the fish.

It worked so well that I also decided to try it with chicken and lamb. It is equally good. Either use meat juices from a roast to moisten the cucumbers or substitute white wine.

**TO ROAST WITH ROASTED
COHO SALMON** (page 247)

3 teaspoons unsalted butter

5 large hothouse cucumbers (5 pounds), trimmed, peeled, quartered lengthwise, and cut into 1¾-inch lengths (approximately 9½ cups)

3¼ ounces fresh gingerroot, peeled, trimmed, and roughly cut into ¼- to ½-inch dice (about ⅓ cup)

7 cloves garlic, smashed, peeled, and coarsely sliced (3 tablespoons)

4 teaspoons ground cumin

2 teaspoons kosher salt

**IF NOT ROASTED WITH
ROASTED COHO SALMON**

Above ingredients *and*

One 8-ounce container nonfat yogurt (¾ cup)

¼ cup white wine or deglazing juices of your choice

To make with salmon: Place a rack for cucumbers on lowest level of oven. Place another rack for fish in center level of oven. Heat oven to 500°F.

Butter a 14 x 12 x 2-inch roasting pan. Combine the cucumbers, ginger, and garlic in a single layer in the pan. Place pan on lowest rack. Roast for 20 minutes while roasting fish.

After removing the fish from the oven, stir cumin and salt into the cucumbers. While deglazing the fish pan, return cucumbers to oven about 5 more minutes. Stir in yogurt sauce from fish.

To roast cucumbers without salmon: Place a rack in bottom of oven. Heat oven to 500°F. Butter a 14 x 12 x 2-inch roasting pan. Combine cucumbers, ginger, and garlic in a single layer in the pan. Roast for 20 minutes. Remove from oven, stir in salt and cumin, and return cucumbers to oven for an additional 5 minutes of roasting. Stir in the yogurt and white wine.

*E*GGPLANTS

EGGPLANT IS A FAVORITE VEGETABLE—REALLY A FRUIT—IN MEDITERRANEAN CUISINES AND ALMOST EVERY ASIAN CUISINE. It is a boon to vegetarians since it has a deep taste and rich flesh that various authors have called meaty.

There are as many methods and recipes for cooking eggplant as there are varieties. Roasting has certain advantages. It minimizes the amount of oil used in the cooking. Unlike grilling, it ensures a cooked vegetable by the time the surface is done. The underdone eggplant one often gets from the grill in even the fanciest restaurants is mildly nauseating. Eggplant needs to be fully cooked. Roasting eggplant tends to evaporate excess juices, which can be bitter.

The most commonly thought of "roasted eggplant" is not truly roasted at all; rather, it is baked in its skin, and only the pulp is used. I have included the basic timing on page 340 and a sample recipe using the pulp, Sort-of-Italian Eggplant Caviar (page 348).

There is one rather unusual and virtually oil-less technique for cooking eggplant slices (page 340) that turns them a light golden brown and slightly puffy. I like it so well that I have shown off the results in Roasted Vegetable Towers (page 346), a spiffy first course easy enough to do for the family, fancy enough for any dinner party. This method is an ideal way to cook eggplant slices for dishes such as vegetable lasagne, eggplant Parmigiana, or vegetarian sandwiches.

Other than this, large eggplants do not really roast well as the flesh turns unpleasantly custardy. Roast medium eggplants weighing eight ounces or less. Halve them lengthwise or roast small ones weighing three ounces or less. whole if desired.

I thought I knew a decent amount about eggplant, having eaten it in America; Italy (melanzana and many related regional names); France (aubergine from the Arabic al-badinjân); Spain (berenjena); Turkey; Greece; Japan; in Thai, Vietnamese, and Chinese (according to Barbara Tropp, my authority on Mandarin, ch'ieh tsu) restaurants; and even in England, where culinary experts now call it aubergine, but where it was eggplant until fairly recent times.

It wasn't until I lost myself for a day in my treasured hoard of reference books and gardening catalogs while trying to sort out the many shapes, sizes, colors, and names of eggplants, that I learned all of the above names. When I finally got to the out-of-print but brilliantly written, helpful, and chock-full of information *Vegetables in South-East Asia*, by the ardent gardener and botanist G.A.C. Herklots, I finally figured out the sonic boom that tied all the names together. I learned about varieties

I will probably never see, and got a better handle on the history of this extraordinary food.

Eggplants grow wild in Southeast Asia, including India, and have done so since time immemorial. At some point they underwent selective cultivation. They don't crop up in Chinese literature until the fifth century, or in Europe, until sometime between the thirteenth and sixteenth centuries. It seems that one of the many Indian names for eggplant is *bengen*. From there it is easy to see how the name followed the customary trade route to the Arab-speaking world and onward, being modified according to the pronunciation of each language, just as the fruit itself was modified by the climates, growing seasons, and tastes of each culinary tradition.

I undertook the search not for the pure joy of learning but to sort out the confusion brought on by the market-to-market variation of names for the relatively newly arrived Japanese and other far more exotic—to me—eggplants. In sharing my findings, I have decided to organize the eggplants by size rather than color or Latin name because size makes the greatest difference in roasting eggplant. They are all *Solanum*. Most are *Solanum melongem*, but there are many other subvarieties as well.

The better new varieties and most of the Asian, Near Eastern, and European varieties are almost without bitterness and, unless overgrown, have small seeds. All eggplants should be firm, glossy, and without blemishes when bought or picked. The calyx, or cap, at the stem end should be firmly attached and not curling back. The calyx is not edible. It can be removed with the least loss of eggplant by prying it up with your fingers and cutting it off just where it meets the eggplant. Sometimes, when I halve smaller eggplants for roasting, I cut right through the calyx and leave it attached for prettier presentation and greater retention of any marinating liquid.

Large glossy purple eggplants, the kind generally available in America, can weigh up to five pounds. Above one and a half pounds, they are not really any good, except baked for their pulp or sliced. For other roasting, use those eight ounces each or smaller. In 1946, Vilmorin, the great French seed house, issued a dictionary and called the very large purple ones "l'aubergine monstreuse de New York." The monster name persists in many gardening catalogs. There are many other large eggplants in addition to the large purple ones. Some of the best are agora, or larga, which is a creamy white blushed with reddish-pink splotches, and the violetta di Firenze, which can be dark oxblood in color and is notable for its odd lobed shape, like Cinderella's carriage pumpkin. These lobes give slices a seductive, scalloped shape.

My favorite eggplants are medium to small—but not tiny—weighing at most eight ounces, but usually only three to four. Many eggplants are long and slender, such as

Chinese eggplants, which go from a narrow stem end to become slightly wider and rounded at the other end, curving on the way. The ones in Chinese paintings tend to start out white and flush to lavender at the round end. One such is Asian Bride, which fruits in small clusters of two or three. Barbara Tropp has had the experience of getting all white ones. The kind most available in Chinese markets are a bright lavender, which unfortunately—like all colors of eggplant—darkens to almost beige in cooking.

The Chinese eggplants are very similar to the Turkish, which can be pale or purple, the Neapolitan violetta lunga, and the French violette longue. The French violet is more purple than the Italian, and I have no idea what it means. All can be used in recipes calling for Chinese eggplant.

The French have cultivated a delicious, thin-skinned, purple eggplant that is absolutely straight, like a zucchini. A recent development is a dark pink cultivar, which I haven't seen. There are many offspring. All will be called "de Barbentane" (barbentane-style). They are six to eight inches long and about two inches in diameter. They are very good for sautéing or using in stews with their skins on. They can be used in recipes calling for Chinese eggplant, although they may sometimes be slightly heavier and require a little longer cooking.

In this country, we have recently begun to grow, under the name "fingerlings," an Asian variety that is purple and straight like the de Barbentane, but smaller: three to seven inches long and three quarters to one and a quarter inches in diameter. They grow in clusters. I have had great luck with them in Vermont as they have a short growing season. I prefer them at the four-inch length.

The Japanese use Chinese eggplants; but the true Japanese eggplant is small, shaped like an asymmetrical pear, purple, weighs three to four ounces, and is four inches long. Very similar is the baby, which is about three inches long and weighs about three ounces. The smaller Japanese eggplants and the babies can be used interchangeably. The larger Japanese eggplants can be used like the Chinese.

The baby should not be confused with the Italian bambino, which is very small—one to one and a half inches long—like our dwarf eggplant. Bambinos are usually used for pickling, like the truly tiny "pea" eggplants of Southeast Asia, which are very bitter.

Any of the shapes and sizes of these many eggplants can be white; but it is small white ovoid ones looking like chicken fruit that gave us the name eggplant. There are many other colors. I have cooked orange eggplants. Mine were round and about three and a half inches in diameter. I understand there are also egg-shaped orange ones, but I have not run off to search for them because I found the ones I did cook to have tough skins and big seeds: not good. I have read of light green eggplants with yellow markings called "Madras" in a European catalogue; but little other information was given. I will try planting them and see how they are. Future experimentation seems endlessly possible.

EVEN WHEN ROASTING eggplant, there will be a choice of recipe and technique. When eggplants are small, three to four ounces, they can be roasted whole or cut in half lengthwise. Larger eggplants, from four to eight ounces, should be cut in half lengthwise and roasted twenty-five to thirty minutes. Eggplants over eight ounces do not roast well when cut in half as their flesh develops a custardy texture. They need to be cut across into half-inch-thick slices and roasted for thirty minutes, with the slices turned over every ten minutes for even browning. Large eggplants may also be roasted whole when the puréed flesh is desired for dips and soups.

WHOLE LARGE EGGPLANT

1 large whole eggplant (1 to 1½ pounds); makes about 1½ cups cooked shredded flesh

Put eggplant, usually no more than 2 at a time, on an ungreased baking sheet. Bake on center rack of 400°F oven for approximately 1½ hours, or until the eggplant bursts and its center becomes very tender. As it becomes fully cooked, it will deflate like a pricked balloon and the skin will char slightly. This is ugly but correct.

Remove the pan of cooked eggplant from the oven and immediately, using 2 forks, tear the eggplant open. Scrape out the pulp onto the hot baking sheet. Let it sizzle and brown slightly. This will help some of the juices to evaporate. Discard the dry skin. Remove the pulp to a bowl and continue to shred the pulp finely with the forks. The pulp can be puréed in a food processor or blender, but the seeds will get crushed and the mixture may become bitter.

TOTAL ROASTING TIME: about 1 hour 30 minutes

NOTE: Use in Hidden Depths Eggplant with Pasta (page 343), Creamy Eggplant Soup (page 349), and Sort-of-Italian Eggplant Caviar (page 348).

LARGE EGGPLANT SLICES

1 to 1½ pounds (1 eggplant), sliced; serves 3 to 4 as a side dish

Trim ends from eggplant. Cut across to make 15 slices ½ inch thick. Place slices in smallest pan that will hold them comfortably. Slick slices and pan with ⅓ cup fat.

Roast in center of 500°F oven for 10 minutes. Turn. Roast 10 minutes more.

TOTAL ROASTING TIME: 20 minutes

MEDIUM EGGPLANT HALVES

It is a nice idea to add a bit of flavor to whatever fat you are using. Crushed garlic or any mixture of fresh or dried herbs would be a good addition. Citrus juice, pomegranate juice, white wine, vinegar, Sherry, or vermouth are delicious as the liquid.

2 pounds eggplant (4, about 8 ounces each), halved lengthwise; serves 8 as a side dish, 4 as a first course

Cut each eggplant in half lengthwise, calyx removed or not, to make a total of 8 pieces. Place halves cut side down in smallest pan that will hold them comfortably. Slick halves and pan with ¼ cup fat adding optional seasonings if desired. Add 2 tablespoons liquid. Roast in center of 500°F oven for 25 minutes.

TOTAL ROASTING TIME: 25 minutes

SMALL EGGPLANT HALVES (baby purple, fingerling, Japanese, or Chinese eggplants)

2 pounds small eggplants (8, about 4 ounces each), halved lengthwise; serves 8 as a side dish, 4 to 5 as a first course

Cut each eggplant in half lengthwise to make a total of 16 pieces. Place halves cut side down in smallest pan that will hold them comfortably. Slick halves and pan with ¼ cup fat. Add 2 tablespoons stock, white wine, vinegar, Sherry, or vermouth. Roast in center of 500°F oven for 10 minutes. Turn halves over. Roast 15 minutes more.

TOTAL ROASTING TIME: 25 minutes

WHOLE SMALL EGGPLANTS (baby or small Japanese eggplants)

1½ pounds small eggplants (8, about 3 ounces each); serves 4 to 8 as a side dish

Place whole eggplants in smallest pan that will hold them comfortably. Slick eggplants and pan with 1 tablespoon fat. Roast in center of 500°F oven for 15 minutes. Shake pan to turn eggplant. Roast for 10 minutes more.

TOTAL ROASTING TIME: 25 minutes

Roasted eggplant with green herb spread

MAKES 8 HALVES; SERVES 4 AS
A FIRST COURSE, 8 AS A SIDE DISH

TOTAL
ROASTING
TIME:
20 *to* 25
minutes

THIS RECIPE USES the large dark purple eggplant found in most stores today. For best results, use eggplants weighing no more than eight ounces. Larger eggplants have too many seeds, and the flesh takes on an unpleasant custardy texture.

The herbal mixture topping the eggplant halves is so rich and thick it almost looks like a green mayonnaise. The eggplant can be marinated up to eight hours before cooking.

To make more—leftovers are good at room temperature the next day—cook seven to eight eggplants of the eight-ounce size (fourteen to sixteen halves) in an 18 x 13 x 2-inch roasting pan with double the marinade. The timing is the same. Leftovers can also go into Hidden Depths Eggplant with Pasta (page 343).

4 to 5 cloves garlic, smashed, peeled, and chopped into medium pieces

1 tablespoon fresh lemon juice

5 tablespoons olive oil

½ bunch (½ ounce) fresh thyme, leaves picked off stems

½ bunch (¼ ounce) fresh oregano, leaves picked off stems

1 teaspoon kosher salt

Freshly ground black pepper, to taste

4 small eggplants (up to 8 ounces each), stem end trimmed but calyx left on

In the blender, put the garlic, lemon juice, and 2 tablespoons of the oil. Blend until smooth, stopping to scrape down the sides once or twice with a rubber spatula. Add another 2 tablespoons of oil, the thyme, oregano, salt, and pepper. Blend until smooth, scraping once or twice. Reserve.

Cut eggplants in half lengthwise. Using a small kitchen knife, deeply score the flesh in a diamond pattern. It doesn't matter if the knife pokes through the skin on the bottom; deep cutting is important so that the marinade can be rubbed in. Plop some of the marinade spread onto each half. Vigorously rub and poke the spread all the way down into each slit and slather the rest on top.

Pour the last tablespoon of oil into a 12 x 8 x 1½-inch roasting pan. Use already oily hands to rub oil all over the bottom and sides of the pan. Arrange eggplant halves in pan cut side up. Let marinate at room temperature for at least half an hour.

About 20 minutes before cooking the eggplant, place rack in center of oven. Heat oven to 500°F. Roast eggplant 20 minutes. It should be well browned on top. Do not turn over. If not brown enough, roast 5 minutes more. Serve warm or at room temperature.

Hidden depths eggplant with pasta

MAKES 4 CUPS; SERVES 4 TO 6 AS
A FIRST COURSE, 2 OR MORE
AS A MAIN COURSE

THIS IS A complex-tasting—not mak-ing—pasta dish. The caper and anchovy tastes give a surprising depth of flavor and enough salt so that the dish needs no more. I originally made it because I had leftover Roasted Eggplant with Green Herb Spread.

I soon found myself roasting a whole large eggplants (340) just to make this dish, using a one-pound eggplant and throwing in a handful of garlic cloves coated with olive oil to roast after an hour of the eggplant's roasting time. Use these in this recipe instead of sautéing garlic as indicated in what follows. The recipe can be doubled and made ahead.

8 cloves garlic, smashed, peeled, and finely chopped (about 2 tablespoons), or roasted whole with the eggplant

¼ cup olive oil

1 recipe Roasted Eggplant with Green Herb Spread (page 342) or Basic Eggplants: Whole Large Eggplant (page 340), cut into 1-inch pieces

½ cup rinsed and drained capers

3 tablespoons anchovy paste

½ cup red wine

¼ cup red wine vinegar

Freshly ground black pepper, to taste

1 pound rigatoni or bucatini

½ cup toasted pine nuts, optional

Put garlic, if uncooked, in a medium 1½-quart saucepan with the oil and cook over low-ish heat until softened, or use roasted garlic. Add eggplant and capers. Stir. Add remain-ing ingredients except the pasta and pine nuts. Cook until warm throughout. If using right away, boil salted water and cook pasta. Drain, reserving a few tablespoons of the water. Return pasta to warm pot with reserved water. Add heated sauce. Toss. Serve warm, topped with pine nuts, if using.

Tex-Mex roasted baby eggplant

MAKES 12 TO 16 HALVES; SERVES 8 AS A
FIRST COURSE OR A SIDE DISH

TOTAL ROASTING TIME: 20 *to* 30 minutes

THESE ARE SPECTACULARLY good. The only problem is they must be started the day before needed. If that's inconvenient, make them two or three days ahead.

Good hot, good cold, good as a first course, good as an hors d'oeuvre, good as a side dish—no problem. If you wish to make more eggplant halves, see page 341.

6 to 8 baby eggplants (2 pounds), or small Japanese eggplants, or long, thin, Chinese, or other similarly shaped eggplants; with stem end trimmed but calyx (leaves at stem end) left on, halved lengthwise

½ cup canola oil

6 cloves garlic, smashed and peeled,

⅓ cup fresh lime juice

⅓ cup loosely packed cilantro, finely chopped

2 jalapeños or 2 Basic Jalapeños (page 383), seeded, deribbed, and finely minced

1½ teaspoons kosher salt

With the skin side down, use a paring knife to score the flesh diagonally, crisscrossing to form a diamond pattern. Cut as deeply as possible without piercing the skin.

Make the marinade by combining the remaining ingredients. Place the eggplant halves in the dish, cut side down. Rub the marinade into and over the eggplant halves. Marinate at least overnight—up to 2 days is fine—in the refrigerator. Before roasting, let the eggplant come to room temperature.

Place rack in center of oven. Heat the oven to 500°F. Place eggplant, cut side down, in a 12 x 8 x 1½-inch roasting pan. Pour marinade over eggplant and move them around slightly to permit some marinade to get under halves. Roast the eggplant 15 minutes. Remove from oven. Turn to skin side down, spooning some of the marinade on top. Roast until soft, for 10 to 15 minutes more.

Let the eggplant cool in the liquid. Remove from the liquid with a slotted spoon and serve at room temperature.

Roasted Chinese eggplant with balsamic marinade

MAKES 10 HALVES;
SERVES 4 TO 6
AS A FIRST COURSE

TOTAL
ROASTING
TIME:
20 *to* 30
minutes

I LIKE TO make this with the slender, lavender, Chinese eggplants; but other slender eggplants such as the French Barbentane, or the Italian violetta lunga, or even the small Japanese make very satisfactory substitutes. The eggplants make an attractive addition to a mixed vegetable hors d'oeuvre, in which case, the ten halves should serve as many people.

Careful deep scoring of the eggplant flesh lets the flavors permeate it in a dramatic way. Score all the way down to the skin without cutting it.

4 cloves garlic, smashed and peeled

2 teaspoons kosher salt

Freshly ground black pepper, to taste

¼ cup balsamic vinegar

¼ cup olive oil

5 Chinese eggplants (about 8 ounces each, 1½ pounds total), stem end trimmed but with calyx left on, cut in half lengthwise, and flesh scored deeply in a diamond pattern

Place rack in lowest level of oven. About 20 minutes before roasting, heat oven to 500°F.

In a mortar with a pestle, or on a cutting board with a knife, smush the garlic with the salt and pepper until it is a smooth paste. Put the vinegar in a small bowl. Whisk in the paste until it is smooth. Whisk in olive oil until smooth. Pour mixture into an 18 x 13 x 2-inch roasting pan. Put the eggplant in the pan. Rub mixture all over, especially into the cut flesh. Arrange each half cut side down in the pan.

Leave eggplant to marinate at room temperature for 4 to 8 hours. Roast until browned, 20 to 30 minutes, depending on the freshness and size of the eggplant. I like them cooked a full 30 minutes to get a maximum of browning and caramel flavor. When stuck with the tip of a sharp knife, the eggplant should be soft throughout—there should be no resistance.

Eggplant may be served warm from the oven or made ahead and served at room temperature. If made ahead, reheat briefly in a 500°F oven about 10 minutes.

Roasted Japanese eggplant with Asian glaze

MAKES 16 HALVES

I'M EXTREMELY FOND of Asian Glaze and use it on any number of foods in addition to vegetables. It seems to have a natural affinity for the small, pear-shaped, glossy black Japanese eggplants; but any eggplants weighing about four ounces each could be used, particularly the Italian babies. If you want to end up with more pieces, put twenty-eight halves (fourteen eggplants) in a medium pan or forty-four or more halves (twenty-two plus eggplants) in a large pan. Multiply the glaze recipe as needed. The large quantities make this a good party dish, but remember the pan must fit the quantity: Too few eggplants in a large pan will burn; too many in a small pan will not brown.

8 Japanese eggplants (about 1½ pounds), stem end trimmed but with calyx left on, cut in half lengthwise, and flesh scored deeply in diamond pattern

2 tablespoons olive oil
1 recipe Asian Glaze (page 33)

Put the eggplant in a 14 x 12 x 2-inch roasting pan. Pour the oil in the pan. Rub the oil all over the pan and over each piece of eggplant. Pour the glaze over the eggplant. Rub the glaze into each piece deep into the cut flesh. Let marinate at room temperature for at least 30 minutes, or up to 3 to 4 hours. Turn occasionally.

About 20 minutes before ready to roast, place rack in center of oven. Heat oven to 500°F. Arrange eggplant cut side down in pan. Roast 10 minutes. Remove from oven and, using a spatula, scrape up eggplant halves and turn them over. Return pan to oven, back to front, and roast for 15 minutes more. Serve warm.

Roasted vegetable towers

SERVES 4 TO 6 AS A FIRST COURSE

TOTAL ROASTING TIME: *see facing page*

THIS HAPPY ASSORTMENT of roasted sliced vegetables can be served simply in one large, overlapping layer on a platter with anchovies, whole or in bits, on top; but I like the drama of this presentation, which can be brought in on a platter or on individual plates. I use my own roasted peppers because they add good vinegar to the dish. Fire-roasted peppers from a store-bought jar can be substituted. Drain and rinse them and then marinate in good vinegar while the vegetables are roasting.

Two cans of anchovies that have been halved will please anchovy lovers.

Although this recipe makes about fifteen towers, I find it's just about right for four to six people for a first course, depending on the size of the eggplant you find. It's surprising how many of these guests will eat. I prefer this dish warm, but it can made ahead and served at room temperature.

⅔ cup olive oil

1 large eggplant (1¼ pounds), cap and blossom ends removed, cut across into ½-inch-thick slices (about 15)

One 2-ounce can flat anchovies or 2 cans, if you really like them

4 zucchini (about 4 ounces each, 1 pound total), trimmed and cut across into ½-inch-thick slices (about 4 cups)

3 small onions (about 4 ounces each, 13 ounces total), peeled, halved, and cut across into ¼-inch-thick slices (about 17 pieces)

Kosher salt, to taste

Freshly ground black pepper, to taste

4 Basic Whole Red Bell Peppers (page 382), seeded, deribbed, and cut into 1½-inch pieces

Place a rack in center of oven and another on lowest level. Heat oven to 500°F. If 2 ovens are available, place 1 rack in the center of each.

Pour ⅓ cup of the oil into the bottom of an 18 x 13 x 2-inch roasting pan. Swirl around so that the bottom is completely covered. Quickly swoosh each slice of eggplant through the oil. Do not soak slices in the oil or blot them. Arrange slices in one layer. Open can of anchovies and drizzle their oil over the eggplant. Reserve anchovies.

Pour the remaining olive oil into another roasting pan of the same size. Swirl as before. Quickly swoosh each slice of zucchini through the oil. Arrange slices in the center of the pan. Repeat with the onion slices, arranging them on either side of the zucchini so zucchini remains in the middle.

Place pan of zucchini and onion on lowest rack. Roast for 15 minutes. Add pan of eggplant to center rack. Roast for 10 minutes more. Turn the eggplant over with a spatula. Roast another 10 minutes. Remove both pans from oven. Carefully turn all slices with a spatula, trying to keep them intact.

Reverse position of pans, putting the one with the onions and zucchini on the center rack and the pan with eggplant on the bottom. Roast another 10 minutes. Remove the eggplant. Roast onions and zucchini 15 minutes more.

To serve, lightly salt and pepper vegetables and build towers: Start with a slice of eggplant. Top with a slice of onion. If it falls apart a bit, not to worry. Follow with 2 to 3 slices of zucchini. Then add a piece of roasted pepper. Sprinkle over this any loose pieces of onion. Finish off with a piece of anchovy. Build towers until all ingredients are used.

TOTAL ROASTING TIME: eggplant, 30 minutes; zucchini and onions, 45 minutes

Sort-of-Italian eggplant caviar

MAKES 3 CUPS

TOTAL
ROASTING
TIME:
1
hour
30
minutes

LARGE EGGPLANTS CAN be "roasted" if only the pulp is wanted. This pulp recipe is spiffy. When a group of friends tasted it, they were strongly reminded of guacamole, for which it would make a good substitute on the numerous occasions when available avocados are less than perfect. I find the flavors more Italian than Mexican. A real advantage of this recipe is that the finished dip is not the customary beige but a brilliant green thanks to all the basil, which also makes the dish fairly peppery. I use four large cloves of garlic, but many will prefer smaller cloves in a smaller amount.

2 large eggplants (1¼ pounds each)
½ cup olive oil
¼ cup fresh lemon juice
1½ cups loosely packed basil leaves

3 to 5 cloves garlic, smashed, peeled, and cut into medium pieces
1 teaspoon kosher salt
½ cup finely chopped (not minced to powder) fresh flat-leaf parsley

Place rack in center of oven. Heat to 400°F. Put eggplants on an ungreased baking sheet and roast for 1½ hours. They will sag and possibly burst, look ugly, and be very tender inside.

While the eggplants are in the oven, combine all remaining ingredients except parsley in a blender, and blend until a smooth green cream with no dark spots.

Remove eggplants from oven. Using 2 forks, immediately tear each eggplant open. Scrape out the pulp onto the hot baking sheet. Let it sizzle and brown. This will help some of the juice to evaporate. If there are still puddles of juice, sponge them up. Discard dry skins.

Put pulp into a large bowl. Continue to pull it apart until finely shredded, almost chopped. Thoroughly mix in basil mixture and parsley. Cover and refrigerate for up to 3 days, or until 20 minutes before serving.

Creamy eggplant soup

MAKES 7 CUPS; SERVES 6

TOTAL
ROASTING
TIME:
1
hour
30
minutes

ROASTED EGGPLANT MAKES a surprisingly creamy soup. I call this "creamy" and not "cream of," even though the soup does have a cup of cream in it. I sometimes cheat and use a half cup of cream and a half cup of milk. The creaminess really comes from the puréed eggplant. The cream is there for color and sweetness. The purée has to be made in a food mill, which removes all the seeds and any strings. Otherwise, it must be pushed through a sieve, which is no fun.

2 large eggplants (1½ pounds each)

4 cups Basic Chicken Stock (page 42)
    or canned, skimmed of all fat

1 cup heavy cream

½ teaspoon ground cumin

Kosher salt, to taste

Freshly ground black pepper, to taste

Place rack in center of oven. Heat to 400°F. Put eggplants on an ungreased baking sheet and roast for 1½ hours. They will sag and possibly burst, look ugly, and be very tender inside. Remove eggplants from oven. Using 2 forks, immediately tear each eggplant open. Scrape out the pulp onto the hot baking sheet. Let it sizzle and brown. This will help some of the juice to evaporate. If there are still puddles of juice, sponge them up. Discard dry skins. There will be 2 ample cups of shreds.

Place food mill with finest disc in place over a non-aluminum pot and force the eggplant through the mill. You will have to stop from time to time to scrape off the bottom of the disc with a rubber spatula. The purée is somewhat viscous. Scrape off the disc or the remainder of the eggplant won't get puréed. Makes scant 2 cups of purée. Add the remaining ingredients and bring just to the boil. Simmer for 5 minutes.

eNDIVES

WHAT AMERICANS CALL ENDIVE IS THE PALE GREEN, SECOND GROWTH OF A CHICORY. We also call it Belgian endive. The Belgians call it witloof and the English, chicory. Here we eat endive raw in salads, but it is also delicious cooked, as is common in Europe as with other chicories, such as the red ones. Treviso, a slender redhead similar to our Belgian endive, can replace it in these recipes, but do not use the round one from Verona that looks like a stunted cabbage.

Of course, there are young and tender chicories that are usually eaten raw, such as the plant Americans—to confuse matters—actually call chicory. The French and English call young, pale yellow-green chicory frisée. It is a popular salad green and is never cooked. However, older chicories of all sorts can be and are cooked.

BASIC WHOLE ENDIVES

IMAGINE USING OLIVE oil as the fat and tarragon vinegar, stock, or orange or lemon juice as the liquid for a fabulous first course. Mix and match from there.

1 pound whole endives (4, about 4 ounces each); serves 2 to 4 as a side dish or first course

Using a small sharp knife, trim around root end of each endive to remove any tough edges and brown spots. Place whole endives in smallest pan that will hold them comfortably. Slick endives and pan with 2 tablespoons fat. Roast on lowest level of 500°F oven for 15 minutes. Turn. Roast another 15 minutes. Turn. Roast 15 minutes more. Remove. Sprinkle endives with 2 tablepoons plus 1 teaspoon liquid. Serve hot or cold.

TOTAL ROASTING TIME: 45 minutes

Mahogany roasted endives

MAKES 12; SERVES 6 TO 12
AS A SIDE DISH

TOTAL
ROASTING
TIME:
30
minutes

"MAHOGANY" REFERS TO the glorious color the pale green heads achieve after roasting, and not, fortunately, to any woody texture. They become meltingly soft. The rich flavor goes well with almost any roasted meat or fish. Change the type of stock according to what the endive is served with. In a pinch, chicken broth out of a can would probably be neutral enough to go with anything. For vegetarians, use a vegetable stock, as this is a great friend to grains such as bulgur or quinoa.

The fat can vary as well. I use goose fat and goose stock to go with Simple Roast Goose (page 78). It is divine.

¼ cup goose fat or other fat

2 tablespoons unsalted butter

12 endives (about 4 ounces each), trimmed

¼ teaspoon kosher salt

Freshly ground black pepper, to taste

⅓ cup stock (depends on what else is being served or is on hand)

Place rack in bottom of oven. Heat oven to 500°F.

Melt fat and butter in a 14 x 12 x 2-inch roasting pan on the stove top over low heat.

Turn off heat. Put endives in the pan and turn each in the melted fat. Arrange endives in 2 rows in the pan, alternating positions so top of one endive is next to bottom of another. Salt and pepper lightly.

Put in oven and roast for 15 minutes. Shake pan, remove from oven, and turn each endive on its side. Roast 15 minutes more. Pour or spoon off the fat. If making ahead, reserve at this point. Pour a little of the stock onto each endive. Leave in the pan until ready to serve. Reheat briefly if needed or desired.

Escarole: see Endives

*f*ENNEL

FENNEL IS TWO DIFFERENT PLANTS. One is a tall—well over my head—frondy herb that looks like giant dill. Its stalks become woody, and it is often dried and used on the fire for grilling fish in the South of France, where it grows wild, as it does along the roadsides in California. Then there is Florence, or bulb, fennel, which is a vegetable that has similar fronds. It is not a true bulb, but instead a swelling of the stem just above ground level. Both plants produce seeds that are used as a seasoning in savory and sweet dishes.

The vegetable roasts most satisfactorily in slices cut lengthwise from top to bottom right through the stem end. Roasted fennel slices (below) can be used on their own as a vegetable or assembled with other vegetables to make a dish. They can be made ahead and kept in the refrigerator for several days. Before cutting and cooking fennel, trim a very thin slice off the bottom as it is likely to be hard. Then, with a vegetable peeler, remove any discolored or coarse-looking spots on the outside of the fennel.

Fennel is particularly nice in fish and chicken dishes. See the Index for ideas.

Roasted sliced fennel bulb

MAKES 1¼ CUPS; SERVES 4 AS A SIDE DISH

THIS IS AN unusual side dish that can be served hot or cold. When serving it as a hot vegetable, consider replacing the olive oil with melted butter and the lemon juice with a quarter cup of rich stock.

TOTAL ROASTING TIME:
30
minutes

1 fennel bulb (1¼ pounds), trimmed, with tops and tough outer leaves removed and fronds reserved, cut lengthwise through the core into ¼-inch-thick slices so that pieces stay together

3 tablespoons olive oil
1 tablespoon fresh lemon juice
Kosher salt, to taste
Freshly ground pepper, to taste

Place rack in lowest position of oven. Heat oven to 500°F.

Put the fennel slices in a 14 x 12 x 2-inch roasting pan. Drizzle 1 tablespoon of the oil over the slices. Gently toss until all slices are evenly coated. Arrange slices in a single layer so that they touch as little as possible.

Roast for 15 minutes. Turn carefully with a spatula, trying to keep the slices intact. Roast for 15 minutes more.

Drizzle with remaining oil, lemon juice, salt, and pepper. Serve hot or allow to cool.

Chop feathery bits of reserved fennel fronds. Sprinkle over slices just before serving.

Capered fennel salad

SERVES 4

TOTAL
ROASTING
TIME:
see page 354

This delicious cold first course contrasts the smoky anise flavor of the fennel with the rich, seemingly oily sweetness of roasted pepper. The peppers can roast at the same time as the fennel, but use preprepared peppers, if available. The juices from the two vegetables marry to make the dressing.

3 large red bell peppers (1½ pounds), ½ recipe Basic Whole Red Bell Peppers (page 382), or 1½ cups fire-roasted peppers from a jar, drained and rinsed

3 tablespoons olive oil

1 fennel bulb (1¼ pounds), trimmed, with tops and tough outer leaves removed and fronds reserved, cut lengthwise through the core into ¼-inch-thick slices so that pieces stay together

½ cup balsamic vinegar

1½ tablespoons drained and rinsed capers

⅛ teaspoon kosher salt

1 tablespoon chopped fennel fronds

Freshly ground black pepper, to taste

Place 1 rack on top level of oven and another rack on lowest level. Heat oven to 500°F.

Rub a 12 x 8 x 1½-inch roasting pan and the peppers with 1 tablespoon of the olive oil. Put the fennel slices in a 14 x 12 x 2-inch roasting pan. Drizzle 1 tablespoon of the oil over the slices. Gently rub slices until evenly coated. Arrange slices to touch as little as possible. Roast peppers on top rack and the fennel slices on the bottom rack for 15 minutes.

Use a spatula to turn peppers and fennel, trying to keep fennel intact. Roast 15 more minutes. Turn peppers again. Remove fennel slices. Roast peppers 15 minutes more. Meanwhile, let fennel cool and drizzle with remaining oil to keep from drying out. Refrigerate fennel if making ahead.

continued

After the peppers have roasted a total of 45 minutes, the skins will be scorched and black, which is exactly how they should be. Using tongs or a spatula, immediately transfer peppers to a brown paper bag or large plastic storage bag. Seal bag. Put bag either in the sink or in a pan. As the peppers sweat, the bottom of the bag will get very damp. If using a brown paper bag, don't try to pick it up, or the bottom will fall right out. Let cool.

Using fingers, peel the charred skin off of each pepper and rinse each pepper with cold running water, if need be. Remove core and seeds as well. Leave pepper pieces as large as possible, but don't worry if they shred some. All the scraps are tasty, too.

Pack peppers into a clean glass container. Fill jar with balsamic vinegar until peppers are covered. Seal tightly. Let marinate in refrigerator 2 to 3 hours. Recipe may be prepared several days ahead up to this point.

Before serving, allow peppers and fennel to come to room temperature. To serve on individual plates, arrange 2 pieces of fennel with the root ends pointing toward each other in the center of the plate. Place 2 large, or several small, pieces of red pepper across from each other in the 2 open spaces. When the 4 plates are prepared, sprinkle the capers evenly over each.

The liquid that remains in the fennel container can be used as a dressing. Add to it 1 tablespoon of marinade from the peppers and the salt. Mix. Pour over each serving. Top with a sprinkling of chopped fennel fronds and a grind of black pepper.

TOTAL ROASTING TIME: peppers, 45 minutes; fennel, 30 minutes

g ARLIC

GARLIC MAY BE MY FAVORITE MEMBER OF THE *ALLIUM* FAMILY, ALTHOUGH ALL OF THEM, IN ALL SIZES, FROM LEEKS TO SHALLOTS TO SCALLIONS TO ONIONS, ARE CONSTANTLY COOKED IN MY KITCHEN. However, one needs to know something about garlic to enjoy it thoroughly.

The most commonly seen garlic in America has a white skin, which is also called the paper, surrounding the entire head. The skin surrounding each clove is also white. When I can get them, I prefer the French kind of garlic, which has reddish skin and somewhat smaller heads with smaller cloves. It is generally sweeter and crisper. There is also a gray-skinned variety, which I have never seen in the market, but it is very good as well. Elephant garlic, as its name suggests, is huge and has huge cloves. While it is certainly easier to peel than smaller heads it is often over the hill, and I really don't like the flavor, so I don't suggest it in this book.

Mostly, I roast individual cloves in their skins and let people suck the goodness out with their teeth. People who like garlic are generally the kind who will enjoy doing this when they find the cloves sprinkled around their roast chicken or even stewed chicken.

Heads often need to be peeled and so do individual cloves for chopping or for use whole in a recipe. It is not laborious.

To remove outer paper and separate cloves: Place the whole head (or heads) on a cutting board on a strong table or on counter. Cover loosely with a dish towel, which will keep cloves from flying around the kitchen. Whack the head sharply with a heavy pot. Lift the towel. The cloves should have broken apart. Discard the root end and any loose paper.

To peel: Replace cloves on board, cover again, and whack again with pot. To peel only a few cloves, hit them one by one with the flat side of a heavy chef's knife, keeping the hand that isn't holding the knife with palm flat and on top of the blade to keep it from wobbling. Hold the handle of the knife so that it extends over the edge of the table or counter, avoiding smashing a hand along with the garlic. Remove the skins from the individual cloves. Cut off the root end of each clove.

In addition to removing the paper and peel, smashing the garlic also makes it sweeter when used raw or only lightly cooked. Smashing kills what is a living plant and prevents it from using its skunklike self-defense maneuver of making a nasty stink when bitten, keeping underground animals from eating it. Long-cooked garlic, such as roasted garlic, gets very sweet in any case, so it is not necessary to smash whole heads or cloves to be cooked in their skins.

Garlic will vary in freshness and size. It is best in the late spring just after it has been dug up. The individual cloves are the starting point for new plants, and sometime during the year, depending on how the head has been stored, the cloves will begin to sprout. Even before you can see the sprout greenly poking out, the sprout— what the French call the *germe*—is busy forming inside the clove. As it develops, using the flesh of the garlic for food, it becomes bitter. It can be removed, or the clove degermed, by either cutting the clove in half lengthwise or prying it open where it has been split by vigorous whacking. The tip of a sharp knife inserted under the sprout will easily remove it.

Since the sprout eats the garlic, as time goes on the garlic will be almost all eaten except for the cellulose cell walls. Even if the sprout is removed, garlic this old is of no use. After removing the sprout from viable cloves, some of the clove is gone.

Make up for this by adding an extra clove of garlic to a recipe. Which brings up the point that all garlic cloves are not created equal. Numbers of cloves in a recipe are given for convenience. If the cloves are huge, use only two thirds of the number called for in the recipe. If they are teeny, double the amount.

BASIC
GARLIC

THE NUMBER OF servings depends on how much your guests like garlic—from a few cloves to one head per person. In general, if doing only a small number of heads, not twenty or so for a party all roasted around a bird or leg of lamb, look for a gratin, soufflé, custard, or other small ovenproof dish in which to roast the garlic. If heads are roasted around a main-course roast, fat may not need to be added; there may be sufficient in the pan. Just make sure there is liquid in the pan so the garlic will not burn.

WHOLE HEADS GARLIC

2 heads garlic; serves 2 to 4 as a side dish

Slice off the top ½ inch of heads across the stem end. Trim root end just enough to clean, leaving cloves attached. Use the smallest ovenproof dish or pan that will hold heads comfortably in a single layer without touching. Slick garlic heads and container with 1 teaspoon fat. Add ¼ cup water or stock. Roast on center rack of 500°F oven for 25 to 30 minutes.

TOTAL ROASTING TIME: 25 to 30 minutes

INDIVIDUAL CLOVES GARLIC

1 head garlic, separated into cloves, unpeeled (½ cup); serves 1 to 2 as a side dish

Use smallest ovenproof container that will hold garlic cloves comfortably. Slick cloves and container with 1 teaspoon fat. Roast on center rack of 500°F oven for 20 to 25 minutes, or until largest cloves are soft to the touch.

TOTAL ROASTING TIME: 20 to 25 minutes

Roasted garlic purée

MAKES ⅓ CUP

TOTAL
ROASTING
TIME:
25 *to* 30
minutes

JUDGE HOW MUCH of this to make for guests. I can happily smush the smoky-tasting, cooked garlic out of an entire head and eat it slathered on slices of hearty country bread or Roasted Bread (page 367). The uses for this purée are endless.

To make extra to have on hand, multiply the recipe and, to store, mix with one tablespoon of olive oil for each recipe. It keeps in a tightly sealed container in the refrigerator for a week. The mellow, smooth flavor is a fine addition to pasta sauces. Mixed with mayonnaise, the purée makes a sauce for roasted vegetables or can be spread in between layers on a potato or rutabaga gratin.

2 heads garlic	Kosher salt, to taste
1 teaspoon olive oil	Freshly ground black pepper, to taste
¼ cup Basic Chicken Stock (page 42) or canned	

Place rack in center of oven. Heat oven to 500°F.

Turn garlic heads on their sides and cut off about ½ inch from the stem end so that the white flesh of almost every clove is revealed. Trim off a minimal amount from the root end just to clean; the cloves must stay attached. Remove any of the outer papery skin that is flaking off.

Put oil and garlic in a small gratin or other ovenproof dish just large enough to hold the whole heads. Using your hands, rub the garlic with oil. Pour in stock.

Roast 25 to 30 minutes, or until largest cloves are soft to the touch. Remove. Allow to stand for about 10 minutes.

When garlic is cool enough to handle, drain off liquid and reserve. Remove garlic to a cutting board. Turn heads on their sides. Hold one head at a time by its root end. With the back of a chef's knife, push softened cloves from their skins, pressing downward and moving the knife from root to stem end. Rotate bulb to push on all sides of the head.

Discard the emptied skin and paper. With a knife or fork mash the soft garlic cloves to a pulp. Salt and pepper to taste. Some of the reserved liquid can be added to make a thinner purée. The extra liquid can be added to vegetable soups.

Jalapeños: see Peppers

Jerusalem Artichokes: see Sunchokes

*L*EEKS

LEEKS USED TO BE THE ASPARAGUS OF THE POOR; NOW THEY ARE THE ASPARAGUS OF THE RICH. Rich or poor, I love them. They are one of the mildest members of the *Allium* family, and I can well understand why the Welsh have taken these attractive vegetables as their national symbol. Even very young, leeks are not ordinarily eaten raw, and only the part of their green leaves nearest to the white are eaten at all unless the leek is very well cooked and pureed into soup or used as a flavoring for stock. It is the white of the leek that is prized.

The growing of leeks starts in trenches, and as they push upward, dirt is continually heaped around them to deprive them of sun and keep them white. They can be kept in the ground until the ground gets so frozen that the leeks are impossible to pull. Once pulled, they must be refrigerated because they do not have paper over them like onions and garlic, which can be stored at room temperature.

To clean and trim leeks: Because they have loose dirt heaped around their leaves as they grow, leeks can be very dirty and difficult to clean. I first cut off the leaves about two inches above the white part. I stuff the greens into a bag and refrigerate them to use another day. (I don't wash them at this point as they may get bruised.) I then turn to the root end, from which I cut all the roots and a thin slice of the leek, being careful to leave enough root end to keep the leaves attached to each other. Now, I give the leeks a quick rinse. While I run very cold water into the sink to fill it, I make a four-inch slit down into the top of the green end and through the leaves. I turn the leek halfway around and make a second cut at a right angle to the first. The tops of the leaves are now in four pieces, yet attached to the remainder of the leek. I make two similar cuts into the white end of the leek, but only about an inch and a half long. I try to make these cuts so that they are not in line with the first cuts.

By now the sink is full, and I soak the leeks for about twenty minutes. I remove the leeks from the water, clean the sink thoroughly to make sure no bits of sand are clinging to it, refill the sink, and soak the leeks again. At this point, I peek into the leeks' interiors to scout for sand. If I see some, I repeat the soaking process. By now the leeks are clean and ready for cooking. They can be stored in the refrigerator for a day if they are very well wrapped. Leeks that are to be sliced either into fine lengthwise strips or across into rounds or half-moons will be easier to soak and clean after cutting.

I like whole leeks meltingly well cooked and the rounds, half-moons, and thin strips crisply cooked, sautéed until done but not mushy, or blanched to the same texture in boiling salted water. Roasting is an efficient way to thoroughly brown whole leeks prior to braising or to turn the small bits crisp and brown.

Weights of leeks: The very largest leeks can be woody, and even one is too much for a single portion. Keep these for soups and stocks. Small ones of four ounces each, medium ones of six ounces each, and large ones up to eight ounces each are all suitable for roasting. All weights are before trimming—as you buy them in the store. To roast baby leeks, which look much like scallions, see Basic Scallions (page 405). Since leeks vary so much in size, they can run anywhere from two to six leeks per pound.

BASIC
LEEKS

REMEMBER, WEIGHTS ARE before trimming, with all their green leaves, just as you buy them. After trimming, about half the weight is lost. Weigh and count when buying or before cleaning to ensure you have enough. Roast only one size at a time. Obviously, the number of leeks in a pound will vary with the weight of each, as will the number of leeks in a serving.

WHOLE LEEKS

2 pounds untrimmed leeks (about 8 small, 6 medium, or 4 large); serves 2 to 4 as a side dish or first course

Thoroughly wash and trim leeks. Use smallest pan that will hold leeks comfortably in a single layer. Slick leeks and pan with 3 tablespoons fat. Roast on center rack of 500°F oven for 15 minutes. Turn. Roast another 7 minutes. Remove from oven. Add 1 cup water or chicken stock. Roast 10 minutes. Turn. Roast for 10 minutes more for maximum browning.

TOTAL ROASTING TIME: 42 minutes

SLICED LEEKS

THESE DELICIOUS, FRIZZLED and crisp leek bits can be sprinkled over just about any dish to add flavor and texture. The Indonesians serve crisped garlic and shallots the same way. This method is a lot easier than deep-fat frying. Watch carefully so they don't burn.

3 medium untrimmed leeks (1¼ pounds), sliced; serves 4 to 6 as a garnish (makes 1 cup cooked)

Trim greens and root ends from leeks. Quarter lengthwise. Cut across into ¼-inch-thick slices (2 cups). Rinse thoroughly. Dry. Use smallest pan that will hold slices comfortably. Slick slices and pan with 2 tablespoons fat. Roast on center rack of 500°F oven for 6 minutes. Turn. Roast for 6 minutes more.

TOTAL ROASTING TIME: 12 minutes

Roasted, then braised leeks

SERVES 6 AS A FIRST COURSE,
10 TO 12 AS A SIDE DISH

TOTAL
ROASTING
TIME:
42 *to* 52
minutes

My SON THINKS that Thanksgiving isn't Thanksgiving without braised leeks. Over the years, I have made them, start to finish, on top of the stove; browned on the stove and then finished in the oven; pale in the oven; and in the microwave. Last year, I roasted them. He approved and so did all the other people down the long table. I certainly approved, since it is much easier on the cook. I didn't have to stand over them as they browned; but I got them to a lovely golden brown color and then was able to braise them in the same pan. The timing is forgiving. Once the broth is poured on, a slightly longer or shorter cooking time will not make a noticeable difference in the final result.

You may want to try roasting and braising as well; but be prepared. There will be a fair amount of smoke during the browning due to all the sugar in the leeks. Turn the fan on and/or open a window. Once the liquid is added, there is no more smoking. You might want to make this in the morning and then follow the reheating instructions at the end of the recipe. Using a pan small enough so that the leeks fill the pan will help reduce the amount of smoke. Any of the leek-flavored stock left in the pan after cooking is a savory head start on a soup, if I can stop from drinking it myself. I prefer to use smaller leeks, since they are usually more tender. Check the browning five minutes early to see if the leeks are brown enough.

6 tablespoons unsalted butter, melted

3 tablespoons olive oil

12 medium leeks (5 pounds), trimmed and washed well

2 cups Basic Chicken Stock (page 42) or canned (see Note), plus up to 1½ cups additional broth

Kosher salt, to taste

Place rack in center of oven. Heat oven to 500°F.

Put butter and oil in a 14 x 12 x 2-inch roasting pan. Swirl around so that bottom is covered. Arrange leeks in the pan so that they are as flat as possible. Roast 15 minutes. Remove pan from oven; use tongs or a fork to turn leeks over. Roast 7 minutes longer. Remove from oven, turning again so the whitest, or palest, side is facing up. Add broth. Return pan to oven, reversing position, back to front. Roast 10 minutes. Turn leeks for maximum browning. Roast 10 minutes more. If you can get only large leeks, roast them longer—about 10 minutes longer—once the broth is added. Add ½ cup extra broth.

Sprinkle with salt. (The amount of salt needed will vary according to the saltiness of the stock.) Serve warm or at room temperature.

The leeks can be prepared ahead. About ½ hour before ready to serve, heat oven to 500°F. Add another cup of chicken stock. Reheat for 10 minutes.

NOTE: These are more delicious with a gelatinous broth. Store-bought broth is generally not gelatinous. *To enrich broth with gelatin:* While leeks are cooking, put broth into a heat-proof measuring cup. Sprinkle ½ envelope of gelatin over the broth. Let sit for 10 minutes. Place measuring cup in a small saucepan. Fill saucepan with just enough water to come halfway up the side of the measuring cup. Heat until broth is warm and gelatin has dissolved or melt in microwave oven. Use stock.

*M*USHROOMS

THERE IS AN ENORMOUS WORLD OF MUSHROOMS OUT THERE IN THE SHOPS AND THE NATURAL WORLD. Unfortunately, one needs to learn a lot about wild mushrooms before picking them; but it is great fun and wild mushrooms truly have a stronger, better taste than cultivated ones. In France, pharmacists must be trained to judge mushrooms, and all the forager has to do is take the haul to the nearest pharmacy to find out whether the mushrooms are edible and what type(s) they are. In any case, never eat mushrooms raw that grow in forests where there are beavers. You can get what Vermonters call "beaver fever," an acute case of the runs that must be cured by a doctor's strong medicine. I have restricted myself here to store-bought mushrooms.

All mushrooms will need to be cleaned before cooking. Avoid soaking in water whenever possible, as mushrooms are like sponges and sop up the water. Most store-bought mushrooms will be relatively clean. Buy only those that look clean, are not mushy, and whose surfaces haven't turned color or hardened. For roasting, the stems should be cut off close to the cap. The dirty ends of the stems should be cut off and the stems kept for stocks, stews, and sauces. The palm of your hand, a paper towel, or at most, a damp paper towel, wiped firmly over the mushrooms, should be all that is required to clean them.

The ordinary, store-bought white button mushroom is not suitable for roasting. Those readily available that roast well are portobellos, fresh shiitakes, whole or sliced porcinis, and creminis.

FOR ROASTING, ALWAYS select mushrooms with larger, fleshy caps. These mushrooms, when cooked, will have an intense flavor and are meant to be presented on their own as a handsome first course perhaps on a slice of Roasted Bread (page 367), as an accompanying vegetable, or as part of a vegetable medley platter (page 314).

PORTOBELLOS

1 pound whole portobello mushrooms (4, about 4 ounces each); serves 4 as a side dish

Remove stems. Wipe caps clean. Use smallest pan that will hold portobellos comfortably in a single layer. Place in pan, stem side down. Slick portobellos and pan with 6 tablespoons fat. Roast on second level from bottom of 500°F oven for 6 minutes. Turn, changing position of each mushroom in pan for even roasting. Roast for 6 minutes more.

TOTAL ROASTING TIME: 12 minutes

CREMINIS

It is better to buy creminis that are loose rather than in packages to ensure large, even cap sizes.

1¾ to 2 pounds creminis (14, 2 to 2½ ounces each, 2½ to 3 inches in diameter); serves 3 to 4 as a side dish or a first course

Remove stems. Wipe caps clean. Use smallest pan that will hold creminis comfortably. Place in pan, stem side down. Slick creminis and pan with ¼ cup fat. Roast in center of 500°F oven for 7 minutes. Remove. Turn, changing position of each mushroom in pan for even cooking. Roast 5 minutes more.

TOTAL ROASTING TIME: 12 minutes

SHIITAKES AND BOLETUS (PORCINIS OR CÈPES)

While the large fresh shiitakes look handsome when presented as a first course and taste somewhat better since they are fleshier, smaller caps can be roasted the same way and are nice for surrounding a roasted main course. For smaller caps, use more shiitakes and a larger pan. Five of the largest caps (eight small) will fit into an 12 x 8 x 1½-inch pan; six to eight large (twelve small) in a 14 x 12 x 2-inch pan, and twelve large (sixteen small) in an 18 x 13 x 2-inch pan. Larger pans require more oil, but adjust the amount accordingly: Use one and a half times as much oil for the medium-size pan and double the oil for the largest-size pan. Allow two large caps and four to five smaller ones per person. The small ones will take the same time to cook as the larger ones.

Fresh boletus (porcinis or cèpes) are too special and too expensive to waste as a garnish. Always use them as a first course on their own or with other compatibly seasoned roasted vegetables.

Unlike portobellos and creminis, which both cook for twelve minutes total, these require twenty minutes total. Sprinkle with seasonings and lemon juice just before serving.

6 large fresh shiitake mushrooms (about 2 ounces each, 4 to 4³⁄₄ inches in diameter); serves 6 as a side dish

6 to 8 fresh boletus mushrooms (each about 3 inches in diameter and ³⁄₈ inch thick); serves 6 as a first course; 4 large porcini mushrooms (³⁄₈ inch thick); serves 4 as a first course

For whole mushrooms, remove stems and wipe caps clean. If slicing, trim end of stem and cut through cap and stem into ³⁄₈-inch-thick slices. Use smallest pan that will hold mushrooms comfortably. Place in pan, stem side down for caps. Slick mushrooms and pan with 2 tablespoons fat. Roast in center of 500°F oven for 10 minutes. Turn. Roast for 10 minutes more.

TOTAL ROASTING TIME: 20 minutes

Roast shiitakes with soy

SERVES 6 AS A SIDE DISH OR
FIRST COURSE

TOTAL
ROASTING
TIME:
20
minutes

FRESH SHIITAKE MUSHROOMS are becoming more common in our markets. I thought we might honor them with vaguely Japanese seasonings. The large caps make a handsome first course and can be presented on a few shiso leaves or on a thin bed of mizuna. Since these are often unavailable, consider watercress or fresh green cilantro (coriander). The smaller caps are extremely attractive surrounding Roasted Cod with Pacific Rim Glaze (page 273) or a whole fish with the same glaze.

To use smaller caps or make a larger quantity of either size—often desirable—see Basic Mushrooms: Shiitakes and Boletus (page 362).

6 large fresh shiitake mushrooms (about 2 ounces each, 4 to 4¾ inches in diameter), stems removed and caps wiped clean

1½ tablespoons canola or other neutral oil
½ tablespoon sesame oil
1 teaspoon tamari soy sauce
Juice of ½ lemon

Place rack in center of oven. Heat oven to 500°F.

Arrange mushrooms, stem side down, in a 12 x 8 x 1½-inch roasting pan. Drizzle the oils and soy sauce over mushrooms. Rub oil over the top of each.

Roast for 10 minutes. Turn over. Roast 10 minutes more. Remove mushrooms and juices and sprinkle with lemon juice. Serve warm.

Roast portobello mushrooms with garlic marinade

SERVES 4 AS A SIDE DISH

TOTAL
ROASTING
TIME:
12
minutes

T RY TO FIND caps of the same size. If not, don't worry; the size (diameter) of the caps does not affect the cooking time.

Partner these up with Roasted Flank Steak (page 142) for a quick dinner, or use them as part of a roast vegetable dinner medley. Vary the flavor of the marinade by adding two teaspoons of chopped fresh herbs. A combination of thyme, oregano, and savory works well, as do sage and parsley. Use your imagination. Consider dropping in two teaspoons of Sherry vinegar, or tarragon vinegar mixed with chopped tarragon.

4 portobello mushrooms (¾ to 1 pound total), stem ends trimmed and caps wiped clean
6 cloves garlic, smashed, peeled, and roughly chopped

½ cup olive oil
1 teaspoon kosher salt
Freshly ground black pepper, to taste

Using a small kitchen knife, cut the stems off the flat mushroom caps. Reserve stems in the refrigerator in a sealed plastic bag or container.

Put the garlic in the blender with 2 tablespoons of the oil. Blend until smooth. Scrape down sides with a rubber spatula. Add remaining oil and salt and pepper. Blend until smooth. Put the mushrooms in a 12 x 8 x 1½-inch roasting pan. Using the spatula, scrape out all the garlic purée from the blender into the pan. Rub the purée into both sides of each mushroom cap. Leave to marinate for at least ½ hour, or up to 5 to 6 hours, turning occasionally if more time is available.

About 20 minutes before roasting the mushrooms, place a rack on the second roasting level from the bottom of the oven. Heat oven to 500°F. (If also making the Roasted Flank Steak, page 142, roast the steak on the lowest rack.) Arrange mushrooms so that they touch as little as possible, with stem sides down. Roast 6 minutes. Turn. Roast for 6 more minutes. Serve warm or at room temperature.

Roasted creminis with orange-cumin glaze

SERVES 4 TO 5 AS A SIDE DISH OR FIRST COURSE

TOTAL ROASTING TIME: 12 minutes

ADJUST THE CUMIN to flavor the creminis depending on how they will be served. If they are to go with a strongly flavored meat, use the full two teaspoons. If making up a batch to eat as part of a vegetable medley or to eat on top of a slice of good, thick-cut Roasted Bread (page 367) as a first course, a half teaspoon less will do.

14 cremini mushrooms (2 to 2½ ounces each, 2½ to 3 inches in diameter, 1¾ to 2 pounds), stems removed and caps wiped clean
5 tablespoons canola or other neutral oil

1½ to 2 teaspoons ground cumin
½ teaspoon kosher salt
¼ cup fresh orange juice
Freshly ground black pepper, to taste

Place rack in center of oven. Heat oven to 500°F. Put the mushrooms in a 12 x 8 x 1½-inch roasting pan. Combine remaining ingredients in a small bowl. Pour over mushrooms. Turn mushrooms in liquid so that both sides are well coated. Arrange in a single layer stem side down.

Roast for 7 minutes. Remove from oven. Turn mushrooms over and move the pieces nearest the edge of the pan into the center and those in the center to the outer edges. Roast 5 minutes more. Serve warm.

Roast porcinis with pleasure

SERVES 4 TO 6 AS A FIRST COURSE

TOTAL
ROASTING
TIME:
20
minutes

Among the mushrooms, almost nothing beats porcini, for my money. (In the case of porcini, that's a lot of money.) When caps or slices are roasted, they turn a warm, golden brown and are good hot or at room temperature as a lavish first course. They are too special to be just an accompaniment unless you want the classiest roast chicken on the block.

Porcinis are one of the large *Boletus* family of mushrooms. Perhaps the most prestigious and certainly the best for roasting are the *Boletus edulis*, commonly called "porcini" in Italy and "cèpes" in France. They do grow in the Americas. They are seasonal and must come from the wild, usually by way of a trusted supplier. The season will vary, depending on the part of the world from which the mushrooms come. In Vermont, I begin to find them in late August, and they can go on—depending on temperature and rainfall—through October.

Porcini can be found in a wide range of sizes with caps going from barely an inch and a half across to handsome devils whose velvety, chestnut brown caps reach five to six inches in diameter. The underside of the caps does not have gills as with most mushrooms, but instead a fine sponge or foam that is creamy and should not be mushy or discolored. The delicious and edible stems have the shape of old-fashioned newel posts; they taper at either end and swell in the middle and may—in the smaller mushrooms—reach almost the width of the cap.

Never discard these stems. When slicing large porcinis to roast, slice right through the cap and the attached stem. When roasting whole caps of smaller porcinis (those whose caps are only three-eighths of an inch at the thickest point), snap off the stems and cut them into neat, small cubes to sauté as an addition to mushroom dishes such as Sauté of Mushrooms (page 163) or soups. The stems may be somewhat striated in black. If it seems better, scrape them with a sharp knife before cutting.

I cannot really say how many slices can go in a pan at one time since the mushrooms vary so much in size. The important thing is to use a pan just large enough to hold the number of slices you are making. One or two caps or one large slice makes a first-course portion to serve on top of a piece of Roasted Bread (page 367) or naked on a plate. This is lavish food. To multiply the recipe, see Basic Mushrooms: Shiitakes and Boletus (page 362).

6 to 8 porcini caps (about 3 inches in diameter and ⅜ inch thick) or 4 slices large porcini, caps wiped clean, stem ends trimmed, caps, slices, and stems sliced ⅜ inch thick

2 tablespoons fabulously good olive oil

½ teaspoon kosher salt

Freshly ground black pepper, to taste

OPTIONAL INGREDIENTS

1 clove garlic, smashed, peeled, and mashed to a paste with the salt

1 tablespoon additional olive oil

2 teaspoons total of 3 fresh herbs (flat-leaf parsley, thyme, oregano, savory, sage, tarragon, chervil, or chives), finely minced

¼ teaspoon tarragon, red wine, or balsamic vinegar

Place rack in center of oven. Heat oven to 500°F.

Arrange mushrooms stem side down for caps and flat for slices in smallest pan that will hold them comfortably. Drizzle oil over mushrooms. Rub oil over top sides of each.

Roast 10 minutes. Turn each mushroom over. Roast for 10 more minutes. Remove. Sprinkle both sides of all with salt and pepper and optional ingredients, mixed together, if using.

Roasted bread

MAKES 8 PIECES OR MORE IF USING LARGER PAN

TOTAL ROASTING TIME: 8 *to* 10 *minutes*

An EASY WAY to present roasted vegetables, particularly mushrooms, as a first course is to put them on top of a crunchy, golden slice of roasted bread. Bread with good texture is addictive on its own, particularly with a full-flavored olive oil.

I try to find thick-crusted Italian country loaves with the bread not cottony but having a nice texture with some large holes. I cut the loaves across into one-inch-thick slices and then cut the slices so that I end up with pieces that are three and a half to four inches wide. Regular Italian or French loaves work as well. If the breads are narrow in diameter, slice them on the diagonal to get larger pieces.

When choosing a pan, be sure that the bread slices just fit. Otherwise, there will be smoking. A medium-size pan will hold about twelve slices, a large one about sixteen. As the number of slices to be roasted is multiplied, multiply the oil accordingly, but use a little less. A pastry brush works much better for applying the oil than simply dipping the slices in the oil, which tends to use too much. No pastry brush? Dip a piece of paper towel in the oil and use it to dab the slices.

The oil can be varied or flavored. A good variation for serving Italian-style roasted vegetables on Roasted Bread is to infuse some sliced garlic in the oil over low heat for about five minutes before slicking oil over bread.

These roasted croutons can get slightly blackish brown around the edges. I think that's delicious, but if that is offensive, check the color from time to time.

1 loaf Italian bread, ends trimmed off (on the diagonal), sliced across or on the diagonal into 1-inch-thick slices	¼ cup olive oil for every 8 slices

Place rack on upper level of oven. Heat oven to 500°F.

Leave slices whole or cut, as need be, to make pieces about 3½ to 4 inches across at widest point.

Pour oil into a 12 x 8 x 1½-inch roasting pan. Using a pastry brush, brush oil on both sides of bread slices so that they are evenly coated. Arrange slices in pan. Roast for 5 minutes. Remove pan and turn the slices. Return pan to oven back to front. Roast 3 to 5 minutes more.

Onions

ONIONS MAY BE OUR MOST-USED CULINARY VEGETABLE. It is hard to imagine Creole, Cajun, Italian, Spanish, and Central and South American cooking without the onion's almost ubiquitous use in the refritos and soffritos, the basic aromatic sautés that form the bases of most dishes. Hungarian cooking would be impoverished without onions. We use them raw in salads and on hamburgers, fry them into crisp rings, enjoy onion soups and soubise types of sauces that have onions as the predominant component, pickle them, and put them into Gibsons.

It is astonishing that in recipes so little attention is paid to onions' diversity in color, size, type, and flavor. Although much attention has been drawn in recent years to the sweetness of some onions (Vidalias, Mauis, and Walla Walla Sweets), aside from an occasional reference to color—red, white, or yellow—or size, few specifications are normally given.

At different times of the year, plain, yellow, or white onions can vary wildly in strength. They also vary according to variety. A whole dish can be ruined by following the quantities in a recipe and using onions that are excessively strong. How can you tell? Tasting is the best test; but if you find your eyes streaming when cutting onions, that is a good clue. What does the cook do? Use fewer onions or substitute leeks or shallots. Avoid onions that are sprouting, are green at the core, or have brown mushy rings or spots inside. They will have unpleasant, off flavors.

Large onions with thick layers will give a coarse chop unless mashed, which makes them almost impossible to brown because so much of their juice has been released. If you want a fine chop or mince, use smaller onions with thinner layers. For the same reason, try to avoid chopping them in the food processor, which tends to mash the onions. Large onions will also make thicker rings.

Roasting onions is a simple way to brown with a minimal amount of fat and attention. It is frequently done for stocks and stews. On their own or as ingredients, browned onions are used in so many forms in the kitchen that I give many cooking times which are needed to figure out when the onions should be added to a pan in which other foods are roasting or when to put a separate pan of them into the oven with another roasting food—sometimes they will need to go in first.

I have not included separate roasting times for the smallest onions, pearl onions, which can be red or white. Follow the timing for Really Small Whole Onions (page 370) if you are willing to do the work of cutting the stem end off of each and then peeling by hand. (The easiest way to peel small onions is to blanch them, at which point they will be too wet to roast well.)

After roasting onions, the pan can be deglazed with a liquid to use in stews or soups. If you have enough left over, either the Whole Onions (below) or the Roasted Onion Flowers (page 372) can be used to make the delicious Roasted Onion Soup with Cannellini Beans (page 373). This soup is so popular, I make a batch of onions just for it.

Onion relatives—shallots, leeks, scallions, and garlic—are listed alphabetically.

BASIC
ONIONS | WHOLE ONIONS

WHOLE ONIONS VARY in size and color. Large onions up to fourteen ounces each can be roasted successfully.

1½ pounds onions (4, about 6 ounces each); serves 4 as a side dish

Whole onions may be peeled or not before cooking. Place onions in smallest pan that will hold them comfortably. Slick onions and pan with 2 to 3 tablespoons fat.

continued

Roast in center of 500°F oven, turning onions in pan halfway through cooking time.

TOTAL ROASTING TIME: Large onions (up to 14 ounces each), 45 minutes; medium onions (up to 10 ounces each), 40 minutes; smaller onions (from 4 to 6 ounces each), 30 minutes

REALLY SMALL WHOLE ONIONS

I TEND TO roast small onions to use in stews and other foods. Sometimes I roast them with a chicken or a small leg of lamb. They take the same amount of time and can surround the meat in the pan. They require only a tablespoon and a half of fat when roasted with meat because the cooking meat will provide more. These onions may also be used in the same way as the cippolines (pages 375–377).

1 pound really small round onions (approximately 2 cups raw, 26 to 30 onions about ½ ounce each, ¼ to ½ inch in diameter) or cippolines (3½ cups raw); serves 4 to 5 as a side dish

Using a small sharp knife, peel the papery skin off each onion. Trim around the root end to remove any hard or brown bits. Place onions in smallest pan that will hold them comfortably. Slick onions and pan with 3 tablespoons fat. Roast in center of 500°F oven for 15 minutes. Shake pan vigorously to turn onions. Roast another 15 minutes. Shake. Roast for 15 minutes more.

TOTAL ROASTING TIME: 45 minutes

ONION SLICES (WHITE OR RED)

WHEN MAKING LARGER quantities, divide the onions between two pans on two different racks, switching pans halfway through the cooking, or use a larger pan for all of the slices. The cooking time will almost double.

1 pound onions (4, about 4 ounces each), sliced; serves 4 to 6 as a side dish

Peel onions. Cut across into ¼-inch-thick slices or separate into rings. Place onion slices in smallest pan that will hold them comfortably. Slick slices and pan with 2 tablespoons fat. Place 1 rack on lowest level of oven and another rack in center. Roast on bottom rack at 500°F for 15 minutes. Turn slices. Roast another 15 minutes. Move pan to center rack. Roast 15 minutes more.

TOTAL ROASTING TIME: 45 minutes

ONION WEDGES

OF THE MANY vegetables tested for this book, these rank among the best-glazed. If smaller onions are used, there will be only about four wedges in each. If using red onions, check about five minutes before end of time given; they may cook more quickly.

2½ pounds onions (4, about 10 ounces each, or 10, about 4 ounces each), sliced; serves 6 as a side dish

Peel onions, keeping root ends intact. Halve onions from stem to root. Cut each half of a larger onion lengthwise through the root end into 3 to 4 wedges to make 6 to 8 wedges per onion. Cut each half of a smaller onion lengthwise through the root end into 2 wedges to make 4 wedges per onion. Place wedges in smallest pan that will hold them comfortably in a single layer. Slick wedges and pan with 3 tablespoons fat. Roast in center of 500°F oven for 15 minutes. Remove pan and turn wedges. Return pan to oven, reversing position back to front for even browning. Roast 15 minutes more.

TOTAL ROASTING TIME: 30 minutes

CHOPPED ONIONS

WHEN A LARGE quantity of chopped onions needs to be browned to include in a dish, to flavor another vegetable, or to serve as a topping for sliced roasted or grilled meats, this method is a winner. While smaller batches can be made, it is convenient to have extra on hand in a container in the refrigerator. Also, for the health conscious, there is a saving in the amount of fat used with larger quantities. Regardless of the quantity made, less fat is used than would be used for sautéing.

This is a technique that liberates the cook from watching and stirring constantly. There is little danger of scorching onions, which happens so easily when they are sautéed on top of the stove. Onions come out golden and meltingly soft. Just remember to set the timer and to toss and turn the onions well to mix them. If using fewer onions and therefore a shallower layer, check them the last two stirrings. They may brown more quickly.

It may seem that all the onions in the world are being cut up; but they shrink away when cooked. Ten cups raw reduce to two cups when cooked. The work is lessened appreciably by using larger onions. While any fat can be used, half butter and half olive or canola oil is a good combination. The butter increases the browning and adds flavor. The oil keeps down any smoking, reduces the amount of saturated fat, and, in the case of olive oil, adds another good flavor.

4 ½ pounds onions (5 to 6, about 13 ounces each), chopped; makes 2 cups cooked

Peel onions. Roughly chop into ¼-inch dice (10 cups). Place chopped onions in smallest pan that will hold them comfortably in a thin layer. Slick onions and pan with ¼ cup fat. Roast in center of 500°F oven for 15 minutes. Toss and turn. Roast another 15 minutes. Toss and turn. Roast 15 to 20 minutes more. If using as a sauce or topping, salt and pepper to taste.

TOTAL ROASTING TIME: 45 to 50 minutes

Roasted onion flowers

SERVES 6 AS A SIDE DISH

TOTAL
ROASTING
TIME:
45
minutes

THERE ARE FASHIONS even in vegetable preparation. There was a fad at one time for deep-fried onions looking like flowers. They are a lot of work, and the fat sputters alarmingly. This is an improved substitution that not only looks spectacular on the plate but also is fun to eat and loved by guests. I often put each onion onto a separate plate next to the main course plate. Onion devotees will like them as a first course.

These may be scary because tips sometimes get very brown, almost black, and look burned. Be reassured. After one taste, everybody will enjoy them.

This works equally well with red or white onions. The four- to six-ounce size of onion is best. They open up and brown evenly and fit nicely on the dinner plate. Roast as many onions as there are guests. They get one apiece. Leftovers, if there are any, are perfect for Roasted Onion Soup with Cannellini Beans (page 373).

6 small red or white onions (4 to 6 ounces each), peeled and cut through in an X from top just down to root, but root end left intact

2 to 4 tablespoons olive oil

Place rack in center of oven. Heat oven to 500°F.

Cut just enough root end of each onion so onions will stand up in the pan. Pour 2 tablespoons of the oil into a 14 x 12 x 2-inch roasting pan. Rub oil around so that it covers the bottom and sides of the pan. Rub each onion. Arrange onions as far away from each other as possible so they will have room to open up. Roast for 30 minutes. Remove from oven to check dryness of pan, which will vary according to age and size of onions. If pan is dry, drizzle remaining oil over and around onions. Roast 15 more minutes. Onions should be browned and soft. If some of the tips are too black, just snip them off with kitchen scissors. Serve right away.

Roasted onion soup with cannellini beans

MAKES 4⅔ CUPS; SERVES 4

THIS SOOTHING, SMOKY-flavored onion soup is welcome during the winter. Make an extra batch of the base for it using just the first two ingredients. Freeze the base. After defrosting, continue with the remaining ingredients. The whole soup freezes well for about three weeks. The amount of onion used is from about a cup of leftovers. Canned cannellini make it extra easy.

3 cups Basic Chicken Stock (page 42)
  or canned

1 cup leftover roasted onions

1⅔ cups cooked cannellini beans or one
  19-ounce can white cannellini beans,
  drained and rinsed

2 teaspoons kosher salt, or less if using
  canned broth

2 teaspoons red wine vinegar

½ bunch (1½ ounce) fresh basil, washed,
  leaves stacked, rolled, and cut across
  into thin strips (about ¾ cup)

¼ cup freshly grated Parmesan cheese,
  optional

In a blender, combine 1 cup of the stock with the onions. Blend until smooth, stopping once to scrape down sides of blender.

Using a rubber spatula, scrape contents of the blender into a medium-size saucepan. Add remaining stock, beans, salt, and vinegar. Heat until just warm throughout. Stir to combine ingredients completely. Once soup is warm, add half the basil. Stir in with Parmesan, if using. Sprinkle the remaining basil over each serving.

Red onions

WHILE RED ONIONS can be used interchangeably with white or yellow onions, they tend to be sweeter and moister than their cousins. For eating raw, they must be cut shortly before using. Unless they are being combined with a lot of acid, as in a salsa, they will darken unpleasantly.

Crisp red onion rings

SERVES 8 AS A SIDE DISH

TOTAL ROASTING TIME: 50 minutes

ROASTING USES MUCH less fat than deep-fat-frying and is more enjoyable. The crisped rings will look very dark—mahogany-brown—when roasted. Don't worry, they are not burned. Roasting them this long is what gives them their smoky flavor.

I particularly like to serve these rings on top of Sweet Potato Slices (page 398) for a contrast of color and texture and complementary sweetness.

¼ cup olive oil

About 5 red onions (1¾ pounds), peeled and sliced into ¼-inch-thick rounds

¼ teaspoon kosher salt

Place rack on lowest level of oven. Heat oven to 500°F.

Pour the oil into an 18 x 13 x 2-inch roasting pan. Swirl the pan until the oil evenly covers the bottom.

Gently pull apart the rings in each onion slice. As rings are separated, put them in the oiled pan. Toss rings in the oil until all are coated. Arrange rings to touch as little as possible.

Roast 25 minutes. Remove from oven and turn rings over with a spatula. Roast for 25 minutes more. Remove to a platter. Sprinkle with salt and serve.

If serving with roasted sweet potato slices, make a pile of the potatoes on the platter first. Top with red onion rings, sprinkle with salt, and serve. This combination is delicious with Roasted Boneless Loin of Venison (page 219).

Cippolines and other small whole onions

THE CIPPOLINE—a small, flat white onion—has an August harvest in its native Italy and is really only good September through February. Since the season is short and the onions are highly prized in Italy and along the French Riviera (once part of Italy), there are many recipes for pickling them after they are cooked. While the onions can be peeled and boiled before pickling, I don't like the flavor nearly as well as when they are well browned instead. The easiest way is roasting.

When cippolines are in season, roast and marinate lots of them and put them up in refrigerated jars. They are perfect as part of a mixed hors d'oeuvre or as an accompaniment to pâté.

Cippolines are now available in the United States either loose or in eight-ounce bags, each of which holds eight to nine onions (meaning there are sixteen to twenty in a pound). The easiest way to prepare them is to cut off the root end, peel off the skin, and then trim off any stalk. The stalk sits in a sort of hollow in the top of the onion. It is essential to dig in slightly with the tip of a sharp knife to get all of the stalk out. I don't know why, but these always need to be rinsed after peeling and trimming.

Small round onions, red or white and as small as pearl onions in size, can be substituted for cippolines in the recipes below. Use the timing for Really Small Whole Onions (page 370).

If you want to use the onions immediately after roasting, sprinkle them with salt, pepper, your choice of vinegar, and a little sugar or honey. Shake them in the pan and return to the oven until the sugar or honey is just melted.

Roasted and marinated cippolines

MAKES 4½ CUPS; SERVES 6 TO 8 AS
A SIDE DISH

TOTAL
ROASTING
TIME:
30
minutes

I LOVE THESE. They are sweet and sour without the addition of any honey or sugar because the onions are so sweet. I usually keep some in the refrigerator. The only problem in counting on them as emergency guest rations is that they seem to disappear mysteriously. I may be the culprit, since they are just as good cold as warm, which makes them ideal on a buffet or as part of a mixed hors d'oeuvre plate. Warm, they can be part of a vegetable medley main course or a side dish with roasted birds or meats.

Due to the amount of sugar in the onions, it is very important to remove them from the roasting pan as soon as they are done, or they will stick.

¼ cup olive oil

3 pounds cippolines (10 to 11 cups), peeled

½ cup balsamic or red wine vinegar

½ cup water

1 tablespoon kosher salt

Place rack on lowest level of oven. Heat oven to 500°F.

Pour the oil into a 14 x 12 x 2-inch roasting pan. Roll each cippoline in the oil. Roast 15 minutes. Turn. Roast for 15 minutes more.

Remove cippolines immediately from pan with a slotted metal spoon, otherwise they will stick. Cippolines may be used at this point as a side dish or in a stew.

Reserve cippolines in a large bowl. Put roasting pan over medium-high heat. Pour in the vinegar and water. Bring the liquid to a boil, scraping up the brown glaze on the bottom of the pan. Add the salt. Cook 5 minutes. Pour liquid over cippolines. Let cool.

Pack cippolines into sterilized glass jars with tightly fitting lids. Cover with the liquid. If the liquid does not completely cover, top with more vinegar.

Once jars are completely cooled, they may be stored in the refrigerator, where they will keep for several months.

Roasted cippolines Riviera

MAKES 4½ CUPS; SERVES 6 TO 8 AS
A SIDE DISH

TOTAL
ROASTING
TIME:
30
minutes

IN TIMES THAT are far from antique and that I remember with great fondness, almost every restaurant along the French Riviera presented a seductive table of hors d'oeuvre variés, or the staff would parade by your table bringing first the vegetable hors d'oeuvre, then the fish, and finally the meats and sausages. I still go to the Colombe d'Or, in St.-Paul-de-Vence because—in addition to having a spectacular view—they preserve this custom. A standard and always welcome element of these "cascades" of hors d'oeuvres was this dish (sometimes made with other small onions). The name would vary according to the town you were in, the birthplace of the chef, or the supposed celebrity of the locale; "Monegasque" after Monaco was a favorite name.

It may be harder to find the "cascade"; but I can make the onions and have them at home in their sweet-and-sour sauce of an alluring orangy red.

3 pounds cippolines (10 to 11 cups),
    peeled
¼ cup olive oil

FOR THE MARINADE
¾ cup white wine vinegar

⅔ cup golden raisins
One ½-gram vial stem saffron
3 tablespoons tomato paste
Freshly ground black pepper, to taste

Roast cippolines as in Roasted and Marinated Cippolines (page 376).

During the last 15 minutes of roasting cippolines, combine all marinade ingredients in a small pan. Bring to a boil over medium heat, reduce to a simmer. Roast until cippolines come out of oven. Place roasting pan with cippolines on the stove over medium heat. Pour simmering liquid into pan. Stir with a wooden spoon, scraping pan with wooden spoon to deglaze.

Fill sterilized jars with the hot cippolines and marinade. If liquid does not cover all the cippolines, top off with more white wine vinegar. Let cool completely. Let flavor develop for at least 2 days before using. Will keep for several months in the refrigerator.

PARSNIPS

PARSNIPS ARE A HOMELY, OLD-FASHIONED ROOT VEGETABLE JUST BEGIN-
NING TO CREEP BACK INTO FAVOR WITH TRENDIER COOKS. Pulled and cooked
after first frost, they are sweet. Too many will ruin a soup or stew; but just the right
amount will lend a hint of sweetness and perfume.

In addition to roasting parsnips to eat as a vegetable, consider roasting some
until brown enough for a stew. If you work it right, you can roast them with carrots,
turnips, onions, and/or tomatoes at the same time, all in one pan or in different
pans (see Parsnip Slices, below, and Roasted Vegetable Combination, page 379).

BASIC
PARSNIPS

PARSNIPS GLAZE WONDERFULLY at high heat. Those new to roasting may be afraid that
the parsnips will come out overcooked, and they may be unhappy with what appears
to be a slight charring of the surface. The delicious taste will convert the skeptic.
There is so much flavor, they may not even need salt and pepper. Roasting works
best on parsnips that weigh up to four ounces or are one and a quarter inches in
diameter. Smaller are even better. They are perfect with Simplest Roast Chicken
(page 23) or as part of a medley of vegetables for a vegetarian meal.

WHOLE PARSNIPS

*1½ pounds whole parsnips (9 to 10, about 2½ ounces each); serves 3 to 4 as a
side dish*

Trim and peel parsnips. Place parsnips in smallest pan that will hold them comfortably in a single layer. Slick parsnips and pan with 1 tablespoon fat. Roast in
center of 500°F oven for 15 minutes. Turn. Roast 15 minutes more.

TOTAL ROASTING TIME: 30 minutes

PARSNIP SLICES
Parsnip pieces cooked like this are good simply sprinkled with salt and eaten as is
or added to stews and soups. The pieces will be nicely browned throughout with
color ranging from light to very dark brown.

*2 pounds parsnips (12 to 13, about 2½ ounces each), halved and sliced; serves 6 as
a side dish (makes 3 cups cooked)*

Trim and peel parsnips. Cut in half lengthwise and slice across into ½-inch-thick pieces (6 cups). Place slices in smallest pan that will hold them comfortably. Slick slices and pan with 2 tablespoons fat. Roast in lowest level of 500°F oven for 15 minutes. Turn. Roast for 15 minutes more.

TOTAL ROASTING TIME: 30 minutes

Roasted vegetable combination

MAKES 5 CUPS; SERVES 8 TO 10 AS A SIDE DISH

TOTAL ROASTING TIME: 30 minutes

THIS COMBINATION USES carrots, turnips, and parsnips and is a wonderful way to save time in the kitchen because these three vegetables roast remarkably well together. The combination can be used in a variety of ways: as a vegetable dish (see Balsamic Vegetable Trio, page 380), combined with leftover roasted meat for a stew, or puréed for a side dish or as the base of a soup that is thinned with stock.

2 tablespoons unsalted butter, melted

6 to 7 medium carrots (1 pound), trimmed, peeled, cut in half lengthwise, and sliced across into ½-inch-thick pieces (3 cups)

6 to 7 parsnips (1 pound), trimmed, peeled, cut in half lengthwise, and sliced across into ½-inch-thick pieces (3 cups)

About 4 turnips (1 pound), trimmed, peeled, and roughly cut into ½-inch-thick pieces (2½ cups)

Place rack on lowest level of oven. Heat oven to 500°F.

Put melted butter, carrots, parsnips, and turnips in a 14 x 12 x 2-inch roasting pan. Toss until pieces are lightly coated with the butter. Roast for 15 minutes. Remove from oven. Use a spatula to toss and turn pieces well. Move the pieces nearest the edge of the pan into the center and those in the center to the outer edges, to allow the maximum browning. Roast 15 minutes more. Most pieces will be nicely browned. Serve warm.

Balsamic vegetable trio

MAKES 5 CUPS; SERVES 8 TO 10 AS
A SIDE DISH

TOTAL
ROASTING
TIME:
30
minutes

THIS ROOM-TEMPERATURE SIDE dish cum salad makes good use of Roasted Vegetable Combination. The balsamic vinegar warms up the colors of the parsnips and turnips, making them look like water chestnuts in a Chinese dish. The trio is perfect for a buffet, or for serving over quickly sautéed bitter greens as a vegetarian main course.

Putting a kielbasa sausage in the center of the oven halfway through the vegetable cooking time turns the vegetables into a hearty, hot dinner to serve with beer, or a Cahors or Barbera red wine, and mustard. Simply slice the sausage and mix the vegetables with the vinegar.

1 recipe Roasted Vegetable Combination (page 379)

⅓ cup balsamic vinegar

1½ teaspoons kosher salt

Prepare Roasted Vegetable Combination. When it's cooked, remove from roasting pan to medium-size bowl. Pour vinegar and salt over vegetables. Using a slotted spoon, toss gently. Let cool to room temperature, tossing occasionally.

HOT KIELBASA WITH BALSAMIC VEGETABLE TRIO: Place a second rack in the center of the oven. Prick a ring of kielbasa sausage in about 6 different spots with the tip of a sharp knife. Put in small roasting pan. After vegetables have roasted 15 minutes, roast sausage on center rack. for remaining 15 minutes, or until warm throughout.

To serve, slice ring of sausage on the diagonal into 10 to 20 pieces. Arrange sausage on top of vegetables. Serve warm.

*P*EPPERS

WE ARE USED TO TALKING ABOUT "ROASTED PEPPERS" AND SEEING VARIOUS *CAPSICUMS* (POD PEPPERS), SWEET OR HOT, GREEN, ORANGE, RED, OR PURPLE, CALLED "ROASTED" ON MENUS AND IN SHOPS. Generally, they are actually broiled or grilled, sometimes right over a stove-top burner.

In a perverse fit, I decided to actually roast them. There turned out to be great advantages to the method. Instead of doing the peppers one by one on top of the stove or grill and carefully and constantly turning them or cooking them under the broiler, where they have to be turned frequently and must be watched carefully, the peppers are arrayed—as many at a time as you can put into a pan in a single layer—on the top shelf of an oven heated to 500°F. The peppers roast from the heat under them and from the reflected heat above. The result is reliable, and a large quantity is easy to do at one time.

Peeling jalapeños and other hot peppers with thin skins, particularly the small ones, is a great bore and I almost never do it. However, a quantity can be roasted at one time and peeled afterward, which makes it easy. If the peppers are large and hot, such as gypsy peppers and poblanos, that need peeling before stuffing, follow the cooking time for Basic Italian Frying Peppers (page 383). The peeling technique is the same as that for bell peppers (page 382).

Since peppers have seasons—late summer and fall—like other vegetables, buy them when they are good, plentiful, and cheap. Roast them, peel them, put them up in olive oil or vinegar (preferably balsamic), and refrigerate them to use as desired throughout the year. It is a lot less expensive than buying jars of roasted peppers in the market. The oil is better for storage. The vinegar is better than brine and has no salt. Both the vinegar and the oil from the stored peppers can be used for cooking and salad dressings.

It is not essential to put up roasted peppers. They are good just after preparation, with salt and either a little vinegar—for once, I don't like lemon juice—or olive oil. In addition to being a classic part of an Italian antipasto, peppers can be used to make endless simple first-course preparations with a little vinaigrette. Use roasted peppers instead of out-of-season tomatoes in a salad with mozzarella and a leaf or two of fresh basil, and make the vinaigrette with a little prepared mustard. Shred some Belgian endive lengthwise, put the peppers over them, and top with a few capers. Or put them over some arugula and top with anchovies, small black olives, or very thin slices of Parmesan.

THIS RECIPE CAN be changed to accommodate any number of peppers that need to be roasted. Don't bother to roast the expensive purple peppers because they lose their beautiful amethyst color. Yellow, red, and orange peppers are nicest. This quantity of peppers fits and blackens in a 14 x 12 x 2-inch roasting pan. Tightly pack and cover with oil or vinegar to keep. To use the roasted red bell peppers, see Capered Fennel Salad (page 353) and Roasted Vegetable Towers (page 346).

3 pounds red bell peppers (6 large); makes 3 cups cooked

Place whole peppers in smallest pan that will hold them comfortably. No fat is needed. Roast on highest level of 500°F oven for 15 minutes. Turn. Roast another 15 minutes. Turn. Roast 15 minutes more.

TOTAL ROASTING TIME: 45 minutes

To peel roasted bell peppers: Pepper skins will be scorched and black, which is exactly right. Use tongs or a spatula to immediately transfer peppers to brown paper bags or large plastic storage bags. Seal bags. Put bags in either the sink or a large pan. Avoid countertops that will stain. As the peppers sweat, the bottoms of the bags will get very damp. Don't try to pick up a brown paper bag or the bottom might fall out. Leave to cool.

With fingers, peel the skin off of each pepper. Remove core, ribs, and seeds. Leave pieces as large as possible, but don't worry if they shred some. All the scraps are tasty too. Use peeled, roasted peppers as needed or put them up to use later.

To store: Tightly pack peppers into glass containers, cover with olive oil or balsamic vinegar, and seal. Keeps in refrigerator indefinitely.

Italian frying peppers

THESE PALE GREEN, pointed peppers have thin skins that don't even need to be removed after roasting. The flesh is thinner than that of bell peppers, and the shorter roasting time used for them doesn't char the skin, which can therefore be eaten. Unfortunately, the season for these is short—July and August. Enjoy them when available in a pasta sauce or on their own, as part of an antipasto. Leave whole. They do not have to be deribbed; they are mild.

THESE ARE NOT the peppers to put up. See page 381 for those. Instead, consider these in a first course, contrasted with peppery, dark green watercress, perhaps a thin slice of provolone, and a little oil, vinegar, and salt.

1 pound Italian frying peppers (8, about 2 ounces each); serves 8 as part of an antipasto, 3 as a first course

Leave peppers whole or core each pepper from the top and remove all the seeds without further cutting the peppers. Place peppers in smallest pan that will hold them comfortably. Slick peppers and pan with ½ teaspoon fat. Roast in center of 500°F oven for 10 minutes. Shake pan to move peppers. Roast 5 minutes more.

TOTAL ROASTING TIME: 15 minutes

WHEN JALAPEÑOS ARE cheap, roast, peel, and pack whole into sterilized jars and cover with vinegar, or roast and peel the jalapeños, split them in half lengthwise, and remove the seeds before packing. If covered with vinegar, they will keep refrigerated for six months. If not covered with vinegar, they will keep, well wrapped, in the refrigerator for up to a month. Use about one third the quantity of the seeded, chopped jalapeños for fresh as a substitute. They are strong. A pound of peppers will fill a 12 x 8 x 1½-inch roasting pan.

1 pound jalapeño peppers (16, about 1 ounce each); makes 2 cups cooked when left whole; makes ¾ cup cooked when cored, seeded, deribbed, and chopped medium

Place peppers in smallest pan that will hold them comfortably. Slick peppers and pan with ½ teaspoon fat. To cook unpeeled peppers, roast in center of 500°F oven for 10 minutes. Shake pan to move peppers. Roast 5 minutes more. If roasting peppers for peeling, cook 5 minutes longer.

TOTAL ROASTING TIME: Unpeeled, 15 minutes; peeled, 20 minutes

To peel jalapeño peppers: As soon as peppers come from oven, cover loosely with a towel. When they are cool enough to touch, peel off skins.

Roasted red pepper spread

MAKES ⅔ CUP; SERVES 4 AS
A FIRST COURSE

THIS IS A recipe that has haunted me ever since I introduced it in *Food for Friends*. With each succeeding book, I tried a new variation. This is close to the original. There is absolutely no tradition but my own behind this bright red and rich-tasting spread, which I like to serve as a dip, on crostini, at drinks time, at the opening of the meal, on a few leaves of lettuce as a first course, or even as a pasta sauce. I like it so much I always make a triple quantity.

1 recipe Basic Whole Red Bell Peppers
(page 382)

3 large black olives, pitted

4 flat anchovy fillets or 2 tablespoons
drained and rinsed capers

2 sprigs fresh flat-leaf parsley leaves,
or 6 basil leaves

2 teaspoons olive oil

1½ teaspoons fresh lemon juice or
balsamic vinegar

Kosher salt, to taste

Freshly ground black pepper, to taste

Place the peppers, olives, anchovies, and parsley on a cutting board. Using a large chef's knife and working with a rocking motion, chop the ingredients until minced. Make sure as you chop to distribute the ingredients evenly and that they are not chopped too finely—the mixture shouldn't be puréed. Transfer the pepper mixture to a small bowl and beat in the olive oil and lemon juice. Add salt and pepper. The amount of salt will vary, depending on the olives and anchovies that are used.

This spread can also be made in a food processor by placing the peppers, olives, anchovies, and parsley in the work bowl and processing with very quick on/off motions until the ingredients are finely minced. Add the lemon juice and olive oil and process until barely incorporated. Add salt and pepper.

Roasted Italian frying peppers and whole tomatoes with linguine

MAKES 4 CUPS SAUCE; SERVES 6 AS A FIRST COURSE, 4 AS A MAIN COURSE

TOTAL
ROASTING
TIME:
20
minutes

THIS HAS THE taste of late summer, which is the only time this dish should be made. It is nice to be able to cook the vegetables together and know that they will come out right.

This sauce is light even though rich with flavor. Linguine seems to match it perfectly. Heavier pastas such as rigatoni or penne weigh the freshness down. If there is no good linguine, use spaghettini. This is a healthy meal, only two tablespoons of oil—olive at that—and an ample supply of vegetables. Don't add cheese. It too makes the dish taste less fresh. If a spicier dish is desired, substitute two to three jalapeños for one of the frying peppers.

1 pound linguine

About 8 Italian frying peppers (1 pound), cored from top to remove seeds

About 4 tomatoes (2 pounds), cored

6 cloves garlic, smashed, peeled, and thinly sliced lengthwise

2 tablespoons olive oil

1½ teaspoons kosher salt

Freshly ground black pepper, to taste

¼ cup water, wine, or stock, for deglazing

½ bunch (1½ ounces) fresh basil, rinsed well, stems removed, leaves stacked, rolled up, and cut across in thin strips, optional

Place rack in center of oven. Heat oven to 500°F. If you are eating right away, fill a large covered pot with salted water and bring to boil for the pasta. If not, make sauce ahead and hold at room temperature for 3 to 4 hours.

Put peppers, tomatoes, and garlic in an 18 x 13 x 2-inch roasting pan. Pour the oil into the pan. Rub the oil all over the bottom of the pan and over each pepper, tomato, and slice of garlic. Roast 10 minutes. Shake the pan to move things around. Roast 10 minutes more. There should be plenty of juice in the pan from the tomatoes, but if things look too dry and the garlic is too dark, add ¼ cup water. Scrape roasted vegetables into a medium-size bowl. Add salt and pepper.

Place roasting pan over medium–high heat. Add liquid. Bring to a boil. Cook briefly, using a wooden spoon to scrape up any blackened and cooked-on bits. Reduce heat to a simmer. Let liquid reduce by half. Add to vegetables in bowl. With a small kitchen knife, roughly cut through peppers and tomatoes in bowl. Do not cut too much; leave in large chunks.

continued

Meanwhile, after the vegetables have roasted for 8 minutes, put the pasta in the boiling salted water. Cook for 12 minutes. Strain, reserving a little of the cooking water. Return pasta to its cooking pot. Add the roasted vegetables and the reserved cooking water. Toss over low heat until warm throughout. Add basil, if using.

POTATOES

ROASTED POTATOES ARE PRACTICALLY PROVERBIAL AND ARE ONE OF THE EASIEST AND MOST SUCCULENT VEGETABLES TO MAKE EITHER ON THEIR OWN OR TO SURROUND CHICKEN, MEAT, OR FISH AS IT ROASTS. A check of the timings for Basic Potatoes (pages 387–392) makes it easy to figure out when to put potatoes in with a roast. Such timings are actually given in some recipes, such as Roast Chicken with Crispy Potatoes (page 25).

These timings are for potatoes as separate events; but potatoes are included in many dishes in other parts of the book. Roasting potatoes uses much less fat than pan-frying for a very similar result. All roasted potatoes can be made ahead and reheated for five minutes in a 500°F oven. Season potatoes with salt, pepper, and fresh herbs after roasting or when reheating.

It is always important to know a little bit about the kind of potatoes that does best in a given dish. Roasted Monkfish Felix (page 280) and Red Snapper Potato Salad (page 260), for instance, will do best with waxy potatoes. Others need floury potatoes, the kind that are boiled for mashing.

To turn leftover roasted vegetables into soup: Use one third as much by volume of the floury potatoes as vegetables. Peel and cook the potatoes, put through a food mill, combine with vegetables such as roasted leeks or parsnips that have been puréed already in a food processor or blender, thin as desired with stock, and season.

The most common floury potatoes are baking potatoes, the large brown ones—such as russets from Idaho or Maine—which are more floury than the thin-skinned yellowish ones that are often called California bakers. Other all-purpose floury potatoes are the round, brown potatoes often called Maine or Long Island potatoes.

The most common medium-sized waxy potatoes are red new potatoes.

Potatoes have always been available in many colors of skin and flesh and in many shapes and sizes; but those indications alone do not determine a potato's texture. There are potatoes with purple or blue skins and lavender flesh that are waxy and others that are floury. Round potatoes describe themselves. Fingerlings are shaped like a small link sausage.

This book usually calls for Idaho potatoes—baking potatoes—and new potatoes. If you are lucky enough to have other kinds available to you, substitute them on the basis of what the store, gardening catalogue, or your experience tells you. Large yellow Finns, for instance, can be used in place of baking potatoes. Russian bananas or the red fingerlings would make a superior substitution for other new potatoes.

Potatoes can be roasted with their skins on or off, whether whole or cut up. It's a matter of choice. A great part of the nutritional value is in or just under the skins. For roasting whole, smaller potatoes will be more succulent than larger ones. Those with blue and pink flesh will keep their color.

As with most roasting recipes, the ones for potatoes can be multiplied up to the point at which they no longer fit comfortably into a single layer in your pan. Making too many roasted potatoes never seems to be a problem. They generally get eaten.

BASIC
POTATOES

POTATOES FALL INTO three categories: waxy, medium-waxy, and floury, going from low to high starch. The medium-waxy potatoes can become more floury with age, and young (small and new) floury potatoes will be more waxy. Some of the waxy potatoes are carola, Russian banana (also called yellow-fleshed banana fingerlings), rose gold, la rouge, and la soda (the last two are both small and red). The red fingerlings—ruby crescent and ruby—are also waxy. La ratte is an old variety of waxy fingerling that is all the rage in France and England. Joël Robuchon uses it to make his fabulous mashed potatoes. Unfortunately, since rattes have very little starch, the mashing and beating in of unbelievable amounts of butter can only be done at the last minute because they cannot be reheated. The lack of starch means that they will ooze out their butter.

Among the medium-waxy potatoes are Caribé (white flesh and purple skins), Yukon gold (yellowish flesh), red cloud (red skins and somewhat dry white flesh), the standard Eastern potatoes—superior, Kennebec, Maine, Delaware, and Long Island—and Peruvian blue (blue inside and out). The floury potatoes are red bliss, belrus, Green Mountain, and russet. There are hundreds more varieties, and the enterprising gardener can have a field day trying them out.

I often find that the bigger the potato gets, the starchier—more floury—it will be. While baby Yukon golds picked early in the season are considered only medium-waxy, I find large ones to be quite floury and the same to be true of the Eastern potatoes.

Floury potatoes

Baking or other floury potatoes can be roasted in wedges, thick slices, or cubes, lightly coated with butter, oil, goose or duck fat, or bacon drippings. I don't know if anybody else remembers a coffee can to which bacon drippings were added each morning after breakfast. Few of us eat that way anymore. The fat rendered by roasting Basic Lardoons (page 392) can be used, and the lardoons strewn over the potatoes after roasting. Use only the amount of fat called for. Save extra lardoons, refrigerated, to add to a salad or stew.

Floury potatoes generally need to be cut into larger pieces or thicker slices than waxy potatoes so that they will remain whole. Each baking potato weighs about ten ounces.

FLOURY POTATO SLICES

A small roasting pan (12 x 8 x 1½ inches) holds one potato cut into ½-inch-thick slices; a medium pan (14 x 12 x 2 inches) holds two sliced potatoes; and a large pan (18 x 13 x 2 inches) holds three sliced potatoes.

10 ounces floury potatoes (1 large), cut into ½-inch slices; makes 1½ cups, serves 2 to 3 as a side dish

Potato may be peeled or skin left on and washed. Trim ends from potato. Cut potato across into ½-inch-thick round slices. Place slices in smallest pan that will hold them comfortably in a single layer. Slick potato slices and pan with 1 teaspoon fat. Roast on center rack of 500°F oven for 15 minutes. Turn potatoes with a spatula, scraping along bottom of pan to scoop up any slices that stick. Roast 10 minutes more. Transfer slices to a plate lined with paper towels.

TOTAL ROASTING TIME: 25 minutes

DICED FLOURY POTATOES

A small roasting pan (12 x 18 x 1½ inches) holds one potato cut into ½-inch dice (2 cups); a medium pan (14 x 12 x 2 inches) holds two diced potatoes (4 cups); and a large pan (18 x 13 x 2 inches) holds four diced potatoes (8 cups).

10 ounces floury potatoes (1 large), cut into ½-inch dice (2 cups); makes 1½ cups, serves 2 to 3 as a side dish

Potato may be peeled or skin left on and washed. Trim ends from potatoes. Cut potato lengthwise into ½-inch-thick slices. Cut slices into ½-inch squares. Place dice in smallest pan that will hold them comfortably in a single layer. Slick potato dice and pan with 1 teaspoon fat. Roast on center rack of 500°F oven for 10 minutes. Turn potatoes with a spatula, scraping along bottom of pan to scoop up any dice that stick. Roast 10 minutes more. Transfer dice to a plate lined with paper towels.

TOTAL ROASTING TIME: 20 minutes

FLOURY POTATO WEDGES

A small roasting pan (12 x 8 x 1½ inches) holds a pound and a quarter of potatoes, about twenty-four wedges.

4 to 4½ pounds floury potatoes (8 large, about 8 to 10 ounces each), cut into wedges; serves 6 to 8 as a side dish

Potatoes may be peeled or skin left on and washed. Cut in half lengthwise, then across. Cut each section lengthwise into 3 to 4 wedges. Place potatoes in the smallest pan that will hold them comfortably in a single layer. Slick wedges and pan with 3 tablspoons fat. Roast on second rack from bottom of 500°F oven for 15 minutes. Remove pan. Turn potatoes with a metal spatula, scraping along bottom of pan to scoop up potatoes. Roast another 20 minutes. Remove. Turn. Roast 20 minutes more.

TOTAL ROASTING TIME: in animal fat, 40 minutes; in oil, 50 minutes

Waxy potatoes

See page 387 for a discussion of waxy potatoes. There is no difference in cooking time between different colors of waxy potatoes. Waxy potatoes are given here as new potatoes, eight to ten to the pound with a diameter of 1½ to 2 inches. Larger potatoes, whole, halved, and in quarters may take a few minutes longer.

WHOLE WAXY POTATOES

2¾ to 3 pounds new potatoes (about 22); serves 5 as a side dish

Potatoes may be peeled or skin left on and washed. Place whole potatoes in smallest pan that will hold them comfortably in a single layer. Slick potatoes and pan with 2 tablespoons fat. Adjust timings for fat used. Roast on center rack of 500°F oven for 15 minutes. Remove pan. Turn potatoes with a metal spatula, scraping along bottom of pan to scoop up potatoes. Roast another 15 minutes. Turn. Roast 15 minutes more.

TOTAL ROASTING TIME: in animal fat, 40 minutes; in oil, 50 minutes

WAXY POTATO HALVES

A small roasting pan (12 x 8 x 1½ inches) holds ¾ to 1 pound of potatoes, halved (3 cups); a medium pan (14 x 12 x 2 inches) holds 1¾ pounds of potatoes, halved (6 cups); and a large pan (18 x 13 x 2 inches) holds 2½ pounds of potatoes, halved (10 cups).

¾ to 1 pound waxy potatoes (8 to 10), cut into halves (3 cups); serves 4 to 6 as a
*   side dish (makes 2½ cups cooked)*

Potatoes may be peeled or skin left on and washed. Cut potatoes in half lengthwise. Place halves cut side down in smallest pan that will hold them comfortably in a single layer. Slick potato halves and pan with 2 teaspoons of fat. Roast on center rack of 500°F oven for 15 minutes. Remove pan. Turn potatoes with a spatula, scraping along bottom of pan to scoop up any that stick. Roast 15 minutes more. Turn again. Roast 5 minutes more. Transfer halves to a plate lined with paper towels.

TOTAL ROASTING TIME: in animal fat, 30 minutes; in oil, 35 minutes

WAXY POTATO QUARTERS

A small roasting pan (12 x 8 x 1½ inches) holds 1 pound of potatoes, quartered (2¾ cups); a medium pan (14 x 12 x 2 inches) holds 1¾ pounds of potatoes, quartered (5½ cups); and a large pan (18 x 13 x 2 inches) holds 2¼ pounds of potatoes, quartered (9 cups).

1 pound waxy potatoes (10 to 11, about 1½ to 2 inches in diameter), cut into quarters (2¾ cups); serves 4 to 6 as a side dish (makes 2¼ cups cooked)

Potatoes may be peeled or skin left on and washed. Cut potatoes lengthwise into quarters to form wedges. Place wedges cut side down in smallest pan that will hold them comfortably in a single layer. Slick potato wedges and pan with 2 teaspoons fat. Adjust timings for fat used. Roast on center rack of 500°F oven for 15 minutes. Remove pan. Turn potatoes with a spatula, scraping along bottom of pan to scoop up any wedges that stick. Roast 15 minutes more. Transfer halves to a plate lined with paper towels.

TOTAL ROASTING TIME: in animal fat, 25 minutes; in oil, 30 minutes

WAXY POTATO SLICES

A small roasting pan (12 x 8 x 1½ inches) holds 9 ounces of potatoes sliced ¼ inch thick (2 cups); a medium pan (14 x 12 x 2 inches) holds 18 to 20 ounces of sliced potatoes (4 cups); and a large pan (18 x 13 x 2 inches) holds 1¾ to 2 pounds of sliced potatoes (7 cups).

9 to 10 ounces waxy potatoes (5 to 6), cut into ¼-inch-thick slices; serves 3 to 4 as a side dish (makes 1½ cups cooked)

Potatoes may be peeled or skin left on and washed. Trim ends from potatoes. Cut potatoes across into ¼-inch-thick round slices. Place slices in smallest pan that will hold them comfortably in a single layer. Slick potato slices and pan with 1 teaspoon fat. Adjust timings for fat used. Roast on center rack of 500°F oven for 15 minutes. Remove pan. Turn potatoes with a spatula, scraping along bottom of pan to scoop up any slices that stick. Roast 5 minutes more. Transfer slices to a plate lined with paper towels.

TOTAL ROASTING TIME: in animal fat, 17 minutes; in oil, 20 minutes

DICED WAXY POTATOES

A small roasting pan (12 x 8 x 1½ inches) holds 10 ounces of potatoes cut into ¼-inch dice (1½ cups); a medium pan (14 x 12 x 2 inches) holds 20 ounces of diced potatoes (3 cups); and a large pan (18 x 13 x 2 inches) holds 2 pounds of diced potatoes (5 cups).

10 ounces new potatoes (5 to 6, 1½ to 2 inches in diameter), cut into ¼-inch dice (2 cups); makes 1 cup; serves 2 as a side dish

Potatoes may be peeled or skin left on and washed. Trim ends from potatoes. Cut potatoes lengthwise into ¼-inch-thick slices. Cut slices into ¼-inch squares. Place dice in smallest pan that will hold them comfortably in a single layer. Slick potato dice and pan with 1 teaspoon fat. Roast on center rack of 500°F oven for 10 minutes. Remove pan. Turn potatoes with a spatula, scraping along bottom of pan to scoop up any dice that stick. Roast 10 minutes more. Transfer dice to a plate lined with paper towels.

TOTAL ROASTING TIME: in animal fat, 15 minutes; in oil, 20 minutes

BASIC LARDOONS

MANY CLASSIC RECIPES such as coq au vin call for lardoons. This is an easy way to make them. The quantity can be increased by using a larger pan. In addition to the lardoons, you will get a quarter cup bacon grease, which can be used to roast potatoes or to sauté chicken. Do not shake the pan; there is too much grease. Instead, turn with a metal spatula.

1 slice of slab bacon (about 7 ounces, 1 inch thick), cubed; makes ½ cup cooked

Cut bacon slice into ¼-inch cubes (1⅔ cups). Place bacon cubes in smallest pan that will hold them comfortably in a single layer. Roast in center of 500°F oven for 6 minutes. Turn. Roast 6 minutes more.

TOTAL ROASTING TIME: 12 minutes

Roast red new potatoes with garlic and rosemary

SERVES 4 TO 5 AS A SIDE DISH

TOTAL
ROASTING
TIME:
30
minutes

IF THE GUESTS like garlic, add more garlic cloves to this recipe. The potatoes go very well with a simple dish such as Simple Roast Leg of Lamb (page 186).

The potatoes can be peeled or not. Peeling takes extra time, but something very nice happens to peeled potatoes: They turn an excellent dark brown color and puff up on the outside. Peeled potatoes can stick a bit to the pan. Be sure to scrape the bottom of the pan to get up any browned bits.

Larger potatoes need to roast longer. The amount can be increased by increasing the pan size.

3 pounds waxy red new potatoes (1½ to 2 inches in diameter), peeled

2 tablespoons olive oil

Kosher salt, to taste

Freshly ground pepper, to taste

5 to 10 cloves garlic, unpeeled

1 tablespoon chopped fresh rosemary leaves

Place rack in center of oven. Heat oven to 500°F. Place potatoes in a 12 x 8 x 1½-inch roasting pan. Drizzle oil over potatoes. Rub the oil over the potatoes and the inside of the pan. Sprinkle with salt and pepper.

Roast for 15 minutes. Turn potatoes over with a metal spatula. Scrape spatula along bottom of pan to scoop up any crisp bits. Add garlic. Roast 15 more minutes. Sprinkle on the rosemary. Turn potatoes and garlic with spatula so that rosemary mixes in. Roast 10 minutes more. Potatoes should be easy to pierce with the tip of a sharp knife.

Roast new potatoes with dill

TOTAL
ROASTING
TIME:
40
minutes

SERVES 4 TO 5 AS A SIDE DISH

ANY SMALL WAXY new potato—red, white, gold, or blue—can be used. This is particularly good with fish. The dill will darken in color. If going for aesthetics, cut up some extra dill and reserve to sprinkle on the finished dish. Never chop dill too small, or it will taste gritty.

3 pounds waxy new potatoes (about 1½ inches in diameter unless oval, in which case a little less), peeled or not

2 tablespoons unsalted butter, at room temperature

Kosher salt, to taste

Freshly ground black pepper, to taste

2 tablespoons chopped fresh dill

Place rack in center of oven. Heat oven to 500°F. Place potatoes in a 12 x 8 x 1½-inch roasting pan. Place small dabs of butter around potatoes. Rub some of the butter over the potatoes and the inside of the pan. Sprinkle with salt and pepper.

Roast for 15 minutes. Turn potatoes over with a metal spatula. Scrape spatula along bottom of pan to scoop up any crisp bits. Roast another 15 minutes. Sprinkle on the dill and turn potatoes with spatula to incorporate dill. Roast 10 minutes more. Potatoes should be easy to pierce with the tip of a sharp knife.

Crisp potatoes

TOTAL
ROASTING
TIME:
50
minutes

SERVES 6 TO 8 AS A SIDE DISH

ANY FLOURY POTATO, such as an Idaho baker, can be used to make these browned, delicious wedges. Fill up the largest pan available. The pieces always get eaten, no matter how few guests show up. Serve with Tarragon Roast Chicken (page 30).

If you don't trust my predictions about the likely disappearance of the potatoes, reduce the quantities proportionately and use a smaller pan.

About 8 large Idaho potatoes or other floury type (4 to 4½ pounds)

3 tablespoons unsalted butter, at room temperature

Kosher salt, to taste

Freshly ground black pepper, to taste

Place rack on second level from bottom of oven. Heat oven to 500°F.

Peel the potatoes. Cut in half lengthwise, then in half across. Cut each piece lengthwise into 3 wedges by holding the knife so the blade points in at an angle as you cut into the potato. As wedges are cut, put them in an 18 x 13 x 2-inch roasting pan. Dot potato wedges with butter. Arrange in pan so that they touch as little as possible. Sprinkle with salt and pepper. Roast 15 minutes. Remove from oven. Use the flat back side of a metal spatula to scrape up potatoes and turn over. This helps them to cook and brown evenly. Roast another 15 minutes. Remove. Turn. Roast 20 minutes more. Serve warm.

Melting potatoes
(Not-on-Your-Diet)

SERVES 8 TO 10

TOTAL
ROASTING
TIME:
55
minutes

ONE OF THE BEST, it is the most sinful recipe from a nutritional point of view. I would gladly sacrifice fat and butter for several days to eat as many of these potatoes as I can. The problem with making them is that people tend to eat potatoes rather than the main dish. Friends have begged me to make these. A pound and a half of potatoes serves four people and can be made in a small roasting pan. This seems like a waste of effort. If I really thought the larger amount of potatoes wouldn't get eaten, I would probably make them anyhow and finish roasting just those I thought would get eaten with the last fifteen minutes of extra-butter roasting. I would indulge myself the next day by letting the leftover potatoes come to room temperature while the oven heated, and then finish them. Goodness knows, these potatoes plus a green salad and a glass of wine would make me happy.

The cooking time will be the same for new potatoes and baking potatoes; either can be used. The wedges of baking potatoes will get a crisper crust that contrasts adorably with the floury insides. The reds are good, but firmer. All the liquid and fat gets absorbed during the cooking, and the potatoes still shrink.

I frequently make this dish on a rack at the bottom of the oven as Simplest Roast Chicken (page 23) roasts, especially if I'm making more than one chicken at a time and potatoes cannot fit around them in the pan. A smallish bird roasts for fifty minutes, like the potatoes. A larger chicken can continue to roast while the potatoes wait outside the oven. Finish off the potatoes while deglazing the chicken's roasting pan.

For the ultimate flavor and glazing, use six tablespoons of goose fat instead of butter and olive oil; but do use a tablespoon of butter for the final heating. If using all butter rather than an olive oil and butter combination, the potatoes will brown and roast more quickly. Follow the alternate times in the recipe.

3 tablespoons unsalted butter, cut into 6 pieces, plus 1 tablespoon reserved in refrigerator

3 tablespoons olive oil

6 large baking potatoes (3 pounds)

1 teaspoon kosher salt

Freshly ground black pepper, to taste

2 cups Basic Chicken Stock (page 42) or canned (see Note)

Place rack in top third of oven. Heat oven to 500°F.

Put the 3 tablespoons of butter into an 18 x 12 x 2-inch roasting pan. Set the pan over medium heat just until the butter has melted. Remove. Add the olive oil.

Peel the potatoes. Cut in half lengthwise, then cut each half in half again across. Cut each quarter into 3 wedges. Put them in the roasting pan. Roll wedges in butter and oil until evenly coated. Arrange so that they touch as little as possible. Sprinkle with salt and pepper.

Roast for 15 minutes. Turn wedges with a pancake turner. Roast another 10 minutes. Turn again. Roast 10 minutes more. Remove pan from oven. Turn wedges again, making sure to turn the white sides of each wedge faceup. Add the stock. Return to oven for a final 15 minutes. The potatoes can be made up to this point and held for 4 to 6 hours. (*If using all butter*, roast 10 minutes, 5 minutes, 5 minutes, add stock, and roast 15 minutes.)

When ready to serve, dot the wedges with small pieces of the reserved tablespoon of butter. It is much easier to break up the butter into teeny pieces when it is cold. If the potatoes have been at room temperature, roast 15 minutes. If they are still warm, 5 minutes will do nicely. Remove potatoes to a platter right away or they will stick to the pan.

NOTE: Canned broth lacks the gelatin that makes this dish so sumptuous in texture. To enrich, see Note on page 361. Canned broth usually has lots of salt. Add no more.

Seaside melting potatoes

SERVES 8 TO 10 AS A SIDE DISH

TOTAL
ROASTING
TIME:
55
minutes

THIS IS A variation of Melting Potatoes (page 395) that roasts in the same way. A hint of the ocean comes through with the fish stock, and a fresh taste with the dill. Perfect to serve with a whole roasted fish (page 240).

7 tablespoons olive oil

About 6 large baking potatoes (3 pounds)

1 teaspoon kosher salt

Freshly ground black pepper, to taste

½ teaspoon dill seed

2 cups Basic Fish Stock (page 243)

2 teaspoons chopped (medium-fine) fresh dill

Juice of 1 large slice of fresh lemon, seeds removed, optional

Follow recipe for Melting Potatoes, substituting the olive oil for the butter. Start with 6 tablespoons of the oil in the roasting pan, wedges sprinkled with the salt and pepper. Combine the dill seed with the stock. Drizzle the last tablespoon of the oil over the potatoes at the end, when returning to oven for reheating. When ready to serve, top potato wedges with fresh dill. Squeeze on juice from lemon if using.

Mildly curried roast vegetables

SERVES 4 AS A SIDE DISH, 6 AS A
MAIN COURSE SERVED WITH RICE

TOTAL
ROASTING
TIME:
45
minutes

1 floury potato, such as Idaho (8 ounces), peeled and cut in half lengthwise, then across, each quarter cut into 4 wedges

3 tablespoons canola or other neutral oil

2 medium onions (1 pound), peeled and each cut into 6 to 8 wedges

3 medium carrots (4 ounces each), trimmed, peeled, and cut across into ½-inch slices (1 cup)

¼ pound green beans, ends trimmed, snapped in half (1 cup)

1 red bell pepper (8 ounces), stemmed, seeded, deribbed, and cut into 1-inch pieces (1½ cups)

6 cloves garlic, peeled

2 tablespoons curry powder

1½ cups Roasted Plum Tomato Sauce (page 419) or one 14-ounce can plum tomatoes, drained and crushed

2 cups broccoli florets (1 head)

1 cup Basic Chicken Stock (page 42) or canned, or vegetable stock

2 teaspoons kosher salt

4 grinds black pepper

2 tablespoons fresh lime juice

continued

Place rack in center of oven. Heat oven to 500°F.

Put potato wedges in an 18 x 13 x 2-inch roasting pan. Drizzle with 2 tablespoons of the oil. Rub potatoes and pan with oil. Roast 15 minutes. Remove. Move potatoes to the sides of the pan. In the center, add the onions, carrots, green beans, red pepper, and garlic. Drizzle with remaining 1 tablespoon of oil. Roast 15 minutes.

Meanwhile, combine the curry powder with the tomato sauce. Pour tomato sauce over vegetables and toss with a spatula. Place broccoli around outer edges of pan, on top of tossed vegetables. Roast for 15 minutes more. Remove and transfer all vegetables and juices to a large serving bowl. Put roasting pan over high heat and add stock. Bring to a boil, scraping the bottom of the pan to remove any crisp bits. Let reduce by half. Add salt, pepper, and lime juice. Pour sauce over vegetables. Serve warm.

Sweet potatoes

SWEET POTATOES ARE roots not potatoes (tubers) at all and they are not yams, although, to add to the confusion, some kinds of sweet potatoes have been given "yam" as part of their common name. Do not use yams for these recipes.

BASIC
SWEET
POTATOES

SWEET POTATO SLICES

1½ pounds sweet potatoes (3 to 4, about 7 ounces each), sliced; serves 4 as a side dish

Peel sweet potatoes. Cut across on the diagonal into ¼-inch-thick slices. Place sweet potato slices in smallest pan that will hold them comfortably in a single layer. Slick slices and pan with 2½ tablespoons fat. Place 1 rack in center of the oven and another on the second level from the bottom. Roast on center rack of 500°F oven for 25 minutes. Remove pan and turn each slice. Return pan to lower rack of oven, back to front. Roast 25 minutes more.

TOTAL ROASTING TIME: 50 minutes

SWEET POTATO WEDGES

1½ pounds sweet potatoes (3 to 4, about 7 ounces each), cut into wedges; serves 3 to 4 as a side dish

Peel sweet potatoes. Cut in half lengthwise, then across. Cut each section into 3 to 4 wedges. Place sweet potato wedges in smallest pan that will hold them comfortably in a single layer. Slick wedges and pan with 3 tablespoons fat. Roast on center rack of 500°F oven for 15 minutes. Remove. Turn. Roast for 15 minutes more.

TOTAL ROASTING TIME: 30 minutes

Puffed sweet potato slices with crisp red onion rings

TOTAL ROASTING TIME:
50
minutes

SERVES 8 AS A SIDE DISH

THIS RECIPE COMBINES two vegetables, which can be made separately. Together, their contrast in taste, texture, and color makes the dish an instant hit. Use three large roasting pans and three oven racks. If two pans and racks are all that are available, halve the sweet potatoes—remember there will be less. Everything cooks for 50 minutes, so once it's in the oven, it's easy.

FOR THE SWEET POTATOES

5 tablespoons olive oil

About 6 medium sweet potatoes (3 pounds), peeled and sliced across on the diagonal into ¼-inch-thick pieces

½ teaspoon kosher salt

FOR THE RED ONIONS

¼ cup olive oil

About 5 red onions (1¾ pounds), peeled and sliced into ¼-inch-thick pieces

¼ teaspoon kosher salt

There will be enough sweet potato slices to fill two 18 x 13 x 2-inch roasting pans. A third pan of the same dimensions will be fine for the onions. About 20 minutes before ready to roast, place 1 rack in the center of the oven, another in the lower third, and 1 in the bottom for the onions. Heat oven to 500°F.

For the sweet potatoes: Pour half the oil into 1 of the roasting pans. Smear it around. Using half of the sweet potato slices, take each one and swish both sides quickly through the oil. Do not blot or soak the pieces in the oil. Arrange pieces in the pan so that they do not touch. Repeat in the second pan. Sprinkle ¼ teaspoon of salt over each panful of slices.

For the onions: Pour the oil into the roasting pan. Swirl the pan until the oil evenly covers the bottom. Gently pull apart the rings in each onion slice. As rings are separated, put them into the oiled pan. Toss rings in the oil until all are coated. Arrange rings to touch as little as possible. Sprinkle with salt.

Place all 3 pans in oven: onions on lowest rack with sweet potatoes on the other two. Roast 25 minutes. Remove 1 pan at a time from oven and use a spatula to turn over each sweet potato slice and each onion ring. Return pans to oven back to front. Put the pan that was on the highest rack on the middle one and vice versa. Roast 25 minutes more.

Pile sweet potatoes on a serving platter. Top with red onion rings, sprinkle with salt, and serve. Delicious with Roasted Boneless Loin of Venison (page 219).

Maple-glazed roasted sweet potatoes

SERVES 3 TO 4 AS A SIDE DISH

TOTAL
ROASTING
TIME:
30
minutes

A TEXAN FRIEND feels that the syrup on these richly brown wedges transports her down memory lane: "It tastes like when I was a child and got to eat masses of sweet potatoes with brown sugar and—even better—with marshmallows toasty and fluffy on top." To get even more Southern, use cane or dark Karo syrup in place of the maple syrup. Add some marshmallows on top for the last five minutes of cooking if you must.

3 to 4 sweet potatoes (about 7 ounces each, 1½ pounds total), peeled

3 tablespoons unsalted butter
3 tablespoons maple syrup

Place rack in center of oven. Heat to 500°F.

Cut the sweet potatoes in half lengthwise, then across. Cut each section lengthwise into 3 wedges.

Use smallest pan that will hold sweet potatoes comfortably. Melt butter in it on top of stove. Remove from heat, and place sweet potatoes in pan, and turn wedges in butter. Roast for 15 minutes. Remove pan from oven and toss sweet potatoes with maple syrup. Roast for 15 minutes more. Sweet potatoes should be easy to pierce with the tip of a sharp knife. Immediately remove to serving plate or sweet potatoes will stick to pan. Soak pan.

*r*ADICCHIO

Radicchio is one of the many chicories. For more general information, see Endives (page 350). The radicchios are the burgundy-red endives, of which the most commonly seen outside of Italy is the round variety from Verona. In Italy these chicories are generally eaten cooked, not raw. My favorite to cook is the variety from Treviso, which is sometimes made into a salad with thinly sliced fennel and a lemon and olive oil dressing.

Treviso has thin, pointy heads like Belgian endive, although the leaves are a good bit less tightly furled and are longer. There is enormous variation in weight and length of heads among Trevisos available in the market. I generally cut smaller heads, about four ounces each, in half lengthwise, and I cut large heads, which can go up to ten ounces each, in quarters lengthwise. The roasting time will not change. Even if large heads are cooked whole, there will be only a small increase in cooking time. Check these larger heads by inserting the point of a sharp knife just above the root end. The knife should meet no resistance.

One of the great pleasures of roasting Treviso rather than grilling it is that it cooks all the way through. Both methods of cooking turn the color a disappointing brown; but the appealing, slightly bitter flavor more than makes up for the loss of color.

The round Verona can be substituted (split the heads from top to bottom) as can Belgian endives when Treviso is unavailable.

BASIC
TREVISO

SIMPLY ROASTED, TREVISO makes a good side dish with Roasted Rack of Veal (page 212), Simplest Roast Chicken (page 23), or Roasted Red Snapper with Tarragon (page 259). One to two small halves, or two to three large quarters, will make a serving. Sprinkle the roasted Treviso with ¼ cup balsamic vinegar, or 1½ tablespoons fresh lemon juice, or ½ cup stock right when it comes out of the oven. Season with salt and pepper to taste.

1¾ pounds Treviso (5 small heads, about 4 ounces each; 2 large heads, about 10 ounces each, or an assortment), sliced; serves 6 to 8 as a side dish

Using a small sharp knife, trim Treviso of any brown spots. Cut small heads in half lengthwise; cut large heads into quarters lengthwise. Place Treviso pieces in smallest pan that will hold them comfortably in a single layer. Slick Treviso and pan with ¼ cup fat. Roast on lowest level of 500°F oven for 10 minutes. Turn. Roast 10 minutes more.

TOTAL ROASTING TIME: 20 minutes

Toasty Treviso with mozzarella and anchovies

SERVES 4 AS A FIRST COURSE

TOTAL
ROASTING
TIME:
20
minutes

WHAT A WONDERFUL complexity of flavors—salty, bitter, sweet, and unctuous—comes from a very simple preparation. I serve this as a first course or the way Italians might, as a course on its own, *contorno*, after the main course instead of salad and cheese. Used this way, two small halves or three large quarters make a serving.

The number of anchovies used depends on the size of the Treviso and whether the guests are really wild for them. Large quarters of ten-ounce heads will need three anchovy fillets to run the length of each piece. Smaller heads of four ounces will only need two anchovies per half. Medium heads can be a compromise between the two. Different-sized heads can be mixed, but don't stint on the toppings. A half pound of mozzarella may be enough if sliced very thinly. Think proportional representation.

No Treviso? Use endive or Verona radicchio cut in half lengthwise, putting as many as will fit comfortably in the pan.

1⅓ pounds Treviso radicchio (2 to 5 heads, depending on size)	16 to 24 flat anchovy fillets (two to three 2-ounce cans)
1 teaspoon kosher salt	¾ pound fresh mozzarella, cut into ⅛-inch-thick slices (2 to 3 slices per piece of Treviso)
2 cloves garlic, smashed and peeled	
¼ cup olive oil	

Place rack on lowest level of oven. Preheat oven to 500°F.

Trim the Treviso, removing any dark and discolored parts on the outer leaves and stems. If heads are large, 10 ounces each, cut lengthwise into quarters, leaving stem intact; if small, 4 ounces each, cut lengthwise into halves.

Put the salt, garlic, and oil in a blender. Blend until they form a smooth purée. (Alternatively, garlic and salt may be smushed in a mortar with a pestle and oil whisked in.) Place Treviso in an 18 x 13 x 2-inch roasting pan. Pour garlic mixture over Treviso. Coat each piece well. Roast 10 minutes. Turn. Roast for 5 minutes.

Remove pan. Place anchovy fillets lengthwise in strips along the center of each piece of Treviso. Cover with mozzarella. Roast for 5 minutes more, until mozzarella is brown and melting at edges. Remove to a platter or plate.

*R*UTABAGAS

I ROASTED RUTABAGAS OUT OF A SENSE OF DUTY TO THE COMPLETENESS OF THIS BOOK. I don't generally like them. The taste is strong, and they can be stringy. Roasted rutabagas surprised me. The wedges hold their shape well and brown evenly, and their pumpkin-colored flesh looks pretty on the plate. Somehow, the flavor of the rutabaga mellows with roasting and makes a lovely contrast to the sweet richness of a roast fresh ham.

The rutabaga is also known and sold in local stores as wax turnip, yellow turnip, and Swedes. It is under-loved, perhaps because it is hard to cut and often waxed on the outside. Once rutabagas are halved, the rest of the cutting up and the peeling are fairly simple.

BASIC
RUTABAGAS

1 rutabaga (1 to 1½ pounds), cut into wedges; serves 4 to 5 as a side dish

Peel rutabaga. Cut into quarters. Cut each quarter into 1-inch-wide wedges. Place rutabaga wedges in smallest pan that will hold them comfortably. Slick wedges and pan with 1 tablespoon fat. Roast on center rack of 500°F oven for 15 minutes. Turn. Roast 20 minutes more.

TOTAL ROASTING TIME: 35 minutes

*R*oasted rutabaga wedges

SERVES 8 TO 10 AS A SIDE DISH

TOTAL
ROASTING
TIME:
35
minutes

R UTABAGAS HAVE SO much flavor that they need little seasoning. A little salt is probably enough, along with a sprinkling of malt vinegar—the slightly sweet, dark brown kind with added caramel is particularly nice—or a full-tasting red wine vinegar points up the flavor. Adjust quantities by using the instructions in Basic Rutabagas.

2 to 3 rutabagas (3 pounds), peeled
3 tablespoons olive oil

Kosher salt, to taste
3 tablespoons malt vinegar or red
    wine vinegar

Place rack in center of oven. Heat oven to 500°F.

continued

Cut rutabagas in half lengthwise. Insert the edge of the knife into the rutabaga so that it is secure. Lift up your arm, bringing the knife and rutabaga off the chopping block. Swiftly bring your arm down onto the chopping block. This momentum helps safely push the knife through. Cut each half across its width. Cut each piece into 4 to 5 wedges, each about 1 inch wide.

Put oil and rutabaga wedges into a 14 x 12 x 2-inch roasting pan. Toss until wedges are lightly coated with oil. Arrange pieces so that one flat side of each is flat down so that they touch as little as possible. Roast 15 minutes. Remove pan from oven and use a small spatula or fork to turn each piece onto its other flat side so it browns. Roast for 15 minutes more. Remove pan from oven, turning each piece onto its curved, or least brown, side. Roast for 5 minutes more. Pieces should pierce easily with the tip of a sharp knife but still be firm. Wedges will be evenly and richly browned. Sprinkle with salt and vinegar.

Roasted rutabaga picnic salad

MAKES 2½ CUPS; SERVES 2 TO 4 AS
A SIDE DISH

THIS SALAD IS zestier than a potato salad, with a prettier color than most. It is good in early fall, made with the first rutabagas. I make it when I have leftover Roasted Rutabaga Wedges (page 403). Prepare the salad the day it will be used. Leftover cooked rutabagas will keep in the refrigerator up to two days in advance. To increase the quantity of rutabaga wedges, see Basic Rutabagas (page 403).

2 cups Roasted Rutabaga Wedges (page 403), roughly cut into 1-inch dice

1 small red onion (4 ounces), peeled and cut into small dice (½ cup)

1 tablespoon Basic Mayonnaise (page 303) or store-bought

2 teaspoons fresh lemon juice

½ teaspoon kosher salt

Freshly ground black pepper, to taste

1 tablespoon Roasted Garlic Purée (page 357), optional

1 bunch (4½ ounces) watercress, cleaned and stems snapped off, plus extra to put under salad, optional

Put the rutabaga and onion in a small bowl. In a separate, smaller bowl, whisk together the mayonnaise, lemon juice, salt, pepper, and garlic purée, if using, until smooth. Pour mayonnaise mixture over rutabaga and onion. Mix gently until pieces are lightly coated.

Break off leaves of watercress. Add. Mix gently. Serve on a bed of watercress if desired.

SCALLIONS

THE CHINESE, THE JAPANESE, AND AMERICANS USE SCALLIONS. It was a shock when I had previous books converted for the British to find that the British do not. They happily use spring (green) onions, which form bulbs; baby leeks, which are straight like American scallions but are flatter and tougher and need to be cooked, like big leeks; and wild onions or wild leeks, which many of us call "ramps." I think it's a shame to be deprived of the crisp freshness of raw scallions, with the white and the green parts often used differently. Ramps can smell and taste somewhat rank when raw. Cooked, they are sweet and delicious. Cover the green leaves with some foil for part of the time so they don't dry out.

Roasted, green onions, ramps, and scallions will cook in the same way. The only thing to keep in mind is the necessity of choosing a pan just big enough to hold them flat. Turn on the exhaust fan or open a window here. Once again, members of the onion (*Allium*) family have a lot of sugar, which may caramelize and smoke.

The sweet brownness is delicious, which is why I bother with roasting. Also, roasting is easier and uses less fat than trying to get the same effect in a skillet. A grill will char the scallions before they cook through. Ramps are thin enough to cook on a grill.

BASIC
SCALLIONS

QUANTITY CAN BE increased to the limit of the size of your pan.

12 ounces scallions (20, about 4 bunches); serves 5 to 6 as a side dish

Trim root ends of scallions. Cut lengths into 8-inch-long pieces, including all of the white and some of the green. Use smallest pan that will hold scallions comfortably in a single layer. Slick scallions and pan with 2 tablespoons fat. Roast in center of 500°F oven for 8 minutes. Turn. Roast for 3 minutes more.

TOTAL ROASTING TIME: 11 minutes

Roasted, then braised scallions

SERVES 5 TO 6 AS A SIDE DISH

TOTAL
ROASTING
TIME:
16 *to* 17
minutes

IF WE THINK of the relationship between scallions and leeks, or indeed, use baby leeks, this recipe makes instant sense. I often add a little bit of lemon juice after the cooking, especially if serving the scallions cool at the start of a spring meal, much the way one serves asparagus.

1 tablespoon unsalted butter, melted

1 tablespoon olive oil

4 bunches (12 ounces) scallions (about 20), root ends trimmed and lengths cut lengthwise into 8-inch slices, including all the white and some of the green

½ cup Basic Chicken Stock (page 42) or canned

¼ teaspoon kosher salt (omit if using canned chicken broth)

Place rack in center of oven. Heat oven to 500°F.

Put butter, oil, and scallions in a 14 x 12 x 2-inch roasting pan. Turn scallions in the butter so that they are lightly coated. Roast 8 minutes. Remove pan from oven. Use a fork to turn scallions over. Return pan to oven, back to front. Roast 3 minutes more. Add stock and salt, if using, and roast 3 to 4 minutes more. If serving hot but not immediately, remove from oven after adding stock. Just before serving, roast 4 minutes longer. Serve warm or at room temperature.

Fettuccine with roasted scallion-tomato sauce

SERVES 4 AS A MAIN COURSE, 6 AS
A FIRST COURSE

TOTAL
ROASTING
TIME:
15
minutes

T HIS STARTS LIFE with some leftovers from the Basic Scallions (page 405). To serve more people, use a full recipe of scallions and double the amount of tomatoes. If the pan isn't big enough for all of the tomatoes, add a third rack to the oven. The richness of egg-noodle fettuccine is smooth and sexy with the sauce; but leaner, nonegg linguine or even angel hair is fine, although the angel hair needs a little extra oil to keep the thin strands from clumping. Don't move to a heavier pasta; the sauce is light and elegant. It can be made ahead.

2 teaspoons olive oil

6 medium ripe tomatoes (5 to 6 ounces each, 2 pounds total), cored and cut into 4 wedges

1 cup Basic Scallions (page 405), roughly snipped into 1- to 2-inch-long pieces

Kosher salt, to taste

Freshly ground black pepper, to taste

8 ounces fettuccine

If there are no leftover roasted scallions, roast the scallions and tomatoes in 2 pans at the same time. Otherwise, just proceed with the tomatoes.

Place 1 rack in upper section of oven for tomatoes. (If making roasted scallions, place another rack in the center of the oven and proceed as recipe directs.) Heat oven to 500°F.

Put oil and tomatoes in a 14 x 12 x 2-inch roasting pan. Rub wedges with the oil until all are lightly coated. Rub some of the oil onto the sides of the pan. Arrange wedges with a flat side down so they touch as little as possible. Roast for 8 minutes. Remove pan. Use a small spatula or fork to turn each wedge onto its unbrowned flat side. Return pan to oven back to front. Roast 7 minutes more.

Meanwhile bring a large covered pot of salted water to a boil for the pasta.

In a medium-size saucepan, combine the tomatoes with all the juices from the pan and the scallions with all their juices. Heat until warm throughout. Add salt and pepper.

Cook pasta. Strain. Toss with sauce.

Shallots

SHALLOT BULBS ARE USUALLY SHAPED LIKE CLOVES OF GARLIC, BUT GROW SINGLY OR TWO TOGETHER, NOT IN HEADS. Their pinkish-brown papery covering when removed reveals shallots that are either a deep lavender pink or gray. The French prefer the gray. In the United States, I see the pinkish ones almost exclusively. Along the Riviera, in Spain, Italy, and the Midi (really the South; isn't that perverse?) of France, I have bought shallots the same pinkish-red and of a similar shape, but they are huge, a full three to four inches long and are generally sliced to roast on top of fish or vegetables. I was unable to buy them near home for testing, but would expect them to roast wonderfully like the other *Alliums* and to have a cooking time somewhere between the large shallots described below and medium onions (pages 369–370).

Shallots turn a rich brown and are heavenly. I see no point in playing around with them. I serve them just as they come from the oven, as a side vegetable or as part of an hors d'oeuvre plate or a main course vegetable medley. If there are leftovers or a variation is desired, prepare as for Roasted and Marinated Cippolines (page 376).

As a side vegetable, shallots go well with Simplest Roast Chicken (page 23), Simple Roast Capon (page 51), and any of the roast lamb recipes.

BASIC SHALLOTS

BASIC THESE MAY be; but basic does not adequately describe the pleasure they give. Shallots of the size discussed first are readily available in the stores. The larger size is sometimes available and should be pounced on by all right-thinking cooks.

MEDIUM SHALLOTS

1 pound shallots (18 to 20, about 1 ounce each), peeled; serves 4 to 6 as a side dish

Peel and trim shallots (3 cups). Use smallest pan that will hold shallots comfortably in a single layer. Slick shallots with 1 tablespoon olive oil. Roast on lowest level of 500°F oven for 5 minutes. Shake pan to move shallots around. Roast another 10 minutes. Remove pan from oven. Turn. Return pan to oven back to front. Roast 5 minutes more.

TOTAL ROASTING TIME: 20 minutes

LARGE SHALLOTS

These are the *Allium* lover's equivalent of caviar. They all get eaten. Use a smaller pan and the same timing if there are fewer shallots. I use olive oil, as butter may burn.

4½ pounds large shallots (32, about 2¼ ounces each) peeled; serves 10 to 12 as a side dish

Peel and trim shallots (10 cups). Use smallest pan that will hold shallots comfortably in a single layer. Slick shallots and pan with ¼ cup olive oil. Roast on lowest level of 500°F oven for 5 minutes. Shake pan to move shallots around. Roast for another 10 minutes. Remove pan from oven. Turn. Return pan to oven, back to front. Roast 15 minutes more.

TOTAL ROASTING TIME: 30 minutes

Spring onions: see Scallions

Summer squashes

WHILE ZUCCHINI ARE ALSO SUMMER SQUASH, I THOUGHT MOST PEOPLE WOULD LOOK FOR THEM UNDER "ZUCCHINI," THOUGH SOME MAY LOOK UNDER COURGETTES. The material here refers to yellow crooknecks, with the knobbly skin, and the smoother yellow squash. There is one odd thing about yellow squashes; it is almost impossible to overcook them. That doesn't hold true for yellow zucchini, another squash entirely.

BASIC
YELLOW
SUMMER
SQUASHES

THE EASIEST WAY to remove the seeds is to scrape them out with a teaspoon. If they are obdurate, run the tip of a knife lengthwise along both sides of the seeds; then scrape.

2 pounds yellow summer squash (4, about 8 ounces each); serves 4 as a side dish

Trim each squash. Cut each across in half. Cut each half lengthwise into 4 pieces. Remove seeds. Use smallest pan that will hold squash comfortably in a single layer. Slick pieces and pan with ¼ cup fat. Add ¼ cup water or stock. Roast on upper level of 500°F oven for 15 minutes. Turn. Roast 15 minutes more.

TOTAL ROASTING TIME: 30 minutes

Roasted yellow squashes in a mint bath

SERVES 6 TO 8 AS PART OF A FIRST COURSE
OR MAIN COURSE

TOTAL
ROASTING
TIME:
45
minutes

THIS IS AS fresh-tasting as summer and just as attractive. I like it best at room temperature as an addition to an antipasto platter or as part of a vegetarian main course.

The preparation can be done up to eight hours ahead, with the squash left to marinate, covered, at room temperature. It is extremely important to have the oven rack in the top position. A panful of roasted Basic Asparagus (page 318) or Roasted Cherry Tomatoes with Basil (page 419) could be slipped onto the center rack of the oven for the last twelve minutes of the roasting time, and a pan of Basic Shallots (page 408) onto the bottom rack for the last fifteen minutes of roasting. This would make a stunning assortment as an accompaniment or first course.

4 medium yellow summer squash
    (2 pounds), trimmed, each cut across
    in half and each half cut lengthwise
    into 4 pieces, seeds scooped out
¼ cup fresh lemon juice

¼ cup olive oil
¼ cup tightly packed fresh mint leaves,
    chopped medium-fine
1 teaspoon kosher salt

Place rack in top level of oven. Heat oven to 500°F.

Check slices of squash to see that pieces are not larger than 5 inches long by 1¼ inches wide. Any larger and the squash will not cook evenly.

In a small bowl, combine the lemon juice, oil, mint, and salt. Pour into a 14 x 12 x 2-inch roasting pan. Arrange squashes in pan, with thinner pieces in the center of the pan and larger pieces around the edges, so that squashes fit tightly and don't leave a lot of surface space showing. Roll the squashes in the oil mixture. Roast 30 minutes. Remove pan from oven. Use a fork or a spatula to turn pieces over. Roast 15 minutes more. May be served warm from the oven, or made ahead and served at room temperature.

WINTER SQUASHES

WINTER SQUASHES SUCH AS DELICATA, GOLDEN NUGGET, AND SWEET DUMPLING ARE BETTER BAKED THAN ROASTED.

There are two exceptions: sliced buttercup and acorn squash for very basic preparation either as a side vegetable or as an ingredient.

Summer squashes roast well. Use the instructions for Basic Yellow Summer Squashes (page 409), or, for the very tender summer squashes, emulate Zucchini (page 424).

All the seeds roast to be a splendid, nutrition-filled treat. See page 413.

Acorn squash

THERE COMES A time toward the very end of summer when I hate my acorn squashes. Their vines trail everywhere, like those of other members of the very American *Curcurbita* family. The heavy fruits roll over everything that gets in their way. I am moved to wonder if the Narragansett Indians, who named squash, practiced a form of humorous oenomatopoeia. Come midwinter, when the perfect, glossy, dark gourds are a little splotched with orange and still loyally waiting to be cooked, I bless them.

BASIC
ACORN
SQUASH

GENRALLY SPEAKING, I find that acorn squash is best baked or cooked in a microwave oven. Sometimes I want to prepare acorn squash simply, without adding butter and maple syrup or any other sweetness, to get flesh that serves as an ingredient—not watery, as from the microwave—instead of a potato. Then, I roast.

When it is difficult to get the squash to sit still and not roll in the pan, cut off a tiny slice at the bottom (blossom end) of each half.

1 whole acorn squash (1½ pounds); serves 2 as a side dish

Cut squash in half and remove seeds. Use smallest pan that will hold halves comfortably. Brush cavity of each half with ½ teaspoon fat. Roast, flesh side up, on center rack of 500°F oven for 40 to 45 minutes. When done, squash pierces easily with the tip of a sharp knife.

TOTAL ROASTING TIME: 40 to 45 minutes

Roasted buttercup squash with chile oil

SERVES 3 TO 4 AS A SIDE DISH

TOTAL
ROASTING
TIME:
15 *to* 20
minutes

THESE SMALL, DARK green squashes, deeply ribbed, with a paler green top knot like a brioche, may be dappled with orange. Cut across into slices, they make a pretty and unusual roasted vegetable. Slicked with a little fat and sprinkled with salt and pepper, they are simple and good. Add a little more fat and more seasonings and it's a standout. While I have used chili powder to season the slices when serving with roast pork, good alternatives are ground cumin, ground anise to accompany fish, or a little bit of ground cinnamon and nutmeg to go with southern Mediterranean food.

Having tried a version with sugar on the slices, I can report that the taste and browning did not improve. The sugar gets very hot and splatters—not a good idea.

1 whole buttercup squash (1 pound), halved, seeded, and cut across into 16 slices

3 to 4 tablespoons canola or other neutral oil

1½ teaspoons chili powder

½ teaspoon kosher salt

Freshly ground black pepper, to taste

Peel squash slices with a sharp paring knife.

Place rack in center of oven. Heat oven to 500°F.

Place slices in a 12 x 8 x 1½-inch roasting pan. Combine oil, chili powder, salt, and pepper. Toss with squash slices. Roast for 5 minutes. Shake pan to turn more pieces. Roast 5 minutes more. Shake pan again. Roast 5 to 10 minutes more.

IF TIME ALLOWS, letting seeds dry will shorten the roasting time. This works for any seeds. Peek from time to time to make sure they are not getting too brown. Timing varies with the kind of seed and the amount of moisture. The ideal result is a golden toasty color with the seeds cooked through. The amount of salt is up to you. To serve as a snack with a drink, more salt gets more drinkers.

As soon as the seeds have been removed from the squash, put them into a sieve and run cold water over them, rubbing them gently to remove as much sticky surrounding fiber as possible. This can be done while the squash is cooking, or before. If the seeds are left sitting around too long, it is hard to remove the fiber. Drain and place on several sheets of paper towel. Rub some more with extra paper toweling if need be to remove remaining fiber. Allow to dry.

1 pound buttercup squash; yields about ½ to ¾ cup toasted seeds

Remove fibers from seeds. Rinse. Dry. Use smallest pan that will hold seeds comfortably in a single layer. Slick seeds and pan with 1 tablespoon canola oil. Roast in center of 400°F oven for 10 minutes. Turn. Roast for 5 minutes more. If necessary, turn again and roast for 5 to 10 minutes more.

TOTAL ROASTING TIME: 15 to 25 minutes

Adelle's favorite roasted seeds

MAKES ¾ CUP

TOTAL
ROASTING
TIME:
20 *to* 25
minutes

THROUGHOUT MEXICO, THIS is a favorite salty snack, usually made with pumpkin seeds. Adelle serves them in a beautiful blue and white Mexican pottery bowl and ushers them in with sangria and margaritas. A small saucer filled with cut limes is always brought along to squeeze over the spicy seeds. Don't squeeze the juice on ahead of time; the seeds get soggy.

The amount and strength of chili powder (a clear red, without cumin or other added seasonings) is a question of taste. It makes sense to make a bigger batch of these; multiply the recipe as needed. Roasted seeds can be left at room temperature for a day or so or stored in a covered jar in the refrigerator for months. If refrigerated, toast in microwave oven or at 300°F in a conventional oven just until warm.

¾ cup squash seeds, fibers removed, rinsed	½ teaspoon salt
	½ to ¾ teaspoon pure chili powder
1 tablespoon canola oil	1 lime, halved and seeded

Place rack in center of oven. Heat oven to 500°F.

Put seeds in a 12 x 8 x 1½-inch roasting pan. Drizzle with oil, rubbing to lightly coat the seeds and pan with oil. Sprinkle salt and chili powder over seeds. Roast for 10 minutes. Scoop up and turn seeds over with a spatula. Roast 10 to 15 minutes more. To serve, squeeze lime juice over seeds.

SUNCHOKES (JERUSALEM ARTICHOKES)

A NATIVE-AMERICAN FOOD, BEING PROMOTED AS "SUNCHOKES," THIS IS A TUBER THAT IS NEITHER FROM JERUSALEM NOR AN ARTICHOKE. It grows prolifically and has often been used as cattle feed. In France, during World War II, Jerusalem artichokes were one of the few readily available foods. Cattle and famine have probably given these a bad name, along with the fact that these ovoid tubers used to be knobby and hard to peel. In their new sunchoke incarnation, they have become quite smooth.

They are at their best during cold weather and store well. The season is from late September through February.

These starchy little tubers serve the same purpose on a plate as potatoes, but have a more assertive flavor. Like turnips, they balance rich foods such as duck.

BASIC
SUNCHOKES

1 pound Jerusalem artichokes (about 24 pieces); serves 4 to 6 as a side dish

Peel sunchokes. Cut pieces that are larger than 1-inch long in half lengthwise. Use smallest pan that will hold sunchokes comfortably in a single layer. Slick sunchokes and pan with 2 teaspoons olive oil. Roast in center of 500°F oven for 8 minutes. Turn. Roast 8 minutes more.

TOTAL ROASTING TIME: 16 minutes

Crispy, creamy roasted Jerusalems

SERVES 4 TO 6 AS A SIDE DISH

TOTAL
ROASTING
TIME:
16
minutes

Fʀᴏᴍ ᴀᴄʀᴏss ᴛʜᴇ table these look like pommes soufflées, but they offer a surprise. The teeth crunch through the firm, crisp crust to sink into soft and floury centers.

If the available Jerusalem artichokes are longer than an inch, cook them five minutes longer, until done all the way through and rid of any green taste.

1 pound Jerusalem artichokes (about 24 pieces, each about 1 inch long), peeled and any larger pieces halved lengthwise	2 teaspoons olive oil Kosher salt, to taste Freshly ground black pepper, to taste

Place rack in center of oven. Heat oven to 500°F.

Put artichoke pieces and oil in a pan just large enough to hold them. Rub pieces with oil until lightly covered. Roast for 8 minutes. Shake pan vigorously to turn pieces. Roast 8 minutes more. Pieces should be a very dark brown. Sprinkle with salt and pepper to taste. Serve right away.

*t*ᴏᴍᴀᴛᴏᴇs

Tᴏᴍᴀᴛᴏᴇs ᴏғ ᴀʟʟ sᴏʀᴛs ʀᴏᴀsᴛ ᴡᴏɴᴅᴇʀғᴜʟʟʏ ᴛᴏ ʙᴇ ᴇᴀᴛᴇɴ ᴀs ᴀ sɪᴅᴇ ᴅɪsʜ ᴏɴ ᴛʜᴇɪʀ ᴏᴡɴ ᴏʀ ᴛᴏ ʙᴇ ᴜsᴇᴅ ɪɴ sᴏᴜᴘs, sᴛᴇᴡs, ᴀɴᴅ sᴀᴜᴄᴇs. Whole roasted tomatoes are a common ingredient in stocks. Roasting adds color and a dimension of flavor to what is already an extraordinary food. When tomatoes are less than ideal (even green at the center)—as they are for a major part of the year—roasting concentrates their flavor and provides a better alternative to canned tomatoes for many uses.

It is hard to be as precise as I would like to be with these recipes because at different times of the year, tomatoes will vary in size, flavor, and amount of juice. If the tomatoes are wonderfully ripe, reduce the amount of oil and cooking time slightly. Check for tinges of brown on skins that are crinkly and stop roasting. If using midwinter plum tomatoes, roast them until they crack.

All tomatoes roast better whole in the skin than cut or peeled. For cut tomatoes, top-of-the-stove cooking, or medium- to low-temperature baking or broiling are the routes to go. Once tomatoes have been roasted, it is easy to peel them by pulling off the skins as soon as the tomatoes are cool enough to touch.

To make a seedless, skinless sauce: Roast the tomatoes whole and purée through a food mill. All sizes and colors of tomatoes can be used for sauce, varying flavor, and allure. Timing for roasting tomatoes goes by the size and shape of the tomato.

I wouldn't be surprised if tomatoes were found to be the world's most popular vegetable. They erupted out of Central America in many colors, sizes, and shapes to take over Italian cooking and have spread their flavors and seeds to India, China, Africa, and the world at large. Even in England, where the amount of sun hours is not propitious to the ripening of tomatoes, most home gardeners still attempt to grow them. In the United States, tomatoes are the favorite vegetable (yes, I know, fruit) for home growing. Over the years many kinds of tomatoes have been hybridized, and the recent, laudable interest in heirloom seeds has expanded the sorts available.

The three main sorts of tomato are cherry (small and round or Shmoo-shaped like pears), plum (midsize and ovoid), and the enormous variety of larger tomatoes, other than those two, that are used for cooking and eating raw. All can vary in color from pale green—usually not ripe but good—through yellow, gold, and orange to reds of various hues and on to colors that are really purple or purple brown. Yellow and golden tomatoes generally have less acidity, which is good for some people's stomachs, but not for all dishes and not for canning.

Cherry tomatoes, particularly the very smallest, are generally eaten raw as a snack. Sometimes, instead of being popped into mouths they are popped raw into salads as a booby trap for the unwary eater. We seldom think of cooking them. I start cooking them in early summer, when they are the first tomatoes ripe in the garden. In winter, the best tomatoes I have had were the somewhat larger cherry tomatoes still on the vine, imported from Italy at great price. All the cherry tomatoes, including the pear-shaped ones, roast wonderfully and make an especially sweet sauce. Once roasted and put throught the fine screen of a food mill, each three pounds of cherry tomatoes will give about two and a half cups purée. You may want to reduce the purée somewhat on top of the stove for a better consistency.

Plum tomatoes have a high flesh-to-juice-and-seed ratio, good for use in sauces and purées. These are the sort found in cans marked "Roma" or "San Marzano." Roast away.

The variability among the round larger tomatoes, from "Big Boys" to beefsteaks, is huge not only in size, color, and flavor, but in the ratio of flesh and juice to seeds and skin. So it is impossible to give accurate yields of purée for all. For a sort of medium yield, each five pounds of tomatoes that are roasted and put through the fine screen of a food mill will give about eight cups of purée. It can be reduced somewhat on top of the stove for a better consistency.

BASIC
TOMATOES

WHOLE CHERRY TOMATOES, SMALL TOMATOES, AND EXTRA-LARGE TOMATOES

The smallest cherry tomatoes take only twenty to twenty-five minutes to roast, but larger cherry tomatoes, the kind on the stem in the stores in the winter, and small regular tomatoes take twenty-five to thirty minutes.

The commonly available basket of cherry tomatoes weighs about a pound and a quarter and contains approximately twenty tomatoes. A pound and a half fits in a small pan (12 x 8 x 1½ inches). Five pounds fills my largest pan (18 x 13 x 2 inches). If puréed through a food mill for an intense orange-colored sauce, the larger amount of roasted tomatoes will make about six cups. Greater amounts of tomatoes need a little more oil. The skins pop off easily after roasting. But why bother?

Summer, when tomatoes are really ripe, is the only time to roast most regular tomatoes, unless a couple are roasted along with other ingredients to add to a stock. Eight-ounce tomatoes will cook in twenty minutes or less and need little oil. They are an excellent vegetable hot or cool, skins on or off, with roast chicken or fish. Sprinkle with salt, pepper, finely cut fresh basil, chives, dill, or lemon balm. I don't think they need anything else; but butter or cream can be added when serving hot and a little olive oil when serving cold.

Stores don't normally sell tomatoes that weigh a pound each; but I can't resist boasting a little about those from my garden. I simply slip the skins off these and serve them, one per person, slathered with herbs, salt, pepper, and a tiny bit of olive oil on a bed of watercress.

1½ pounds cherry tomatoes (4 cups); serves 6 as a side dish

5 pounds cherry tomatoes (about 90, ¾ ounce each); serves 20 as a side dish (makes 6¼ cups purée)

5 pounds small tomatoes (10, about 8 ounces each); serves 10 as a side dish

6 pounds extra-large whole tomatoes (6, about 1 pound each); serves 6 as a side dish or first course

Remove stems. Use smallest pan that will hold tomatoes comfortably in a single layer. For 1½ pounds cherry tomatoes or 8-ounce or 1-pound tomatoes, slick tomatoes and pan with 1 tablespoon fat; for 5 pounds cherry tomatoes, use 2 tablespoons fat. Roast in center of 500°F oven for 10 minutes. Shake pan. Roast another 10 minutes. Shake pan. If using extra-large tomatoes, turn. Roast 5 to 10 minutes more.

TOTAL ROASTING TIME: 20 to 30 minutes

CHERRY TOMATO PURÉE: Place food mill fitted with finest disc over a bowl or pot. Force tomatoes through mill. From time to time, stop to scrape bottom of disc with rubber spatula to allow all tomatoes to pass through mill. Purée may be used as is, reduced over very low heat to thicken further, or stored in the freezer in airtight containers for 3 to 4 months.

WHOLE PLUM TOMATOES

Roasted plum tomatoes merit separate instructions because they are so often used in recipes and, when time is available, in sauce. When they are puréed through a food mill, the result is richly red.

In summer, when plum tomatoes are riper and sweeter, roasting may take only twenty minutes. In winter, when tomatoes are harder, they take five minutes longer. Two pounds of plum tomatoes will fit in a small (12 x 8 x 1½-inch) pan. Six pounds fill a large (18 x 13 x 2-inch) pan.

Since I often use these as a replacement for the inferior canned plum tomatoes, I find it useful to know the yield for different sizes of canned tomatoes. A fourteen-ounce can will make a cup and a half of mush for sauce after draining off a cup of liquid. A twenty-eight-ounce can, as you might suspect, makes twice as much.

2 pounds plum tomatoes (about 12, 2 to 4 ounces each); makes 2 cups cooked (3 cups purée)

6 pounds plum tomatoes (about 36, 2 to 4 ounces each); makes 6¼ cups cooked (9¼ cups purée)

Remove stems. Use smallest pan that will hold tomatoes comfortably. Slick tomatoes and pan with 1 to 3 tablespoons fat. Roast in center of 500°F oven for 10 minutes. Shake pan. Roast for 10 minutes more.

TOTAL ROASTING TIME: 20 minutes

PLUM TOMATO PURÉE: Place food mill fitted with finest disc over a bowl or pot. Force tomatoes through mill. From time to time, stop to scrape bottom of disc with rubber spatula to allow all tomatoes to pass through the mill. Purée may be used as is, reduced over very low heat to thicken further, or stored in the freezer in airtight containers for 3 to 4 months.

Roasted cherry tomatoes with basil

SERVES 3 AS A SIDE DISH

TOTAL ROASTING TIME: **25** *minutes*

MEDIUM TO LARGE cherry tomatoes make an extraordinary vegetable when roasted. Thinly sliced strips of basil, tossed in after the tomatoes have cooked, wilt and give a welcome peppery taste.

Garlic lovers can add six unpeeled cloves. The tomatoes will be soft and have a smoky, roasted flavor.

1½ pounds cherry tomatoes, stemmed (4 cups)

1½ tablespoons olive oil

Scant ½ teaspoon kosher salt

2 tablespoons basil leaves, stacked in piles, rolled up, and thinly sliced across

Place rack in center of oven. Heat oven to 500°F. Place tomatoes in smallest pan that will hold them comfortably. Drizzle oil over tomatoes. Rub the oil over the tomatoes and pan. Sprinkle with salt. Roast 10 minutes. Shake the pan to move the tomatoes around. Roast 15 minutes more. Remove. Add the basil. Toss lightly. Serve warm.

Roasted plum tomato sauce

MAKES 2¼ CUPS

TOTAL ROASTING TIME: **20** *to* **25** *minutes*

THIS SAUCE, INTENTIONALLY coarse in texture and robust in taste, is good year-round on pasta that has been tossed with a little extra olive oil or over cold leftover roast fish or chicken.

8 to 16 plum tomatoes (2 to 4 ounces each, 2 pounds total) and

1 tablespoon olive oil or

One 14-ounce can plum tomatoes, drained

1½ teaspoons kosher salt

2 tablespoons olive oil

1½ tablespoons tomato paste

2 cloves garlic, smashed, peeled, and minced

If using fresh tomatoes: Place rack in center of oven. Heat oven to 500°F.

Place tomatoes in a 12 x 8 x 1½-inch roasting pan. Drizzle 1 tablespoon of the oil over tomatoes. Rub tomatoes to lightly coat with oil. Roast 10 minutes. Shake pan to move tomatoes around. Roast 10 to 15 minutes more.

Cool 10 minutes. Slip off skins and remove hard stem end from each tomato. Place tomatoes in a medium bowl.

Whichever tomatoes used, crush them into a thick chunky purée by squeezing repeatedly through fingers. Add the salt, 2 tablespoons oil, tomato paste, and garlic. Combine well.

Cool, creamy roasted tomato soup

MAKES 8 CUPS; SERVES 8

TOTAL
ROASTING
TIME:
25
minutes

THIS IS REALLY a summer soup and depends on wonderful ingredients and the hot day or evening that makes cold soup a treasure. If smaller tomatoes are used, the timing will be different (see Basic Tomatoes, page 417).

The flavor evoked by roasting the tomatoes is amazing. When they're simply puréed, it seems too good to be true. Serve this soup with confidence to even the pickiest critics. It's a silky bit of heaven with the cream. For someone on a major no-fat regime, use a bit of nonfat yogurt or nothing at all in place of the cream.

6 large tomatoes (5 pounds, ¾ to 1 pound each total), cored

4 cloves garlic, unpeeled

1 tablespoon olive oil

2 teaspoons kosher salt

¼ cup water, optional

Freshly ground black pepper, to taste

2 tablespoons chopped fresh mint, plus leaves for garnish

3 tablespoons snipped or finely chopped fresh chives

1 cup heavy cream, optional

Place rack in center of oven. Heat oven to 500°F.

Put tomatoes and garlic in a 12 x 8 x 1½-inch roasting pan. Add oil. Rub oil all over tomatoes, garlic, and bottom of pan. Sprinkle with salt. Roast for 15 minutes. Turn tomatoes over and pour in water if there is not plenty of juice in the pan or if the garlic is getting too brown, or almost black. Roast 10 minutes more.

Remove pan. Place a food mill, fitted with a fine mesh, over a large bowl. Pour entire contents of pan into food mill. Strain garlic, tomatoes, and all the juice through the mill. Be sure to strain through all the yummy juices at the end—there is lots of flavor there. Add pepper. Let cool to room temperature, then refrigerate. Liquid may be made ahead and held at this stage for 1 or 2 days, tightly covered in the refrigerator.

When ready to serve the well-chilled soup, stir in the mint, chives, and cream, mixing well. Top each serving with a sprig of mint.

Roasted curry tomato soup

MAKES 9 ½ CUPS; SERVES 8

TOTAL
ROASTING
TIME:
25
minutes

A WARMING SOUP to serve hot or cold, this is fairly spicy. I would tend to leave the seasonings as is when making to serve well chilled. A dollop of sour cream or low-fat yogurt can be put on top of each serving to minimize the spiciness which, in any case, is much less pronounced when the soup is cold. If guests like only mild spices, reduce the curry powder to a quarter cup and the paprika to two tablespoons.

This can even be made well with the hard, pinkish plum tomatoes, running about two ounces each, that are found throughout the winter. In summer, when tomatoes are riper, cook them five minutes less.

1 head garlic, separated into cloves and
  unpeeled

20 to 24 plum tomatoes (2 to 4 ounces
  each, 4 pounds total)

2 medium onions (1 pound), peeled and
  chopped fine (2½ cups)

2 tablespoons olive oil

2 tablespoons kosher salt, or less if using
  canned broth

⅓ cup curry powder

3 tablespoons sweet paprika

3 cups Basic Chicken Stock (page 42)
  or canned

3 tablespoons fresh lemon juice

Place rack in center of oven. Heat oven to 500°F.

Put garlic, tomatoes, and onions in an 18 x 13 x 2-inch roasting pan. Drizzle with the oil. Toss until vegetables are lightly coated. Sprinkle with salt. Roast for 10 minutes. Remove pan from oven. Add curry and paprika. Toss and turn vegetables with a metal spatula. Roast for 15 minutes more.

Place food mill with finest disc over a large non-reactive pot. Pour half the pan's contents into the mill. Stop from time to time to scrape off the bottom of the disc with a rubber spatula. Add chicken stock to purée and bring just to the boil. Stir, scraping bottom of pan so that purée does not stick. Reduce heat to medium and cook until hot throughout. Remove from heat and add lemon juice. Taste for salt.

*t*URNIPS

TURNIPS GET SHORT SHRIFT IN MOST KITCHENS, WHICH IS A PITY. Young turnips are delicious thinly sliced when eaten raw, or cut into wedges and deep-fat fried. Old and woody turnips are really only good for mashing.

Young, middle-aged, and even old turnips (as long as they have not gotten woody) are delicious roasted. Do not roast them sliced; it just doesn't work. Do eat them as soon as they come out of the oven and are crisp and delicious. As they sit, they get mushy.

BASIC
TURNIPS

TURNIPS HAVE LOTS of flavor and need little else to be added. They are also a good addition to stews such as lamb. Butter will give the turnips a deeper glaze than oil, but canola or olive oil will be more healthful and neutral.

DICED TURNIPS

2 pounds turnips (8, about 4 ounces each); serves 3 to 6 as a side dish
(makes 3 cups cooked)

Trim and peel turnips. Cut into ½-inch dice. Use smallest pan that will hold pieces comfortably. Slick turnip pieces and pan with 2 tablespoons fat. Roast on lowest level of 500°F oven for 10 minutes. Turn. Roast 15 minutes more.

TOTAL ROASTING TIME: 25 minutes

TURNIP WEDGES

2 pounds turnips (8, about 4 ounces each); serves 3 to 6 as a side dish

Trim and peel turnips. Cut in half lengthwise. Cut each half into 3 wedges (48 wedges total). Use smallest pan that will hold wedges comfortably in a single layer. Slick wedges and pan with 2 tablespoons fat. Roast in center of 500°F oven for 15 minutes. Turn. Roast another 7 minutes. Turn. Roast 5 minutes more.

TOTAL ROASTING TIME: 27 minutes

NOTE: See Roasted Vegetable Combination (page 379).

Tamari turnips

SERVES 6 AS A SIDE DISH

TOTAL
ROASTING
TIME:
25
minutes

THIS QUICKLY ROASTED turnip recipe to serve tepid uses tamari soy sauce as a base for a somewhat Japanese flavor, good with Roast Pork Loin with Asian Glaze (page 167), Roasted Coho Salmon (page 247), or Simple Roasted Scallops (page 290).

2 tablespoons canola or other neutral oil

About 6 turnips (2 pounds), trimmed, peeled, and roughly cut into ½-inch-thick pieces

2½ ounces fresh gingerroot, trimmed, peeled, and chopped into medium pieces

2 tablespoons tamari soy sauce

2 tablespoons mirin

3 tablespoons rice wine vinegar

Place rack in lowest level of oven. Heat oven to 500°F.

Put oil and turnip pieces in a 14 x 12 x 2-inch roasting pan. Toss until pieces are lightly coated with the oil. Roast 15 minutes. Remove from oven. Use a spatula to toss and turn pieces well: Move the pieces nearest the edge of the pan into the center and those in the center to the outer edges to get maximum browning. Roast 10 minutes more. When done, turnips should be easily pierced with the tip of a sharp knife, but still firm.

While the turnips are roasting, combine gingerroot, tamari soy sauce, mirin, and vinegar in a blender. Blend until smooth.

Place turnips in a medium bowl. Pour liquid over turnip pieces while they are still warm. Toss lightly to combine. Cool to room temperature, tossing occasionally, and serve.

Honey-glazed turnip wedges

SERVES 4 AS A SIDE DISH

TOTAL
ROASTING
TIME:
27
minutes

THE OUTSIDES OF these wedges develop a honey-bear brown crunch encasing the floury soft inside. The sweet glaze brings out the full turnip flavor.

2 tablespoons olive oil

3 turnips (about 4 ounces each, 12 ounces total), trimmed and peeled

½ cup honey

1 tablespoon hot water

Pinch of ground cinnamon

Pinch of ground nutmeg

¼ teaspoon kosher salt

Place rack in center of oven. Heat to 500°F. Pour oil into a 12 x 8 x 1½-inch roasting pan. Swirl oil in pan until bottom is evenly covered.

Cut turnips in half. Cut each half into 3 wedges. Roll wedges in oil until evenly covered. Arrange wedges with a flat side touching the pan, each wedge touching the others as little as possible.

Roast 15 minutes. Remove from oven. Use a fork to turn each piece over onto the other flat side, and return pan to oven back to front.

Roast 7 minutes more. While wedges are roasting, combine the remaining ingredients in a small measuring cup. Blend well with a small whisk. Reserve.

Remove turnips from oven. Pour reserved honey mixture over wedges. Gently toss until well coated. Arrange wedges so that curved sides touch the pan. Roast for 5 minutes more. When done, turnips should be easily pierced with the tip of a sharp knife. Remove to platter. Serve right away.

ZUCCHINI

ZUCCHINI ARE SLIM, STRAIGHT SUMMER SQUASH, BEST EATEN BEFORE THEY GET TOO LARGE AND THE SEEDS BECOME OVERLY PROMINENT. The most frequently seen zucchini are green; but there are very good yellow ones as well. Related squash are the long, somewhat serpentine southern Italian cocozzelle or gogozze that can be grown at home. These are too large to be roasted whole, but they can be cut in pieces or sliced and cooked according to the instructions for Whole Zucchini.

WHOLE ZUCCHINI

Timing is for small to medium zucchini, which use very little fat. Roasted in olive oil and cooled, these make a pleasant addition to an antipasto or main-course vegetable medley. Sprinkle with salt when serving.

3½ pounds zucchini (8 small to medium, 6 to 8 ounces each); serves 8

Trim zucchini of hard stem on blossom end. Use smallest pan that will hold zucchini comfortably in a single layer. Slick zucchini and pan with 2 teaspoons fat. Roast in center of 500°F oven for 15 minutes. Turn. Roast 10 to 15 minutes more until well-browned.

TOTAL ROASTING TIME: 25 to 30 minutes

ZUCCHINI HALVES

These taste particularly creamy with melted butter as the fat.

3½ pounds zucchini (8 small to medium, 6 to 8 ounces each), halved; serves 8 as a side dish

Trim zucchini of hard stem on blossom end. Cut in half lengthwise. Use smallest pan that will hold zucchini comfortably in a single layer. Slick zucchini and pan with 3 to 4 tablespoons fat. Roast in center of 500°F oven for 15 minutes. Turn. Roast 10 to 15 minutes more.

TOTAL ROASTING TIME: 25 to 30 minutes

ZUCCHINI SLICES

1 pound zucchini (2 small to medium, 6 to 8 ounces each), sliced; serves 2 as a side dish (makes 1¼ cups cooked)

Trim zucchini of hard stem on blossom end. Cut across into ½-inch-thick slices (2½ cups). Use smallest pan that will hold zucchini comfortably. Slick zucchini and pan with 1 tablespoon fat. Roast in center of 500°F oven for 10 minutes. Turn. Roast another 10 minutes. Turn. Roast 10 minutes more.

TOTAL ROASTING TIME: 30 minutes

NOTE: See Roasted Vegetable Towers (page 346).

ZUCCHINI CHUNKS

2 pounds zucchini (4 to 5 small to medium, 6 to 8 ounces each); serves 4 as a side dish (makes 4 cups cooked)

Trim zucchini of hard stem on blossom end. Cut into quarters lengthwise. Cut quarters across into 1½-inch pieces (about 8 cups). Use smallest pan that will hold chunks comfortably. Slick zucchini and pan with 1 tablespoon fat. Roast on center rack of 500°F oven for 10 minutes. Shake pan to move pieces. Roast 10 minutes more. If not planning to serve immediately, roast slightly less time as the retained heat continues to cook the zucchini chunks, making them soft and mushy.

TOTAL ROASTING TIME: 20 minutes

Zucchini chunks with citrus and mint

SERVES 4 AS A SIDE DISH

TOTAL
ROASTING
TIME:
20
minutes

4 to 5 zucchini (2 pounds), trimmed, quartered lengthwise, and cut across into 1½-inch-long chunks

1 tablespoon canola or other neutral oil

1 teaspoon kosher salt, plus ½ teaspoon, optional

2 tablespoons fresh orange juice

2 teaspoons fresh lemon juice

2 tablespoons chopped (medium-fine) fresh mint leaves

Freshly ground black pepper, to taste

Place rack in center of oven. Heat oven to 500°F.

Place zucchini chunks in a 14 x 12 x 2-inch roasting pan. Toss with the oil and the 1 teaspoon of salt.

Roast 10 minutes. Shake pan vigorously to move pieces around in pan. Roast 10 minutes more. If not planning to serve immediately, roast slightly less time as the retained heat continues to cook the zucchini chunks, making them soft and mushy.

Transfer zucchini and roasting liquid to a medium-sized bowl. Add orange juice, lemon juice, mint, and black pepper. Stir to combine. Taste and add the remaining salt, if using.

Roasted zucchini halves with dilled lemon oil

TOTAL
ROASTING
TIME:
30
minutes

MAKES 16 HALVES; SERVES 6 TO 8 AS
A SIDE DISH

Pair this vegetable with the Roasted Flank Steak (page 142) and Basic Mushrooms: Portobellos (page 362). Each cooks on a different rack level, all in the same oven. Dinner is a one-oven affair. The roasted zucchini can be made a few hours ahead and reheated in a 500°F oven for about 5 minutes. Add a few more minutes to get them even browner.

Eight zucchini make sixteen halves, which usually feed eight guests. To feed a few more, a large pan can hold up to ten zucchini, using the same amount of marinade. To make a smaller amount, fill a small roasting pan with four zucchini and use half the marinade.

8 small zucchini (3½ pounds), trimmed	3 tablespoons olive oil
½ tablespoon fresh lemon juice	1½ teaspoons kosher salt
1 bunch (1½ ounces) fresh dill, thick ends of stems removed	Freshly ground black pepper, to taste

Cut zucchini in half lengthwise. Using a small kitchen knife, deeply score the flesh in a diamond pattern. For the best results, make a sawing motion with the knife to cut the flesh. If the bottom is pierced in a few spots, it won't matter. Put halves, skin side down, in an 18 x 13 x 2-inch roasting pan.

Put the remaining ingredients in a blender. Whirl until smooth. Using a rubber spatula, scrape out all the flavored oil over the zucchini. Thoroughly rub oil into each piece, making sure to smush it into each slit. Leave to marinate at room temperature, turning occasionally, for at least 1 hour, or if there is time, up to 6 hours.

About 20 minutes before roasting the zucchini, place rack in center of oven. Heat oven to 500°F. Arrange halves in pan cut sides up so that liquid drools in. Roast 15 minutes. Turn halves over. Roast for 15 minutes more. Serve hot or at room temperature.

SOME FRUITS

These are what I think of as fruits until someone comes along to tell me that they are really vegetables: pears flushed with rose and gold; peaches, fuzzy and sweetly perfumed; and pineapples spurting juice from their harsh, spiny shells. All fruits do not roast well. Bake apples; the skin turns leathery if roasted, and if peeled, the flesh turns to mush. Roasting is fine for applesauce or for apple sections that golden glow brown next to roast meat, but it's not for a whole fruit.

Fruit for roasting must have skins that are pleasant when roasted—peaches; or the fruit must retain its shape when peeled and roasted—pears; or the peel like that of papaya and pineapple must act like a container for the roasted flesh.

Unlike other foods for roasting, fruits do not need to be at their ripe peak, which is a good thing as so much of the fruit in stores is less than perfect. However, the fruit should not be blemished. Roasting concentrates the flavor of the fruit by evaporating water and by caramelizing natural sugars. The fruits will taste as if they are much better than nature has created them; but better is better and will give more succulence.

Most roasted fruits are coated with a glaze which may be sweet or savory. The fruits can be served as a dessert or as an accompaniment to meats like duck, pork, and game. The taste is rich, but only a small amount of fat is added to aid in glazing. The glaze is usually spooned over the fruit one or more times during the roasting. Take this opportunity to turn the pan in the oven; most ovens have hot spots. If the fat is butter, the fruit will taste much better eaten warm. If the fruit is to be served as a dessert, it can normally be roasted while the main course is being eaten. If it is being used as an accompaniment to a main course, roast on another shelf in the same oven, or precook and reheat.

Glazes can be interchanged between the fruits for added variety.

Unless using a deep roasting pan, put the cooking dish on a baking sheet. Depending on the ripeness of the fruit and the depth of the pan, the glazes can sometimes get a bit lively and pop over the sides onto the floor of the oven. The sugar in these glazes can burn and cause smoke; it's not from the roasting fruit.

Specific pans are called for so that there will be enough room for the fruit as well as the glaze. Generally, I stay with glass or ceramic for the longer-cooking fruits. If the pan called for is unavailable, place the fruit in the pan available and pour water over the fruit, measuring it. Adjust the glaze quantity so that the pan, with the glaze in it, is never filled more than within a half inch of the rim. Metal pans such as pie plates will give much darker glazes and fruits, and may require more topping up with water. Soak the pans as soon as roasting is finished.

Roasted apricots

SERVES 2

TOTAL
ROASTING
TIME:
15
minutes

THERE ARE MANY different kinds of fresh apricot. None of them seems to be truly ripe unless picked from one's own tree. Roasting intensifies the flavor of firm apricots and softens them. If truly splendid apricots are available, eat them sun warm, out of hand. The apricots here need to be served with a large spoon or a small knife and fork. There are pits in those lightly brown speckled delights. For pitless roasted apricots, see the following recipe; they will be messy although delicious.

This recipe can be made two ways. The first quantities of sugar and seasoning make apricots that can be served as a slightly tart side dish with roast pork or game. The second quantities will make a dessert-worthy flavor.

Any number of apricots can be made that will fit comfortably—not squashed—into a flat ceramic or glass baking dish. Four will fit in a one-quart soufflé, eight in a large pie dish. More can be put in a lasagna dish. After the first four apricots, do not double or quadruple the butter. Use an extra teaspoon for six apricots, two teaspoons for eight. Add another tablespoon for ten to twelve. Sugar and seasonings should increase proportionately to the apricots.

As a dessert, they are nice with vanilla ice cream, the cooking liquid poured over (two tablespoons per person), and a crisp cookie. Because of the butter, these are best served warm. Two apricots make a serving.

1 tablespoon unsalted butter	4 apricots (2 to 3 ounces each)
1 or 2 teaspoons sugar	1 tablespoon fresh lemon juice
⅛ teaspoon or 1 pinch of cayenne pepper	

Place rack in center of oven. Heat oven to 500°F.

In a small saucepan, melt butter with sugar and cayenne. (I usually do this for 45 seconds in a microwave oven directly in a 1-quart soufflé dish.) Roll apricots in butter and set on their stem end. Roast for 15 minutes. Remove from oven. Pour on lemon juice and serve.

Almond roasted apricots

SERVES 3

TOTAL
ROASTING
TIME:
10
minutes

THIS IS EXTREMELY delicious and messy. Even with the almond replacing the removed stone, the apricots sink into a blob. I like them so much I thought I'd share the recipe in any case.

6 whole fresh apricots (about 1 pound)
2 tablespoons unsalted butter, plus
    ¼ teaspoon for the pan
3 teaspoons sugar

1 teaspoon lemon zest
¼ teaspoon ground nutmeg
6 whole blanched almonds

Place rack in center of oven. Heat oven to 500°F.

Using a small sharp knife, cut away a ½-inch section from the top of the apricot. Work the tip of the knife down into the apricot and remove the pit. Repeat for all apricots.

In a small bowl smush together the butter, sugar, zest, and nutmeg. Place 1 almond in each apricot cavity. Top with a small amount of the butter mixture. Lightly butter a 9-inch Pyrex dish. Arrange apricots in dish so they do not touch. Roast for 10 minutes.

Apricots will burst apart. Served warm, they are delicious with ice cream.

Roasted papaya with curried lime sauce

SERVES 6

TOTAL
ROASTING
TIME:
12
minutes

THIS IS A wonderful way to make use of all those hard, green papayas that always seem to be on sale in the markets. Don't worry that they are not ripe. Buy and use them right away.

Good on their own, the papayas go to papaya heaven with some cold heavy cream served in the well of each, where it swirls with the dark brown of the sugar. A less lavish topping is low-fat yogurt.

The papaya can be prepared ahead, left with a bit of lime juice poured into each half, and covered with plastic while dinner is cooked and served. Roast them while the main course is being eaten.

1 teaspoon Madras curry powder
6 tablespoons packed dark brown sugar
¼ cup fresh lime juice

3 green papayas
Heavy cream or yogurt (low-fat or regular), optional

Place rack in center of oven. Heat oven to 500°F.

In a small bowl combine the curry powder, sugar, and lime juice. Stir with a small whisk or fork until well combined. Cut papayas in half lengthwise. Using a spoon, scoop out the seeds. Taste them. If the seeds are not bitter, rinse them and reserve for topping.

Put the papaya halves into a 14 x 12 x 2-inch roasting pan. Pour about 1 tablespoon of the curry mixture into each. Rub it around the rim and into the flesh. Roast for 12 minutes. Remove immediately to a platter. Serve warm with a splash of cream or dollop of yogurt in the center of each, if desired.

Whole roasted peaches with ginger syrup

SERVES 8

TOTAL
ROASTING
TIME:
22 to 30
minutes

THE LIQUID CAN be made ahead but will harden a bit. Just before roasting, reheat the liquid and pour evenly over each peach. It is better to use firm peaches. Even hard and out-of-season peaches can be elevated to succulence by this method. Parts of the peach skin will turn mahogany brown. Don't worry. They are not burned but delicious.

8 large peaches (6 ounces each), skins on and stems removed

1 cup water

½ cup packed dark brown sugar

4 tablespoons unsalted butter

4 tablespoons Triple Sec

½-inch piece fresh gingerroot, peeled and minced fine

¼ cup fresh lemon juice

Place rack in center of oven. Heat oven to 500°F. Put a baking sheet on the center rack.

With a small, sharp knife, prick each peach in 3 different places around the top and the base. This will keep the peaches from bursting open as they roast. In a 10-inch tart pan or pie dish, arrange peaches so that they do not touch.

In a small saucepan combine water, sugar, butter, Triple Sec, and ginger. Bring to a boil, then reduce heat to medium. Stirring occasionally, cook only until sugar has dissolved completely. Remove from heat. Add lemon juice. Stir.

Drizzle some of the warm syrup over each peach, letting it run down the sides and into the pan. Use all the glaze. Place the pan in the oven on top of the baking sheet. This will keep your oven clean if any basting juices cascade over the sides of the pan.

Roast for 10 minutes. Remove pan from oven and, using a pastry brush, baste the peaches with the liquid that collects in the bottom of the pan. Return to the oven, turning the pan, so that peaches brown evenly. Roast for 12 to 15 minutes more. Prick peaches to see if they are done. Peaches don't need to be totally soft. When pushed on the side with a spoon they should give a bit and not feel hard at the center. If they are too hard, continue to roast 5 minutes more. Some of the peaches might be very dark on top; they will taste wonderful.

Pears with honey glaze

SERVES 8

TOTAL
ROASTING
TIME:
55
minutes

As with all fruits, but especially pears, results—amount of juice particularly—will depend on the variety and ripeness. I had best results with firm Bosc pears, their skins a dark yellow russet, the flesh firm with a nicely tart edge to the flavor. Anjous, with their greenish yellow skin, are also good but lack the balancing tart edge and can be a tad soft. Comice, with its yellow to red skin, is the queen of eating pears, perfect with some Brie or Gorgonzola; but its excellence is wasted in cooking, where it turns mushy. Pear William also become mushy when cooked. Bartletts, generally available, can be substituted.

It is nice that pears for roasting can be underripe, as pears should never be bought ripe but instead ripened once gotten home; otherwise they are grainy.

Pears can be roasted up to the 45-minute point and reserved in their roasting pan. Just before ready to serve, put back in a 500°F oven for 10 minutes.

To vary the flavor, substitute a peeled stick of fresh ginger, a piece of preserved ginger, or a petal of a star anise in each pear cavity instead of the cloves.

8 firm Bosc pears (see Note)	4 tablespoons unsalted butter, melted
Zest and juice from 2 lemons ($\frac{1}{3}$ cup juice)	6 tablespoons honey (type may vary according to flavor desired)
8 whole cloves	$\frac{3}{4}$ cup water if needed

Place rack in center of oven. Heat oven to 500°F. Place a baking sheet on center rack.

Peel pears. Leave stems intact. Core out the bottoms using the sharp end of a vegetable peeler. Remove enough flesh to scoop out the seeds. Working over a $13\frac{1}{2}$ x $9\frac{1}{2}$ x 2-inch ovenproof glass or ceramic baking dish, or a 10-inch round such as a ceramic quiche dish or a glass pie plate, rub each pear with some of the lemon juice. Stick a clove into the cavity of each pear along with some lemon zest. Arrange pears in the dish so that there is as much room between them as possible.

In a small bowl, whisk together the butter, honey, and remaining lemon juice. Using a pastry brush, paint each pear with the honey mixture.

Cut 8 pieces of aluminum foil about 2 inches square. Cover the stem and very top of each pear with 1 square of the foil.

Place the dish on the baking sheet and roast for 50 minutes. Every 15 minutes, baste each pear with the liquid that collects in the bottom of the dish. Depending on the juiciness of the pears, the liquid will start to thicken after about 25 minutes. If the bottom of the dish gets too dry, add the water.

After 50 minutes, remove the foil caps. Roast 5 minutes more. Pears should be nicely browned. Pierce the pears with a skewer to see if they are soft but not mushy. If not easy to pierce, continue to roast for 10 minutes more.

Remove from oven. Using the pastry brush, coat pears well with the glaze in the bottom of the roasting dish. Remove from pan.

Serve at once with a spoonful of glaze for each pear, or reserve and serve at room temperature.

NOTE: If using Bartletts, there may be no need for the additional water. Remove the Bartletts after about 40 minutes roasting time if they are getting too soft.

Roasted pears with Asian glaze

SERVES 4 TO 8

TOTAL
ROASTING
TIME:
55 *to* 60
minutes

THIS IS AN intensely flavored side dish to go with a variety of roasted meats, notably Roast Pork Loin with Asian Glaze (page 167). Although cooking them in the same roasting pan as the pork saves space, I find that it slows me down when trying to entertain. So I roast these for the first forty-five minutes as directed in this recipe, then remove from the oven and cover loosely with foil. The pears will continue to cook. When the pork loin has cooked for forty minutes, I add the pears to the roasting pan and let them heat up for the last 5 minutes.

These savory pears can also be used as a first course on an endive and watercress pillow.

This recipe can be multiplied as needed. Six to eight pears will fit in a ten-inch quiche pan or ceramic pie plate and eight to ten in a 13½ x 9½ x 2-inch ovenproof glass or ceramic baking dish. Two pears can be roasted, using half of the glaze and the smallest gratin, flat baking dish, that is available.

Bartlett pears, with their generous juices, are perhaps my favorite for this dish. Bosc do well but may need some extra water especially if the pears are cooked in a quicker-browning metal pie plate. There needs to be at least a quarter of an inch of liquid in the bottom of the roasting pan or the glaze will scorch.

1 recipe Asian Glaze (page 33)

1 cup water with 1 tablespoon rice
   vinegar added

4 firm pears

2 tablespoons fresh lemon juice

4 pieces star anise

Place rack in center of oven. Heat oven to 500°F.

Make Asian Glaze. After scraping the glaze from the blender into a small bowl, pour the cup of vinegar water into the blender. Blend for a few seconds, just to combine the left-over glaze ingredients with the water. Pour into another bowl and reserve.

Peel each pear. If the pears have stems, leave them on. Use the sharp end of the vegetable peeler to hollow out the bottom of each pear. Scoop out enough to remove the seeds.

Rub each pear with some of the lemon juice. Place the pears in a 9-inch pie pan, preferably aluminum or other metal.

Using a pastry brush, paint each pear with the glaze. Paint inside the hollow as well as the outside of each pear. Using small pieces of foil about 2 inches square, make a little cap to cover the stem and top of each pear. Place a piece of star anise inside of each pear hollow.

Set in the oven and roast. Add the reserved vinegar water after 10 minutes, swirling it around in the pan with the pastry brush, then brushing pears with this mixture. Roast 45 minutes more, basting each pear with the liquid in the bottom of the pan, and turning the pan for even browning every 15 minutes. Depending on the juiciness of the pears, the liquid will start to thicken after about 20 minutes. If the bottom of the pan gets too dry, add another ½ cup of water.

After 55 minutes all but the hardest pears should be just about done. Before removing the foil caps, test the pears with a skewer. They should be soft and easy to pierce. If done, remove caps. If not, roast 5 minutes more .

Test the pears again with a skewer to make sure they are soft and easy to pierce. All but the very hardest pears should be done at this stage. If still hard and foil caps have been removed, replace the foil caps, add water if needed, and roast another 15 minutes.

Remove from oven. Using the pastry brush, coat pears well with the glaze in the roasting pan.

Serve at once, with some of the glaze for each pear, or reserve and serve at room temperature. If serving pears later, as the pears come to room temperature, periodically coat them with the glaze.

Sugar-glazed pineapple

SERVES 4

TOTAL
ROASTING
TIME:
15
minutes

THIS IS A quick and easy dessert recipe. Roasting only enhances the sharp, fresh, bite of the pineapple. All the sugars caramelize, just as one would hope. The pineapple can be cooked up to several hours ahead. Pour all the juices back over each pineapple quarter and return to the oven for about ten minutes just before serving.

1 pineapple (2½ pounds)

⅓ cup rum, preferably dark

⅔ cup packed dark brown sugar

Trim the pineapple leaves, leaving 3 to 4 inches. Using a large kitchen knife, cut the pineapple in half lengthwise. Cut each half lengthwise again, so there are 4 quarters.

Cut the tough center strip out of each quarter. Holding a quarter of the pineapple with one hand, cut the bottom of the pineapple flesh away from the skin: Start at the top near the leaves and cut down along the side and around. Detach the fruit from the skin, reserving both. Cut fruit across into 6 sections. Repeat for other 3 quarters.

Combine rum and sugar in a small bowl. Stir until dissolved. Dip each quarter of pineapple into the glaze. Return each quarter to its spot in the skin, so each quarter looks whole.

Place the 4 pineapple quarters in a 12 x 8 x 1½-inch roasting pan. Drizzle the remaining glaze over each. Set aside and let marinate for 30 minutes.

About 20 minutes before roasting, place rack in center of oven. Heat oven to 500°F.

Roast for 15 minutes. Remove quarters from pan right away or pineapple can stick. Serve warm.

Red plums with spiced syrup

SERVES 6

TOTAL
ROASTING
TIME:
20
minutes

BLACK PLUMS WORK equally well in this recipe when they are the same size as the red ones, about three to three and a half ounces each. The flavor and the shiny ruby-colored cooking syrup are very alluring. Handle the cooked fruit with care as the skin gets very thin and fragile rather than brown. The fruit and syrup can be transformed into an outstanding compote.

¾ cup water

½ cup sugar

Pinch of ground nutmeg

Pinch of ground allspice

Pinch of ground cinnamon

2 tablespoons fresh lemon juice

12 to 14 red plums (2½ pounds), stems removed

Place rack in center of oven. Preheat oven to 500°F. Place a baking sheet on center rack.

In a small saucepan, combine the water, sugar, nutmeg, allspice, and cinnamon. Bring to a boil, then reduce heat to medium. Stirring occasionally, cook only until sugar has dissolved completely. Remove from heat. Add lemon juice. Stir.

Arrange plums in a 12 x 8 x 1½-inch roasting pan with their stem ends down. Plums will stand upright this way and cook more evenly. Pour a small amount of the syrup over each plum. Let it trickle down the sides and into the pan. Use all the syrup.

Put pan on baking sheet and roast for 15 minutes. Using a pastry brush, baste the plums with the liquid that collects in the bottom of the pan. Turn plums onto their sides. Continue to roast 5 minutes more. Remove carefully as there will be lots of juice.

Plums may be served warm with a puddle of the syrup, 2 plums for each guest. Serve with vanilla or—even better—cinammon ice cream or frozen yogurt. If a thicker glaze is desired, reduce as instructed below.

PLUM COMPOTE: Let fruit cool enough to handle. Using a small kitchen knife, remove fruit from the pit. The roasted fruit is soft, so it is easiest to place each plum on cutting surface. Cut straight down the sides, parallel with the pit. Put the pieces of cut fruit into a small bowl. The pieces will give off more juice as they sit.

Pour off collected juices into a small heavy-bottomed saucepan. Reduce liquid over high heat for 5 to 10 minutes, until reduced by half. Reserve. Serve as a sauce with plums. Very good paired with pound cake or used as a filling for cream puffs or a classic Paris Brest, or serve the compote over ice cream, vanilla frozen yogurt, or angel food cake.

There will be 3 cups starting with the recipe.

i NDEX